Windows 2000 Domains & Active Directory

Aleksey Tchekmarev

alist

Copyright (c) 2001 by A-List, LLC
All rights reserved.

No part of this publication may be reproduced in any way, stored in a retrieval system of any type, or transmitted by any means or media, electronic or mechanical, including, but not imited to, photocopy, recording, or scanning, *without prior permission in writing* from the publisher.

A-List, LLC
c/o CHARLES RIVER MEDIA, INC.
20 Downer Avenue, Unit 3
Hingham, MA 02043
781-740-0400
781-740-8816 (FAX)
chrivmedia@aol.com
http://www.charlesriver.com

This book is printed on acid-free paper.

All brand names and product names mentioned in this book are trademarks or service marks of their respective companies. Any omission or misuse (of any kind) of service marks or trademarks should not be regarded as intent to infringe on the property of others. The publisher recognizes and respects all marks used by companies, manufacturers, and developers as a means to distinguish their products.

Windows 2000 Domains & Active Directory
By A. Tchekmarev
 ISBN: 1-58450-080-8
 Printed in the United States of America

01 01 7 6 5 4 3 2 1

A-List, LLC titles are distributed by Charles River Media and are available for site license or bulk purchase by institutions, user groups, corporations, etc. For additional information, please contact the Special Sales Department at 781-740-0400.

Book Editors: Jessica Mroz, Olga Kokoreva

CONTENTS

Introduction 1

PART I. DEPLOYING WINDOWS 2000 DOMAINS 5

Chapter 1. Active Directory Concepts and Terminology 7
LDAP as a Cornerstone of Active Directory 8
    Informational model 9
    Naming Model 13
    Functional Model 15
    Security Model 20
    LDAP Ports 20
DNS Records Registered by Windows 2000-based Domain Controllers ... 20

Chapter 2. Configuring and Troubleshooting Windows 2000-based Domains ... 25
Placing FSMO Roles 26
Native Mode Domains 27
Replication Issues 27
    Intra- and Inter-site Replication 27
    Urgent Replication 29
    Replication of Group Policy Objects (GPOs) 29
    Monitoring Replication 30
Some Troubleshooting Tips 34
    Logging Diagnostic Events 34
    Internal Errors During Replication 35
    Verifying a Windows 2000 Server Status 35

Chapter 3. Deploying Active Directory 39
Windows 2000 DNS Server 40
    Prerequisites 41
    Installing a Windows 2000 DNS Server 42
    Verifying the DNS Configuration 44
    Configuring Windows 2000 DNS for Use with Legacy DNS 46
Installing Domain Controllers 50
    Creating a Domain Controller 50
    Deleting a Domain Controller 61
    Unattended Installing and Removing of Active Directory 62
Adding Domain Members 64
    Setting the DNS Suffix 64
    Windows 2000-based Workstations and Standalone Servers 65
Connecting a Windows NT 4.0-based BDC to a Windows 2000 Domain ... 66
Switching to Native Mode 67

Establishing Trusts	68
Verifying the State of Trusts	70
Creating Shortcut Trusts	70
Establishing Trusts with Windows NT 4.0-based Domains	72

PART II. ADMINISTERING ACTIVE DIRECTORY — 73

Chapter 4. Domain Manipulation Tools — 75

Basic Active Directory Administrative Snap-ins	76
Common Topics	77
Making a Custom MMC Console	78
Browsing the *Tree* Pane in a Snap-in's Window	78
Choosing Columns for Displaying	79
Exporting the List of Objects	79
Customizing Snap-ins	80
Active Directory Users and Computers Snap-in	82
Connecting to Domain or Domain Controller	82
Contents Displaying Options	84
Active Directory Sites and Services Snap-in	92
Active Directory Domains and Trusts Snap-in	93
Using User Principal Names (UPN)	94
Verifying Trusts	97
ADSI Edit Snap-in	98
Connecting to Namespaces	98
Editing Attributes of Active Directory Objects	100
Creating a Custom Query	101
Creating Active Directory Objects	103
Working with Global Catalog	103
Active Directory Schema Snap-in	104
Installation	104
Modifying the Schema	105
Extending the Schema	106
Group Policy Snap-in	111
Linking to a Group Policy Object (GPO)	111
Creating and Deleting a GPO	115
Selecting a Domain Controller	115
Configuring Group Policy Objects	116

Chapter 5. Common Administrative Tasks — 119

Using the *RunAs* Command	120
Running Administrative Tools from the Context Menu	120
Starting a Tool from the Command Prompt	122
Remote Administration	125
Installing Administrative Snap-ins Selectively	126
Querying Active Directory	128
Configuring *Search* Option on a Computer	128

Contents   v

   Manipulating Directory Objects _____ 129
      Using the *Active Directory Users and Computers* Snap-in _____ 130
      Adding Members to a Group _____ 131
      Adding Users and Groups to Domain _____ 131
   Publishing Folders and Printers _____ 135
      Pubprn.vbs Script _____ 136
      Connecting to Shared Resources _____ 136
   Managing FSMO Roles in the Forest _____ 137
      Finding FSMO Role Owners _____ 137
      Transferring and Seizing FSMO Roles _____ 140
   Refreshing Group Policy _____ 141
   Triggering Replication _____ 142
      The *Active Directory Sites and Services* snap-in _____ 143
      Replication Diagnostics Tool (RepAdmin.exe) (ST) _____ 143
      Active Directory Replication Monitor (ReplMon.exe) (ST) _____ 144
   Delegating Administrative Control _____ 145
   Auditing Access to Active Directory Objects _____ 148
   Recovering Active Directory _____ 150
      General Considerations _____ 150
      Backing up Active Directory _____ 152
      Restoring Active Directory _____ 152

PART III. USING TOOLS AND UTILITIES _____ 157

Chapter 6. General Characteristics and Purpose of System Tools _____ 159

   Where Can You Find All These Tools? _____ 160
      Windows 2000 Support Tools _____ 160
      Windows 2000 Resource Kit _____ 160
   Classification by Purpose _____ 161
   Description of Selected Tools _____ 162

Chapter 7. Active Directory Diagnostics and Maintenance _____ 167

   Domain Controller Diagnostic Tool (DCdiag.exe) (ST) _____ 168
      Standard Full Test _____ 169
      Checking Replication _____ 171
      Enterprise Tests _____ 172
   Active Directory Diagnostic Tool (NTDSutil.exe) (Sys) _____ 173
      Authoritative Restore _____ 174
      Domain Management _____ 174
      Files: Managing AD Database Files _____ 175
      IP Deny List _____ 180
      LDAP policies _____ 180
      Metadata Cleanup: Removing Orphaned Domains or Domain Controllers _____ 182
      Roles: Managing FSMO Roles _____ 185
      Security Account Management _____ 187
      Semantic Database Analysis _____ 188

Chapter 8. Network and Distributed Services — **189**

- NLtest.exe (ST) — 190
  - Verifying Secure Channels — 191
  - Viewing Trusted Domains — 193
  - Viewing Information on Network Topology — 194
  - Miscellaneous Options — 196
- Network Connectivity Tester (NetDiag.exe) (ST) — 197
  - Running Tests — 198
  - Refreshing DNS Resource Records Registration (/fix) — 200
- RPC Ping: RPC Connectivity Verification Tool (RK) — 201
  - Server Component (RPings.exe) — 202
  - Client Component (RPingc.exe) — 202
- NTFRSutl.exe (RK) — 204
- DsaStat.exe (ST) — 205
  - Common Statistical Comparison — 206
  - Analyzing Differences between Partitions — 209
- Replication Diagnostics Tool (RepAdmin.exe) (ST) — 212
  - Monitoring Replication Topology — 212
  - Triggering Replication Events — 216
  - Viewing Directory Changes — 219
  - Auxiliary Options — 224
- Active Directory Replication Monitor (ReplMon.exe) (ST) — 226
  - Preparation Steps — 226
  - Log Files — 228
  - Managing Replication — 228

Chapter 9. Manipulating Active Directory Objects — **229**

- Finding Objects in Active Directory — 230
  - Active Directory Search Tool (Search.vbs) (ST) — 230
- Browsing and Editing Active Directory Objects — 232
  - Active Directory Browser (AdsVw.exe) (AD SDK) — 233
  - Active Directory Administration Tool (Ldp.exe) (ST) — 238
- Importing, Exporting, and Batch Modifying Directory Objects — 252
  - Unicode Support — 257
  - LDIFDE Utility (Sys) — 258
  - CSVDE Utility (Sys) — 263
- Windows 2000 Domain Manager (NetDom.exe) (ST) — 266

Chapter 10. Migration Tools — **271**

- Adventures of the *ObjectSID* Attribute — 272
- Active Directory Object Manager (MoveTree.exe) (ST) — 273
  - Moving an OU Subtree — 274
  - Moving User and Group Accounts — 276
- Cloning Security Principals (ClonePrincipal) (ST) — 277
  - Well-known SIDs and RIDs — 277
  - Supported Object Types — 278

ClonePrincipal Components 279
Configuring Migration Environment 279
Cloning Users 282
Cloning Groups 283
ClonePrincipal Samples 284
Finding Groups of a Specific Type 286

Chapter 11. Security Tools 289

ACL Diagnostics (ACLDiag.exe) (ST) 290
   Viewing All Permissions 290
   Viewing the Effective Rights 292
   Verifying Delegation of Control 293
   Comparing with Schema Default Permissions 294
DsACLs.exe (ST) 295
   Viewing Security Settings 295
   Granting and Removing Permissions 296
   Restoring Security Settings 297
Security Descriptor Check Utility (SDCheck.exe) (ST) 298
Kerberos Tray (KerbTray.exe) (RK) 300
Kerberos List (KList.exe) (RK) 302

Chapter 12. Group Policy Tools 305

Group Policy Results (GPResult.exe) (RK) 306
   General Structure of the Tests 306
   Description of Tests 307
Group Policy Verification Tool (GPOTool.exe) (RK) 314
   General Tests 315
   Detailed Information about the Policies 316
   Corrupted Policies 318

PART IV. PROGRAM ACCESS TO ACTIVE DIRECTORY 321

Chapter 13. Active Directory Service Interfaces (ADSI) 323

ADSI as an Administrative Tool 324
Windows Script Host (WSH) 325
Informal View of the ADSI Architecture 325
   Attributes and Properties 326
   ADSI System Providers 326
   Interfaces and Methods 327
   The *ADsSystemInfo* Interface 328
Basic ADSI Programming 329
   Reading Object Properties 330
   Searching Active Directory 330
Active Directory Schema 333
   The Abstract Schema 333
   Extending the Schema 334
IADsTools ActiveX DLL 339

VIII   Contents

Using Visual Basic and VBScript _____ 339
   Converting a Visual Basic Program to a Script _____ 341
   Debugging Scripts _____ 341
   ADSI Error Codes _____ 343

Chapter 14. Using ADSI for Administrative Tasks _____ 345

Object Names Used in This Chapter _____ 346
Reading Information from Active Directory _____ 347
   Saving Results to a Disk File. Reading the Abstract Schema _____ 347
   Retrieving Information from a RootDSE _____ 350
   Retrieving the Actual Attribute List _____ 352
   Retrieving Characteristics of an Object Class from the Schema _____ 353
   Reading Properties of Different Types _____ 355
Searching Active Directory for Objects _____ 357
Manipulating User Objects _____ 359
   Creating a User Account _____ 360
   Resetting the Password _____ 361
   Disabling Accounts _____ 362
   Manipulating Group Memberships _____ 363
Creating Multiple Objects _____ 364
Reconstructing an Object Tree _____ 366
   Moving and Renaming Objects _____ 366
   Deleting Objects _____ 367
Designating a Global Catalog Server _____ 368
How to Find an FSMO Master? _____ 370
Using IADsTools _____ 371
   Initiating Replication _____ 371
   Triggering Knowledge Consistency Checker (KCC) _____ 372
   Viewing the Flags of a Domain Controller _____ 372
   Finding FSMO Role Owners _____ 374
   Various Operations _____ 375
Manipulating Security Descriptors _____ 376
Extending Schema _____ 381
   Creating a New Attribute _____ 381
   Creating a New Class _____ 384

PART V. APPENDIXES _____ 387

Appendix A. Web Links _____ 388

Appendix B. The LDAP and WinNT Providers Support of ADSI Interfaces _____ 390

Appendix C. IADsTools Functions _____ 392

Glossary _____ 395

"How to?" _____ 401

Index _____ 403

INTRODUCTION

At the present time, there are a number of comprehensive books dedicated to both the Windows 2000 system and, in part, one of its most important components — Active Directory (AD). The reader may easily choose to read a book that covers Active Directory's purpose, its advantages and disadvantages, strategies for developing Active Directory in a large corporate network, and other important questions. (For example, one of the definitive sources of information essential for deploying Active Directory is the *Windows 2000 Server Resource Kit Deployment Planning Guide*, which you can download for free at the Microsoft site — see *Appendix A*.) This is the reason I decided not to go over these topics again.

In this book, I've tried to take a look at the more practical problems that come up while *using* Active Directory. In the beginning, I planned to include here detailed recommendations for installing and troubleshooting Active Directory, as well as advice on setting up network services such as DNS, DHCP, etc. However, while preparing the actual book, it turned out that this task was too laborious, and even thousand-page volumes from the *Windows 2000 Server Resource Kit* don't cover all of the problems and their solutions. Therefore, I decided to concentrate on the less-explained questions, as well as to shed some light on a few frequently encountered problems. Even if there isn't an answer for all the problems that might arise, you should at least know which side to come at them from.

It probably won't cross anyone's mind to repair a defective car or a complex electronic device without additional, special tools and facilities. Nonetheless, administrators who work with Active Directory often forget that the problems that come up in the process of working with AD are also impossible to eliminate without the help of the appropriate tools and utilities. Of course, the biggest collection of various tools and utilities is the *Windows 2000 Resource Kit,* which you must obtain on your own. However, most of the tools that you need for working with Active Directory (and that are looked at in this book) are furnished along with the system, and are found in the *Windows 2000 Support Tools*. This book is dedicated, to a large extent, to working with exactly these tools.

Besides, I would like to turn administrators' attention to methods of program access to Active Directory, and in part to scripts that use the *Active Directory Service Interfaces* (ADSI). Scripts can be used to solve many administrative tasks, and you may use already written scripts, after a minimal number of modifications to fit your needs. Creating scripts doesn't necessitate being a highly qualified programmer, which is what I tried to get across in the last two chapters of the book.

The book is geared towards the prepared reader, one who already has some experience working with Windows 2000, and who is familiar with the basic work methods and components of the system (in part, with Microsoft Management Console snap-ins). If you need basic information, you can easily find it in the Help system or in one of many books and articles dedicated to Windows 2000.

Below is a brief summary of each chapter.

Part I. Deploying Windows 2000 Domains:

- *Chapter 1, "Active Directory Concepts and Terminology"*, covers primarily two standards that make up the basis of Active Directory — Lightweight Directory Access Protocol (LDAP) and Directory Naming Service (DNS). Not knowing the concepts and requirements described in these standards can severely impede understanding Active Directory operating mechanisms and the interaction of its components.

- *Chapter 2, "Configuring and Troubleshooting Windows 2000-based Domains"*, gives recommendations that need to be taken into consideration when developing and troubleshooting Windows 2000-based domains.

- *Chapter 3, "Deploying Active Directory"*, tells you what you need to pay attention to before and during installation of Active Directory. Certain typical problems that you may encounter when developing Windows 2000 domains, such as interoperation between Active Directory and a legacy DNS system, are also examined.

Part II. Administering Active Directory:

- In *Chapter 4, "Domain Manipulation Tools"*, we will look at all of the standard tools for administering Active Directory (administrative snap-ins). To use them effectively, the administrator must be aware of certain features and methods of working with them.

- In *Chapter 5, "Common Administrative Tasks"*, we will examine both typical administrative tasks — like working with user and network resources — and tasks specific to Windows 2000 domains, like delegating administrative control, managing FSMO roles, refreshing group policies, searching Active Directory, and others.

Part III. Using Tools and Utilities:

- The main task of *Chapter 6, "General Characteristics and Purpose of System Tools"*, is to give the administrator an idea of what a certain utility is for, and help in choosing the tool to use for a specific task.

- Described in *Chapter 7, "Active Directory Diagnostics and Maintenance"*, are utilities that allow you to determine the health of a single domain controller and the integrity of the Active Directory database replica stored on it.

- *Chapter 8, "Network and Distributed Services"*, covers the utilities that allow you to diagnose problems that arise due to the fact that Active Directory is a distributed network database, that is, problems of connectivity between domain controllers, authentication, and replication.

- *Chapter 9, "Manipulating Active Directory Objects"*, looks at the utilities used for working with Active Directory logical objects — tools for searching for objects of various types and editing their attributes, utilities for exporting and importing objects, and those used for manipulating workstations, domain controllers, and trust relationships.

- In *Chapter 10, "Migration Tools"*, those utilities intended for reorganizing domain trees and migration of objects between forests are examined.

- The tools that allow you to view and manage access permissions on Active Directory objects are looked at in *Chapter 11, "Security Tools"*.

- Examined in *Chapter 12, "Group Policy Tools"*, are those utilities that allow you to test Group Policy Objects (GPOs) and determine the resulting security settings defined by group policies.

Part IV. Program Access to Active Directory:

- *Chapter 13, "Active Directory Service Interfaces (ADSI)"*, will acquaint administrators with ways to programmatically manage Active Directory. The difficult thing about working with the documentation on ADSI is that it is tough for a novice to find what he/she needs in the midst of such a huge amount of unfamiliar information. This chapter gives the reader an understanding of some of the basic concepts, which will be illustrated in the following chapter with examples.

- *Chapter 14, "Using ADSI for Administrative Tasks"*, consists almost completely of program examples. It seems to me that the principles of programming with ADSI are easier to master when you have a specially designed example with commentary. After having understood these basic concepts, it will be much easier to work with documentation that describes in detail all of the interfaces and their methods and properties.

❑ The *Appendixes* include "must-see" and just plain useful references to web resources, a table of ADSI interfaces supported by the main system providers, and a list of all the functions implemented by the IADsTools ActiveX object, which are useful for developing administrative scripts.

❑ The *Glossary* will help you quickly find a short description of an unfamiliar Windows 2000-related term or verify your understanding of this term.

❑ The "*How to*" section is set up like a typical FAQ. In it, you may be able to find the solution you need for a specific problem faster than if you were to simply look through the table of contents or the index.

❑ For finding references to a certain utility or tool in the *Index*, use its *file name*. You can also find references to interfaces, methods, properties, attributes, enumerations, etc. the same way — under their names.

The author can be reached at **ATchekmarev@hotmail.com**. You may use this address to request the listings included in this book.

Conventions

Here are some graphical conventions used in the book:

❑ Names of administrative snap-ins are in bold, for example, "the **Active Directory Users and Computers** snap-in".

❑ Names of Active Directory object attributes, ASDI interfaces, methods, and properties, are shown in italics, for example, *objectSid*.

❑ Certain important words are also marked in *italics*.

❑ If a long command or string displayed on the screen does not fit on one line in the book, the ↵ symbol will be used. For example:

    createusers LDAP://OU=Staff,DC=w2k,DC=dom **cn:**"User User01"
    ↵ **samAccountName:**user-ldap01 **password:**psw1

This means that the line shown should be considered as one, unbreakable line.

❑ As you can see from the previous example, the mandatory elements of a command line — the command name and the parameters — are **in bold** so as to be more visible. The other elements of the command are specific to your situation and are determined by yourself.

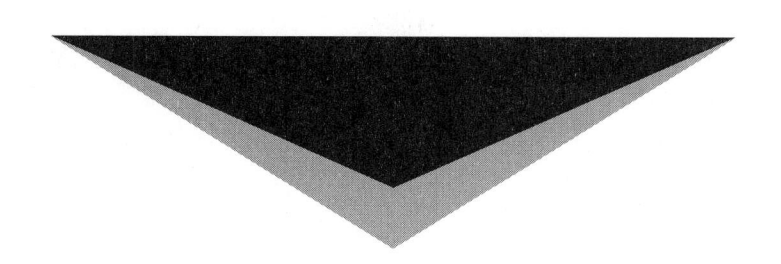

PART I

DEPLOYING WINDOWS 2000 DOMAINS

Chapter 1. Active Directory Concepts and Terminology

Chapter 2. Configuring and Troubleshooting Windows 2000-based Domains

Chapter 3. Deploying Active Directory

Chapter 1
Active Directory Concepts and Terminology

The purpose, advantages, organization, and role of Active Directory for Windows 2000-based domains have already been well described in many books and articles. If you are not familiar with Active Directory basics so far, the comprehensive information can be easily found. In this chapter, I'd like to discuss some aspects of two Internet standards that appeared long before Active Directory, but are very closely related to it. These standards are Lightweight Directory Access Protocol (LDAP v3) and Domain Name System (DNS). There are also two reasons for my decision to focus on these standards. First of all, I think that a better understanding of LDAP basics will help to better understand Active Directory design, which is needed for building queries, working with various administrative tools described in this book, and — even more so — for programming Active Directory. Secondly, experience shows that DNS is often a source of errors when configured contrary to Active Directory requirements. That is why I'll try to describe in detail all records that must be registered on a DNS server, and later — in *Chapter 3, "Deploying Active Directory"* — I'll also consider an example of using a legacy DNS system for deploying Active Directory.

LDAP as a Cornerstone of Active Directory

Active Directory services — as a whole — require a good understanding of LDAP protocol basics. Familiarity with and knowledge of LDAP are also necessary for working with many tools and utilities, such as the Active Directory Administrative Tool (Ldp.exe), **ADSI Edit** snap-in, Search.vbs script, LDIF Directory Exchange utility (LDIFDE.exe), and others, and are needed for scripting as well. This concerns all four LDAP models discussed below. Some Active Directory specific terms and concepts are also considered.

> **NOTE**
>
> All main features of LDAP v3 are described in RFC 2251 through RFC 2256. Refer to these RFCs for more information. You may also find links to other related standards there.

Informational model

The informational (data) model of the LDAP protocol, and therefore, of Active Directory as well, is based on X.500 — the International Standards Organization (ISO) special standard defining a distributed directory service. This standard proposes an object-oriented data model; it therefore includes such terms as class, instance, and inheritance.

Schema

The schema defines classes and attributes, from which all directory objects can be derived. The schema itself is stored in the directory as a set of objects.

Classes

Each directory object is an instance of one or more classes defined in the schema. In general, every object inherits from at least one structural object class and zero or more auxiliary object classes. There are three types of classes:

- *Abstract classes* serve as templates for deriving new abstract, auxiliary, and structural classes. Abstract classes cannot be instantiated in Active Directory, i. e. you cannot create a directory object of an abstract class. The definition of an abstract class can include any number of auxiliary classes.

- *Structural classes* are derived from abstract or structural classes and inherit all attributes of all parent classes. Active Directory objects can only be instances of structural classes. The definition of a structural class can include any number of auxiliary classes.

- An *auxiliary class* is derived from an abstract or auxiliary class and can be included in the definition of a structural, abstract, or auxiliary class. The defined class inherits all attributes of the auxiliary class listed in the *mustContain*, *systemMustContain*, *mayContain*, and *systemMayContain* properties. Auxiliary classes cannot be instantiated in Active Directory. The definition of an auxiliary class can include any number of auxiliary classes.

Attributes

Attributes contain the data used to describe the defined classes. Attributes may be mandatory or optional, single- or multi-valued. An attribute is identified in the schema by a name and an OID (object identifier). Attributes are defined in RFC 2252 and RFC 2256. Here are the examples of attributes (the *lDAPDisplayName* and *attributeID* attributes of the *attributeSchema* objects in the Schema container):

- nTSecurityDescriptor (1.2.840.113556.1.2.281)
- distinguishedName (2.5.4.49)

RootDSE Object

Every LDAP v3-complaint server has an individual DSA-Specific Entry object — *RootDSE* — defined in RFC 2251. This attribute is the root of Directory Information Tree (DIT), but is not a part of any naming context (partition). It defines the directory server's configuration and capabilities. RootDSE has properties that can be retrieved programmatically (see *Listing 14.2*) or by using a query tool (such as Ldp.exe or Search.vbs). To query a RootDSE, specify an empty (null) base DN, a base scope, and a filter `objectClass=*`. (Search operations will be considered a bit later.) It is possible to bind to a specific server, or use a server-less query. In the latter case, the first available LDAP server (a Windows 2000-based domain controller) will respond. Here is an example of the RootDSE data:

```
    1> currentTime: 11/29/2000 11:15:57 Central Standard Time Central
Daylight Time;
    1> subschemaSubentry:
CN=Aggregate,CN=Schema,CN=Configuration,DC=w2k,DC=dom;
    1> dsServiceName: CN=NTDS Settings,CN=W2KDC2,CN=Servers,
CN=W2K-site,CN=Sites,CN=Configuration,DC=w2k,DC=dom;
    3> namingContexts: DC=subdom,DC=w2k,DC=dom;
CN=Schema,CN=Configuration,DC=w2k,DC=dom;
CN=Configuration,DC=w2k,DC=dom;
    1> defaultNamingContext: DC=subdom,DC=w2k,DC=dom;
    1> schemaNamingContext: CN=Schema,CN=Configuration,DC=w2k,DC=dom;
    1> configurationNamingContext: CN=Configuration,DC=w2k,DC=dom;
    1> rootDomainNamingContext: DC=w2k,DC=dom;
    16> supportedControl: 1.2.840.113556.1.4.319;
1.2.840.113556.1.4.801; 1.2.840.113556.1.4.473;
1.2.840.113556.1.4.528; 1.2.840.113556.1.4.417;
1.2.840.113556.1.4.619; 1.2.840.113556.1.4.841;
1.2.840.113556.1.4.529; 1.2.840.113556.1.4.805;
1.2.840.113556.1.4.521; 1.2.840.113556.1.4.970;
1.2.840.113556.1.4.1338; 1.2.840.113556.1.4.474;
1.2.840.113556.1.4.1339; 1.2.840.113556.1.4.1340;
1.2.840.113556.1.4.1413;
```

```
    2> supportedLDAPVersion: 3; 2;
    12> supportedLDAPPolicies: MaxPoolThreads; MaxDatagramRecv;
MaxReceiveBuffer; InitRecvTimeout; MaxConnections; MaxConnIdleTime;
MaxActiveQueries; MaxPageSize; MaxQueryDuration; MaxTempTableSize;
MaxResultSetSize; MaxNotificationPerConn;
    1> highestCommittedUSN: 9267;
    2> supportedSASLMechanisms: GSSAPI; GSS-SPNEGO;
    1> dnsHostName: w2kdc2.subdom.w2k.dom;
    1> ldapServiceName: w2k.dom:w2kdc2$@SUBDOM.W2K.DOM;
    1> serverName: CN=W2KDC2,CN=Servers,
CN=W2K-site,CN=Sites,CN=Configuration,DC=w2k,DC=dom;
    1> supportedCapabilities: 1.2.840.113556.1.4.800;
    1> isSynchronized: TRUE;
    1> isGlobalCatalogReady: TRUE;
```

(Notice numbers that indicate the number of values in attributes.)

RootDSE contains the following standard attributes (refer to RFC 2251 and 2252):

- **altServer** — references to other servers that can be used when this server becomes unavailable. This attribute may be absent.

- **namingContexts** — the list of naming contexts stored on the server. Notice that in our example the domain naming context refers to the *subdom.w2k.dom* domain, but two other contexts — schema and configuration — refer to the root domain: *w2k.dom*. These contexts should be used when searching the directory.

- **subschemaSubentry** — the name of a *subschema* entry (or the *abstract schema*; see *Chapter 13, "Active Directory Service Interfaces (ADSI)"*). This object contains definitions of available attributes and classes.

- **supportedControl** — the Object Identifiers (OIDs) of the controls that the server supports. This attribute may be absent.

- **supportedExtension** — the Object Identifiers (OIDs) of the extended operations that the server supports. This attribute may be absent.

- **supportedLDAPVersion** — the LDAP versions supported by the server.

- **supportedSASLMechanisms** — the Simple Authentication and Security Layer (SASL) mechanisms supported by the server. This attribute may be absent.

In addition, Active Directory supports the following attributes:

- **configurationNamingContext** — the Configuration naming context.

- **currentTime** — the current time.
- **defaultNamingContext** — the default context for the server. By default, this is the DN of the domain where the server is located.
- **dnsHostName** — the server's DNS name.
- **dsServiceName** — the name of the directory service.
- **highestCommittedUSN** — the highest USN committed to the database on this server.
- **ldapServiceName** — Service Principal Name (SPN) for the server, used for mutual authentication.
- **rootDomainNamingContext** — the name of the forest where the server is located.
- **schemaNamingContext** — the Schema context.
- **serverName** — the distinguished name of the server object.
- **supportedCapabilities** — the Object Identifiers (OIDs) of the capabilities that the server supports.
- **supportedLDAPPolicies** — supported LDAP policies.

There are also two important operational attributes:

- **isSynchronized** — TRUE, if initial synchronization of this Active Directory replica with its partners has been completed (i. e. a newly promoted server can advertise itself as a domain controller).
- **isGlobalCatalogReady** — TRUE, if the DC has not simply been *promoted to be* a Global Catalog server, but has already advertised itself as a GC server.

Attribute Syntax

The attribute syntax (see RFC 2252) defines the type of the attribute (a Unicode string, a number, an octet string, etc.), byte ordering, and the matching rules for comparisons of property types. The syntaxes of LDAP attributes are named by OIDs. Examples of syntaxes include:

- Distinguished Name (1.3.6.1.4.1.1466.115.121.1.12)
- UTC time (1.3.6.1.4.1.1466.115.121.1.53)

Directory Entry (Object)

Entry is an instance of a specific structural class, and in Active Directory is usually called *object*. An object can be either a container or a leaf. It is uniquely identified by its relative distinguished name (RDN) and distinguished name (DN).

Naming Model

The naming model defines how directory objects can be uniquely specified. The OSI directory model uses distinguished names for that purpose.

Distinguished Name (DN)

A *distinguished name* is unique in the forest (DIT) and serves as a primary key for a directory object. DN consists of relative distinguished names (RDN), which represent branches in the directory information tree.

Here is an example of an object distinguished name (CN stands for Common Name, OU means Organizational Unit, and DC means Domain Component):

- CN=John Smith,OU=Staff,DC=w2k,DC=dom

Relative Distinguished Name (RDN)

A relative distinguished name uniquely identifies objects in a container. The RDNs consist of an attribute naming specifier and a value, for example:

- CN=Domain Controllers
- OU=Staff
- DC=w2k-domain

Other Names Used in Active Directory

- *User Principal Names* — The User Principal Name (UPN) consists of the user logon name and a UPN suffix (the current or root DNS domain name, or a specially created shortened name), for example, `JohnS@w2k` or `John@w2k.dom`. UPN is intended for simplified logon and can be used for logging on the network on a computer that can belong to any domain in the forest.

- *Fully Qualified Domain Name (FQDN)* is also known as the *full computer name*, i. e. a concatenation of the host name and the primary DNS suffix, for example:

    ```
    w2kdc2.subdom.w2k.dom
    ```

- *Globally Unique Identifiers* — The Globally Unique Identifier (GUID) is a 128-bit number, which uniquely identifies the object when it is created. It never changes and ensures addressing the object even if it has been renamed or moved.

- *SAM (Pre-Windows 2000) Account Names.* SAM account names are required for compatibility with down-level clients. A SAM name must be unique in a domain.

- *LDAP Uniform Resource Locator (URL).* LDAP URLs are used by LDAP-enabled clients for accessing Active Directory objects. LDAP URLs can also be used as binding strings in scripts and applications, for example (the server name is optional):

    ```
    LDAP://w2kdc4.w2k.dom/CN=John Smith,OU=Staff,DC=w2k,DC=dom
    ```

- *Active Directory Canonical Name.* Canonical names are used in the Windows 2000 user interface for displaying object names. A canonical name is similar to the distinguished name without the naming attribute specifiers (DC, CN, etc.). For example, the canonical name for the LDAP URL shown above is:

    ```
    w2k.dom/Staff/John Smith
    ```

Referrals

In a multi-domain forest, complete directory information is not available on a single domain controller. (You can only obtain a subset of attributes of all objects from a Global Catalog server.) You need to have a mechanism that will redirect the query from a DC to the DC that stores the requested object. This mechanism may also be required if the object is located in another naming partition on the same server (i. e. if you specify the domain naming context as the search base and want to find objects that can be stored in either Schema or Configuration partitions).

To inform a client that the server does not have a copy of the requested object, the requested server uses an LDAP *referral* in accordance with RFC 2251. In an ideal case, the referral indicates the DC that stored the necessary object. The server can generate referrals to other DCs according to the *cross-reference* objects stored in the directory. Cross-references allow every DC to be aware of all directory partitions in the forest. The references are stored in the Configuration container, and are therefore replicated to every DC in the forest. Hence, any DC can generate referrals to any other domain in the forest, as well as to the Schema and Configuration partitions. Cross-references can be created either automatically or manually by an administrator.

Functional Model

The functional model describes the operations that can be done with information stored in a directory using the LDAP protocol. You need to be able to access information, and read and update it as well. These operations are implemented in somewhat different ways for various tools, but the main concepts and parameters remain the same.

Authentication

The authentication operations allow the user to establish a connection with a DSA and get the right to access the stored information.

- **Open** — this command creates and initializes a connection block, and then opens a connection to the DSA
- **Bind** — this command initiates a protocol session to the DSA and authenticates the client to the DSA
- **Unbind** — this command terminates a session, frees all resources associated with the session, and closes a connection

Interrogation

The interrogation methods describe ways of retrieving information.

Search

The search operations retrieve information based on user criteria.
- **Search base** — The distinguished name of a directory object (called the *base object*) from which the search begins (e. g. `DC=w2k,DC=dom` or `OU=Stuff, DC=w2k,DC=dom`).

> **NOTE**
>
> The search base can also have the "<GUID=...>" format (the angle brackets are included!) (e. g. "<GUID=0855ae368790cb4b8726cf37cb2222a5>").

- **Search scope** — defines the depth of searching relative to the search base (Fig. 1.1 shows scopes for a domain object). There are three options:

  - **Base**. Only the base object is searched (i. e. you'll work with properties of the base object only).

  - **One level**. The *children* of the base object are searched; the base object itself and *grandchildren* are excluded.

  - **Subtree**. The entire subtree is searched, beginning with and including the base object (i. e. all "visible" objects in the subtree).

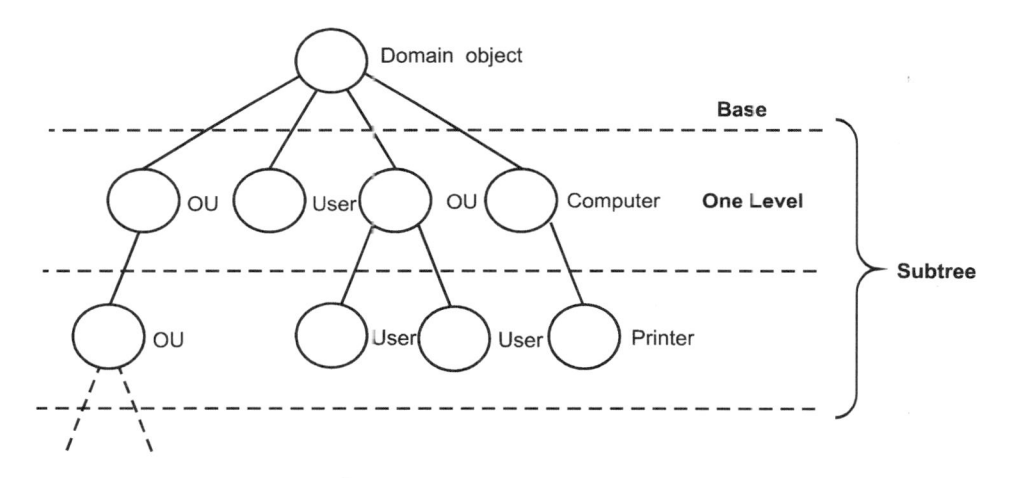

Fig. 1.1. The search scopes for a domain object (which is the *search base*)

  - **Filter**. A rule (see RFC 2254) for selecting objects in the subtree (e. g. (cn=*) or &(objectCategory=Person)(cn=d*)). (See below.)

  - **Selection**. A list of attributes returned from the selected objects that match the filter.

  - **Optional controls**. LDAP search filters (RFC 2254) that define specific criteria. (See examples of using some LDAP controls in *Chapter 9, "Manipulating Active Directory Objects"*.)

Types of Filters

The following table shows a few examples of search filters:

Condition	Filter
Equality match	`(sAMAccountName=jsmith)`
Partial match	`(name=s*)` or `(name=*s*)`
Comparing with a value	`(uSNChanged>=10000)` or `(CN<=Sales)`
Presence of object	`(objectClass=*)`
Logical AND of two conditions (users with names that begin with 'H')	`(&(objectClass=user)(cn>=h))`
Logical OR of two conditions (objects with names that begin with 'A' OR 'H')	`(|(cn=a*)(cn=h*))`
Logical NOT (all users with name that begin with 'A' except 'Administrators')	`(&(objectClass=user)(cn=a*)(!(cn=adm*)))`
Binary (attributes with syntax 2.5.4.1)	`(attributeSyntax=\32\2e\35\2e\34\2e\31)`

Selection Options

Usually, you provide the list of object attributes returned by a query. There are, however, a few special cases:

- If you only need the objects' DNs rather than their attributes, specify OID `1.1` as the selection

- It is possible to specify the attribute OID instead of its name; for example, you can replace `objectClass` with `2.5.4.0`

Example. Listing Attributes replicated to Global Catalog

Let's consider, as an example, how to view all attributes replicated to Global Catalog. You may use any search tool, such as the Search.vbs script or the Ldp.exe utility. (For more information, see *Chapter 9*.) Here is a sample command:

```
search "LDAP://CN=Schema,CN=Configuration,DC=w2k,DC=dom"
    /C:"(&(objectClass=attributeSchema)
```

✧ (isMemberOfPartialAttributeSet=*))"
✧ /P:ADsPAth,attributeID,attributeSyntax,isSingleValued,
✧ lDAPDisplayName,oMSyntax

The query produces a result similar to the following (only one entry from the list is shown):

```
...
ADsPAth = LDAP://CN=User-Principal-Name,CN=Schema,CN=Configuration,
   ✧ DC=w2k,DC=domattributeID = 1.2.840.113556.1.4.656
attributeSyntax = 2.5.5.12
isSingleValued = True
lDAPDisplayName = userPrincipalName
oMSyntax = 64
...
```

Compare

The compare operation returns a Boolean result (TRUE or FALSE) based on the comparison of an attribute value with a specified value.

Administrative Limits and Query Policy

The LDAP server resources that are available to clients requesting LDAP queries, paged result sets, and sorted result sets are limited by the Default Query Policy. Administrative limits constitute the query policy objects which are stored in the container CN=Query-Policies,CN=Directory Service,CN=Windows NT,CN=Services in the Configuration partition. If there are no assigned policies, all domain controllers use the default query policy. A site policy can also be assigned. But if a specific policy has been assigned to a domain controller, this policy overrides any others. It seems that there is no UI for assigning a policy to a site. You can do this by manually editing the *queryPolicyObject* attribute of the *NTDS Site Settings* object of the *nTDSSiteSettings* class object. Use the **ADSI Edit** snap-in. It is also possible to use the ModifyLDAP.vbs script (see below).

Query policy applies to the following LDAP query-related operations:

❑ **Search**. By default, you cannot obtain a result set whose size exceeds 1000 rows. You need to use a paged search to perform operations that generate a significant amount of information. It is also easy to exceed the default timeout set for a search operation.

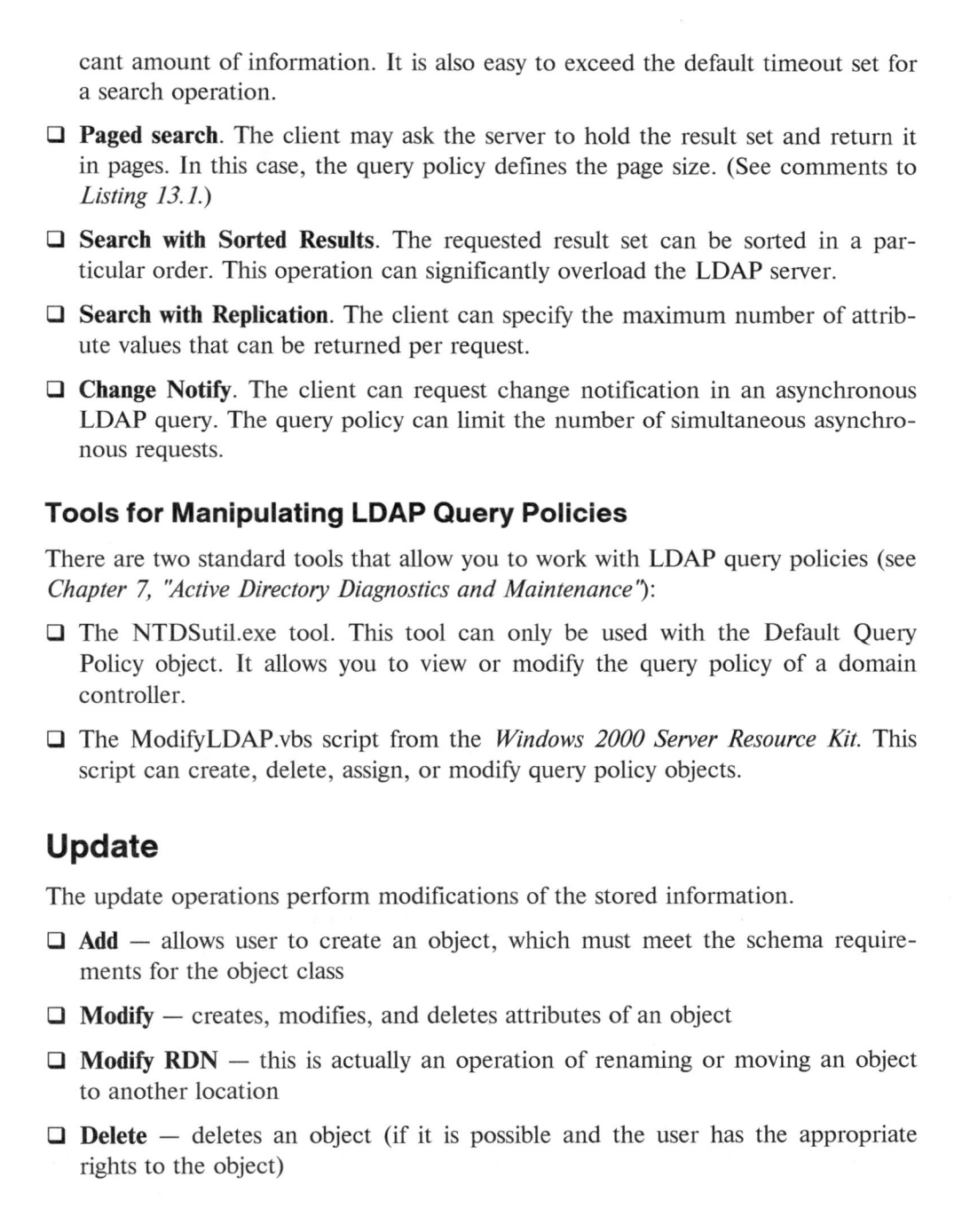

- **Paged search**. The client may ask the server to hold the result set and return it in pages. In this case, the query policy defines the page size. (See comments to *Listing 13.1*.)
- **Search with Sorted Results**. The requested result set can be sorted in a particular order. This operation can significantly overload the LDAP server.
- **Search with Replication**. The client can specify the maximum number of attribute values that can be returned per request.
- **Change Notify**. The client can request change notification in an asynchronous LDAP query. The query policy can limit the number of simultaneous asynchronous requests.

Tools for Manipulating LDAP Query Policies

There are two standard tools that allow you to work with LDAP query policies (see *Chapter 7, "Active Directory Diagnostics and Maintenance"*):

- The NTDSutil.exe tool. This tool can only be used with the Default Query Policy object. It allows you to view or modify the query policy of a domain controller.
- The ModifyLDAP.vbs script from the *Windows 2000 Server Resource Kit*. This script can create, delete, assign, or modify query policy objects.

Update

The update operations perform modifications of the stored information.

- **Add** — allows user to create an object, which must meet the schema requirements for the object class
- **Modify** — creates, modifies, and deletes attributes of an object
- **Modify RDN** — this is actually an operation of renaming or moving an object to another location
- **Delete** — deletes an object (if it is possible and the user has the appropriate rights to the object)

Security Model

To provide secure access to an LDAP server, the LDAP v.3 protocol allows the use of Simple Authentication and Security Layer (SASL) mechanisms. Active Directory supports SASL mechanisms, which include Kerberos Version 5 and MS Negotiate. The *supportedSASLMechanisms* attribute of the RootDSE object stored on a Windows 2000-based domain controller contains two values: GSSAPI and GSS-SPNEGO. GSSAPI means Kerberos, and GSS-SPNEGO stands for NT Negotiate (Kerberos, NT LAN Manager (NTLM), etc.).

LDAP Ports

The connection via the LDAP protocol between a client and DSA uses either a Transmission Control Protocol (TCP) or User Datagram Protocol (UDP). The table below lists the protocol sockets used in different access modes:

Function	Port
LDAP	389
LDAP Secure Sockets Layer (SSL)	636
Global Catalog (GC)	3268
Global Catalog Secure Sockets Layer	3269

DNS Records Registered by Windows 2000-based Domain Controllers

All resource records (20 in total, if the domain controller is the Global Catalog server; 15 if it is not) that each Windows 2000-based domain controller must register on a DNS server, are contained in the *%SystemRoot%*\system32\config\netlogon.dns file. (If your DNS server doesn't support dynamic records update, you need to manually support these records.) An example of such a file is presented below. In this example: server name — w2kdc2.subdom.w2k.dom, domain name — subdom.w2k.dom, root domain name — w2k.dom, site name — W2k-site. The records are sorted for convenience. The real order will differ, but this doesn't

Chapter 1: Active Directory Concepts and Terminology 21

matter. The records for a global catalog server are shown in bold. You can check out all similar records in the DNS snap-in.

```
subdom.w2k.dom. 600 IN A 192.168.0.2
78ac1552-6e3e-4a82-bc5f-78204b0705c5._msdcs.w2k.dom.
    ↳          600 IN CNAME w2kdc2.subdom.w2k.dom.
_ldap._tcp.subdom.w2k.dom. 600 IN SRV 0 100 389 w2kdc2.subdom.w2k.dom.
_ldap._tcp.dc._msdcs.subdom.w2k.dom. 600 IN SRV 0 100 389
    ↳          w2kdc2.subdom.w2k.dom.
_ldap._tcp.pdc._msdcs.subdom.w2k.dom. 600 IN SRV 0 100 389
    ↳          w2kdc2.subdom.w2k.dom.
```
`_ldap._tcp.gc._msdcs.w2k.dom. 600 IN SRV 0 100 3268`
    ↳   `w2kdc2.subdom.w2k.dom.`
```
_ldap._tcp.7050f604-9f15-4536-a592-
    ↳          76d5af2e3487.domains._msdcs.w2k.dom.
    ↳          600 IN SRV 0 100 389 w2kdc2.subdom.w2k.dom.
_ldap._tcp.W2k-site._sites.subdom.w2k.dom. 600 IN SRV 0 100 389
    ↳          w2kdc2.subdom.w2k.dom.
_ldap._tcp.W2k-site._sites.dc._msdcs.subdom.w2k.dom.
    ↳          600 IN SRV 0 100 389 w2kdc2.subdom.w2k.dom.
_ldap._tcp.W2k-site._sites.gc._msdcs.w2k.dom.
    ↳          600 IN SRV 0 100 3268 w2kdc2.subdom.w2k.dom.
gc._msdcs.w2k.dom. 600 IN A 192.168.0.2
_gc._tcp.w2k.dom. 600 IN SRV 0 100 3268 w2kdc2.subdom.w2k.dom.
_gc._tcp.W2k-site._sites.w2k.dom. 600 IN SRV 0 100 3268
    ↳          w2kdc2.subdom.w2k.dom.
_kerberos._tcp.subdom.w2k.dom. 600 IN SRV 0 100 88
    ↳          w2kdc2.subdom.w2k.dom.
_kerberos._udp.subdom.w2k.dom. 600 IN SRV 0 100 88
    ↳          w2kdc2.subdom.w2k.dom.
_kerberos._tcp.dc._msdcs.subdom.w2k.dom. 600 IN SRV 0 100 88
    ↳          w2kdc2.subdom.w2k.dom.
_kerberos._tcp.W2k-site._sites.dc._msdcs.subdom.w2k.dom.
    ↳          600 IN SRV 0 100 88 w2kdc2.subdom.w2k.dom.
_kerberos._tcp.W2k-site._sites.subdom.w2k.dom.
    ↳          600 IN SRV 0 100 88 w2kdc2.subdom.w2k.dom.
_kpasswd._tcp.subdom.w2k.dom. 600 IN SRV 0 100 464
    ↳          w2kdc2.subdom.w2k.dom.
_kpasswd._udp.subdom.w2k.dom. 600 IN SRV 0 100 464
    ↳          w2kdc2.subdom.w2k.dom.
```

As you can see, the first two records have the A (host) and CNAME (alias) types, respectively; the last records have the SRV (service location) type. Let's discuss the purpose of every record in the order that they are presented in the listing above. *DNSDomainName* is the name of the current domain, e. g. `subdom.w2k.dom`. *DNSRootName* is the name of the forest root domain (it can be the *tree* root domain name if there is only one tree in the domain structure), e. g. `w2k.dom`.

> **IMPORTANT!**
>
> Don't confuse a *tree* root domain name (there may be a few in the forest) with the *forest* root domain name (only one)! For example, a forest may include two domain trees with the root domains *w2k.dom* and *w2000.dom*. Only the first created domain — w2k.dom — will be the forest root domain. Therefore, if the global catalog servers appear in the w2000.dom domain (or in its child domains), they will still register the appropriate records in the w2k.dom DNS zone.

`<DNSDomainName>` — a client can use this A record to find a domain controller in the domain using a normal host record lookup.

`<NTDSSettingsGUID>._msdcs.<DNSRootName>` — each domain controller registers this CNAME record for its child object, CN=NTDS Settings,CN=<DCName>,CN=Servers,CN=<SiteName>,CN=Sites, CN=Configuration,DC=<DomainName>, which uniquely identifies this controller in the Active Directory replication topology. A client can use this CNAME record to find any DC in the forest.

`_ldap._tcp.<DNSDomainName>` — a client can use this record to find the LDAP server in the specified domain. Each domain controller registers this record.

`_ldap._tcp.dc._msdcs.<DNSDomainName>` — allows a client to find a DC in the specified domain. Each domain controller registers this record. This record (with different domain names) is used for joining a domain, a tree, or a forest; the current, parent, or root domain name is specified, respectively.

`_ldap._tcp.pdc._msdcs.<DNSDomainName>` — a client can use this record to find the primary domain controller (PDC) in a mixed-mode domain. Only the PDC masters register this record.

`_ldap._tcp.gc._msdcs.<DNSRootName>` — a client can use this record to locate a Global Catalog (GC) server in the forest. Only GC servers register this record.

`_ldap._tcp.<DomainGUID>.domains._msdcs.<DNSRootName>` — a client can use this record to locate a domain controller in the domain specified by the domain GUID. Each domain controller registers this record.

`_ldap._tcp.<SiteName>._sites.<DNSDomainName>` — a client can use this record to find an LDAP server (not necessarily a DC) in the specified domain and site. Each Windows 2000-based DC registers this record for its site.

`_ldap._tcp.<SiteName>.sites.dc._msdcs.<DNSDomainName>` — a client can use this record to locate a domain controller in the specified domain and site. Each domain controller registers this record.

`_ldap._tcp.<SiteName>.sites.gc._msdcs.<DNSRootName>` — allows a client to find a GC server for the forest in the specified site. Only GC servers register this record for their site.

`gc._msdcs.<DNSRootName>` — allows a non-SRV-aware client to find a GC server for the forest.

`_gc._tcp.<DNSRootName>` — a client can use this record to locate a GC server (not necessarily a DC) in the forest. Only an LDAP server that is the GC server registers this record.

`_gc._tcp.<SiteName>._sites.<DNSRootName>` — allows a client to find a GC server (not necessarily a DC) for the forest in the specified site.

`_ldap._tcp.<SiteName>._sites.<DNSRootName>` — a client can use this record to find a LDAP server (not necessarily a DC) in the forest.

`_kerberos._tcp.<DNSDomanName>` — a client can use this record to locate a server (not necessarily a DC) that is running the Kerberos Key Distribution Center (KDC) service in the specified domain. Each Windows 2000-based DC registers this record.

`_kerberos._udp.<DNSDomanName>` — the same as above, but for the UDP protocol.

`_kerberos._tcp.dc._msdcs.<DNSDomanName>` — a client can use this record to locate a server (not necessarily a DC) that is running the Kerberos KDC service in the specified domain and site. Each DC registers this record.

`_kerberos._tcp.<SiteName>._sites.dc._msdcs.<DNSDomanName>` — a client can use this record to locate a Windows 2000-based DC that is running the Kerberos KDC service in the specified domain. Each DC registers this record.

`_kerberos._tcp.<SiteName>._sites.<DNSDomanName>` — a client can use this record to locate a Windows 2000-based DC that is running the Kerberos KDC service in the specified domain and site. Each DC registers this record.

`_kpasswd._tcp.<DNSDomanName>` — a client can use this record to locate a server (not necessarily a DC) that is running the Kerberos Password Change service in the specified domain. Each Windows 2000-based DC that is running the Kerberos KDC service registers this record.

`_kpasswd._udp.<DNSDomanName>` — the same as above, but for the UDP protocol.

> **NOTE**
>
> Notice that all records for global catalog servers refer to the *forest root* domain name.

The following dialog shows how to query the DNS server for the records registered by the Global Catalog servers. (Input commands are in bold.)

```
C:\>nslookup
Default Server:  w2kdc4.w2k.dom
Address:  192.168.0.4
> set type=SRV
> _gc._tcp.w2k.dom
Server:  w2kdc4.w2k.dom
Address:  192.168.0.4
_gc._tcp.w2k.dom        SRV service location:
        priority        = 0
        weight          = 100
        port            = 3268
        svr hostname    = w2kdc4.w2k.dom
_gc._tcp.w2k.dom        SRV service location:
        priority        = 0
        weight          = 100
        port            = 3268
        svr hostname    = w2kdc2.subdom.w2k.dom
w2kdc4.w2k.dom   internet address = 192.168.0.4
w2kdc2.subdom.w2k.dom   internet address = 192.168.2.2
>
```

To re-register the SRV records on a DNS server (provided that it implements dynamic updating), one of the following methods can be used:

- `ipconfig /registerdns` and `netdiag /fix` commands
- Restart the Netlogon service in the **Services** snap-in
- Enter successively `net stop netlogon` and `net start netlogon` at the command prompt

Chapter 2

Configuring and Troubleshooting Windows 2000-based Domains

Certainly, the name of this chapter reflects a huge topic that cannot be fully considered even in a dozen books. I'll discuss only certain issues here, ones that you inevitably encounter in your practice, and that you shouldn't forget about.

Placing FSMO Roles

Every Windows 2000 beginner first learns a piece of good news: all Windows 2000-based domain controllers (DCs) are peers, write operations are permitted on every DC, and all changes are replicated from the originating DC to others (so called multi-master replications). These features are a serious advantage when compared to the rules accepted in Windows NT-based domains. Some time later, the beginner learns some bad news: there are operations when some DCs perform additional functions comparing with other DCs, and instead of the one role available for a DC in Windows NT-based domains — either Primary Domain Controller (PDC) or Backup Domain Controller (BDC) — a Windows 2000-based domain controller can simultaneously perform up to five different roles. These roles are known as Flexible Single-Master Operation (FSMO) roles. (You can easily find a description of each role in the Help system. Open the **Index** tab and enter FSMO as the keyword.)

Here are some guidelines that will help you to properly assign the FSMO roles:

- ❑ Notwithstanding the fact that the PDC Emulator in Windows 2000 domains doesn't play as important a role as the PDC plays in Windows NT domains, you must carefully assign this role. Even in the native mode Windows 2000 domains, the PDC Emulator is used as a primary authority for updating user passwords. By default, it is also selected by the **Group Policy** snap-ins, and you may have trouble editing group policies if the PDC Emulator is inaccessible. All DCs in a domain will synchronize clock with the PDC Emulator. In a multiple-domain forest, the PDC Emulator from each domain will synchronize clock with the PDC Emulator located in the forest root domain. The forest root PDC Emulator should synchronize its clock with an external time source.

- ❑ If a domain has two or more DCs, the Infrastructure Master and a GC server shouldn't be placed on the same DC; however, they need to be connected by a high-speed link to reduce network traffic. (You can ignore this requirement if there is only one DC in a domain, or if each DC in a domain is the GC server.) It is advisable to deploy at least one GC per site. However, it is not typically recommended to designate all DCs in the domain as GC servers, since this produces additional network traffic.

- Place the Schema Master and Domain Naming Master on the same DC and assign this DC as a GC server. This is mandatory to guarantee the uniqueness of names in the forest.
- By default, the first DC installed into a domain owns all of the operations master roles. If you remove Active Directory from this domain controller, all roles are automatically transferred to another available DC. If the demotion process fails, you must manually seize the operations master roles. (See the description of the NTDSutil tool in *Chapter 7, "Active Directory Diagnostics and Maintenance"*.) If, however, the demoted DC was a GC server, you must be sure that there are other GC servers in the forest, and designate a new GC server if necessary.

Native Mode Domains

Keep in mind the following information regarding the mixed and native modes of Windows 2000-based domains:

- It is *impossible to reverse* a domain from native to mixed mode without re-installing Active Directory in this domain.
- It is *not required* that all domains in a tree be in the same mode.
- The native mode has *no impact* on down-level clients such as Windows 9*x*/ME or Windows NT. This is also the case with trusts with Windows NT 4.0 domains. But remember that a trust with any NT 4.0 domain is always explicit, unidirectional, and non-transitive.

Replication Issues

The Active Directory service is a distributed network database, and synchronization of its replicas stored on different domain controllers is vital in order for the service to work. Replication issues are one of the main sources of trouble for an administrator; that is why I'd like to consider some replication-related topics in more details.

Intra- and Inter-site Replication

The concept of site that appears in Windows 2000 domains significantly affects the methods of replicating directory partitions within a site and between sites, as well as the replication transports (protocols).

Replication Transports

The following table lists the rules applicable to the various transports used for different types of replication:

Directory partitions	Within a site	Between Sites	
		The same domain	Different domains
Domain Naming context	RPC over IP	"IP" (RPC over IP)	—
Configuration Schema Global Catalog		"IP" (RPC over IP)	"IP" (RPC over IP) or SMTP over IP
	Uncompressed	Compressed	

"RPC over IP" enables high-speed, synchronous replication. "IP" (as accepted in the **Active Directory Sites and Services** snap-in) enables a low-speed, point-to-point, synchronous replication for all directory partitions. "SMTP over IP" provides low-speed, asynchronous replication between sites and supports only Configuration, Schema, and Global Catalog replication.

Normal Replication Intervals

There are two default methods of replicating object changes in Windows 2000-based forests:

- *Change notification* is used between DCs within a site. If a DC updates an object attribute, it will send notification to its first replication partner within a specified time interval (5 minutes by default). Then, the partner "pulls" the changes from the originating DC. You can change the default interval (300 seconds) by modifying the **Replicator notify pause after modify (secs)** value under the HKLM\SYSTEM\CurrentControlSet\Services\NTDS\Parameters registry key. The originating DC will notify the next replication partner within the time specified by the **Replicator notify pause between DSAs (secs)** registry value.

- Changes are replicated between sites according to a *schedule* (configured for site links and connections). You can configure change notifications between sites too. (Microsoft, however, doesn't generally recommend such a practice.) To do so, point to the **Sites | Inter-Sites Transports | IP** node in the **Active Directory Sites and Services** snap-in, open the **Properties** window, and check the **Ignore schedules** box on the **General** tab.

Urgent Replication

Certain events on DCs are replicated immediately rather than at predefined intervals. This is known as urgent replication. The following events on any domain controller trigger urgent replication between Windows 2000-based DCs in the same site:

- Setting an account lockout after a certain number of failed user logon attempts
- Changing a Local Security Authority (LSA) secret
- Changing the RID Master FSMO role owner

(If a change notification is configured between sites, the urgent replication can be propagated to other sites.)

Urgent replication in Windows 2000 domains is not initiated by the following events:

- Changing the Account Lockout Policy
- Changing the domain Password Policy
- Changing the password on a machine account
- Changing inter-domain trust passwords

If a user changes the password at a specific DC, that DC attempts to urgently replicate the changes to the PDC Emulator. The updated password is then normally replicated to other DCs located in the same site. If the user is repeatedly authenticated by a DC that has not yet received the updated password, this DC refers to the PDC Emulator to check the user credentials.

Replication of Group Policy Objects (GPOs)

Group Policy Objects consist of two parts. One part is located in Active Directory (the *DS part*), and the other part is stored on the hard disk in the SYSVOL volume (the *Sysvol part*). Hence, GPOs are replicated in two ways: by normal Active Directory replication and by File Replication Service (FRS). Forcing one replication doesn't affect the other. That is why you should monitor the consistency of GPOs. For that purpose, use such tools as Active Directory Replication Monitor (ReplMon.exe) or GPOTool.exe that display the DS version and the Sysvol version separately for each GPO.

Monitoring Replication

You may wish to monitor replication events both in a test and a working environment. (The only difference may be in the level of detail given for registering events.) To solve this task, it is possible to use the event logs and performance counters.

Logging Replication Events

You can use the *Directory Service* event log for monitoring such events as the moments of replication request completion, the number, total size, and names of replicated attributes, and so on. The granularity level of logged events is set through the system registry (see below).

Set the *Replication Events* value at the HKLM\SYSTEM\CurrentControlSet\Services\NTDS\Diagnostics registry key equal to 3 or 4 (the difference between the cases will be discussed later). This will help you to see all replication requests, the sequence of replicating directory partitions, and the result of the requests. (Two domain controllers from the same domain — *W2KDC3* and *W2KDC4* — are used in the following examples.) The following two events are logged after each directory partition has been successfully replicated (W2KDC4 asks W2KDC3 for the changes):

```
Event Type: Information
Event Source:      NTDS Replication
Event Category:    Replication
Event ID: 1060
...
User:              Everyone
Computer:  W2KDC4
Description:
Internal event: The directory replication agent (DRA) call completed
successfully.
 - - - - -
Event Type: Information
```

Chapter 2: Configuring and Troubleshooting Windows 2000-based Domains 31

```
Event Source:       NTDS Replication
Event Category:     Replication
Event ID:   1488
...
User:               W2KDOM\administrator
Computer:   W2KDC4
Description:
Internal event: The Directory Service completed the sync request with
```
status code 0.

Any replicated information is logged as an event similar to the following (W2KDC3 asks W2KDC4 for the outbound changes):

```
Event Type: Information
Event Source:       NTDS Replication
Event Category:     Replication
Event ID:   1073
...
User:               W2KDOM\W2KDC3$
Computer:   W2KDC4
Description:
Internal event: The directory replication agent (DRA) got changes
returning 2 objects, 2448 bytes total and entries up to update
sequence number (USN) 100225, with extended return 0.
- - - - -
Event Type: Information
Event Source:       NTDS Replication
Event Category:     Replication
Event ID:   1490
...
User:               W2KDOM\W2KDC3$
Computer:   W2KDC4
Description:
Internal event: The Directory Service finished gathering outbound
changes with the following results:

 Object Update USN: 100225
 Attribute Filter USN: 100225
```
 Object Count: 2
```
 Byte Count: 2448
 Extended Operation Result: 0
```
 Status: 0

To see replication events, set it to at least Level 3. Level 4 allows you to track replication of each changed attribute. (Use this level for debugging only! If a lot of objects are replicated, the number of events in the Directory Service log may be huge. This also significantly affects the performance of the DC.) You can easily find all replicated data by the Event ID. A message (ID 1239) similar to the following is written in the log for all *unchanged* attributes of the replicated objects:

```
Event Type: Information
Event Source:      NTDS Replication
Event Category:    Replication
Event ID:   1239
...
User:              W2KDOM\W2KDC3$
Computer:  W2KDC4
Description:
Property 20002 (whenCreated) of object CN=John
Smith,OU=Staff,DC=w2k,DC=dom (GUID 3b2653cf-76e6-4d35-abf5-
ec4c78fad8ee) is not being sent to DSA a9d28d8e-e681-449f-b1be-
38dadf6f4c06 because its up-to-date vector implies the change is
redundant.
```

If an attribute was changed, it is replicated to another DC, and the message with the ID 1240 will appear in the log:

```
Event Type: Information
Event Source:      NTDS Replication
Event Category:    Replication
Event ID:   1240
...
User:              W2KDOM\W2KDC3$
Computer:  W2KDC4
Description:
Property d (description) of object CN=John
Smith,OU=Staff,DC=w2k,DC=dom (GUID 3b2653cf-76e6-4d35-abf5-
ec4c78fad8ee) is being sent to DSA a9d28d8e-e681-449f-b1be-
38dadf6f4c06.
```

You can filter out events that don't have ID 1240, and quickly check all replicated objects and changed attributes.

Using the Performance Counters

Performance counters are very useful to monitor replication events, especially the replication traffic. To start monitoring, run the **Performance** snap-in (from the Administrative Tools group). Select **System Monitor** and click the **Add** button on the taskpad. Select **NTDS** in the **Performance object** list and add the counters shown in Fig. 2.1. (The *Report View* seems to be the most useful.) All counters have zero values immediately after startup of the DC. (The NTDS performance object has a great number of counters, and I've selected only some of them that are related to replication.)

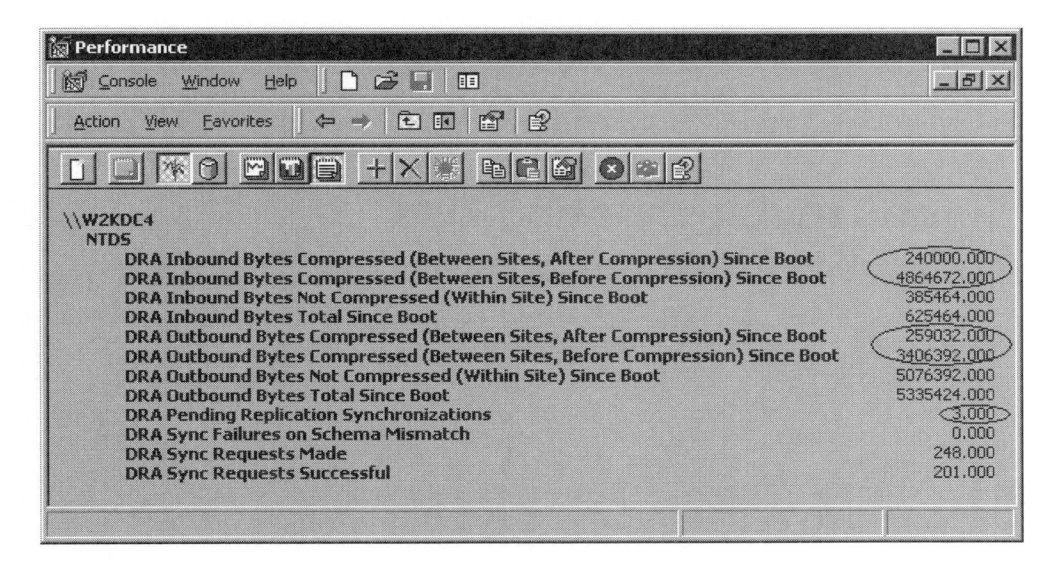

Fig. 2.1. Some of the counters important for monitoring replication

> **NOTE**
>
> As you can see in Fig. 2.1, compression of inbound replication traffic can reach 13 to 1, and 20:1 has been reached for outbound traffic. If the replicated block of information is not large enough (less than 32 Kbytes), compression of inter-site traffic isn't carried out.

You can also create a custom MMC console that will contain a copy of System Monitor Control for each selected domain controller. (Start an MMC console, select **ActiveX Control** in the **Add Standalone Snap-in** window, and find the *System Monitor Control* in the **Control type** list. Repeat this procedure for each desired

DC. Then, select the performance counters from different DCs and add them to the appropriate ActiveX controls.)

The *DRA Sync Requests Successful* value must normally be equal to the *DRA Sync Request Made* value. The values may differ on the DC(s) booted first, while its replication partners may yet be non-operational. Remember the values when all DCs in the network are online and replicated. From that moment on, the difference between these values must not *increase*.

The *DRA Pending Synchronizations* counter displays the number of replication requests that have not been completed yet (any result — a success or a failure — is possible).

The *DRA Inbound/Outbound Bytes Not Compressed (Within Site) Since Boot* counters register both intra- and inter-domain replication traffic, provided this traffic has not been compressed (i. e. replication block size doesn't exceed 32 Kbytes).

Some Troubleshooting Tips

It is not possible to answer each question related to troubleshooting Active Directory. (It is *Microsoft Knowledge Base* that tries to solve this problem, and usually with success!) I'd rather like to consider here a few relatively simple tips, which, nevertheless, could be very useful in various real-life situations. (Don't let the brevity of the tips fool you; this information is quite profound. Try it for yourself in practice.)

Logging Diagnostic Events

The HKLM\SYSTEM\CurrentControlSet\Services\NTDS\Diagnostics registry key contains 19 diagnostic entries that represent the events that Active Directory can register in the Directory Service log. Each entry can have a REG_DWORD value ranging from 0 to 5, which corresponds to the level of granularity of logged events. When the default level 0 is set, only critical events are logged. This is the normal value for most entries. "Super-verbose" level 5 should be used with care, since it causes all events to be logged and is only used for debugging specific problems. If you have encountered an Active Directory-related problem, try to slightly increase the value of the appropriate registry value and reproduce the problem. Don't forget to restore the default value when the problem is resolved.

There are no strict rules for selecting an entry value. You can do this in an experimental way. Use of the Replication Events entry has been discussed above. If, for example, the value of the Garbage Collection entry is set to 3, you can see when the garbage collection starts and completes, as well as the volume of free space in the directory database file. When the value is set to 5, each object deletion will also be logged.

Internal Errors During Replication

There is a kind of replication error that happens when a specific object "prevents" a replication request from being completed. (Remember that you cannot simply delete this object, since deleted objects are also replicated.) *Microsoft Knowledge base article Q265090* describes troubleshooting similar errors that may appear during the replication phase of the server promotion process. A similar approach can also be used for other cases of internal errors related to replication. You should delete the interfering object, decrease the tombstone lifetime to minimum, and wait until the garbage collection entirely deletes the object. This trick has saved my network a few times, when all other means didn't help at all.

Verifying a Windows 2000 Server Status

As you know, a Windows 2000-based server can advertise itself as a domain controller (if it has been promoted to perform such a role), and a Windows 2000-based domain controller can also advertise itself as a Global Catalog (GC) server. There are quite a few cases when you may wish to be sure that this process has been successfully completed. For example, if the File Replication Service (FRS) encounters some trouble, it doesn't initialize the system volume, and the Netlogon service thus cannot share the SYSVOL volume. (The NETLOGON volume also cannot be shared.) This results in problems with applying group policies, as well as many other replication and authentication problems. Here is another situation. The promotion of a DC to a GC server is normally delayed for 5 minutes. But due to replication problems this process can last longer. In both cases, before you begin to locate connectivity, authentication, or other potential problems, you need to be sure that your server *really acts* as a domain controller or a GC server.

Advertising a Server as a Domain Controller

Here are the methods that will allow you to identify whether a Windows 2000-based server is a domain controller after its promotion or normal reboot:

- The HKEY_LOCAL_MACHINE\SYSTEM\CurrentControlSet\Services registry key must contain the NTDS subkey.

- Enter net accounts at the command prompt. The "Computer role" of a domain controller is "PRIMARY" while stand-alone servers identify themselves as "SERVERS".

- Enter net start at the command prompt. The list of running services must contain the Kerberos Key Distribution Center service.

- Enter nbtstat -n at the command prompt. The domain name with the <1C> type must be registered.

- Enter net share at the command prompt. The SYSVOL (*%SystemRoot%*\SYSVOL\sysvol) and NETLOGON (*%SystemRoot%*\SYSVOL\sysvol\<DomainDNSName>\SCRIPTS) shares must exist.

- Use Ldp.exe to view the *isSynchronized* attribute of the RootDSE object. (For more information, see the previous chapter and *Chapter 9, "Manipulating Active Directory Objects"*.) After a server promotion, the system must perform a full synchronization of all directory partitions. When this process is completed, the *isSynchronized* attribute is set to TRUE.

- Use NLtest.exe. (More details are in *Chapter 8, "Network and Distributed Services"*.)

- Use NTDSutil.exe to connect to the domain controller and verify its responding to LDAP queries. (For more information, see *Chapter 7, "Active Directory Diagnostics and Maintenance"*.) You can also use this tool to verify whether the DC knows about the FSMO roles in its domain.

Advertising a Domain Controller as a Global Catalog Server

Assigning a domain controller as a Global Catalog server (for example, in the **Active Directory Sites and Services** snap-in) and *advertising* this DC as a GC server are not the same things. A domain controller can advertise itself as a Global Cata-

Chapter 2: Configuring and Troubleshooting Windows 2000-based Domains 37

log server only after it has *replicated in* all domain partitions existing in the forest at the moment.

You can use the following methods to verify advertising of a DC in the role of Global Catalog server:

- After a DC has been promoted to a GC server, the event with ID 1110 (Event Source: NTDS General; Event Category: Replication) appears in the Directory Service log in Event Viewer. The advertising process completes with the ID 1119 event: "This Windows Domain Controller is now a Global Catalog Server".

- The *Global Catalog Promotion Complete* registry value under the HKEY_LOCAL_MACHINE\SYSTEM\CurrentControlSet\Services\NTDS\Parameters key must be equal to 1.

- Use Ldp.exe to view the *isGlobalCatalogReady* attribute of the RootDSE object. (For more information, see the previous chapter and *Chapter 9*.)

- Use NLtest.exe. (More details are in *Chapter 8*.)

Chapter 3
Deploying Active Directory

An administrator who is not yet closely acquainted with Active Directory must be aware of the two following postulates:

- The terms "creating a domain controller", "installing Active Directory", and "promoting a server" are, in a sense, synonymous because they describe the same process. You cannot install Active Directory without creating a domain controller and vice versa.

- Active Directory or Windows 2000-based domains just don't work without DNS. DNS is one of the "cornerstone" services for a Windows 2000 domain, and you *must* use it in any domain structure based on Active Directory. Is it possible to exploit DNS servers other than Microsoft DNS Server, but these servers must conform to specific requirements. You needn't become a DNS *guru*, but you *have to* be familiar with all DNS essentials and its interoperation with the Active Directory.

Any administrator, even a quite experienced one, should always remember that the DNS is the "heart" of Windows 2000-based domains, and *many*, *many* faults, all very different by nature, derive from an improperly configured DNS system. That's why troubleshooting practically every domain related issue should begin with verifying the DNS configuration. And that's why this chapter begins with a discussion of the Windows 2000 DNS Server.

The chapter doesn't contain step-by-step descriptions of *all* typical operations; instead, it deals with only the most important issues.

NOTE

Name resolving systems, such as DNS and WINS, are a vast, complex theme. There are plenty of good specialized books on TCP/IP, DNS, and Windows 2000 DNS Server in particular, and you may wish to read them to obtain a more profound knowledge of the DNS system in general and its realization in Windows 2000.

Windows 2000 DNS Server

This section deals with various aspects of Windows 2000 DNS Server installation. DNS service is mandatory for Active Directory, and you should be familiar with all DNS requirements in a Windows 2000 environment, which have been discussed in detail in *Chapter 2, "Configuring and Troubleshooting Windows 2000-based Domains"*.

You can skip this section if DNS service has already been deployed in your network and configured according to these requirements.

Be careful! The system *permits* promotion of a server to domain controller (i. e. installation of the Active Directory and creation of a domain) without specifying *any* DNS servers. But this is not a guarantee that your domain will work correctly. Quite the reverse! Nevertheless, it can be useful in some cases (as a prelude to domain deployment) if you thoroughly understand all the details of DNS configuring and its interoperation with Active Directory.

You could, for example, first promote a server to DC, and then prepare a DNS server for dynamic updating of the appropriate zones. Enter the DNS server's IP address in the DC's TCP/IP properties, and reboot the DC (or restart the Netlogon service and execute the `ipconfig /registerdns` command). The result will be an excellent configuration! The same procedure is used when you modify the authoritative DNS server for a domain and want to re-register all necessary DNS records.

Prerequisites

The server providing the DNS Service *must* have a *static* IP address. You shouldn't use the address assigned by a DHCP Server.

Before installing DNS service you must configure the primary DNS domain suffix for the server (see "*Setting the DNS Suffix*" below).

There are three types of Windows 2000 DNS servers:

- **Caching** — A standalone, as a rule, DNS server that doesn't host any authoritative zones after its installation, and therefore only caches the clients' queries.
- **Primary** — The server that hosts an updatable, authoritative zone(s) for some domain(s). Resource records from such a server may be transferred to the secondary servers.
- **Secondary** — The server that hosts a read-only replica(s) of zone(s) transferred from a primary (authoritative) server. However, if both the primary and secondary DNS servers hold an *Active Directory-integrated* zone(s) (which is replicated **only in the same domain**), these servers can be regarded as *peers* that are able to accept updates. Active Directory-integrated zones require a DNS server running on a Windows 2000-based domain controller.

> **CAUTION!**
>
> The Active Directory-integrated zones are stored in the domain partition that is replicated only among domain controllers of the same domain. Even if you create a zone with the same name in different domains, there will be *two different* zones, which results in a big mess in the entire DNS structure. If two DNS servers belong to different domains, one server must be primary for the other one.

Installing a Windows 2000 DNS Server

To install and start DNS Service on a Windows 2000 Server, use the Windows Component Wizard that can be found in the Add/Remove Programs applet in the Control Panel. Select **Network Services** and click the **Details** button. Check the **Domain Name System (DNS)** box and click **OK** and then **Next**. After the system files have been copied (the Windows 2000 Server installation CD will be required) and the service started, you will see the new **DNS** snap-in in the **Administrative Tools** group. The DNS service is now installed on the computer and needs configuration. At first, the new DNS server will work as a caching server and will not be authoritative for any zones. Look up the *DNS Server* log in the Event Viewer to be sure that the service was started successfully.

To configure Windows 2000 DNS server, run the **DNS** command from the **Administrative Tools** menu. The started DNS snap-in has a convenient wizard that helps you in creating zones and resource records.

When you simultaneously install Active Directory and DNS service on a server (the first domain controller in the network), the Active Directory Installation Wizard automatically creates the authoritative zone for this domain (for the forest) on the DNS server. If a DNS server already exists, you must manually create a zone for the new forest and enable dynamic updates of the zone. When a child domain in an existing forest is created, the zone of the forest root domain is used, and the wizard itself creates a DNS domain for this child. But if you add a tree to a forest, you again must *manually* create an authoritative zone for the new DNS namespace. Therefore, you always need to manually create the authoritative zones for every new domain tree, except in the case of simultaneous installation of Active Directory and DNS service on the same server.

Installing a DNS Server and a Domain Controller on the Same Server

By default, the forward domain authoritative zone and the root (".") zone are created as *Active Directory-integrated* and allow *Only secure updates*. This means that only authenticated users can update records. Sometimes, the **Yes** option in the **Allow dynamic updates?** list appears to be a better choice.

Secure updates are only enabled for the Active Directory-integrated zones. When a zone becomes Active Directory-integrated, the appropriate zone file is moved from the *%SystemRoot%*\system32\dns folder to the nested backup folder. At the same time, new objects (of dnsZone and dnsNode types) for the zone are created in the Active Directory in the *System/MicrosoftDNS* container in the domain partition.

> **CAUTION!**
>
> DCpromo doesn't create any *reverse* zones on the DNS server. So, to make the DNS server configuration fully operational, it is recommended that you: manually create an appropriate reverse zone (because some utilities and applications use it), enable dynamic updates for it, and re-register the domain controller address with the `ipconfig /registerdns` command.

The "." zone configured by default makes the DNS server the *root* server, which prevents clients' queries from being sent — forwarded — to the external DNS namespace, e. g. to the Internet. To enable forwarders, you can just delete "." zone. By default, the DNS server's IP address is specified on the **Root Hints** tab in the server's **Properties** window. If you have deleted the "." zone, delete also the server name from this tab.

Secondary Server with Active Directory-integrated zones

You can increase the reliability of your network and install an additional (backup) DC-based DNS server. This task will be very simple if the DNS zone or all of zones are Active Directory-integrated. This means that each DC in the domain contains full DNS information. When you install a new DNS server, it automatically loads zone(s) from Active Directory. You need only to specify the server's IP address in the **Alternative DNS server** field in the **TCP/IP Properties** window on every domain client computer.

Verifying the DNS Configuration

After you have installed DNS service on a Windows 2000 Server, or if you had an already functioning Windows 2000 DNS server, you may wish (rather, *need*) to verify the DNS configuration. It is not enough that you yourself think that all DNS parameters are properly set, rather it is the system and program tests that should confirm that all is working fine.

You must check that the DNS server has the correct forward and reverse zones and that these zones allow dynamic records updates. For that purpose it is helpful to use a general purpose command-line DNSCmd.exe utility from the *Support Tools* pack. You can start it from any computer that has access to the inspected server with DNS service. This utility can perform all operations necessary for remote maintenance of a Windows 2000 DNS server.

> **NOTE**
>
> Using more specialized utilities that also help to verify DNS configuration, such as DCdiag.exe and NetDiag.exe is discussed later in the sections *"Installing Domain Controller"* and *"Adding Domain Members"*.

To verify a zone, use the **/enumzones** command. You will get an output similar to the following (which is the output for the simplest configuration):

```
C:\>dnscmd w2kdc2.w2k.dom /EnumZones
Enumerated zone list:
        Zone Count = 6.
       .                               0   file              Up=0
       0.168.192.in-addr.arpa          1   file   Rev        Up=1
       0.in-addr.arpa                  1   file   Rev  Auto  Up=0
       127.in-addr.arpa                1   file   Rev  Auto  Up=0
       255.in-addr.arpa                1   file   Rev  Auto  Up=0
       w2k.dom                         1   file              Up=1
Command completed successfully.
```

In this case, w2kdc2 is the Windows 2000 Server name, "." corresponds to the cached lookups, w2k.dom is a zone name and the DNS name of the future domain, and 0.168.192.in-addr.arpa is the reverse zone for the private network 192.168.0.0 (255.255.255.0 mask; the address and mask depend on your network configuration). The zones marked as Auto are auto-created zones. To see them in the DNS snap-in, choose the **Advanced** option in the **View** menu.

The `Up=1` parameter indicates whether or not the zone is dynamically updated. You can also check this property of zones (e. g. the `w2k.dom` zone) using the following command. (Be careful, the `AllowUpdate` and other zone properties are case-sensitive!):

```
C:\>dnscmd w2kdc2.w2k.dom /ZoneInfo w2k.dom AllowUpdate
Zone query result:
Dword:   1 (00000001)
Command completed successfully.
```

The value 1 indicates that this zone can be dynamically updated.

You must also verify DNS server responsiveness. It is recommended that you do this before any DC creation, in order to avoid serious domain problems in the future. Enter the following command on the inspected computer (a client, or a server to be promoted):

```
C:\>nslookup 192.168.0.2
```

`192.168.0.2` is the DNS server's IP address, specified in the TCP/IP properties of this computer. The result will be similar to the following output:

```
Server:   w2kdc2.w2k.dom
Address:  192.168.0.2

Name:     w2kdc2.w2k.dom
Address:  192.168.0.2
```

Here, the `Server` reply contains the DNS server name, and `Name` is the resolved name of the specified IP address. In this case the names are the same (because we've asked the DNS server for its own name), but you may want to resolve any other IP addresses if their corresponding host names are registered on the DNS server. You may also verify resolving DNS computer names to the IP addresses.

If you receive any different outputs or error messages, like "Can't find server name for address" or "Default servers are not available", you need to check all TCP/IP properties, the connectivity, and the existence of forward and reverse zones. The DNS server may reply with the aforementioned messages, if, for example, the server is operational but the reverse zone is absent or corrupted.

After a domain controller is created (and especially when the first DC in the forest is created), it is strongly recommended to verify the registration of all necessary SRV records (see *Chapter 1, "Active Directory Concepts and Terminology"*). You can also check an SRV record with the DNSCmd.exe utility by entering, for example, the command:

```
C:\>dnscmd w2kdc2.w2k.dom /EnumRecords w2k.dom _tcp.pdc._msdcs
  /Type SRV
```

```
Returned records:
_ldap 600 SRV    0 100 389 w2kdc4.w2k.dom.
Command completed successfully.
```

This is the SRV record registered by the PDC operations master.

These procedures will help in avoiding some pitfalls of domain functioning. Don't forget to set aside at least a half an hour for DNS testing. Take your time and be thorough, or you could spend days trying to resolve potential problems, such as "why is network reaction so slow?" or "why doesn't the new domain controller replicate data?"

Configuring Windows 2000 DNS for Use with Legacy DNS

If Windows 2000 is deployed in an existing network which already uses DNS service, an interoperation problem may arise if the legacy DNS service doesn't conform to Windows 2000 DNS requirements. This situation is quite typical, but there is a way to achieve a compromise. We shall use the adjective *legacy* for any DNS servers that support neither dynamic records update, nor SRV records (this can be, for example, an NT 4.0 DNS Server or a UNIX DNS server).

You can easily diagnose the problem by looking up the System log after creating the first domain controller. (It's strongly recommended to check all logs when *each* DC is created!) After the domain controller boots, the warning (ID 5773) from Netlogon may appear in the System log:

```
The DNS server for this DC does not support dynamic DNS. Add the DNS
records from the file '%SystemRoot%\System32\Config\netlogon.dns' to
the DNS server serving the domain referenced in that file.
```

Let's discuss how to solve the problem using a scenario. To simplify the situation, we'll use the minimal number of computers. Suppose we have an existing Windows NT 4.0 DNS server authoritative for the "w2k.dom" domain. The server has the forward and reverse zones: w2k.dom and 0.168.192.in-addr.arpa. All clients (including Windows 2000 computers) will use this server as preferred. The second DNS server (based on a Windows 2000 Server) has to be configured to support all updateable resource records for the Windows 2000 domain. The computer's names and addresses are shown in the table below:

Computer's name and role	FQDN	IP address
NT4SRV3 (NT 4.0 DNS server)	nt4srv3.w2k.dom	192.168.0.3

continues

Continued

Computer's name and role	FQDN	IP address
W2KDC2 (Windows 2000 DNS server)	w2kdc2.w2k.dom	192.168.0.2
W2KDC4 (Windows 2000 domain controller)	w2kdc4.w2k.dom	192.168.0.4

By default, the dynamic registration of a host's name and address on the preferred DNS server is enabled, so in our scenario we need to disable registration on all Windows 2000 computers to avoid the error messages in the computers' System logs. To do this, reset the **Register this connection's addresses in DNS** flag on the **DNS** tab in the **Advanced TCP/IP Setting** window.

Creating Authoritative Zones

On the Windows 2000 DNS server we need to create four dynamic authoritative zones, necessary for domain functioning. In our scenario, all these zones' names have the *w2k.dom* suffix.

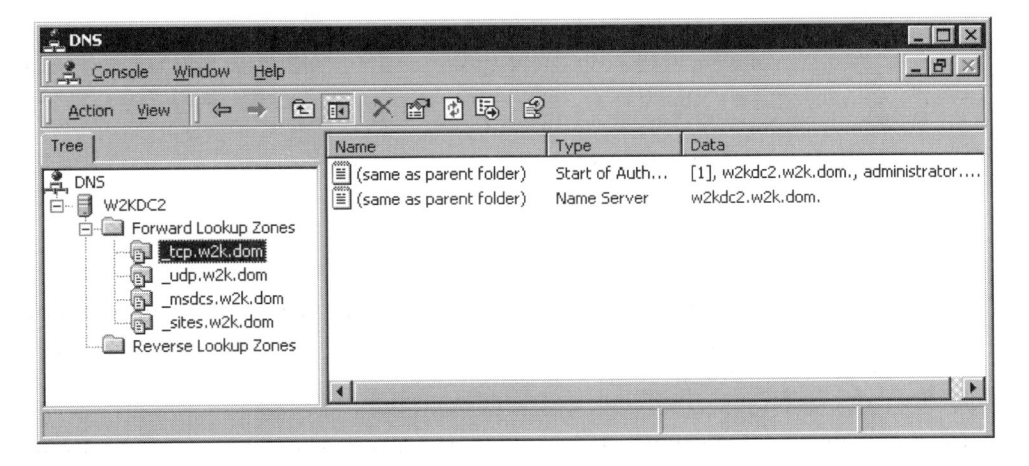

Fig. 3.1. Creating dynamically updateable authoritative zones on the Windows 2000 DNS server

The zones will be the following:

- _msdcs.w2k.dom
- _sites.w2k.dom

- _tcp.w2k.dom
- _udp.w2k.dom

Furthermore, we also have to allow dynamic updates of these zones. Fig. 3.1 illustrates the result obtained in this preliminary step. Notice that each zone has SOA and NS records.

Delegating Dynamic Zones

At the second step, it is necessary to create dynamic zones and delegate them to the Windows 2000 DNS server, where the zones will be stored and updated. All zones are created as subdomains of the authoritative zone w2k.dom.

The result is shown in Fig. 3.2.

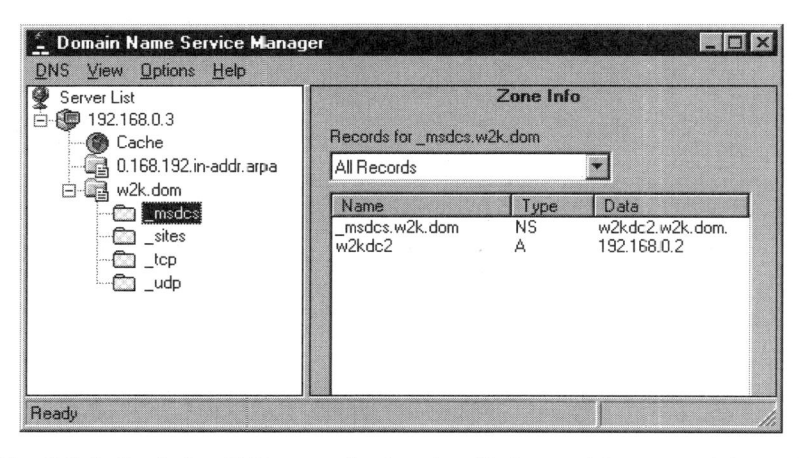

Fig. 3.2. Authoritative DNS server for domain w2k.dom and the zones delegated to the dynamic DNS server W2KDC2

Also, we need to register the following records on the NT 4.0 DNS server:

- Two A records for the Windows 2000 computers with appropriate PTR records
- An A record for the w2k.dom name (this record is needed for finding a domain controller using a simple name lookup)

The latter A record requires additional attention. By design, this record is dynamically updateable. The domain controllers' Netlogon service re-registers it after each system boot. In our case the update is impossible, so an error message will be periodically generated in the System log. You may get rid of the problem by adding the RegisterDNSARecords value (set the value to DWORD 0x0) to the registry in the subkey HKEY_LOCAL_MACHINE\SYSTEM\CurrentControlSet\Services\Netlogon\Parameters.

If you disable registering A records with the subkey RegisterDNSARecords=0, two records are deleted from the netlogon.dns file on the domain controller W2KDC4:

```
w2k.dom IN A 192.168.0.4
```

and

```
gc._msdcs.w2k.dom IN A 192.168.0.4
```

> **CAUTION!**
>
> The RegisterDNSARecords value (being set to 0x0) also prevents the Netlogon service from updating the host (A) record for the gc._msdcs.w2k.dom name. You have to manually add this record and re-register it if the global catalog location is changed.

Resulting Configuration

So, the preliminary steps are over, and the domain controller W2KDC4 is able to update (and first to create) all SRV records.

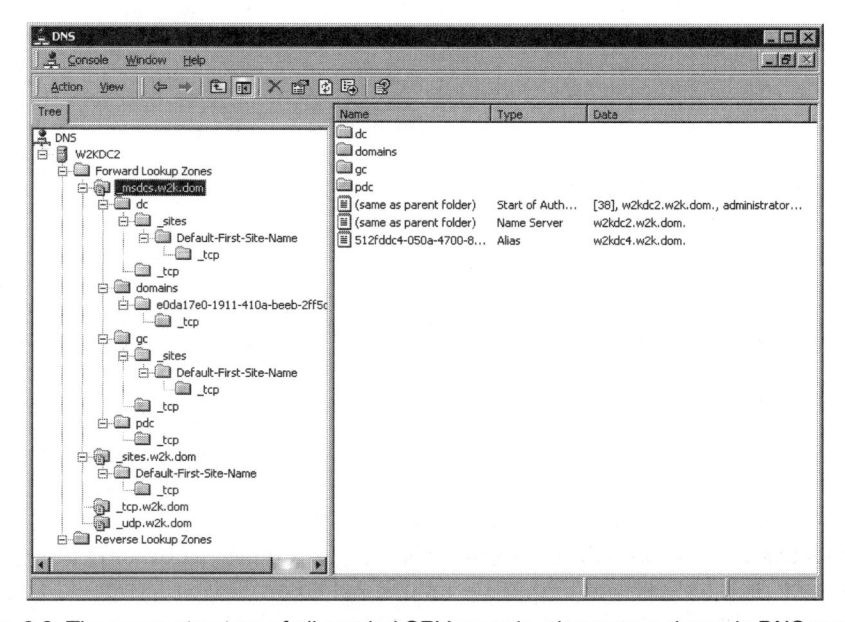

Fig. 3.3. The name structure of all needed SRV records, shown on a dynamic DNS server

You need to restart the Netlogon service or, preferably, reboot the system. After this, you will get all updateable records on the Windows 2000 DNS server (W2KDC2) (see Fig. 3.3).

Now you can (and *should*) check all DNS logs and test the domain controller to be sure that all records have been registered correctly.

Installing Domain Controllers

Creating a Domain Controller

Active Directory can only be installed on an existing Windows 2000 Server. Active Directory installation is a process independent from installing/upgrading the operating system itself. Moreover, you can demote a domain controller (or uninstall Active Directory) to a member (or standalone) server (and promote it again if you wish). The *Active Directory Installation Wizard* is used for both operations. This behavior differs principally from the Windows NT 4.0 "rules", where the role of a server (member server, PDC, or BDC) is specified during installation, and typically cannot be changed without full system re-installation.

Therefore, there are the following ways to create a Windows 2000 domain controller (DC):

❏ Start the Active Directory Installation Wizard on an already installed Windows 2000 Server (standalone or member server). The DCpromo.exe utility is used in such a case. You can work with it either interactively or in unattended mode (see later in this chapter). The result will be a DC in a new domain or an additional DC in an existing domain.

❏ Upgrade a Windows NT 4.0-based domain controller (PDC or BDC). The DCpromo.exe utility is started automatically after the upgrade to Windows 2000 Server is completed and the computer is rebooted.

- A PDC can only be upgraded to a DC in a new domain
- A BDC can be upgraded to an additional DC in an existing domain, or to a member server (if the choice is made not to install Active Directory)

Requirements and Restrictions

The Active Directory can be installed only if several critical conditions are met. The Active Directory Installation Wizard will check different parameters depending on the type of DC that is being created. Among these conditions are the following:

- Active Directory can be installed only on a NTFS 5.0 formatted disk partition.
- This partition must have at least 250 MB of free space.
- If the server is a standalone, only a user that is a member of the local Administrators group can start DCpromo.exe. If the server is a member of a domain, members of the Domain Admins and Enterprise Admins groups can also initiate promotion.
- When creating a new DC in an existing forest, any user that isn't logged on as a domain or enterprise administrator must provide sufficient credentials (a pre-Windows 2000 logon name and a password; names in UPN form, e. g. `admin@w2k.dom`, are not acceptable):
    - Only members of the Enterprise Admins group can create new domains (child domains or new trees). It is possible to have a pre-created new domain in the forest (see NTDSutil.exe in *Chapter 7, "Active Directory Diagnostics and Maintenance"*).
    - The members of the Domain Admins and the Enterprise Admins groups are permitted to add a DC to an existing domain. Some user accounts can also be given rights to join a computer to the domain and create the appropriate replication objects.
- TCP/IP protocol must be installed and configured on the computer. Typically, domain controllers have *static* IP addresses, but conceptually this does not necessarily have to be the case.
- The computer must have the primary DNS suffix. Click **My Computer** on the desktop; then on the **Network identification** tab, first click **Properties** and then **More**. Enter the DNS domain name in the **Primary DNS suffix of this computer** field. This is a *critical* requirement if the computer is going to act as a DNS server. This field will be filled if the computer is a member of a domain, and you needn't change anything. The **Change primary DNS suffix when domain membership changes** box must always be checked.
- An already deployed DNS service must be available. If a legacy or third-party DNS server is used, it should meet the Windows 2000 requirements and be properly configured. If the promoted server will be the first DC and there is no DNS server in the network, you *must* allow the Active Directory Installation Wizard to install and configure the Windows 2000 DNS server.

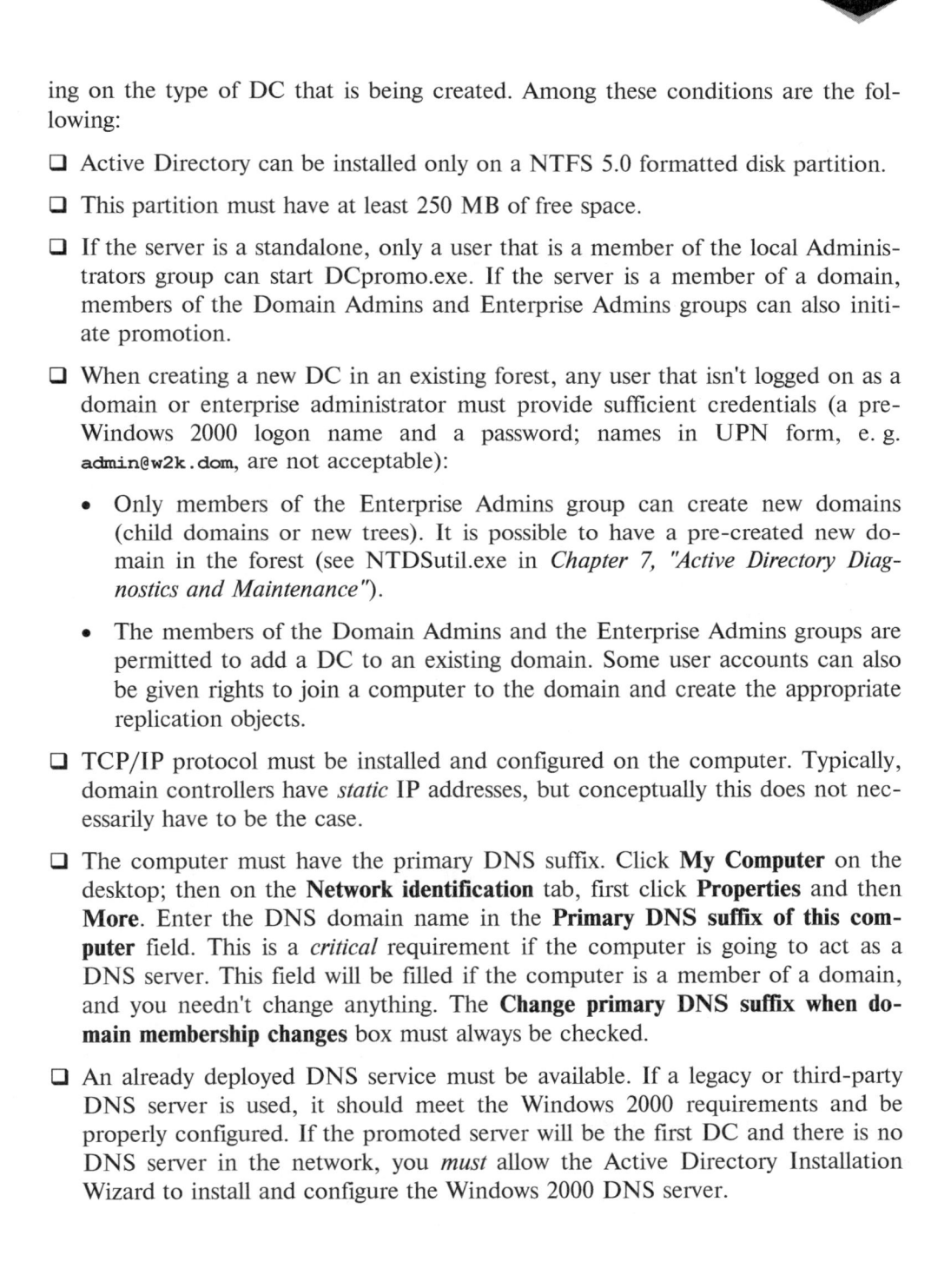

> **NOTE**
>
> A reverse DNS zone is not *required* for Active Directory. Nevertheless, it is recommended to configure one for the other applications that use it.

- The server NetBIOS name must be unique in the domain. The NetBIOS (pre-Windows 2000) name of new domain must be unique in the forest.

- If a child domain (or a new tree) is created, the parent and forest root domains must exist and be accessible. This means that you cannot create a child domain — e. g. subdom.w2k.dom — if the w2k.dom domain does not exist.

- So as not to get hung up in details and in order to considerably simplify the situation, it is possible to say that all **FSMO** masters should be available for starting and successfully completing server promotion. Otherwise, you should always know and remember which **FSMO** masters are required for each specific type of domain controller created.

> **NOTES**
>
> - By default, all domain controllers are created in the *Domain Controllers* OU in the domain partition.
>
> - The computer SID remains the same after the Active Directory installation or removal.
>
> - Let's suppose a server was previously a domain controller and has been demoted, and you again wish to install the Active Directory on to it. It may be useful to delete the folders where the Active Directory files (the database and logs) were stored (by default, the *%SystemRoot%*\NTDS folder is used). Moreover, if the Distributed File System (DFS) is not used on this computer, stop the File Replication Service by using the `net stcp ntfrs` command and delete the contents of the *%SystemRoot%*\ntfrs\jet folder. Then restart the service: `net start ntfrs`.

> **CAUTION!**
>
> At one of the preliminary steps, the Active Directory Installation Wizard asks for your "Directory Services Restore Mode Administrator Password". This password is only used in the logon process after you have pressed the <F8> key in the boot menu and selected the *Directory Services Restore Mode*. The password is not used often, so try not to forget it (this happens!).

Verifying DNS Configuration

This is one of the most important steps in preparing a server for promotion. Any undetected errors in the DNS configuration may result in an inoperable domain controller. The following faults are possible:

- The computer has no settings for the preferred DNS server
- The specified DNS server doesn't host the specified authoritative zone (domain name)
- The authoritative zone exists, but is not updatable

Microsoft has done a great job in extending the functionality of the DCdiag and NetDiag utilities from the *Support Tools* to allow an administrator to verify the DNS configuration in a few seconds. (You can download new versions from the Microsoft website. For additional information on these tools see *Chapter 7, "Diagnostics and Maintenance"* and *Chapter 8, "Network and Distributed Services".*)

If a DNS server's IP address is not specified in the **TCP/IP Properties** window, the `netdiag /test:DsGetDc` or `netdiag /test:DcList` command informs you that

```
The network connections are not configured with preferred DNS
```

and instructions on configuring DNS are following.

The `dcdiag /test:DcPromo` command outputs a message with the error 9852, which means "No DNS servers configured for local system."

The following command reports that you can safely add an additional domain controller in an existing domain (*w2k.dom* in this example):

```
C:\>dcdiag /test:DcPromo /DnsDomain:w2k.dom /ReplicaDC
   Starting test: DcPromo
      The DNS configuration is sufficient to allow this computer
      to be promoted as a replica domain controller in the w2k.dom
      domain.
   ...
      DNS configuration is sufficient to allow this domain controller
      to dynamically register the domain controller Locator records
      in DNS.

   ..................... w2kdc2 passed test DcPromo
```

In such a case you can begin to promote the server. (For compactness, some lines are skipped in this output. Notice that all test runs — successful and failed — end with the same "passed test" line.)

The following output indicates that the authoritative zone exists, but there are no SRV records registered by the existing domain controller:

```
C:\>dcdiag /test:DcPromo /DnsDomain:w2000.dom /ReplicaDC
    Starting test: DcPromo
        This computer cannot be promoted as a domain controller
        of the w2000.dom domain. This is because either the DNS SRV
        record for _ldap._tcp.dc._msdcs.w2000.dom is not registered
        in DNS, or some zone from the following list of DNS zones
        doesn't include delegation to its child zone: w2000.dom, dom
        and the root zone. Ask your network/DNS administrator to perform
        the following actions: To find out why the SRV record for
        _ldap._tcp.dc._msdcs.w2000.dom is not registered in DNS, run
        the dcdiag command prompt tool with the command RegisterInDNS
        on the domain controller that did not perform the registration.
    ...
        DNS configuration is sufficient to allow this domain controller
        to dynamically register the domain controller Locator records
        in DNS.

        ..................... w2kdc2 passed test DcPromo
```

You should verify the DNS configuration and make the DC re-register all its SRV records.

In all cases when updating of an authoritative zone is not enabled on the DNS server (or the server doesn't support dynamic updates), the command output will be similar to the following:

```
C:\>dcdiag /test:DcPromo /DnsDomain:w2k.dom /ReplicaDC
    Starting test: DcPromo
        The DNS configuration is sufficient to allow this computer
        to be promoted as a replica domain controller in the w2k.dom
        domain.
    ...
        This domain controller cannot register domain controller Locator
        DNS records. This is because either the DNS server with IP
        address 192.168.0.4 does not support dynamic updates or the zone
        w2k.dom is configured to prevent dynamic updates.
    ...
```

Detailed instructions on configuring the DNS server are also displayed. You must follow them. To check whether a zone is updatable, it is also possible to use the command

```
dcdiag /test:RegisterInDNS /DnsDomain:w2k.dom
```

which produces a similar output.

Chapter 3: Deploying Active Directory 55

Other parameters of the `dcdiag /test:DcPromo` command allow you to test whether you can create a child domain, new tree, or new forest in the current domain structure. The command's reports are clear, and it isn't necessary to place all them here.

If the preferred DNS server is specified incorrectly or not accessible, or if the authoritative zone didn't configure on the server, the following command will discover the problem and instruct you on what to do:

```
C:\>dcdiag /test:RegisterInDNS /DnsDomain:w2k-new.dom
   Starting test: RegisterInDNS
      Please verify that the network connections of this computer are
      configured with correct IP addresses of the DNS servers to be
      used for name resolution.  If the DNS resolver is configured
      with its own IP address and the DNS server is not running locally
      the DcPromo will be able to install and configure local DNS
      server, but it will be isolated from the existing DNS infra-
      structure (if any). To prevent this either configure local DNS
      resolver to point to existing DNS server or manually configure
      the local DNS server (when running) with correct root hints.

      If the DNS resolver is configured with its own IP address and
      the DNS server is not running locally, the Active Directory
      Installation Wizard can install and configure the local DNS
      server. However, if this server is not connected to the network
      during domain controller promotion then admin needs to
      appropriately configure root hints of the local DNS server
      after the completion of the domain controller promotion.

      ........................ w2kdc2 passed test RegisterInDNS
```

Don't forget that you should also test the DNS configuration (registration of the SRV records) after server promotion has been completed.

> **NOTE**
>
> You can discover more information on additional features of DCdiag and NetDiag in Microsoft Knowledge Base article Q265706.

Running the Active Directory Installation Wizard

There are two ways to start the Active Directory Installation Wizard in interactive mode:

❑ Choose **Start** | **Programs** | **Administrative Tools** | **Configure Your Server**, and then click **Active Directory** in the menu.

❑ Open the **Run** window and enter `dcpromo.exe`.

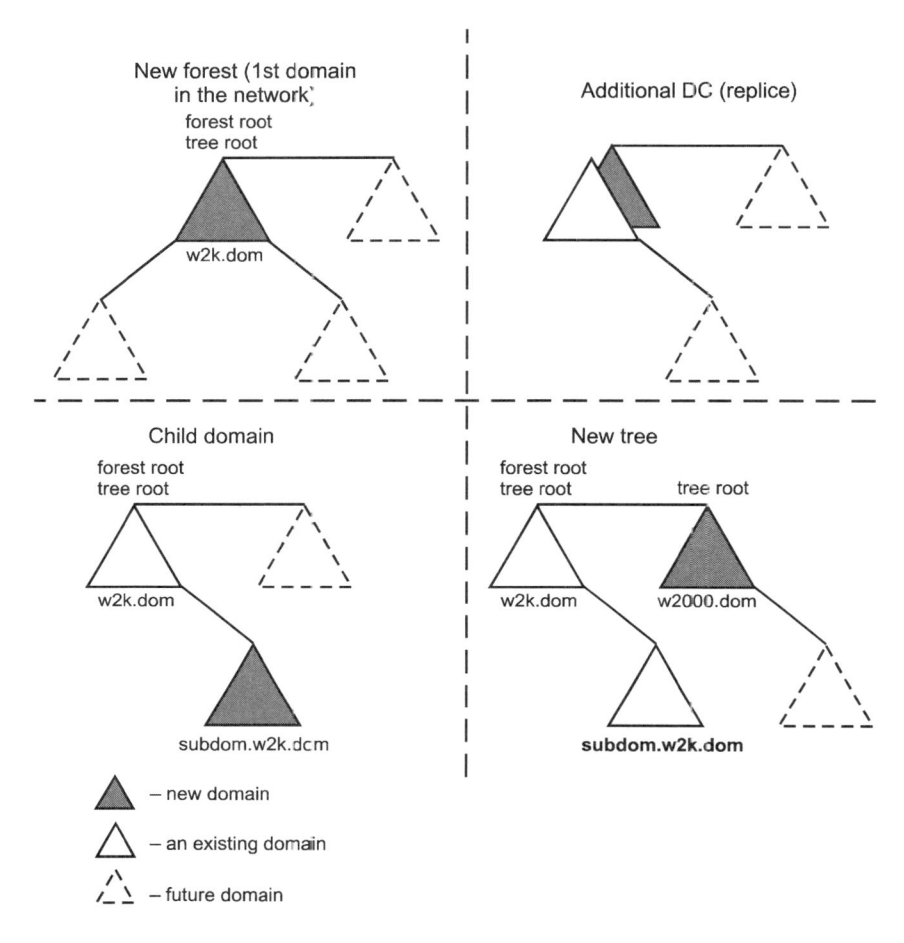

Fig. 3.4. Four scenarios for creating a new domain controller

You have four options for installing the Active Directory; these are graphically represented in Fig. 3.4. The options which you should consequently specify in the wizard's windows are listed below:

1. The first Active Directory installation in the network, or creating a new forest
   - Domain controller for a new domain
   - Create a new domain tree
   - Create a new forest of domain trees

> **NOTE**
>
> Creating a new forest is the only option that doesn't require any existing domain (or domain controller). In all other cases the *Schema* and the *Configuration* partitions are replicated from a source domain controller either in an existing domain (for an additional DC), in the parent (for a child domain), or in the root domain (for a new tree).

2. Additional DC in any existing domain
   - Additional controller for an existing domain
3. Creating a new child domain
   - Domain controller for a new domain
   - Create a new child domain in an existing domain tree
4. Creating a new tree (the root domain with a noncontiguous DNS name) in an existing forest
   - Domain controller for a new domain
   - Create a new domain tree
   - Place this new domain in an existing forest

Depending on the selected option, the wizard will ask you to enter a domain name. It can be the name of an existing domain, parent domain, or forest root domain. It is always recommended to specify *DNS* names because DNS name resolving must already be operational at this stage. Although the wizard can sometimes accept NetBIOS domain names, this doesn't guarantee successful execution of the subsequent Active Directory installation steps.

> **CAUTION!**
>
> At the next step you must specify the domain NetBIOS name. You can choose a name different from the one offered by default if you like (e. g. if the DNS domain name is `w2k.dom`, then the default NetBIOS name will be `W2K`). If Service Pack 1 is not installed on the server, you'll get an error when publishing the printer in the Active Directory (Q255496).

> **NOTE**
>
> During the Active Directory installation, synchronization with existing domain controllers is carried out. It's possible to stop the replication by clicking the **Finish Replication Later** button in the wizard window. The domain controller will advertise itself when the replication has been completed (after the computer reboots).

DNS Server Issues

At a certain moment during Active Directory Installation Wizard execution, the message shown in Fig. 3.5 may appear. It means one of the following:

- There is no DNS server in the network (you are trying to install the DNS server and the domain controller on the same server).
- No address or an incorrect preferred DNS server address is entered in the computer's **TCP/IP Properties** window. (This is a configuration error that the system identifies as the absence of a DNS server.)
- There is no authoritative zone for the new domain on the specified DNS server.

Fig. 3.5. This window warns about potential problems with the preferred DNS server

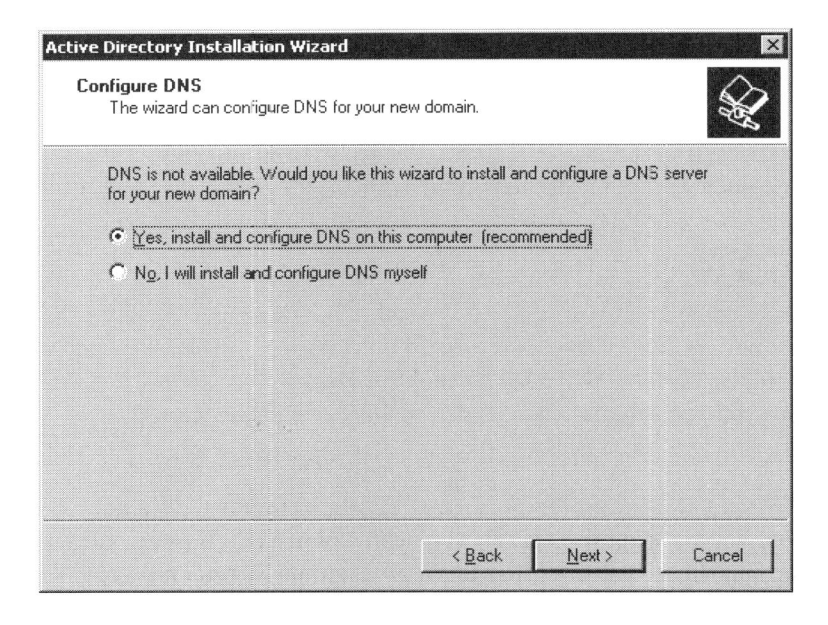

Fig. 3.6. At this point you must decide whether to install the DNS server or not

This window doesn't appear if the DNS server address has been entered correctly and the authoritative zone has been configured on this server, but only if the zone doesn't allow dynamic updates. In such case the window "Configure DNS" (Fig. 3.6) will be next.

This step is a critical point in the installation process, because whether the new domain configuration will work or not depends on what you do here. You have only three alternatives:

- Click **Cancel**, which will terminate the wizard and verify the DNS configuration. You *must* select this option if the promoted server is not the first controller in the domain (forest). If you do not, the Active Directory installation on this server will definitely be unsuccessful: the server will not be able to locate other domain controllers and replicate the Active Directory information from them.
- Agree with the default option and install the DNS server and domain controller on the same computer.
- If you are using a legacy DNS service and have the required subzones delegated to a DNS server that allows dynamic updates, select the **No, I will install and configure DNS myself** option and continue the Active Directory installation.

You may also refuse the default option and continue the installation process if the promoting server is *the only* DC in the network and for some reason you are planning to connect it to a fully configured DNS server only after installing Active Directory and *before* the first DC reboot. This approach may not seem very logical, but is technically quite possible. When the domain controller boots for the first time, it will register all needed resource records on the DNS server (but in the forward zone only, since the wizard doesn't create the reverse zone).

Provided that the DNS configuration fully meets all requirements, you will not see any of the screens described earlier, and the wizard will go to the next step.

Completing and Testing the Installation

After completing the Active Directory installation, the system automatically installs and configures the Windows 2000 DNS Server if this operation has been requested.

After system restart, you can logon to the created domain with local administrator credentials. The local administrator of the server that has been promoted to the first domain controller in a new forest will become a member of the following groups:

- Administrators (built-in local group)

- Domain Admins (is a member of the Administrators group)
- Domain Users (is a member of the built-in local Users group)
- Enterprise Admins (is a member of the Administrators group)
- Group Policy Creator Owners
- Schema Admins

NOTE

Sometimes, while working on the domain controllers in test environments, administrators attempt to logon to a domain using a domain user account, and encounter the "The local policy of this system does not permit you to logon interactively" message. Open the *Default Domain Controllers Policy* GPO, and click the **Computer Configuration | Windows Settings | Security Setting | Local Policies | User Rights Assignment** node. Find the *Log on locally* policy. This policy is *defined* by default, and only the following groups can log on locally: *Account Operators*, *Administrators*, *Backup Operators*, *Print Operators*, and *Server Operators*. Therefore, the "normal" users cannot logon on domain controllers. If you wish (and if security requirements permit), add the *Authenticated Users* or *Everyone* group to this list, and you'll be able to logon locally using any account.

If any applications are running on a Windows NT 4.0-based server that is a member of a Windows 2000 mixed-mode domain, verify that the *Everyone* group is included in the *Pre-Windows 2000 Compatible Access* group with the `net localgroup "Pre-Windows 2000 Compatible Access"` command. If not, type `net localgroup "Pre-Windows 2000 Compatible Access" everyone /add` at the command prompt on a domain controller computer and then restart the domain controller computer.

Log Files

The events that have taken place during Active Directory installation are written in the logs located in the *%SystemRoot%*\debug folder (and are especially useful if the installation crashed):

- csv.log
- dcpromohelp.log
- NetSetup.LOG
- DCPROMO.LOG

- dcpromoui.log
- NtFrs_xxxx.log
- NtFrsApi.log

Deleting a Domain Controller

You cannot *simply* remove a domain controller (DC) from an existing domain structure, since the information about it remains in the Active Directory. The process known as *demotion* allows you to properly remove Active Directory from a DC and automatically update all relative information (if this DC isn't the last one in the network). If the DC is corrupted or has failed, and you cannot successfully perform this operation, you must *manually* cleanup the Active Directory (see *Chapter 7, "Active Directory Diagnostics and Maintenance"*).

After removing Active Directory, the last DC in *any* domain becomes a standalone server that belongs to the *WORKGROUP* workgroup. The DNS suffix of the computer isn't changed.

Requirements

As during Active Directory installation, the other domains (parent or root) must be accessible (otherwise, the demotion will not start). The Active Directory cannot be removed if replication of directory partitions from the demoted server fails. If the demoted DC is an operations master, you need also consider transferring the FSMO roles to other servers. Otherwise the system itself will try to find the appropriate candidates for these roles.

If the last DC in a domain is demoted, this means the deletion of the entire domain. You can only delete a *leaf* domain, i.e. a domain that has no child domains and is not the forest root domain (which can only be deleted last).

Running the Active Directory Installation Wizard

To remove Active Directory from a DC, start the Active Directory Installation Wizard.

You may get the message shown in Fig. 3.7.

Fig. 3.7. Don't delete the last Global Catalog server

Make sure that another GC server exists in the forest. If necessary, designate a new GC server, wait for its advertising, and only then continue the demotion process.

On the next step of Active Directory Installation Wizard you must set or reset the **This server is the last domain controller in the domain** flag. To delete the last DC in a child domain (i.e. to delete this child domain) or in a tree-root domain (i.e. to delete the tree), you must provide the credentials of a member of the Enterprise Admin group. To delete the last DC in a forest (i.e. to destroy the entire forest), you must be logged on as Administrator or as a member of the Domain Admins group. To delete an additional DC, it's sufficient to be logged on as a member of the Domain Admins group.

When the Active Directory has been deleted from a DC, and the demotion process has been completed (after the server reboot), all subdomains with names starting with "_" are deleted from the preferred DNS server (obviously, if the server allows dynamic registration) and the netlogon.dns file is cleared.

Unattended Installing and Removing of Active Directory

Besides the interactive mode, the Active Directory Installation Wizard has an unattended mode similar to the unattended setup of the operating system. All parameters needed for the wizard to operate are written in an answer file that is launched from the command prompt by entering the following string:

```
dcpromo /answer:<answerFile>
```

As in the case of interactive mode, the **Configure Active Directory** window will display all ongoing operations having to do with promoting/demoting the server. If a parameter is missing or incorrect, the wizard will ask the operator for the required or correct value. You may then enter the value and continue the process.

Chapter 3: Deploying Active Directory   63

The description of keys used in the answer file for installing Active Directory (the [DCInstall] section) can be found in the *"Microsoft Windows 2000 Guide to Unattended Setup"*. This file (unattend.doc) is copied to the folder where the *Windows 2000 Resource Kit* is installed, or can be manually extracted from the Windows 2000 operating system CD. In the Windows Explorer, open the \Support\Tools\Deploy.cab file and copy unattend.doc to any location.

The Active Directory can be installed immediately after the Windows 2000 Server setup, or independently at any moment.

To demote a DC (not the last DC in the domain!) to a member server, you need only specify the following parameters (these values are fictitious!) in the answer file:

```
[DCInstall]
UserName              = EntAdmin
Password              = eadm123
UserDomain            = w2k.dom
AdministratorPassword = ladmin123
RebootOnSuccess       = Yes
```

where the first three parameters are the credentials of an Enterprise Administrator, and `AdministratorPassword` is the local administrator password. The last parameter indicates that the computer must reboot after successful demotion.

NOTE

After the wizard completes the requested operation, all specified passwords are deleted from the answer file. So you must enter them again if you want to repeat the operation.

To create an additional domain controller in the *w2k.dom* domain (fictitious), the following parameters are needed:

```
[DCInstall]
UserName              = EntAdmin
Password              = eadm123
UserDomain            = w2k.dom
ReplicaDomainDNSName  = w2k.dom
SiteName              = W2K-site
RebootOnSuccess       = Yes
```

`SiteName` is not a required parameter. It is used here because the domain is situated in a site that has a non-default name (the default site name is *Default-First-Site*).

The following answer file will create the child domain *subdom* of the parent domain *w2k.dom*:

```
[DCInstall]
UserName               = Administrator
Password               = eadm123
UserDomain             = w2k.dom
ReplicaOrNewDomain     = Domain
ChildName              = subdom
DomainNetBiosName      = SUBDOM
ParentDomainDNSName    = w2k.dom
SiteName               = W2K-site
RebootOnSuccess        = Yes
```

Adding Domain Members

When a Windows 2000-based computer joins a Windows 2000 domain, a corresponding computer account is *always* created in the *Computers* container. You then have the option, if you so choose, of moving the account to any desired OU or container. There is, however, an alternative way. It is possible to create an account *before* actually adding the computer to the domain. Pre-create the account in any container, and then add the computer using this account.

Setting the DNS Suffix

Click **My computer** on the desktop, open the **Properties** window, click **Properties** on the **Network Identification** tab, and click **More**. In the opened window (Fig. 3.8) enter the DNS name of the domain to which the computer will belong.

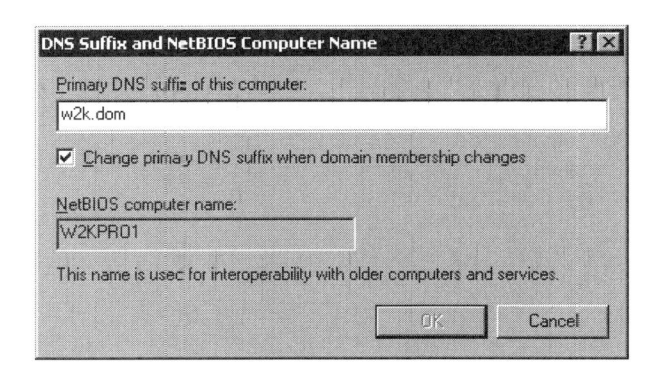

Fig. 3.8. Setting the DNS suffix of the computer

> **NOTE**
>
> You can control the primary DNS suffix by using a group policy. See the *Primary DNS Suffix* policy at the node **Computer Configuration | Administrative Templates | System | DNS Client**.

Windows 2000-based Workstations and Standalone Servers

To add a client computer to a Windows 2000-based domain, you should first verify the client's DNS settings and the availability of a DC that belongs to that domain. The updated version of the NetDiag.exe utility is the best instrument for that purpose. The test command and successful sample output are shown below:

```
C:\>netdiag /test:DsGetDc /d:w2k.dom /v
...
DC discovery test. . . . . . . . . . : Passed

      Find DC in domain 'w2k.dom':
      Found this DC in domain 'w2k.dom':
            DC. . . . . . . . . . . : \\w2kdc4.w2k.dom
            Address . . . . . . . . : \\192.168.0.4
            Domain Guid . . . . . . : {BAF0BAAF-5013-43D3-8FAC-
62CDBBCFA34A}
            Domain Name . . . . . . : w2k.dom
            Forest Name . . . . . . : w2k.dom
            DC Site Name. . . . . . : W2K-site
            Our Site Name . . . . . : W2K-site
            Flags . . . . . . . . . : PDC emulator GC DS KDC TIMESERV
WRITABLE DNS_DC DNS_DOMAIN DNS_FOREST CLOSE_SITE 0x8

      Find PDC emulator in domain 'w2k.dom':
      Found this PDC emulator in domain 'w2k.dom':
            DC. . . . . . . . . . . : \\w2kdc4.w2k.dom
...
      Find Windows 2000 DC in domain 'w2k.dom':
      Found this Windows 2000 DC in domain 'w2k.dom':
            DC. . . . . . . . . . . : \\w2kdc4.w2k.dom
...
The command completed successfully
```

This result indicates that you can add the tested computer to the specified domain.

When a client computer is added to a domain, you may verify that this operation has been successfully completed. The sample output from the following command reports that for some reason the secure channel between the client and the DC has not been established:

```
C:\>netdiag /test:DcList /d:w2k.dom
...
DC list test . . . . . . . . . . . : Failed
    Found DC '\\w2kdc4.w2k.dom' in domain 'w2k.dom'.
    [WARNING] Cannot call DsBind to w2kdc4.w2k.dom (192.168.0.4).
[SEC_E_SECURITY_QOS_FAILED]

The command completed successfully
```

Connecting a Windows NT 4.0-based BDC to a Windows 2000 Domain

You may for some reason need to have the Windows NT 4.0-based Backup Domain Controllers (BDC) in a Windows 2000 domain. The only problem that may (rather, *will*) arise during BDC installation is that the Windows NT 4.0 Setup program creates the wrong type of account. The following error message may appear:

```
The Machine Account for This Computer either does not exist or is
inaccessible.
```

If, for example, the account NT4DC3 was used when installing BDC, the following error is registered in the System Log on the Windows 2000-based domain controller that owns the PDC Emulator FSMO role:

```
...
Event Source:      SAM
...
Event ID:    12298
...
Description:
The account W2KDC3$ cannot be converted to be a domain controller
account as its object class attribute in the directory is not computer
or is not derived from computer. If this is caused by an attempt to
install a pre windows 2000 domain controller in a windows 2000 domain,
then you should precreate the  account for the domain controller with
the correct object class.
```

To pre-create a computer account for a Windows NT 4.0-based BDC, log on to the domain using an administrative account on any Windows 2000 domain member, and perform the following operations:

1. Start the Server Manager (enter `srvmgr` at the command prompt), which is included with Windows 2000. (Don't use the Server Manager from the Windows NT 4.0 installation!)
2. Select **Add to Domain** from the **Computer** menu.
3. Select **Windows NT Backup Domain Controller**, enter the BDC computer name, and click **Add,** then **Close**. An account with "Windows NT Backup" type will appear in the computer list. The account will be created in the "default" *Domain Controllers* OU.

Then you can install a Windows NT 4.0 server as BDC. Or, if the BDC was already installed, it may be necessary to use NetDom.exe to reset the computer account password.

The following steps yield the same result as described above:

1. Using the **Active Directory Users and Computers** snap-in, create a computer object in any container.
2. Using the **ADSI Edit** snap-in, find the *userAccountControl* property (decimal INTEGER type) for the new computer object, and change the value from 4128 (0x1020 — WORKSTATION_TRUST_ACCOUNT) to 8192 (0x2000 — SERVER_TRUST_ACCOUNT).

The third way to create the computer account for a BDC is to install the *Support Tools* pack and enter the following string at the command prompt:

`netdom ADD <BDC-computer-name> /D:<domain-name> /DC`

Switching to Native Mode

If there isn't a Windows NT 4.0 BDC in a Windows 2000 domain, this domain can be switched from the default *mixed mode* to *native mode.*

To change a domain to native mode, use either one of these two snap-ins:

❑ **Active Directory Users and Computers**

❑ **Active Directory Domains and Trusts**

Select a domain and open its **Properties** window. Click the **Change Mode** button on the **General** tab and wait 15 minutes for replication of the changes to all DCs in the domain. To check that the domain is now in the native mode, you may try to create a universal group or to add a domain local group to another local group.

It's convenient to check a domain's mode in the **Active Directory Domains and Trusts** snap-in. You can quickly select any domain in the forest and see its mode.

Establishing Trusts

Creating interdomain trusts is a rather simple operation if one understands the trusts mechanism used in Active Directory. The **Active Directory Domains and Trusts** snap-in is used for all work with any trusts in the Windows 2000 domain structure. You can easily select domains in the snap-in's tree window and look up existing trusts. But to verify, or create, or remove trusts, you must provide the credentials of a user that has rights to modify trusts. Fig. 3.9 and Fig. 3.10 show an example of a domain structure that has all types of trusts.

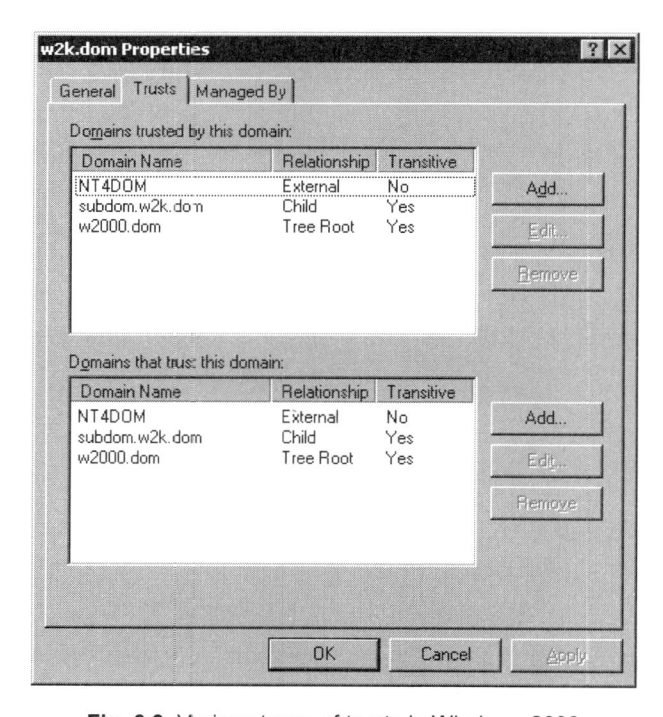

Fig. 3.9. Various types of trusts in Windows 2000

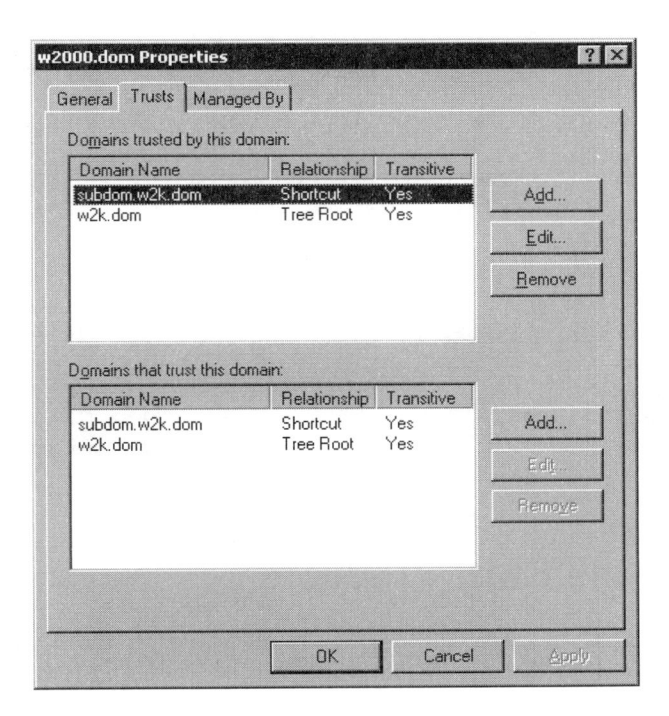

Fig. 3.10. The *shortcut* trust between two domains in the same forest

These are the domains included:

❑ *w2k.dom* — the forest root domain that has a *Child* relationship with its child domain.

❑ *subdom.w2k.dom* — a child domain that has a *Parent* relationship (not shown) with the root domain.

❑ *w2000.dom* — a tree root domain that is connected with the *Tree Root* relationships with the forest root domain.

All of the above mentioned trusts are created automatically, and are transitive. You can, for example, logon to the subdom.w2k.dom domain from a computer that belongs to the w2000.dom domain. To speed up this process, you may want to create an explicit one-way or two-way trust between these domains:

❑ The subdom.w2k.dom and w2000.dom domains are also connected with trusts marked as *Shortcut* (shown only for the w2000.dom domain).

You are also able to establish trust relationships (one- or two-way) with other Windows 2000 forests or Windows 4.0-based domains:

- *NT4DOM* — an independent Windows 4.0-based domain. The relationships with such domains, as with other Windows 2000 forests, are marked as *External*.

> **NOTES**
>
> Let's remember that any trusts are always possible between Windows NT 4.0 and Windows 2000 domains, regardless of the mode in which the latter are working.
>
> Only shortcut or external trusts can be removed. You cannot delete "default" (Parent-Child and Tree Root) trusts using the **Active Directory Domains and Trusts** snap-in. This can only be done by removing the appropriate domain or tree.

Verifying the State of Trusts

The state of all existing trusts can be verified. Select the desired trust on the **Trusts** tab, click **Edit**, and in the open window (funny enough, you cannot *edit* anything in this window) click **Verify**. Normally, you'll get the message: "The trust has been verified. It is in place and active". You may be asked for additional credentials in other domains (e. g. if you test the "parent-child" trust from a child domain, you'll be asked for credentials in the parent domain).

Creating Shortcut Trusts

To create the shortcut trusts, you must specify the appropriate credentials in both trusting and trusted domains.

Let's discuss an example. In the aforementioned domain structure, you may create a shortcut to speed up access from the w2000.dom to the resources in the subdom.w2k.dom domain. The subdom.w2k.dom domain (the *trusting* domain) will then *trust* the w2000.dom (the *trusted* domain):

1. Open the Active Directory Domains and Trusts snap-in, select the trusted domain (w2000.dom), and open the **Properties** window.

2. Click **Add** (to the right of the **Domains that trust this domain** panel).

3. Enter the name of the trusting domain (subdom.w2k.dom), and a password (*any* combination of symbols; the only requirement is that you must repeat it in the trusting domain). Click **OK**.

4. Click **No** when the system asks you "Do you want to verify the new trust?" (You can't verify the trust at the moment because it has not yet been created on the other side of the domain pair.) The trusting domain will appear in the list. Click **OK**.

5. Select the trusting domain (subdom.w2k.dom) and open the **Properties** window.

6. Click **Add** (to the right of the **Domains trusted by this domain** panel).

7. Enter the name of the trusted domain (w2000.dom) and the password entered in Step 3. Click **OK**.

8. Normally, you'll then get the message: "The trusted domain has been added and the trust has been verified".

That's all. A one-way trust has been created. You can check it using the NLtest command. Initially, you have an error on a DC in the subdom.w2k.dom domain (because there is no direct connection between the domains):

```
C:\>nltest /sc_query:w2000.dom
I_NetLogonControl failed: Status = 1355 0x54b ERROR_NO_SUCH_DOMAIN
```

After the trust has been created, you should see:

```
C:\>nltest /sc_query:w2000.dom
Flags: 30 HAS_IP   HAS_TIMESERV
Trusted DC Name \\w2kdc3.w2000.dom
Trusted DC Connection Status Status = 0 0x0 NERR_Success
The command completed successfully
```

You may establish a two-way trust, in which both domains will trust each other. To create the trust in the reverse direction, repeat the procedure described above, but this time start from the other domain in the pair (in our example it would be the subdom.w2k.dom domain). It doesn't matter from which domain — trusted or trusting — one begins to create a trust. The main thing to remember is that every trust is created on *both* sides of a domain pair, and you must use the *same* password.

Establishing Trusts with Windows NT 4.0-based Domains

Basically, the procedure of creating trusts with Windows NT 4.0-based domains is the same as the one described above for Windows 2000 domains. If the trusting domain in the example were a Windows NT 4.0-based domain (named, let's say, NT4DOM), steps 5—8 would look like this:

5. Start the User Manager for Domains, and select the **Policies | Trust Relationships** command.

6. Click **Add** (to the right of the **Trusted domains** panel).

7. Enter the NetBIOS (down-level) name of the trusted domain (W2000) and the password entered in Step 3. Click **OK**.

8. Normally, you'll get the message: "Trusted Relationship with ("W2000" for our example) successfully established".

> **NOTE**
>
> You must establish two-way trusts between domains for migrating from a Windows NT 4.0-based domain to a Windows 2000 domain (which must be in the *native* mode) using the *Active Directory Migration Tool*, *ClonePrincipal*, or similar (third-party) tools.

PART II

ADMINISTERING ACTIVE DIRECTORY

Chapter 4. Domain Manipulation Tools

Chapter 5. Common Administrative Tasks

Chapter 4
Domain Manipulation Tools

This chapter is, maybe, the most illustrated in the book. No wonder! A picture is worth a thousand words! This is not a formal reference to all administrative snap-ins' screens, menus, commands, features, or to the operations that they implement. Neither are all tools discussed. I'd like to make the reader pay attention to certain details and options that are unapparent or which might not be noticed upon first acquaintance with snap-ins intended to manage Active Directory. Using this "know-how" allows you to efficiently organize your workplace.

The chapter unveils certain aspects of using the features of the administrative tools for managing Active Directory. Other typical administrative tasks carried out by these and other tools are discussed in *Chapter 5, "Common Administrative Tasks"*, and in other chapters, where specific tasks are described in detail.

Basic Active Directory Administrative Snap-ins

After a Windows 2000 Server has been promoted to a domain controller, new tools will appear in the **Administrative Tools** group in the Control Panel (Table 4.1).

Table 4.1. Standard Tools for Administering Active Directory

Icon	Tool name	Main operations performed by the tool
	Active Directory Domains and Trusts	Selecting a domain for management in large forests. Viewing the domain operation mode. Creating, verifying, and deleting trusts between domains
	Active Directory Sites and Services	Creating and manipulating sites, transports, and subnets. Managing replication schedules and links. Triggering replication between domain controllers. Setting permissions on objects. Linking GPOs to sites. Enabling DCs to act as global catalog servers
	Active Directory Users and Computers	Creating and manipulating AD objects (users, groups, OUs, etc.). Setting permissions for objects. Linking GPOs to domains and OUs. Transferring FSMO roles
	Domain Controller Security Policy	Editing the **Security Settings** node of the GPO linked to the *Domain Controllers* OU. Use the **Group Policy** snap-in for editing the entire GPO
	Domain Security Policy	Editing the **Security Settings** node of the GPO linked to the domain container. Use the **Group Policy** snap-in for editing the entire GPO

continues

Table 4.1 Continued

Icon	Tool name	Main operations performed by the tool
	Group Policy	Editing GPOs linked to an Active Directory container (site, domain, OU) or stored on a local computer. This snap-in isn't shown in the **Start** menu, but is accessible from other administrative snap-ins or can be added to a custom MMC console

These tools can also be installed on any Windows 2000-based computer included in the forest (domain) as a part of the *Windows 2000 Administrative Tools* pack (see *"Remote Administration"* in *Chapter 5, "Common Administrative Tasks"*). The **Security Policy** snap-ins don't appear in the **Start** menu in this case.

Some other important tools (Table 4.2) for administering Active Directory are included in the *Support Tools* pack. These tools can be regarded as mandatory for an administrator, and are discussed later in this book.

Table 4.2. Some Additional Tools for Maintaining Active Directory (from *Support Tools*)

Icon	Tool name	Main operations performed by the tool
	ADSI Edit (adsiedit.msc)	"Low-level" editing of the Active Directory objects that belong to any partition (domain, configuration, and schema). (The *RootDSE* object is also accessible.) Setting permissions on objects
	Active Directory Administration Tool (ldp.exe)	Searching and modifying Active Directory objects using LDAP queries
	Active Directory Replication Monitor (replmon.exe)	Monitoring replication status and topology. Triggering replication. Monitoring FSMO roles and flags of domain controllers

Common Topics

Since most Active Directory administrative tools have been realized as MMC snap-ins, they all have similar interfaces and basic features. Knowing these features allows you to use all of these tools in the most effective way, and to optimize them to fit your specific tasks. Sometimes, the simple reconfiguration of the UI of an administrative snap-in may even affect some aspects of deploying Active Directory in an enterprise (see a bit later in this chapter *"Choosing Columns for Displaying"*). Let's start discussing the administrative snap-in taking into consideration some common features of snap-ins.

Making a Custom MMC Console

Most of the standard administrative tools can be started from the **Start | Programs | Administrative Tools** menu, or can be added to a custom MMC console. Such tools as the **Active Directory Schema** snap-in or the **Group Policy** snap-in should always be added to an MMC document first:

1. Enter mmc in the **Start | Run** window.
2. Press <Ctrl>+<M>, or select the **Console | Add/Remove Snap-in** command. Click **Add** in the opened window.
3. Select the desired snap-in in the **Add Standalone Snap-in** window, and click **Add**. You can repeat this step for all the snap-ins you need. Then click **Close** and then **OK**.
4. Save the resulting console with any name.

Making your own administrative console may have some valuable advantages:

- ❑ You'll have on hand all instruments you want, which will be configured as you want. For example, you may have snap-ins connected to different domains, or **Group Policy** snap-ins linked to various GPOs.
- ❑ There will be more options for configuring and customizing snap-ins (see below *"Customizing Snap-ins"*).
- ❑ The computer's memory is used more efficiently. A number of tools started separately allocate considerably more memory than the same tools added to a single MMC console.

Browsing the *Tree* Pane in a Snap-in's Window

While working in a snap-in window, don't forget about such simple but timesaving web-style features on the *Standard* toolbar as the **Forward** ⇨ and **Back** ⇦ buttons, the **Up one level** 🖺 button, and the **Refresh** 🔄 button. When pointing to an object, you can view its properties either by selecting the **Properties** command in the context menu, or — a faster way — by clicking the **Properties** button.

Choosing Columns for Displaying

When working with different Active Directory objects, it is possible (and may be very helpful) to display more fields than just the default ones, or to delete unnecessary ones. Select the **Choose Columns** command in the **View** menu, and add or delete the necessary columns in the **Modify Columns** window. Each object will have its own set of fields.

> **NOTE**
>
> When the **Active Directory Users and Computers** snap-in is used for creating new users, the **Full Name** field is generated as concatenation of the **First name** and **Last Name** fields. **Full name**, in turn, determines the value of the *cn* attribute. (You can, however, change this order, if you like — see articles *Q250455* and *Q277717* in the *Microsoft Knowledge Base*.) You may for some reason want to use proprietary naming conventions in your organization. (This can be easily organized by using scripting or batch tools, such as LDIFDE or CSVDE. Manual manipulations are also possible.) For instance, you may wish the *cn* attribute (i. e. the **Full name** field) to have the same value as the *sAMAccountName* attribute (the **Pre-Windows 2000 Logon Name** field) or the same value as a proprietary ID code. No problem. Use the **Find Users, Contacts, and Groups** window rather than the main window of the **Active Directory Users and Computers** snap-in. This window (unlike the snap-in's main window) allows you to sort lines according to the contents of *any* column. "Hide" the **Name** column from view and rearrange the columns in the order most useful for you. Click **Browse** (then **Find Now**) to view the forest tree and go to any location. This window could easily become your favorite administrative feature.

Exporting the List of Objects

To document the objects stored in Active Directory, you can export any currently displayed list into a file for processing or printing from the Word or Excel applications. Point to a container or an object and click the **Export List** button, or select the **Export List** command in the context menu or **Action** menu. You can choose between tab-separated (.txt) and comma-separated (.csv) formats. CSV-files are easily imported into the Microsoft Excel documents.

Customizing Snap-ins

Standard configured administrative snap-ins lack certain useful features that are realized in the Microsoft Management Console (MMC) technology. These features are common for all MMC consoles, but there are many reasons why using them in the *administrative tools* allows an administrator to save a lot of time and effort. See for yourself.

Favorites

In a custom MMC console, the **Favorites** tab will appear near the usual **Tree** tab. You may browse Active Directory in a web-like style, and save the pages you'd like to access quickly. Point to any container in the **Tree** pane, and select **Add to Favorites** in the **Favorites** menu. This feature can be very helpful in large domains that contain many OUs and other objects. Notice also that any container in Active Directory that can be viewed in *different* snap-ins can be designated as favorite. You can, for instance, simultaneously have main OUs from different domains, authoritative DNS zones, DHCP scopes, site connections, etc. all on the **Favorites** tab. Don't forget about traditional browsing features, such as the **Back**, **Forward**, **Up one level**, and **Refresh** buttons.

Creating Custom Taskpads

An administrator may create specialized taskpads for him- or herself (for some routine tasks) as well as for the users that need to carry out certain tasks, or for subordinate administrators to whom control of some OUs or objects is delegated.

Let's discuss an example of how to create a taskpad for administering organizational units. This taskpad will allow us to view all accounts in an OU and perform three predefined operations: create a computer, user, and group.

Select an OU in the **Active Directory Users and Computers** snap-in, and click **New Taskpad View** from the **Action** menu. The *New Taskpad View Wizard* will be started, which will guide you through all necessary steps. At any step of wizard working you can go back and change the selected options or entered information.

Leave the default options in the *Taskpad Display* and *Taskpad Target* steps unchanged. This means that the tab of the created taskpad will appear for each OU in the domain (but not for other domain containers!). Enter the necessary information at the *Name and Description* step. When the wizard has finished (i. e. the

Chapter 4: Domain Manipulation Tools 81

view without task buttons has been generated), check the **Start New Task wizard** box in the last window and click **Finish**. The *New Task Wizard* will start.

The default *Command Type* is **Menu command**. In the *Shortcut Menu Command* step, select **Tree item task** in the **Command source** list (Fig. 4.1). In this case we'll be able to choose the commands for the entire OU. First, select **New->Computer**.

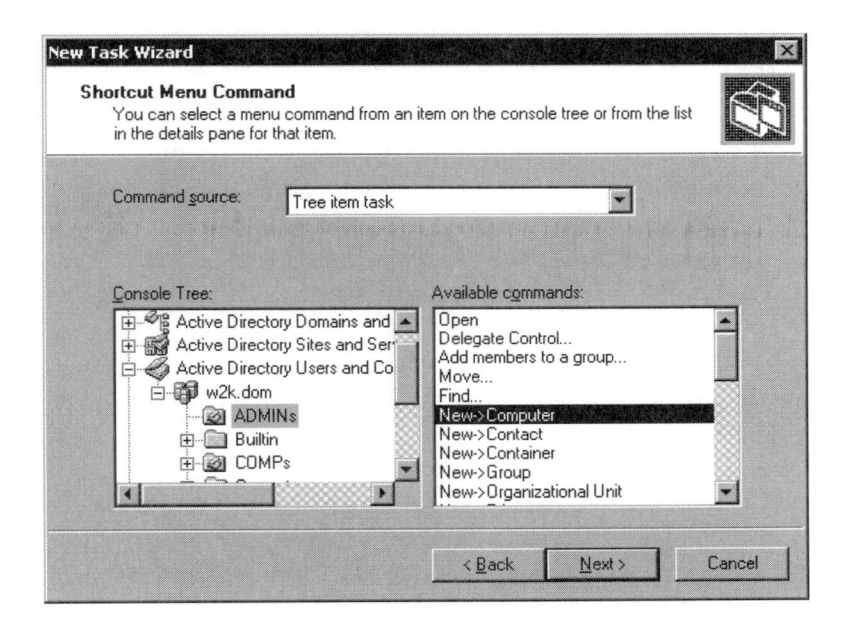

Fig. 4.1. Selecting the source of commands for the new taskpad

At the next step, enter a relevant task name, and a description for this task. Then you can choose a graphical representation for the task. A new task has now been created. To add the other two commands, check the **Run this wizard again** box in the last window of the wizard, and click **Finish**. The wizard will start again. Repeat the necessary steps, the first time selecting **New->User**, and the second time **New->Group**. Fig. 4.2 shows an example of a taskpad created according to the described procedure.

You may add/delete tasks, and/or change the properties (options) of a taskpad, by selecting the appropriate tab and clicking **Edit Taskpad View** in the **Action** menu.

It is possible to define commands (tasks) for a whole container as well as for an individual (selected) object in a container. While browsing the object tree, only those commands that are acceptable for the selected object will be enabled in a taskpad.

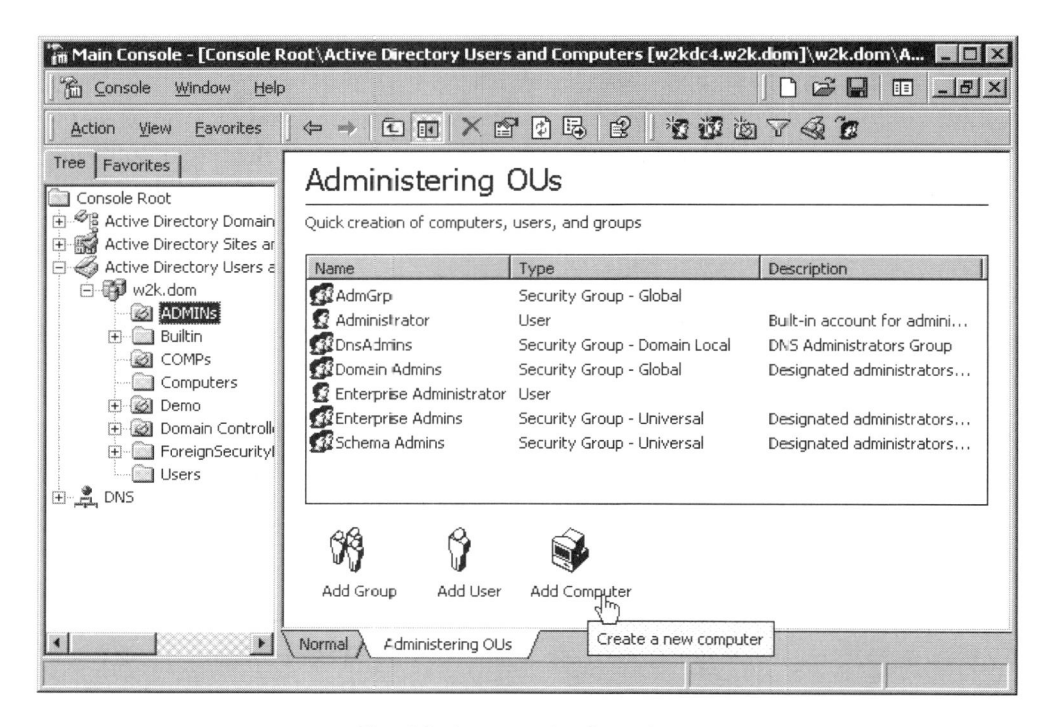

Fig. 4.2. An example of a taskpad

Active Directory Users and Computers Snap-in

The **Active Directory Users and Computers** snap-in is perhaps one of the tools that an administrator will use most often. That is why it is advisable to learn all of the features that this snap-in provides for an administrator. This is especially true if a domain contains thousands of objects, which complicates viewing and manipulating them.

Connecting to Domain or Domain Controller

The **Active Directory Users and Computers** snap-in operates with only one DC — and, therefore, one domain — at a time. By default, this is your current logon domain and DC (unless you've changed domain or DC and checked the **Save this domain setting for the current console box**, see Fig. 4.3). You can choose a domain that you wish to investigate by pointing to the root of the snap-in (or by selecting the domain object from the tree pane) and then selecting the **Connect to Domain** command in the **Action** menu. In the **Connect to Domain** window enter the domain name in the **Domain** field (Fig. 4.3), or click the **Browse** button and select the domain from the expanding domain tree. Notice the **Save this domain setting for the current console** box, which allows you to have a few saved snap-ins configured for different domains.

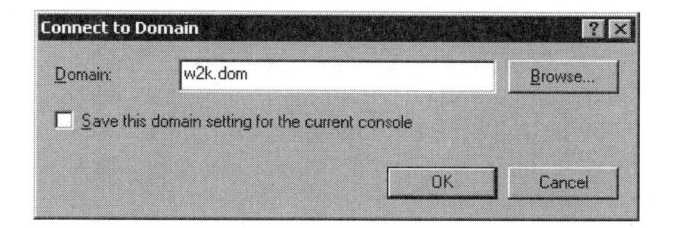

Fig. 4.3. You may choose any domain in the forest to administer

Similarly, you can select any domain controller in the current domain with the **Connect to Domain Controller** command in the **Action** menu. It makes sense to do this when for some reason (e. g. regarding a replication issue) you need to administer a Global Catalog server, or a DC performing a specific FSMO role, such as PDC Emulator. In the **Connect to Domain Controller** window (Fig. 4.4) you can see your current DC's name and the list of available controllers.

Fig. 4.4. Selecting a controller in the domain

Contents Displaying Options

The **Active Directory Users and Computers** snap-in has a few specific features which don't essentially change the administrative options of the snap-in, but significantly affect the scope of objects available for manipulating. These features are discussed below.

Advanced Features Mode

By default, the **Active Directory Users and Computers** snap-in only displays five nodes in basic mode. For some administrative tasks this is not enough, and you need to switch to the *Advanced Features* mode that displays some important "invisible" containers and has additional options. This can be done using the **Advanced Features** command in the **View** menu.

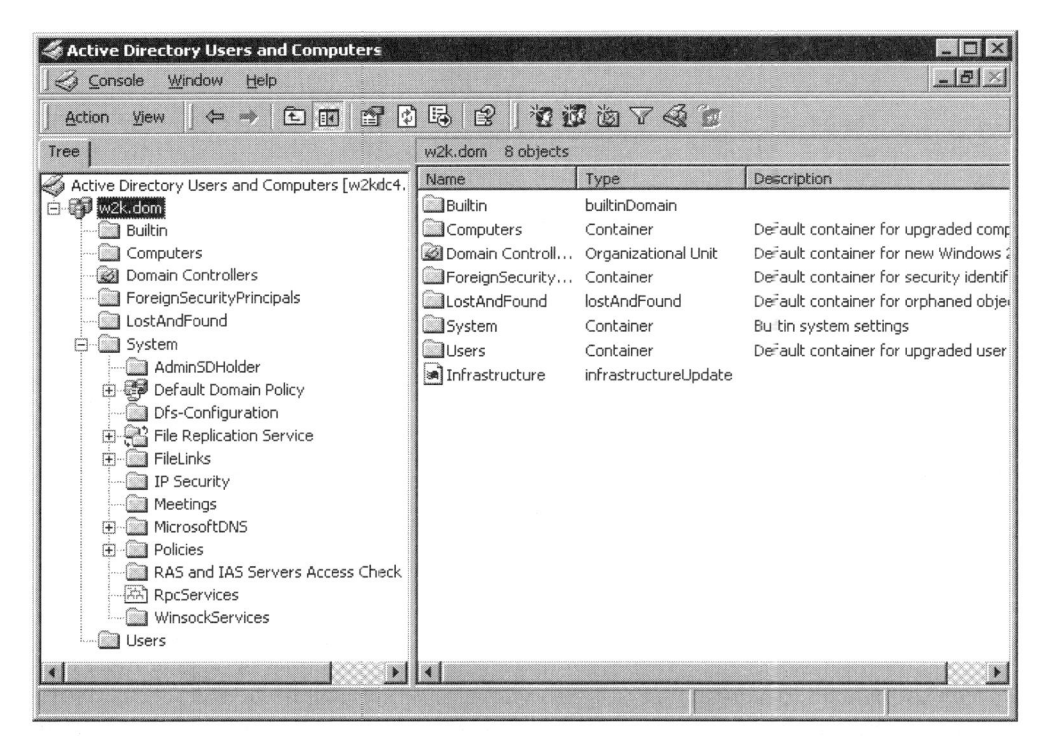

Fig. 4.5. The advanced view of a domain objects tree

Perhaps one of the most valuable nodes shown in advanced mode is the **System** container (Fig. 4.5), which provides access to a number of system objects, for instance, to the *MicrosoftDNS* container that stores DNS zone information if a zone (zones) is (are) Active Directory-integrated.

Even more important is that only in the Advanced Features mode will you have the **Object** and **Security** tabs in the **Properties** window of any Active Directory object. All changes related to delegation of control over some object are displayed in the **Security** tab. For example, if you want to revoke an administrative right from a user or a group, you need to open this tab for the object and delete the appropriate permissions.

There is also one remarkable possibility pertaining to this mode. You might notice that five "default" nodes (plus the possible subdomains) are visible while browsing the **Directory** node in the **My Network Places** folder from Windows 2000-based domain clients (see Fig. 4.6; the root and two child domains are shown.) Sometimes, this information will bother the end users, while other times you may not want end users to be able to access these nodes. You can control the "visibility" of any Active Directory container or object by using an optional Boolean attribute *showInAdvancedViewOnly* (it can be set to FALSE or TRUE, the case of the letters doesn't matter.) The majority of Active Directory objects have this attribute, and you can change its value as needed with the **ADSI Edit** tool (see *"ADSI Edit Snap-in"* later in this chapter.) If an object (container) has this attribute set to TRUE, the object will not be displayed during domain browsing or in the base mode in the **Active Directory Users and Computers** snap-in. This has no affect on the general behavior of the domain. Fig. 4.7 shows the same domain structure that is shown in Fig. 4.6, but the *showInAdvancedViewOnly* attribute has been set to TRUE for some domain objects, so all users in the forest won't be able to see the contents of these domains. (In an actual situation, this may seem too strict a limit, but don't forget that this is only an example!)

> **NOTE**
>
> It is also possible to control the "visibility" of Active Directory objects using access permissions. Both methods have their own *pros* and *cons*; therefore select the most convenient method, depending on your requirements. For example, permissions allow for more comprehensive control, but if you use them, you won't be able to make only selected objects invisible in a container.

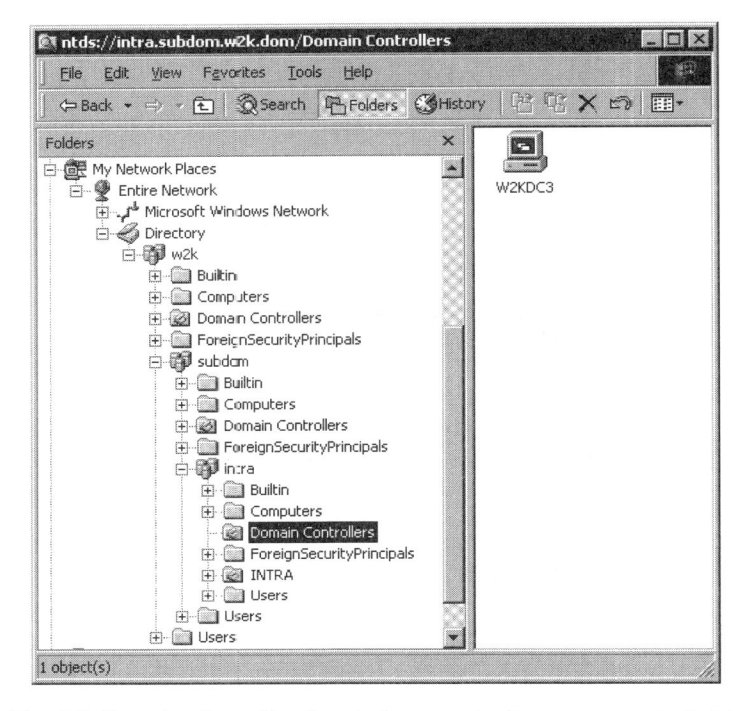

Fig. 4.6. Browsing the entire domain tree may be tiresome or undesirable

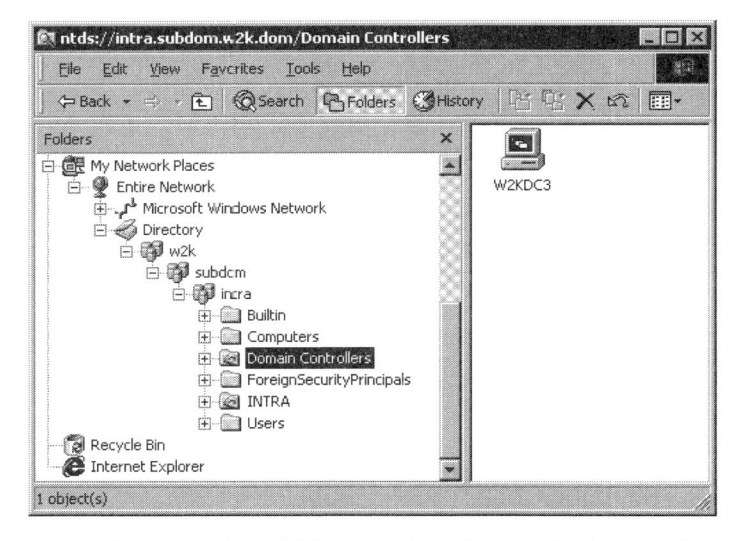

Fig. 4.7. You can entirely disable browsing of parent domains for clients and "hide" unnecessary objects from viewing

Users, Groups, and Computers as Containers

Some Active Directory objects act as containers for other objects. By default, this fact has no visible representation in the **Active Directory Users and Computers** snap-in. Nevertheless, there are situations when you may wish to see all object relations. For example, compare the two screenshots shown in Fig. 4.8 and Fig. 4.9. The first one is a default view of the *Domain Controllers* OU and the *W2KDC4* domain controller; the second one shows the same controller as a container.

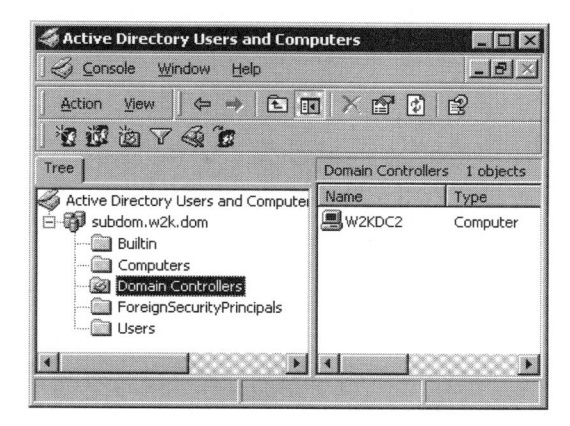

Fig. 4.8. The default view of a domain controller

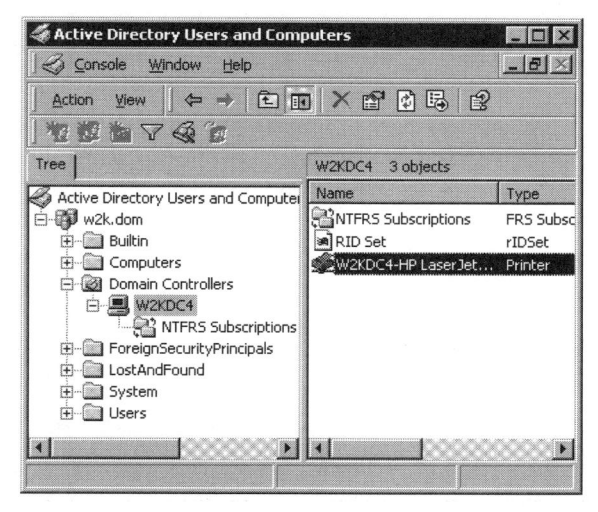

Fig. 4.9. Using *Users, Groups, and Computers as containers* mode for locating a published printer connected to the selected domain controller

As you can see from Fig. 4.9, the domain controller has child objects, in particular, a published printer. You might want to move the printer object to any other OU. This doesn't affect the printer's behavior.

> **NOTE**
>
> All printers are initially published in Active Directory as child objects of relative computers. You may want to gather them in a single OU for users' or administrators' convenience, although the **Search** option is a more convenient way to work with printers.

Filter Options

As the number of objects in Active Directory considerably increases, the time it takes to find specific objects may become unbearably long. However, you can set *a filter* and look up only the desired objects. Select the **Filter Options** command in the **View** menu or click the **Set Filtering Options** button at the Standard toolbar. You can set the types of objects to display from a predefined list, or create your own *custom* filter. The process of creating a filter is intuitively simple. Fig. 4.10 shows a filter for selecting user accounts with names starting with the letter "a". To activate the filter, you must click the **Add** button and place the criteria into the list.

> **CAUTION!**
>
> Using a filter may produce a potential danger when working with containers (OUs). Suppose you have set a filter that displays only computer accounts. You may decide that an OU is empty or holds only unnecessary computer accounts (since it seems it doesn't contain any computers). You might just forget that this OU can contain other objects and inadvertently delete the *entire* OU rather than only the necessary accounts... Therefore, don't forget to turn off any filters when doing such operations as deleting or moving container objects!

> **ATTENTION!**
>
> Many Active Directory objects have the *Name* attribute. Regretfully, the *object* name isn't displayed in the **Fine Custom Search** window in any form. So you must remember yourself all parameters of any added criteria.
>
> Since two or more added criteria are AND-combined, an object is displayed in the snap-in window only if *all* specified conditions are true. OR-combined criteria are not available.

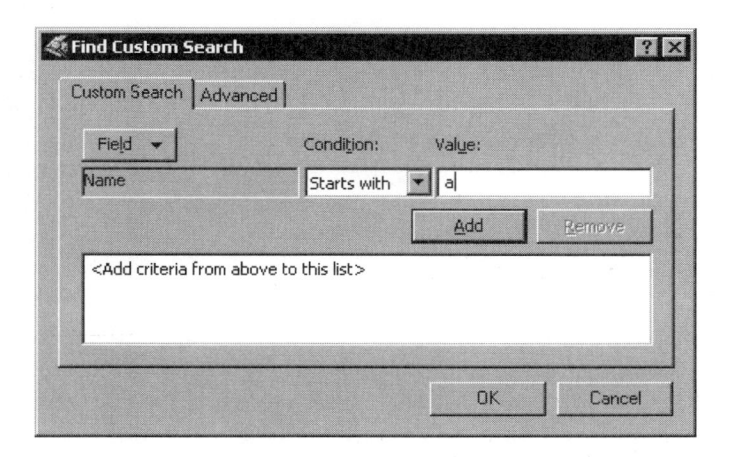

Fig. 4.10. An example of a custom filter

> **CAUTION!**
>
> Filters, especially complex ones, may considerably slow down object display in the snap-in window.

In addition, you can use LDAP queries. Click the **Advanced** tab in the **Find Custom Search** window and enter a query in text format. For example, the following query fetches only non-default user accounts:

```
(&(objectCategory=Person)(objectClass=user)(displayName=*))
```

> **CAUTION!**
>
> All defined custom filters along with the LDAP queries are connected by a logical AND. This means that you may, for instance, define the first filter condition as "Name + Starts with + **a**", and view all user accounts whose names start with "a". If you add the second filter condition defined as "Name + Starts with + **d**" (or add an LDAP query such as (cn=d*)), you won't see user accounts beginning with "a" *or* "d". (You can instead specify an OR-condition in a *single* filter!) You'll see no accounts at all, because there are no accounts whose names start with "a" *and* "d". Therefore, the combination of filter conditions and LDAP queries has to be regarded as a chain of sub-queries within other queries, i. e. as an *intersection of sets*.

Finding Active Directory Objects

Another option that helps to process large numbers of Active Directory objects is the *Find* feature. In a sense, it works as a filter, but has a wider scope: you can find objects in the entire directory (forest), in any domain, or in a selected container. To find an object, you can use the **Find** command in each container's context menu or select a container and click the **Find objects in Active Directory** button on the toolbar.

Search (and advanced search) fields can vary depending on the type of directory objects (users, computers, printers, etc.) Search criteria for advanced operations are composed in the same way as filters and have the same constraints. The *Custom Search* is the most flexible; you can specify practically any attribute of any directory object.

> **NOTES**
>
> When you find users in the **Find Users, Contacts, and Groups** window, the string entered in the **Name** field is verified for matches with *all* user naming attributes — *cn*, *First name*, *Last name*, and *Display name*.
>
> Note that the **In** list has a history of containers (OUs) you've already visited.

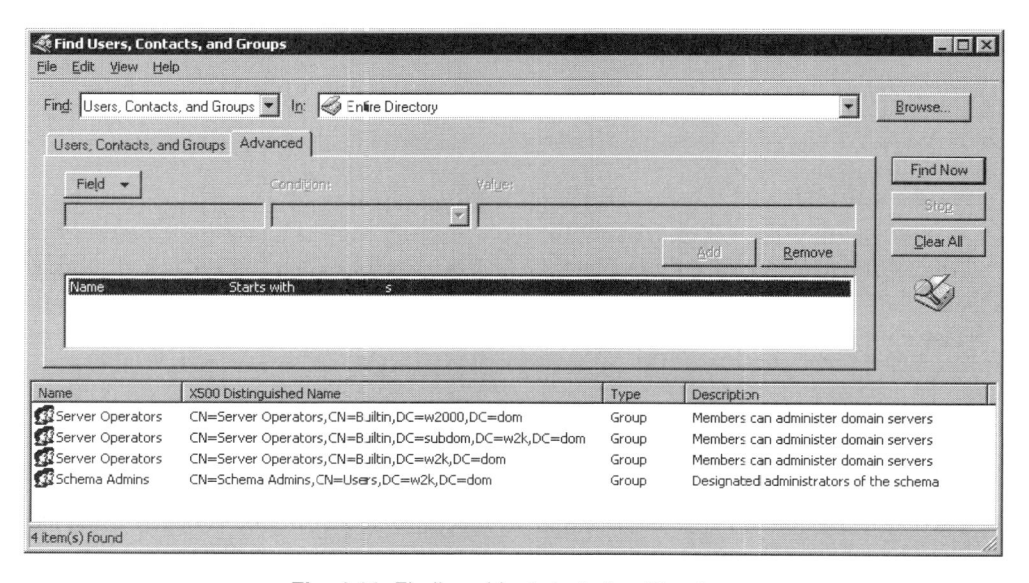

Fig. 4.11. Finding objects in Active Directory

Chapter 4: Domain Manipulation Tools 91

In the window of found objects you can select in the context menus all commands that are available for these objects in the normal snap-in window.

An example of the **Find** window and a sample result is shown in Fig. 4.11. This search query finds all groups in the entire directory with names starting with the letter "s". Maybe the example shown isn't very useful, but notice that you can search the *whole domain forest* (three domains in all) as well as a selected domain or container. Also, it demonstrates that such a group as *Server Operators* is present in all three domains, but only one (root) domain has the *Schema Admins* group.

Fine Tuning the *Find* Window

The display mode shown in Fig. 4.11 isn't the default. To see the distinguished names (i. e. all RDNs of the parent objects) of found objects, click **Choose Columns** in the **View** menu, choose the **X500 Distinguished Name** column and add it to **Columns shown**.

To further filter the result of a find operation, click **Filter** in the **View** menu. The filter bar will appear at the top of the result pane in the **Find** window. How to filter out some groups and users among a number of similar objects is shown in Fig. 4.12.

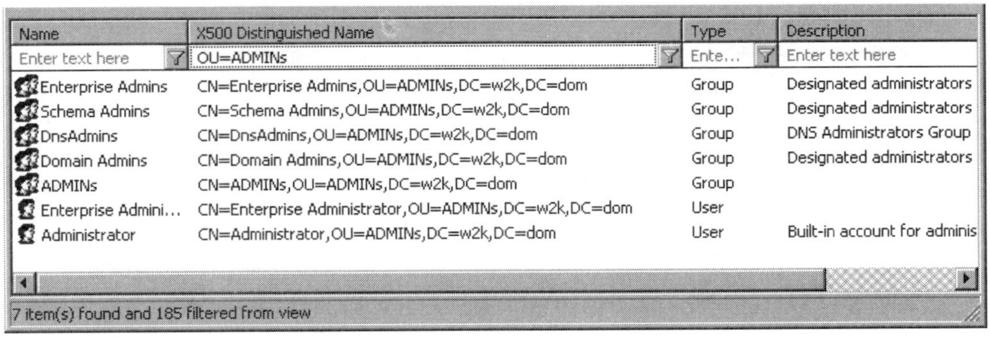

Name	X500 Distinguished Name	Type	Description
Enter text here	OU=ADMINs	Ente...	Enter text here
Enterprise Admins	CN=Enterprise Admins,OU=ADMINs,DC=w2k,DC=dom	Group	Designated administrators
Schema Admins	CN=Schema Admins,OU=ADMINs,DC=w2k,DC=dom	Group	Designated administrators
DnsAdmins	CN=DnsAdmins,OU=ADMINs,DC=w2k,DC=dom	Group	DNS Administrators Group
Domain Admins	CN=Domain Admins,OU=ADMINs,DC=w2k,DC=dom	Group	Designated administrators
ADMINs	CN=ADMINs,OU=ADMINs,DC=w2k,DC=dom	Group	
Enterprise Admini...	CN=Enterprise Administrator,OU=ADMINs,DC=w2k,DC=dom	User	
Administrator	CN=Administrator,OU=ADMINs,DC=w2k,DC=dom	User	Built-in account for adminis

7 item(s) found and 185 filtered from view

Fig. 4.12. Filtering the search results: among all administrators we have selected that ones that belong to the ADMINs OU

NOTE

It is possible to turn on the filter option for clients (by default, the filter is off) by using the *Enable filter* in *Find dialog box* policy in the user's administrative templates.

It is also possible to view the parents of other directory objects: computers, printers, etc. In that case you must add the **Published At** column to the default view of the **Find** window. The canonical names of the parent objects will be displayed in this column. For example, for the *W2KPRO1* computer that belongs to the *w2k.dom* domain and is placed in the *COMPs* organizational unit, the displayed string will be `ntds://w2k.dom/COMPs/W2KPRO1`.

Active Directory Sites and Services Snap-in

The **Active Directory Sites and Services** snap-in is the main GUI tool that allows an administrator to configure Active Directory as a *distributed network service*. (Other administrative tools consider Active Directory as a whole, at a logical level.) You might almost forget about this snap-in in a small, single-site network with just a few domain controllers. But in large networks with many sites, this snap-in becomes one of the main administrative tools.

The **Active Directory Sites and Services** snap-in allows you to perform the following operations:

- Modify forest replication topology (create/delete sites, subnets, links, link bridges, and connections)
- Assign costs to links
- Change schedules and intervals for intra-site and inter-site replications
- Designate bridgehead servers
- Trigger intra-site and inter-site replication events
- Trigger the Knowledge Consistency Checker (KCC) to re-generate replication topology
- Delegate control over sites, subnets, servers, and other containers to users or groups
- Define security and auditing settings for various replication topology objects
- Select Group Policy Objects, link GPOs to sites, and start the **Group Policy** snap-in for editing GPO
- Designate domain controllers as Global Catalog servers

Chapter 4: Domain Manipulation Tools 93

❑ Select LDAP Query policies

In Fig 4.13, you can see the main window of the **Active Directory Sites and Services** snap-in, which displays practically all major elements of network configuration: sites, subnets, inter-site links, connections, and servers (domain controllers). Using and configuring these elements are discussed in other chapters in the book, since it is more advantageous to describe these questions in the context of specific administrative tasks rather than in isolation.

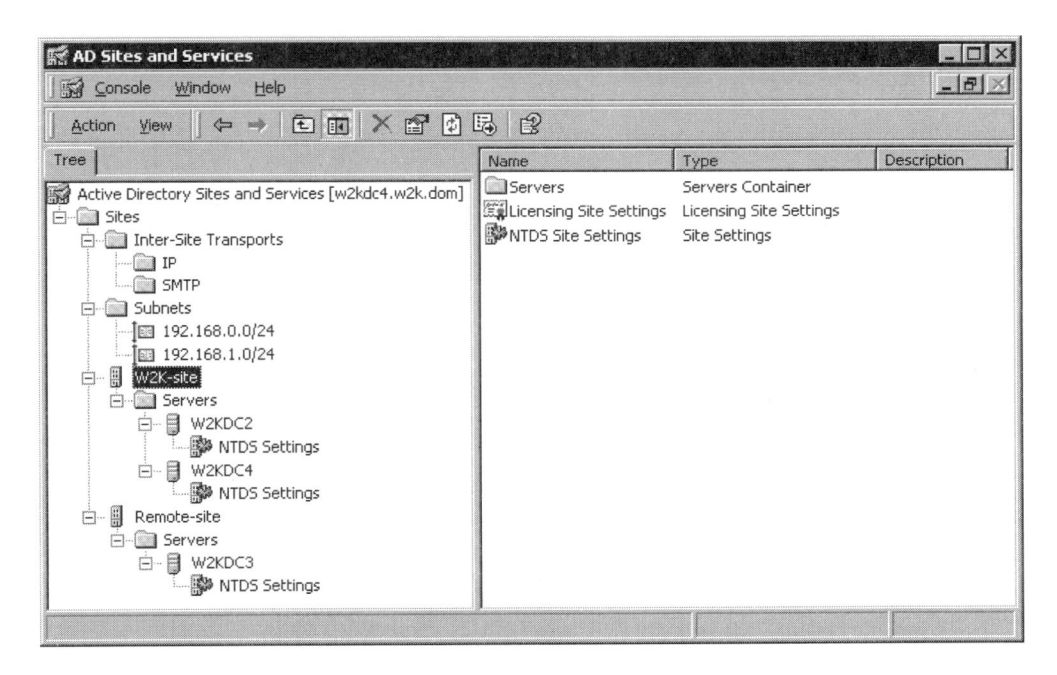

Fig. 4.13. An example of a simple network with two sites

Active Directory Domains and Trusts Snap-in

The **Active Directory Domains and Trusts** snap-in is an enterprise administrator's tool that allows you to easily look up the forest and select a domain for administering. An example of a forest (which contains two tree root domains — *w2000.dom* and *w2k.dom*) represented in the snap-in window is shown in Fig. 4.14.

If you point to a domain in the tree and select the **Manage** command in the context menu or in the **Action** menu, the **Active Directory Users and Computer** snap-in will be started for this domain.

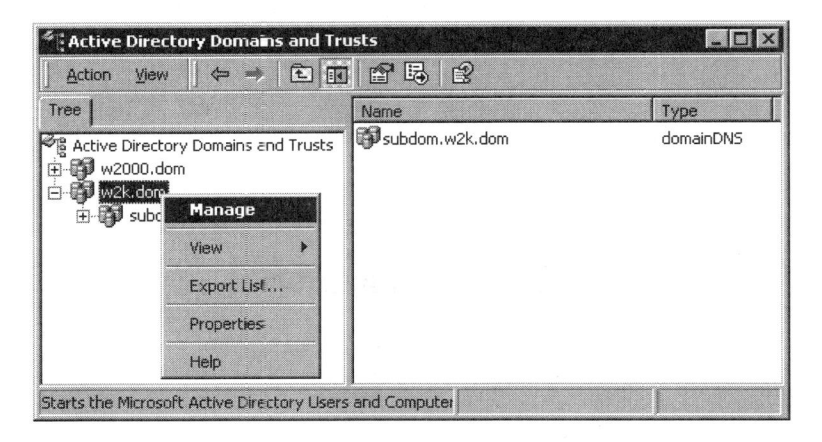

Fig. 4.14. Selecting a domain for management in the enterprise (domain forest)

Using User Principal Names (UPN)

The concept of *user principal names* can considerably simplify the logon process in large domain trees. While logging on, the domain users can use one of two methods for specifying their names:

❑ Entering a UPN name, such as `user@DNSdomainName` (in this case, the domain list becomes unavailable)

❑ Entering a pre-Windows 2000 user name (without the "@" symbol) and then selecting a domain from the list

Each method has certain advantages. But it may be inconvenient to enter long domain names, such as `dom1.comp1.ent1.com`. The first method is in fact just a particular instance of a general format: userName@UPNSuffix. The *default* UPN suffix is the DNS name of that domain where a user account is located. It is possible to add alternative suffixes that can be used *by all users of a domain forest*.

To add a UPN suffix, open the **Active Directory Domain and Trusts** snap-in, point to the root in the tree pane, and select **Properties** from the context menu. Enter a suffix in the **Alternative UPN suffixes** field and click **Add** and **Apply**. The entered suffix (`w2k` in Fig. 4.15) will appear in the dialog box during new user creation.

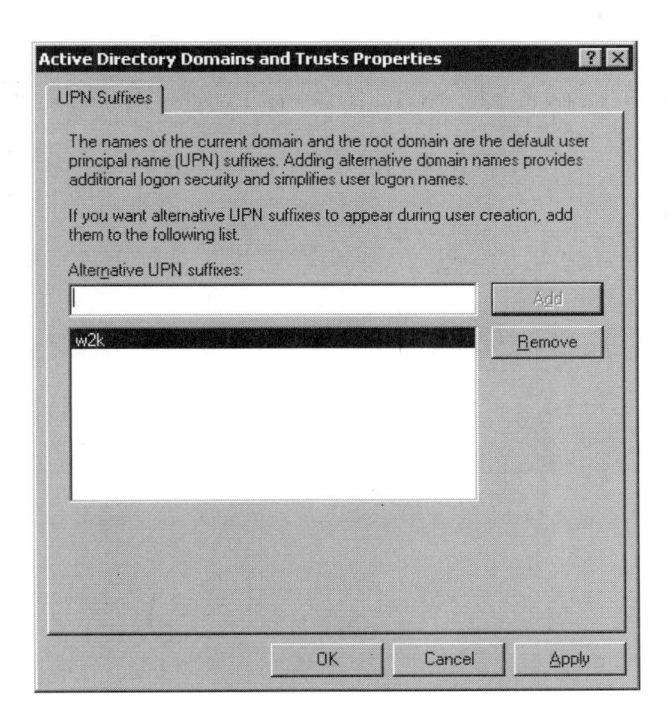

Fig. 4.15. Adding an alternative UPN suffix

Now, you can choose any UPN suffix for a new user (the current domain, parent domain and alternative UPN suffixes) or change the UPN name for an existing user. Let's create, for example, a user with the logon parameters shown in Fig. 4.16. Initially, the *logon* name and the *pre-Windows 2000* name are the same, but you can specify any name you like.

The created user will be able to logon to the domain tree with the following names (the password will be the same for both logon names):

❑ `EAdmin@w2k` — UPN name

❑ `EAdm` (and a domain name selected from the list) — SAM account name

You can also check these names using the **ADSI Edit** snap-in. (`sAMAccountName` is a mandatory attribute, and `userPrincipalName` is an optional attribute.)

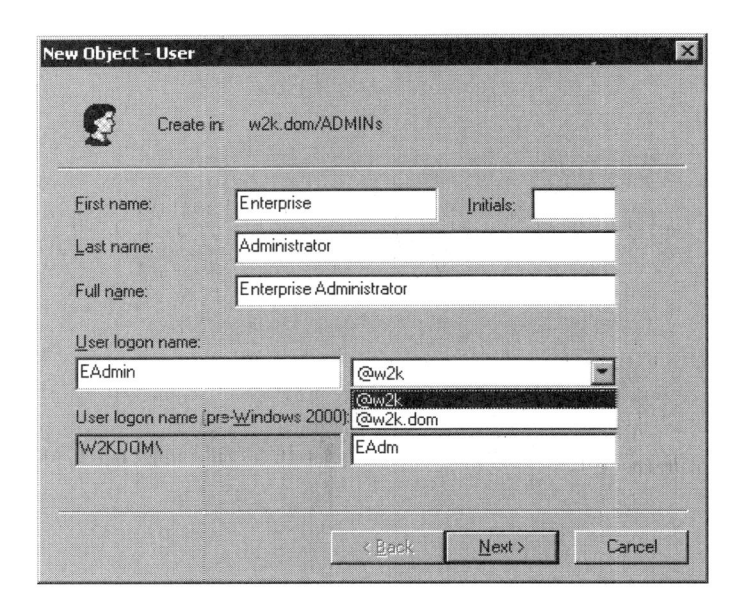

Fig. 4.16. Using UPN suffixes during new user creation

> **NOTE**
>
> Notice that, by default, the 'built-in" Administrator and Guest accounts don't have UPN names.

> **ATTENTION!**
>
> UPN names aren't supported by Windows 9x/ME clients.

Understandably, all account names must be unique. SAM account (pre-Windows 2000) names in the same domain cannot be repeated. A *full name* mustn't be used more than once in an OU. But the same full name *can* be used for accounts in *different* OUs (because the canonical names of objects will differ, e. g. `domain.com/OU1/John Smith` and `domain.com/OU2/John Smith`), provided that the UPN and SAM account names are different (e. g. `jsmith@domain.com` and `johnSmith@domain.com`; `JSMITH` and `JOHNS`).

Verifying Trusts

A domain administrator can use the **Active Directory Domains and Trusts** snap-in for verifying trusts between domains and for creating new trusts. This creating process primarily concerns trusts with Windows NT 4.0 domains. Such trusts must be *manually* created (see *Chapter 3, "Deploying Active Directory"*). But you may also want to create explicit, unidirectional trusts between Windows 2000 domains that belong to different domain trees or even to the same tree. This, for instance, may be required for reducing logon time into a "remote" domain. "Remote" here is related to the "distance" between domains in tree structure. For example, the `dom1.comp1.ent1.com` and `dom2.comp2.ent2.com` domains (Fig. 4.17) can be regarded as "remote", because trusts between trees in a forest are established trough the root domains.

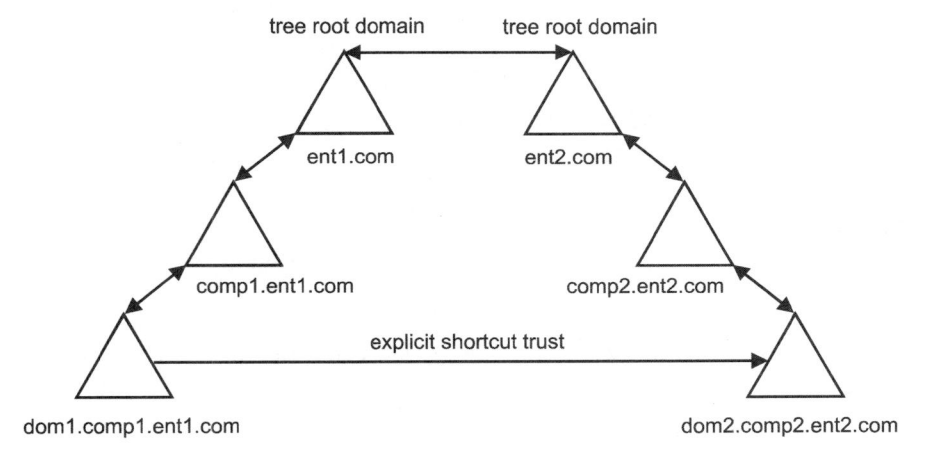

Fig. 4.17. A shortcut trust between two "remote" domains

To check a trust between domains: open the properties window for a domain, select a trust on the **Trusts** tab, click **Edit**, and then **Verify** (in the next dialog box). If the trust is operational, you should get the message: "The trust has been verified. It is in place and active." If the system reports an error and proposes that you reset the trust, confirm the operation. Usually, the trusts will be successfully reset. You can also use the *NetDom* tool for verifying and resetting trusts.

ADSI Edit Snap-in

The **ADSI Edit** snap-in, which is included in the *Support Tools* pack, is a tool that provides "low-level" access to Active Directory. It allows you to perform the following operations:

- Connect directly to any Active Directory object using its distinguished name
- View, move, rename, and modify any attribute of any object
- Tune security settings down to a single attribute
- Perform a query against a whole domain tree and save it
- Create and delete objects of any type
- Work with a global catalog

Connecting to Namespaces

The newly installed **ADSI Edit** snap-in is configured for work with three Active Directory namespaces (contexts, or partitions):

- Domain (DC=domainName,DC=com)
- Configuration (CN=Configuration,DC=domainName,DC=com)
- Schema (CN=Schema,CN=Configuration,DC=domainName,DC=com)

The first namespace is replicated among all DCs that belong to the same domain. The other two are replicated over every DC in the domain tree.

There is one more object to which the **ADSI Edit** snap-in can be connected:

- RootDSE

> **NOTE**
>
> Note that **ADSI Edit** only shows the informational (LDAP) attributes of the RootDSE object. Operational (system specific) attributes, such as *isSynchronized* or *isGlobalCatalogReady* are not accessible.

You can also add the standalone **ADSI Edit** snap-in to any MMC console opened in the author mode. In this case it is added without any connection. If you create your own MMC console, you have a feature such as the **Favorites** tab, which can be very helpful for working with multilevel tree structures and various Active Directory objects (which all have very long LDAP names).

To make a new connection, point the root node in the tree pane and select the **Connect to** command from the context menu. Enter any string you want in the **Name** field and specify the distinguished name of an object, or select a predefined namespace from the **Naming Context** list (Fig. 4.18). You may also enter a domain or server name different from the default one.

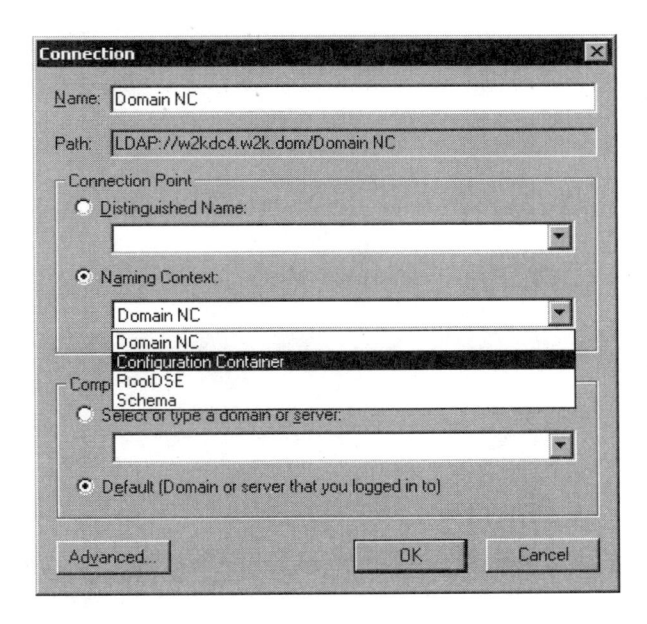

Fig. 4.18. Connecting to a namespace

You can also create a connection to any object while browsing the object tree. Point to an object and select **New Connection from here** in the context menu. All new connections are saved upon exit from the snap-in.

In the **Advanced** window (click **Advanced** in the **Connection** window) you can specify alternative credentials, a port number, or choose the protocol: LDAP or Global Catalog. To view or modify the current properties of a connection, select the **Settings** command from the context menu for this connection. Any connection may be deleted by the **Remove** command.

Editing Attributes of Active Directory Objects

Let's see how to work with the **ADSI Edit** snap-in in the two following examples that contain some tips which may be useful for an administrator.

Example 1. Hiding Directory Objects from Browsing

Using the example of the *showInAdvancedViewOnly* attribute (see "*Advanced Features* Mode" above), let's discuss how to locate attributes of an Active Directory object and modify their values. Suppose we'd like to hide the *Builtin* container from browsing. Point to it in the tree pane of the **ADSI Edit** snap-in and click **Properties** on the toolbar. In the opened window, the **Select which properties to view** dropdown list contains all attributes of the selected object. You can quickly locate an attribute in the list by typing in the first few characters of the attribute's name (Fig. 4.19). When the attribute has been selected, enter the new value TRUE (or true, it doesn't matter) into the **Edit Attribute** field and click **Set,** then **Apply**. (To delete the value of an attribute, click **Clear**. If the attribute is multi-valued, select a value, and click **Remove**.)

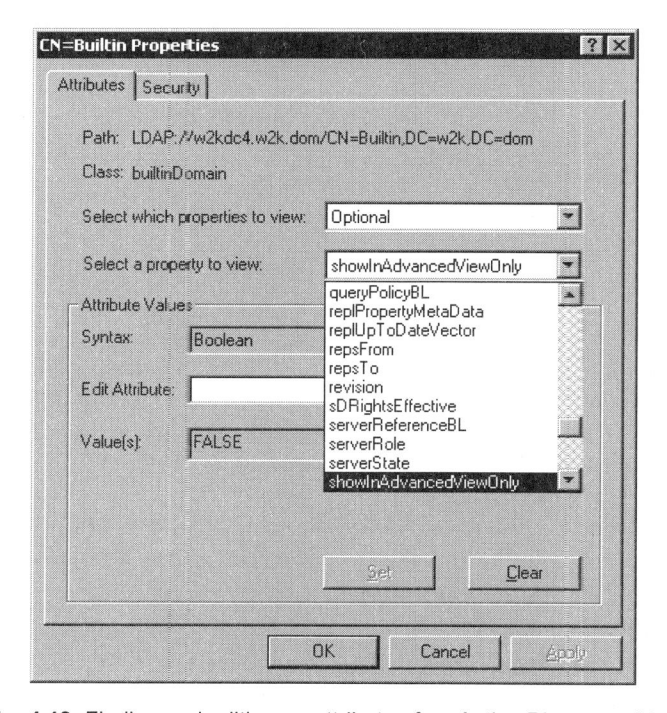

Fig. 4.19. Finding and editing an attribute of an Active Directory object

Example 2. Enabling Creation of Containers through User Interface

This example shows how to modify the schema by using **ADSI Edit**.

By default, you cannot create a new object of *Container* type using the **Active Directory Users and Computers** snap-in. Sometimes it may be useful to have such an option for organizing directory objects. To create this option, it's necessary to modify the schema.

1. If you have not yet connected to the schema name context, do it now.
2. Open the schema folder and find the container class (CN=Container).
3. In the properties window, select the optional *defaultHidingValue* attribute (the default value is TRUE).
4. Enter FALSE in the **Edit Attribute** field and click **Set**, then **Apply** and **OK**.
5. Point to the **Schema** node and select **Update Schema Now** from the context menu.

If the schema cache has been updated successfully, open the **Active Directory Users and Computers** snap-in (restart it, if it was already opened) and check that the container object has appeared in the **Action | New** menu.

Creating a Custom Query

A query in the **ADSI Edit** snap-in is a custom template for displaying only desired objects in the tree pane. This simplifies working with large numbers of objects or objects related to different Active Directory containers. The queries can be created in any Active Directory namespace (partitions), but remember that since a namespace belongs to a specific domain, the queries work within the borders of one domain only.

Let's create a query for all published folders. Point to the node related to the domain context and select the **New | Query** command in the context menu. Give the new query any name you like and click **Browse** to define a container — the root of the search. In our case it will be the root domain (*w2k.dom*). The next step is defining the query itself. You can either directly enter a query in the **Query String** field or click **Edit Query** and start the wizard that helps to create a custom filter (see "*Filter Options*" above, Fig. 4.10). The generated string is displayed in the **Query String** field (Fig. 4.20). (Remember the limitations of custom filters!)

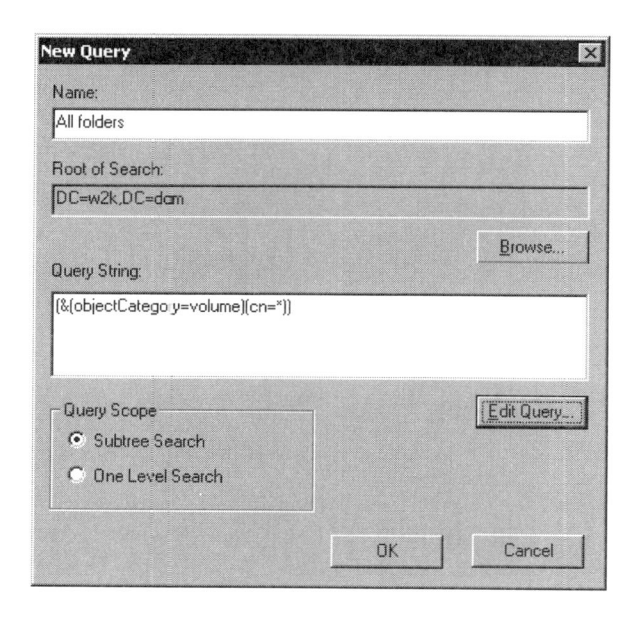

Fig. 4.20. This window contains the parameters necessary for creating a custom query

To see *all* folders, you must specify the "*" character for the folder name. Select the appropriate query scope — **Subtree Search** or **One Level Search**.

An example of the resulting display is shown in Fig. 4.21. Notice (in the **Distinguished Name** column) that the selected folders are related to *different* OUs in the same domain. This means that you've really searched the entire domain.

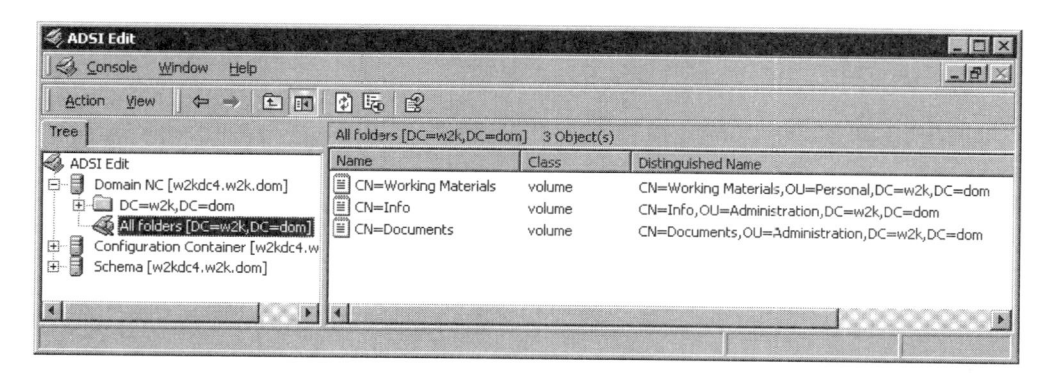

Fig. 4.21. The query that allows you to work with all published folders in the whole domain forest

All queries are saved upon snap-in closing, and refresh upon its loading. You can refresh the contents of a query at any time. To edit a query, select **Setting** from the query's context menu.

Creating Active Directory Objects

Using the **ADSI Edit** snap-in, you can create Active Directory objects of any type. It can hardly be recommended to do so, however, because of a high probability of errors with object attributes: you must be very familiar with the meaning of all mandatory and optional attributes and their valid values. Using the "standard" administrative snap-ins and tools is much preferable.

If, nevertheless, you do decide to manually create an object, point to the desired object in the tree pane and select the **New | Object** command. The wizard will start and ask you for all required values. The list of possible new objects depends on the type of object selected initially. (See also "*Extending the Schema*" in *Chapter 13, "Active Directory Service Interfaces (ADSI)".*)

Working with Global Catalog

The possibility of working directly with a global catalog (GC) server may be helpful while troubleshooting the problems related to GC replication. You can connect to different GC servers and compare the values of stored attributes (see also the description of *DsaStat* in *Chapter 8, "Network and Distributed Services"*). You can also verify the representation of attributes in a GC. (This process can be controlled via the **Active Directory Schema** snap-in, see the next section).

> **NOTE**
> Only some of Active Directory object's attributes are presented in Global Catalog. When you have enabled/disabled replication of an attribute to Global Catalog, you may wish to use the **ADSI Edit** snap-in to verify the presence of this attribute on a GC server.

In general, the procedures for working with Global Catalog are the same as described above. The only difference is that you must select the **Global Catalog** protocol in the **Advanced** window when creating a connection to an Active Directory naming context (partition). It is clear that is impossible to *create* new objects in the Global Catalog.

Active Directory Schema Snap-in

The **Active Directory Schema** snap-in is the preferred GUI tool (the other one is the **ADSI Edit** snap-in; its usage requires that you have a more advanced familiarity with Active Directory's interiors) that allows viewing and modifying of Active Directory classes and the attributes which the classes contain. (Two other ways to extend the schema are scripting and using command-line tools, such as LDIFDE and CSVDE.) This snap-in allows an administrator to view X.500 OIDs of classes and attributes, a range of values for attributes, mandatory and optional attributes for classes, and other meta-information on attributes and classes.

Installation

The **Active Directory Schema** snap-in is installed by default on domain controllers. (This snap-in is also included in the *Windows 2000 Administration Tools* pack, and can be installed on any computer with Windows 2000.) It appears neither in the **Start** menu nor in the Control Panel, and should be manually added to an MMC console. You need only first register the DLL by entering the following command at the command prompt:

```
regsvr32 schmmgmt.dll
```

You should get the message shown in Fig. 4.22.

Fig. 4.22. This message will appear if the DLL-file is registered successfully

If you install *Windows 2000 Administrative Tools* on a computer (see *Chapter 5, "Common Administrative Tasks"*), the appropriate DLL is registered automatically.

After schmmgmt.dll is registered on a computer, you can create an MMC document (which is a console saved with any name you liked) containing the **Active Directory Schema** snap-in, or add the snap-in to an existing custom console.

Modifying the Schema

All modifications of the schema are only permitted on the DC that owns the Schema Master FSMO role. It is highly recommended *not* to bypass this requirement. By default, the modification of the schema is disabled. So, to modify the schema, start the **Active Directory Schema** snap-in (which by default is targeted to the Schema Master) and first set the flag **The Schema may be modified on this Domain Controller** in the **Change Schema Master** window. After this, you can change the schema itself and schema access permissions.

> **ATTENTION!**
>
> By default, only members of the Schema Admins group can modify the schema. It is, however, also possible to grant this permission to other people.
>
> The schema's updates are dumped from cache to disk every 5 minutes. You can manually reload the schema to speed up this process.

Modification, and especially extension of the schema, requires a profound understanding of Active Directory concepts and classes structure, and this could be the theme of a separate book. (Some basic information on this question is given in *Chapter 13, "Active Directory Service Interfaces (ADSI)".*) However, in routine work an administrator may want to perform the following operations (these are the names of checkboxes at the **General** tab in the **Properties** window of an attribute or a class; see Fig. 4.24):

- **Index this attribute in the Active Directory** — Indexing of an attribute speeds up the frequently used query operations that include the attribute.

- **Replicate this attribute to the Global Catalog** — If an attribute is included in GC, you can get the attribute's values when doing forest-wide queries.

- **Deactivate this attribute (class)** — If a newly created (e. g. a test) attribute or class is not yet used (i. e. there are no new objects of that class, or that attribute has not been added to a class) in Active Directory, you may "disable" it. (You cannot *delete* attributes and closses in Active Directory.)

To enable these operations, expand the **Attributes** or **Classes** node in the tree pane and find the desired attribute or class. Open the **Properties** window and set the appropriate flag on the **General** tab.

> **CAUTION!**
>
> After a new attribute has been added to the global catalog, a forest-wide replication is triggered. (This is the case regarding all schema modification operations.) This can result in significant network traffic. Therefore, this operation should not be performed often and should be well planned.

Extending the Schema

Extension of the schema is not a particularly complicated operation, but in fact a very crucial one. You must always remember that all extensions of the schema are not reversible (even if you restore Active Directory from a backup copy!) and may result in significant forest-wide replication traffic.

Let's discuss how to create a new attribute and class with a few examples. (See also about extending the schema in *Chapter 13, "Active Directory Service Interfaces (ADSI)"* and *Chapter 14, "Using ADSI for Administrative Tasks".*)

Creating an Attribute

Before creating an attribute, you must carry out the following operations:

- Choose the attribute's common and LDAP display names according to Microsoft recommendations
- Obtain the base X.500 OID and add your specific attribute ID to it
- Select the attribute's syntax
- Choose the minimum and maximum values for the attribute (optional)

> **ATTENTION!**
>
> The base X.500 OIDs — one for classes and one for attributes — are obtained only *once* for your organization. Then you can add your own increasing IDs to the base OIDs.

When you have gathered all this information, point to the **Attributes** node in the tree pane and click **Create Attribute** in the context menu. Click **Continue** in the warning window. Fill in the fields in the **Create New Attribute** window. (All fields except **Minimum** and **Maximum** are mandatory.) Click **OK**. Fig. 4.23 displays sample information necessary for creating a string attribute.

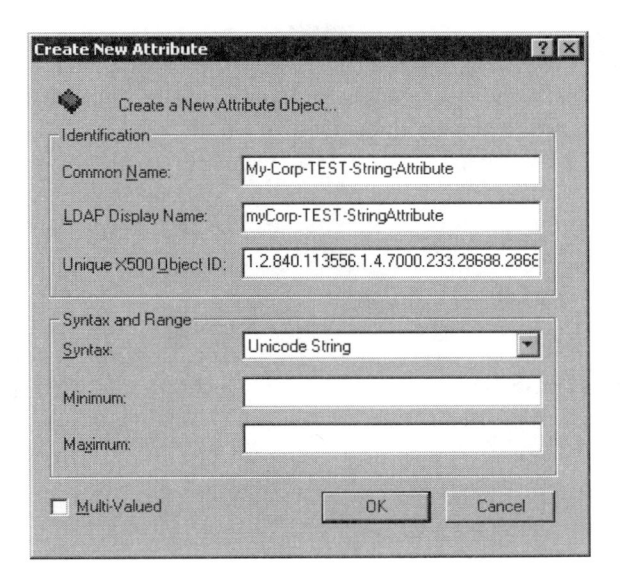

Fig. 4.23. An example of creating a new string attribute

Fig. 4.24. Properties of an attribute

> **ATTENTION!**
>
> If you received the "Schema update failed in recalculating validation cache" error, verify the selected OID. It may appear to be used.

Now you can find the new attribute in the list, view the attribute's properties (Fig. 4.24), give a description to it, and set the necessary flags (checkboxes). At this point, you can use the created attribute, i. e. add it to an existing class(es) (see below and in *Chapter 14*).

Creating a Class

To create a class, you must gather the following information:

- ❏ The class's common and LDAP display names according to Microsoft recommendations
- ❏ The base X.500 OID (and add your specific class ID to it)
- ❏ The type of the class (commonly, *structural*) and the parent class (optional; *top* by default)
- ❏ The lists of mandatory and optional attributes of the class (if a structural or auxiliary class inherits only the attributes from the parent and doesn't have its own attributes, is it really necessary to create such a class?)
- ❏ The possible superior(s) — the container(s), in which creation of the class's objects is permitted

Point to the **Classes** node in the tree pane and click **Create Class** in the context menu. Click **Continue** in the warning window. Fill in the fields in the **Create New Schema Class** window. Fig. 4.25 illustrates this step. Click **Next**.

In the next window (Fig. 4.26) you can add mandatory and optional attributes to the class. If you leave both lists empty, the new class will have only the attributes of the parent class. You can add and remove attributes until you click **Finish**.

> **ATTENTION!**
>
> It is possible to add optional attributes to a class at any time, but the mandatory attributes are added only at the class's creation.

Fig. 4.25. The first step in creating a new object class

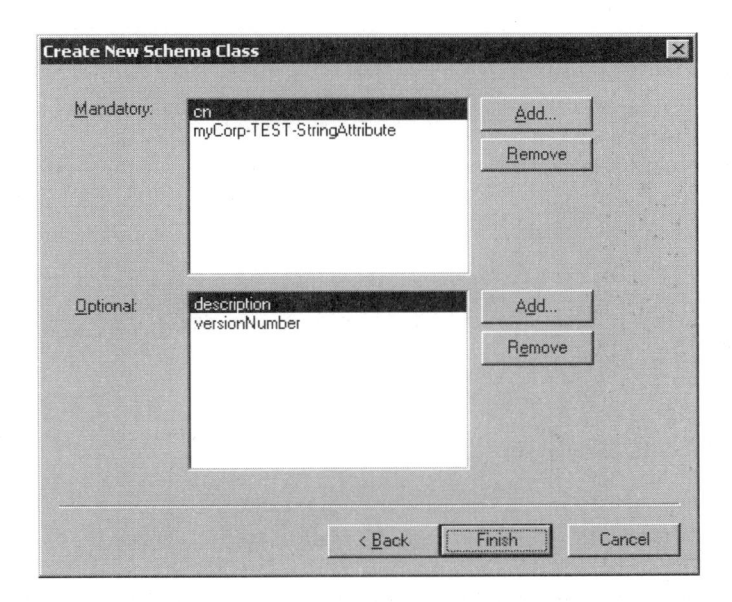

Fig. 4.26. In this window, you can add mandatory and optional attributes

To define a *possible superior* for the new class, select the class from the list, open the **Properties** window, and click the **Relationship** tab (Fig. 4.27). Add the necessary class, click **Apply**, and close the window. Creation of a new class is now complete.

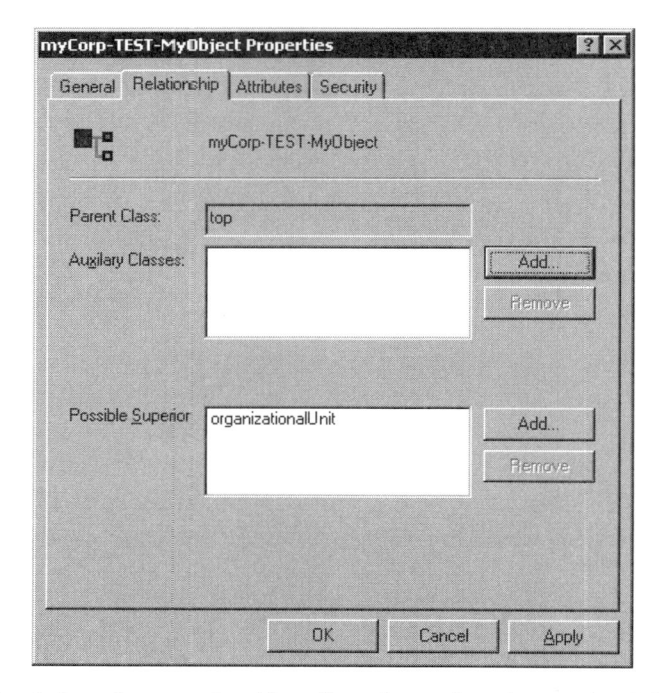

Fig. 4.27. This window allows you to add auxiliary classes to a class and to define containers (possible superiors), in which objects of that class can be created

If the class created is of the *auxiliary* type, you may wish to add it to an existing class. Select a class, open the **Properties** window, click the **Relationship** tab, and add the new class to the **Auxiliary Classes** list (Fig. 4.27).

Adding Attributes to Existing Classes

It is possible to add newly created or existing attributes to classes — new or standard ones. Select the applicable class from the list and open the **Properties** window. You can add necessary attributes to the **Optional** tab at the **Attributes** tab: click **Add** and choose an attribute from the **Select Schema Object** list. Click **Apply** and close the window. Reload the schema or wait until the schema's updates are written to disk. Then the new attributes of the class will be "visible" in other administrative tools.

Group Policy Snap-in

The main purpose of the **Group Policy** snap-in is editing of a group policy object (GPO) stored locally on a computer or in Active Directory, and linked (in the second case) to an Active Directory container: site, domain, or OU.

You should solidly understand the difference between the **Group Policy** snap-in and the **Security Policy — Local**, **Domain Controller**, or **Domain** — snap-ins. (These last three snap-ins are configured by default on every DC; the **Local Security Policy** snap-in is also configured on every client Windows 2000 system.)

The **Group Policy** snap-in works with an *entire* GPO, and can be run from certain administrative snap-ins or from a custom MMC console. It contains both computer and user policies (the **Computer Configuration** and **User Configuration** nodes of GPO).

The **Security Policy** snap-ins deal *only* with the **Security Setting** sub-node of the corresponding GPO, and can be run from the **Start** menu (the **Administrative Tools** submenu). These snap-ins allow you to configure computer policies only.

> **NOTES**
>
> Don't forget about two other important snap-ins — **Security Configuration and Analysis** and **Security Templates** — that also help an administrator to deploy Active Directory security in an enterprise. Due to space limitations and other reasons, these snap-ins are not discussed in this book.
>
> See *Chapter 5, "Common Administrative Tasks"*, about refreshing computer (machine) and/or user policies after editing a GPO's parameters.

Linking to a Group Policy Object (GPO)

A running **Group Policy** snap-in is always linked to a GPO. Therefore, you need to learn two things: how to start the snap-in itself, and how to link it to a GPO.

There are three ways to start the **Group Policy** snap-in:

- ❏ In the **Active Directory Users and Computers** snap-in — select the domain or an OU, open the **Properties** window, and click the **Group Policy** tab (Fig. 4.28).
- ❏ In the **Active Directory Sites and Services** snap-in — select a site, open the **Properties** window, and click the **Group Policy** tab.

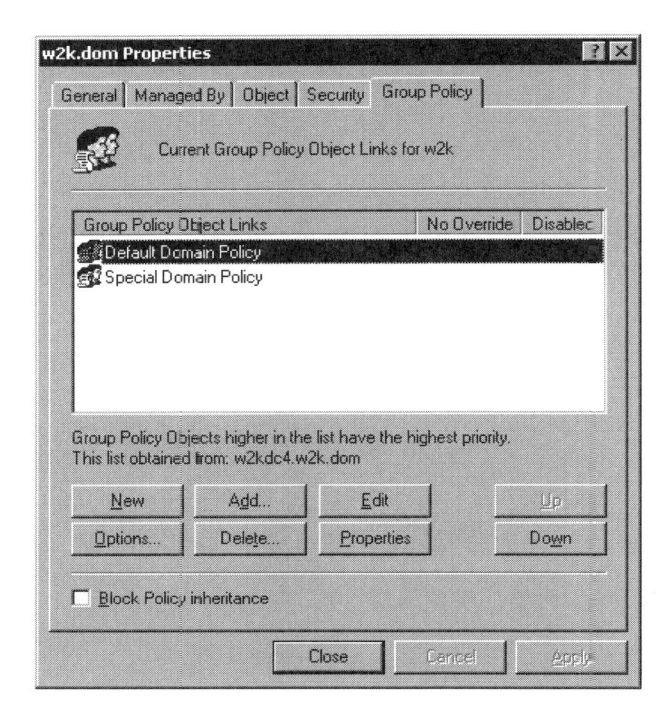

Fig. 4.28. The list of GPOs for a domain container

- Start Microsoft Management Console (enter mmc in the **Run** window) or open a custom MMC console, and add the **Group Policy** snap-in. The **Select Group Policy Object** window allows you to link to the local GPO (default option) on the local computer (it is also possible to select another computer). An alternative option is to open the **Browse for a Group Policy Object** window (by clicking **Browse**) (see Fig. 4.29).

In each of the three cases you have three options:

- *Select* an existing GPO (i. e. already linked) in the list and edit it by using the **Group Policy** snap-in
- *Create* a new GPO
- *Add* (link) an existing GPO to the container

Let's discuss the last case. If you click **Add** at the **Group Policy** tab, the **Browse for a Group Policy Object** window will open. An example of the default view of such a window is shown in Fig. 4.29. (You may click the circled icon and create a new GPO.)

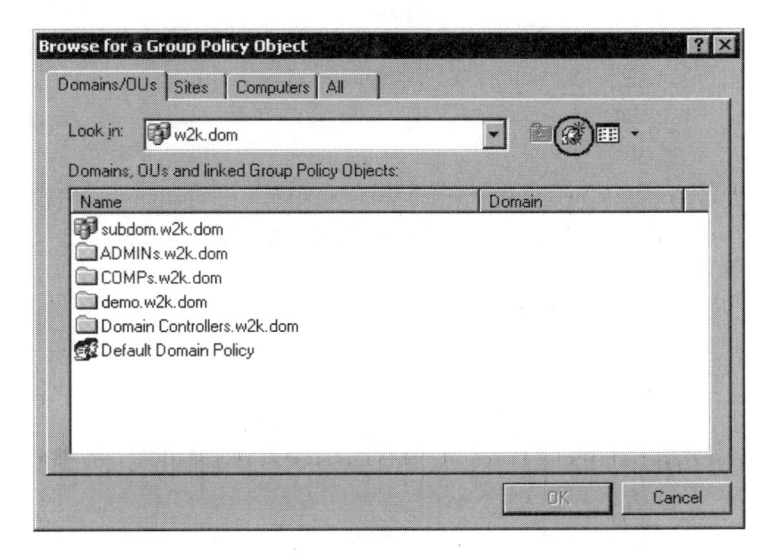

Fig. 4.29. You can see in this window the entire structure of OUs in a domain and the GPOs linked to them

As shown in Fig. 4.30, all GPOs that exist in a domain are listed in the **All** tab, so you can quickly find the necessary GPO.

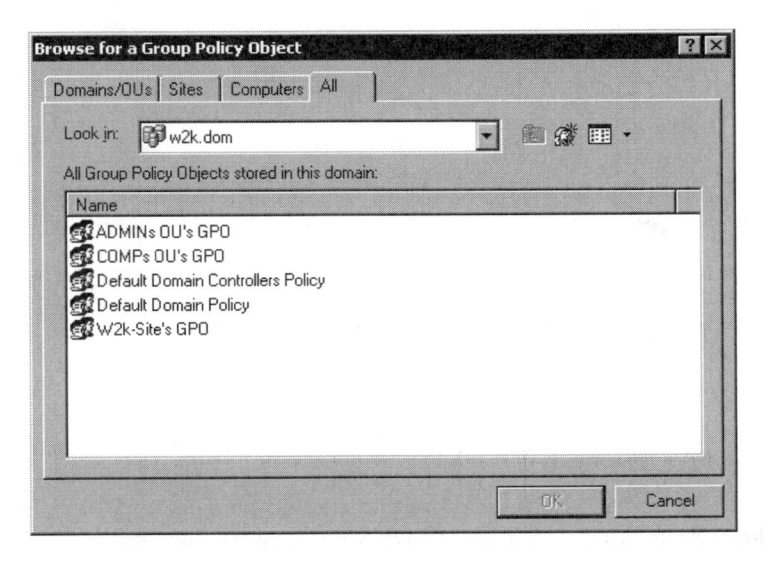

Fig. 4.30. Use this tab to quickly find a GPO that you want to link to the current container

When the **Group Policy** snap-in is opened or a custom MMC console is created, it is not possible to re-link the snap-in to another GPO. You also cannot change the DC with which the default **Security Policy** snap-ins works. This operation can only be done for customer-created MMC consoles with the **Group Policy** snap-in.

You can check which containers the selected GPO is linked to. In the **Group Policy** snap-in's window, point to the root node in the tree pane and open the **Properties** window for the GPO. Click **Links** tab (Fig. 4.31). Select an applicable domain and click **Find Now**. If the GPO is linked to other containers, you'll see their names in the list in addition to the name of the current container.

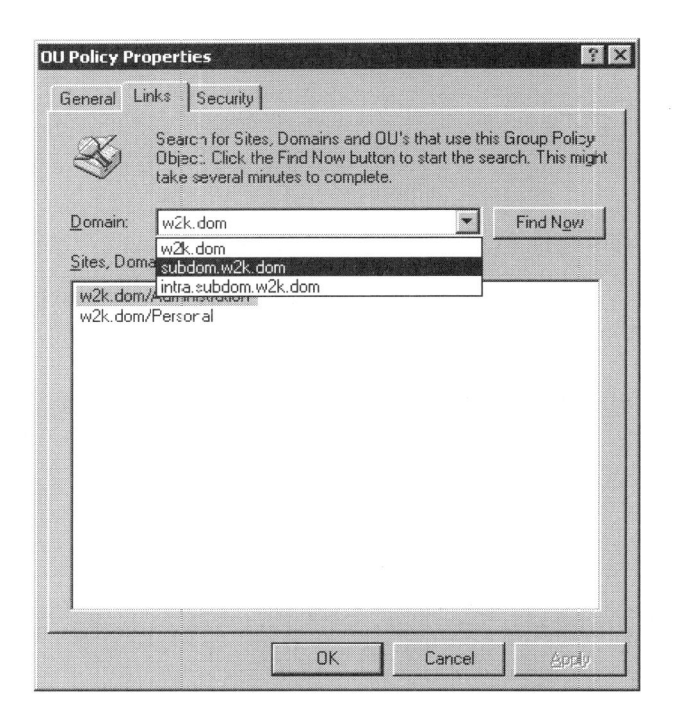

Fig. 4.31. You can quickly check out if the selected GPO is linked to another containers besides the current one

ATTENTION!

It is not advisable to use GPOs in "cross-domain" fashion due to possible security and administrative conflicts.

Creating and Deleting a GPO

To create a GPO, it is sufficient to click **New** at the **Group Policy** tab in a container's **Properties** window, or to click the button in the **Browse for a Group Policy Object** window (see Fig. 4.29). Name the new GPO, and you may then begin editing it.

When you are going to delete a GPO, you have two options:

- **Remove the link from the list** — In selecting this option, you break only the link between the selected GPO and the current container. The GPO remains intact, and you can use it later.

- **Remove the link and delete the Group Policy Object permanently** — As the message indicates, this is a more decisive option, since you not only break the link, but entirely delete the GPO (remember that this GPO can be used by other containers!)

Selecting a Domain Controller

A **Group Policy** snap-in is always targeted to a specific — "preferred" — domain controller. (Notice the **This list obtained from...** line in Fig. 4.28. By default, all **Group Policy** snap-ins started on computers that belong to the sample domain *w2k.dom* will select the same DC.) There are some rules that define this behavior of the snap-in. To verify or change the default settings of a **Group Policy** snap-in, point to the root node in the tree pane and click **View | DC Options** in the context menu. You can select one of the options shown in Fig. 4.32. (This selection may be overridden by a group policy; see below.)

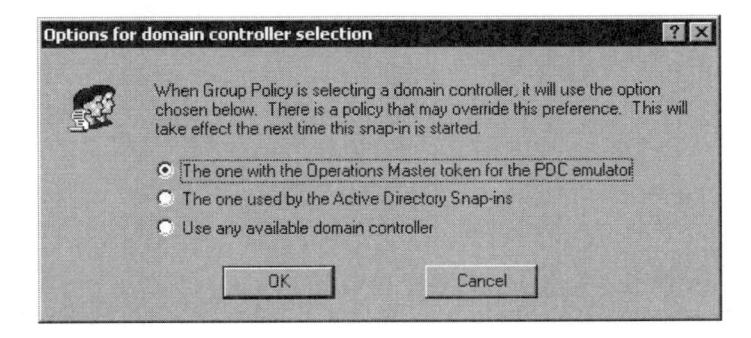

Fig. 4.32. These options determine which DC the **Group Policy** snap-in selects at its startup

It is necessary to comment only the second option. You can start the **Group Policy** snap-in from either the **Active Directory Users and Computers** or the **Active Directory Sites and Services** snap-in which is targeted to a DC (any DC in the forest) at that moment. The **Group Policy** snap-in will obtain a group policy setting from a GPO stored on *that* DC.

The selected option is saved and used at the next run of the snap-in.

> **ATTENTION!**
>
> If the selected DC is not accessible at the snap-in's startup, an error will be reported. Verify the setting (and the policy if defined), and select another option if necessary.
>
> Because the DNS is used for locating GPOs, the errors at the Group Policy snap-in's startup are very often related to the malfunctioning of DNS. Therefore, always verify the DNS configuration when you encounter such errors. Remember that DNS is a dynamic system, and the records registered periodically expire.

There is also a group policy that allows an administrator to define the strategy of selecting a "preferred" DC. Open the *Default Domain Policy* GPO (or other applicable GPO) and select the **User Configuration | Administrative Templates | System | Group Policy** node. Double click the **Group Policy domain controller selection** policy. Click **Enable** and select one of the following options:

- **Use the Primary Domain Controller**
- **Inherit from the Active Directory Snap-ins**
- **Use any available domain controller**

If this policy is disabled or not configured, the **Group Policy** snap-in selects the PDC Operation Master for the domain. When defined, the policy overrides the option selected in the **Group Policy** snap-in.

> **NOTE**
>
> You cannot define the "preferred" DC for **Security Policy** snap-ins.

Configuring Group Policy Objects

There are some common recommendations and tips on using and configuring GPOs. Let's discuss them.

- Disable unused settings in a GPO. This improves performance when a computer or user is logged on to the domain. Open the **Properties** window of the GPO (see Fig. 4.31 where the **Links** tab of this window is shown) and click the **General** tab. Check the appropriate box: **Disable Computer Configuration settings** or **Disable User Configuration settings**. When both boxes are disabled, it means that the GPO is linked to the container, but doesn't affect it.

- For the **Administrative Templates** nodes, you can set the **Show Configured Policies Only** flag (point to a node and set the flag in the **View** menu). This prevents you from viewing not-configured policies. This flag is set for the **Computer Configuration** and **User Configuration** node separately.

- If your system was upgraded from a Windows NT 4.0 and/or you use the older ADM-files, pay attention to the value of the **Show Policies Only** flag in the **View** menu for the **Administrative Templates** nodes. This flag when set prevents old system policy settings from applying to Windows 2000 clients.

- Pay attention to the **Explain** tab in the **Properties** window of each policy. This tab contains a comprehensive description of the policy, which may be a good substitute for many pages of documentation.

Chapter 5
Common Administrative Tasks

This chapter deals with some typical administrative tasks related to Active Directory. (A few operations were already considered in the previous chapter.) All tasks discussed below are carried out using administrative snap-ins or different utilities from the *Support Tools* or the *Windows 2000 Resource Kit*.

Using the *RunAs* Command

Due to security requirements, it is not recommended that you be permanently logged on to the system (domain) with a user account that has full administrative privileges. Windows 2000 offers a very helpful command — *RunAs*. This command allows a system administrator to carry out common tasks using an account with restricted (or "normal" user) rights, and to start a specific command on behalf of a "power" user (this can be an administrator account or an account with some additional rights). Thus, it is not necessary to repeatedly re-register into the system.

Let's consider how to use this command with the administrative snap-ins.

> **NOTE**
> If the RunAs command fails, make sure that the RunAs service is running on the computer (run the **Services** snap-in and check the status of the service).

Running Administrative Tools from the Context Menu

You can select an administrative tool in one of the following ways:

- Select the tool in the **Start | Programs | Administrative Tools** menu.

- Open the window that contains all tools. Click **Start | Programs | Administrative Tools**, and select **Open** or **Open All Users** in the context menu. (The former window only contains the tools created by the user, while the latter one contains all tools installed by default.) Select the tool in the open window.

- Copy (drag and drop) icons of the necessary tools to the desktop. (You may also create one or more folders on the desktop, and copy the icons to them.)

Then, for **Active Directory Domains and Trusts**, **Active Directory Sites and Services**, **Active Directory Users and Groups**, **Domain Security Policy**, **Domain Controller Security Policy**, and certain other snap-ins, you can press and hold

Chapter 5: Common Administrative Tasks 121

<Shift>, and select the **Run as** command from the context menu. (Many snap-ins in the **Administrative Tools** group already have this command in their context menus.) You'll see a window similar to the one shown in Fig. 5.1. Selecting the upper switch allows you to start the tool on behalf of your current account (i. e. with your current privileges). The default (shown) option permits you to enter an administrator's credentials, and start the tool in the "privileged" mode. Note that only the NetBIOS (pre-Windows 2000) domain name can be used in this window!

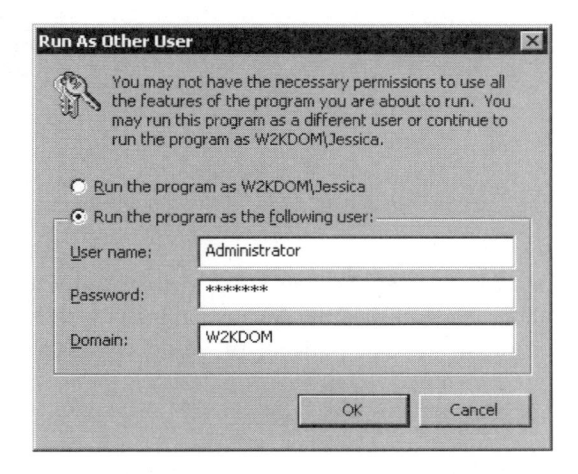

Fig. 5.1. By entering proper credentials in this window, you can start a program on behalf of another user

NOTE

The procedure described above can be used with *any* EXE- or MSC-file, and not only with administrative tools. (See below about running the RunAs command from the command prompt.)

Also, for many administrative tools you can open the tool's **Properties** window and set the **Run as different user** flag. After this operation, the system will *always* propose that you start the tool as another user.

NOTE

Notice also the **Author** command that appears in the context menu of many administrative tools. This command allows you to start a snap-in in author mode and modify it. By default, all tools are saved in **User mode — limited access, single window**, and the

Do not save changes in this console box is checked. To prevent users from changing the administrative snap-ins, you may use the user administrative templates in the **Group Policy** snap-in.

Starting a Tool from the Command Prompt

Using the RunAs command, it is possible to start any executable file — EXE, COM, CMD, BAT, MSC; shortcuts to programs (LNK); and Control Panel items (CPL) — on behalf of a different user. Let's discuss some examples. (You can get complete information on RunAs in *Help* or by running `runas /?`)

> **NOTES**
>
> RunAs cannot be used with some items, such as Windows Explorer, the **Printers** folder, and desktop items.
>
> Usually, it's much more convenient to start MMC tools with RunAs from the command prompt rather than from the **Run** window, because in the first case you'll be able to see possible errors. For frequently used commands, you may want to create shortcuts on the desktop.

Example 1. Work in the Same Domain

Suppose you are currently logged on to the *w2k.dom* domain with a "normal" user account, and want to configure the domain security settings, which requires administrative privileges (see Table 5.1). In the **Run** window or at the command prompt enter the command:

`runas /user:administrator@w2k.dom "mmc dcpol.msc"`

`Administrator` is the name of a user that is a member of the *Domain Admins* group. Enter the administrator's password when prompted.

Example 2. Administering Another Domain

Now, you want to create a user in the *subdom.w2k.dom* domain using the **Active Directory Users and Computers** snap-in. (I. e. you'd like to work in a domain, other then the domain where you are logged on.) Enter the following string:

`runas /netonly /user:SUBDOM\administrator "mmc dsa.msc"`

Chapter 5: Common Administrative Tasks   123

> **NOTE**
>
> As you can see, it's possible to use two formats for representing a user account: UPN format, and standard SAM format — DOMAIN\USER. Both formats are acceptable, although `runas /?` asserts that UPN format is not compatible with the `/netonly` parameter.

Example 3. Verifying User Permissions

RunAs can be very helpful for setting up user permissions on a file or Active Directory objects. To set the necessary permissions for a user, you may start a tool using administrative privileges. At the same time, it's possible to open the command prompt or start a program on behalf of this user and check the resulting permissions. You needn't repeatedly logon to the system using different accounts or use several computers.

Names of Administrative Snap-ins

To use administrative tools with RunAs, you need to know the names of the corresponding snap-ins. Also, some tools can be used only with administrative privileges. Table 5.1 contains information on some important tools.

> **NOTE**
>
> All installed snap-ins are located in the *%SystemRoot%*\system32 folder.

Table 5.1. Some Administrative Tools and the Privileges Necessary to Use Them

Tool name	Snap-in's name	Necessary privileges
Active Directory Domains and Trusts	domain.msc	User
Active Directory Schema	*userCreatedName*.msc	User
Active Directory Sites and Services	dssite.msc	User
Active Directory Users and Computers	dsa.msc	User
Computer Management	compmgmt.msc	User
Distributed File System	dfsgui.msc	User

continues

Table 5.1 Continued

Tool name	Snap-in's name	Necessary privileges
DNS	dnsmgmt.msc	Administrator
Domain Controller Security Settings	dcpol.msc	Administrator
Domain Security Settings	dompol.msc	Administrator
Group Policy (see below)	gpedit.msc	Administrator
Local Security Settings	secpol.msc	Administrator
Routing and Remote Access	rrasmgmt.msc	Administrator
Services	services.msc	User
Snap-ins that aren't displayed in the *Administrative Tools* menu		
Device Manager	devmgmt.msc	User
Disk Management	diskmgmt.msc	Administrator
Local Users and Groups	lusrmgr.msc	User
Shared Folders	fsmgmt.msc	Administrator

By default (when started without any parameters), the **Group Policy** snap-in is targeted to (focused on) the local computer. You have two options: to run this snap-in with a GPO located on a remote computer, or in Active Directory.

In the first instance, you can create a custom MMC console, add the **Group Policy** snap-in to it, link the snap-in to the necessary GPO, and save the console with any name you like. Then you can start the console by its name. This is the "static" approach.

By using the second method, you are exploiting the fact that the **Group Policy** snap-in (the gpedit.msc file) allows you to change its focus (the "dynamic" approach). For example, the following command allows you to open a *GPO stored on a remote computer* (even the local computer specified in the /gpcomputer parameter is regarded as a *remote* one):

```
gpedit.msc /gpcomputer:"w2kdc3.w2k.dom"
```

ATTENTION!

You cannot view and manage the **Security Settings** extension (except for the **IP Security Policies**) of a *remote* computer's GPO. The **Software Installation**, **Remote Installation Services**, and **Folder Redirection** extensions are never displayed for *local* GPOs.

You can also specify the *GPO's distinguished name.*

I'd suggest the following approach. At the command prompt, carry out a search operation by using the Search.vbs script (Ldp.exe can also be used) with parameters similar to:

```
search "LDAP://DC=w2k,DC=dom" /C:(objectCategory=GroupPolicyContainer)
    ↳ /S:subtree /P:AdsPath,displayName
```

On the screen, you'll see the list of all GPOs stored in the domain, for instance:

```
<LDAP://DC=w2k,DC=dom>;((objectClass=GroupPolicyContainer));AdsPath,
displayName;subtree
Finished the query.
Found 9 objects.
...
AdsPath 2 = LDAP://CN={31B2F340-016D-11D2-945F-00C04FB984F9},
    ↳ CN=Policies,CN=System,DC=w2k,DC=dom
displayName 2 = Default Domain Policy
AdsPath 3 = LDAP://CN={6AC1786C-016F-11D2-945F-00C04FB984F9},
    ↳ CN=Policies,CN=System,DC=w2k,DC=dom
displayName 3 = Default Domain Controllers Policy
...
```

You can easily select the necessary policy by its friendly name and use its DN as the parameter. (Don't forget about the *copy-and-paste* feature of the command prompt window.) For example, to open the *Default Domain Controllers Policy* shown above, use the following command (the quotes are mandatory):

```
gpedit.msc
    ↳ /gpobject:"LDAP://CN={6AC1786C-016F-11D2-945F-00C04fB984F9},
    ↳ CN=Policies,CN=System,DC=w2k,DC=dom"
```

This command used with the RunAs will have the following syntax:

```
runas /user:w2kdom\administrator "mmc gpedit.msc
    ↳ /gpobject:\"LDAP://CN={6AC1786C-016F-11D2-945F-00C04fB984F9},
    ↳ CN=Policies,CN=System,DC=w2k,DC=dom\""
```

Remote Administration

To administer Active Directory from a domain client computer, you have the following standard options (in free order):

- ❑ *Terminal Services* allow an administrator to work on a client computer in the same way as when at the server's console. This is the only standard option for

- down-level client computers (Windows NT, Windows 9x) to run the administrative tools, and the only option for low-speed (dial-up) connections. Although many administrative command-line tools can work on remote computers, you need the Terminal Services to get the full functionality of the command prompt on a DC.

- The *Windows 2000 Administration Tools* pack contains practically all administrative snap-ins (see Table 5.2). It is located in the *%SystemRoot%*\system32\adminpak.msi file available on every Windows 2000-based domain controller. You can install the Administration Tools on any computer with Windows 2000, but to use the tools you must be logged on as a user with domain administrative rights.

- You can manually install the selected administrative snap-ins on a client computer (see next section).

Table 5.2. Snap-ins Included in the *Windows 2000 Administration Tools* Pack

Active Directory Domains and Trusts	Internet Authentication Service
Active Directory Sites and Services	Internet Services Manager
Active Directory Users and Computers	QoS Admission Control
Certification Authority	Remote Storage
Cluster Administrator	Routing and Remote Access
Connection Manger Administration Kit	Telephony
DHCP	Terminal Services Client
Distributed File System	Terminal Services Licensing
DNS	Terminal Services Manager
	WINS

Installing Administrative Snap-ins Selectively

For some reason, you may want to install only one or just a few separate administrative tools on a client computer instead of the entire Administration Tools pack. This can easily be done. (But don't forget about security requirements!) You have to carry out the following steps:

1. Copy the necessary snap-ins (files with MSC extension) from the *%SystemRoot%*\system32 folder on a DC to any local folder you wish.

2. Copy the appropriate DLL(s) to the local *%SystemRoot%*\system32 folder or to any local folder.

3. If the DLL has been copied to a folder other than *%SystemRoot%*\system32, you must first change the folder as necessary. To register the DLL, enter the following string at the command prompt:

   ```
   regsvr32 <DLLname>
   ```

4. For example, to register the DLL for the **Active Directory Users and Computers** snap-in, enter `regsvr32 dsadmin.dll`.

Now you may create shortcuts for new snap-ins, and then run them. Of course, you have to be logged on to the domain with appropriate privileges.

The following table contains DLL names for some administrative snap-ins:

Tool name	Snap-in's name	DLL's name
Active Directory Domain and Trusts	domain.msc	domadmin.dll
Active Directory Sites and Services	dssite.msc	dsadmin.dll
Active Directory Schema	*userCreatedName*.msc	schmmgmt.dll
Active Directory Users and Computers	dsa.msc	dsadmin.dll

> **NOTE**
>
> After schmmgmt.dll has been copied to a local computer, you will then be able to add the snap-in to any custom MMC console (since there is no schema snap-in configured by default).
>
> The **Group Policy** snap-in is present on any Windows 2000-based computer by default. Therefore, to use this tool and link it to any domain GPO, you need only to have administrator's privileges in the domain.

Notice that both the **Active Directory Users and Computers** and **Active Directory Sites and Services** snap-ins use the same dsadmin.dll file. Both snap-ins actually provide similar operations (browsing and editing properties) with directory objects. The former enables you to work with the entire domain naming partition of Active Directory. The latter provides access to two containers in the configuration partition, namely, *Sites* and *Services* (you can also view them in the **ADSI Edit** snap-in).

Querying Active Directory

Querying is one of the commonly used operations in network directories, and Active Directory is not an exception. Active Directory may contain a huge number of objects, whose precise locations are frequently unknown. Querying the directory rather than browsing the directory tree is preferable for both users and administrators. Users of Windows 2000 domains have the following instruments (some of them are available to all clients including down-level systems, and others only work on Windows 2000 systems) of finding one or more objects in Active Directory:

- Built-in search features (see the next section) — the friendliest way for a user to find a shared folder or printer, user, group, or other common directory object. All other tools are intended for administrators.

- The **ADSI Edit** snap-in (from *Support Tools*) — using this tool, an administrator can create powerful queries and modify objects in all directory partitions. (See *Chapter 4, "Domain Manipulation Tools"*.)

- The *Search.vbs* script — the simplest tool (from *Support Tools*) that uses the LDAP protocol. (See *Chapter 9, "Manipulating Active Directory Objects"*.)

- *Active Directory Administration Tool* (Ldp.exe) (Support Tools) and *Active Directory Browser* (AdsVw.exe) (Active Directory SDK) — complicated administrative tools that also allow an administrator to browse the directory tree and modify objects. Ldp.exe uses the LDAP protocol and is the only tool that can retrieve deleted objects. AdsVw.exe uses both LDAP and WinNT protocols, and works with Windows 2000 and Window NT domains. (See *Chapter 9*.)

- The Guid2obj.exe utility (from *Windows 2000 Resource Kit* — a specialized tool that can determine the distinguished name of an object from its GUID.

Most of the listed tools require a good understanding of LDAP filter syntax. Only then will you be able to quickly and precisely find or filter out the necessary objects.

Configuring *Search* Option on a Computer

By default, clients — those aware of this option — can search for various Active Directory objects by using the **Find** command from the context menu of a domain displayed in the **Directory** folder (in **My Network Places**). (They can use the **Active Directory Users and Computer** snap-in installed on a client computer.) There are also two more specialized commands in the **Start | Search** menu: **For Printers**, and **For People**.

It is also possible to add a shortcut for the search operation to the desktop or any folder. You need to do the following:

1. Click on the desktop with the right button and select **New | Shortcut**.
2. Enter the following string in the **Type the location of the item** field:

   ```
   rundll32.exe dsquery,OpenQueryWindow
   ```

3. In the next window, enter a name for the shortcut and click **Finish**.
4. You may wish to move the created shortcut to some folder or menu. If so, do it now.

After clicking the shortcut, the user will see a search window similar to one shown in Fig. 4.11. In this window, it is possible to find users, contacts, groups, printers, OUs, etc.

> **NOTE**
>
> I tested this feature on a Windows ME-based computer with the standard DSClient from the Windows 2000 Server CD. Everything works fine! (The feature might also be able to be used on Windows 9*x* systems with the client installed.) Just keep in mind that you mustn't enter a space between the *dsquery* and *OpenQueryWindow* parameters.

Manipulating Directory Objects

There are, in fact, quite a number of tools that allow an administrator to create, delete, and modify one or a number of Active Directory objects. You should be familiar with all (or at least most) of them to be able to choose the most effective tool for specific tasks. Let's list all of the main facilities provided by Windows 2000:

❑ Standard snap-ins installed by default (see *Chapter 4, "Domain Manipulation Tools"*) — universal GUI tools that work with one object only and have modest support for group operations.

- The **Active Directory Users and Computers** snap-in creates users, contacts, groups, computers, printers, shared folders, and OUs
- The **Active Directory Sites and Services** snap-in creates sites, subnets, links, and connections
- The **Active Directory Domains and Trusts** snap-in creates inter-domain trusts

- Specialized administrative GUI tools (see *Chapter 4* and *Chapter 9, "Manipulating Active Directory Objects"*) — tools used for specific operations and for fine tuning and troubleshooting Active Directory.
    - The **Active Directory Schema** snap-in creates attributes and classes
    - The **ADSI Edit** snap-in, Ldp.exe and AdsVw.exe create any types of objects (including objects which cannot be created by any other tools), but are primarily useful for editing attributes
- Tools for import/export (see *Chapter 9*) — command-line utilities that could (and should) serve as powerful tools for administering large-scale Active Directory installation. LDIFDE can also be used for changing the attributes of a number of similar objects.
    - LDIFDE
    - CSVDE
- Utilities intended for specific tasks (see later in this chapter and the *Remote Administration Scripts* in the *Windows 2000 Server Resource Kit*).
    - AddUsers.exe, CreateUsers.vbs, CreateGroups.vbs, and others (NetDom can be used for creating machine accounts in domains)
- ADSI scripts (see *Chapter 13, "Active Directory Service Interfaces (ADSI)"* and *Chapter 14, "Using ADSI for Administrative Tasks"*) — the most flexible of the options, and, in fact, a quite simple way to manipulate Active Directory objects.

Using the *Active Directory Users and Computers* Snap-in

The **Active Directory Users and Computers** snap-in is the main tool that an administrator will use daily to manage various domain resources. The procedure of creating and deleting Active Directory objects is basically the same for all types of objects. There are buttons on the *Standard* toolbar for some of the most used objects:

- **Create a new user in the current container**
- **Create a new group in the current container**
- **Create a new organizational unit in the current container**

You can select one, several, or all created objects and move them into any container or OU in the current domain. As usual, use the <Shift> or <Ctrl> keys for selecting multiple objects.

It is possible to use a user account as a template, and create users with the same properties (group memberships, profile settings, etc.) To start this process, select a template user and click **Copy** in its context menu.

> **NOTES**
>
> Organizational units can only be created in the OU or domain containers.
>
> If you want to move objects between *different* domains in the same tree or non-adjacent trees, you need to use the MoveTree utility from the *Support Tools* (see *Chapter 10, "Migration tools"*).

> **CAUTION!**
>
> Built-in domain local groups cannot be deleted.

Adding Members to a Group

The **Active Directory Users and Computers** snap-in has a feature for "bulk" operations that permits you to add a number of selected users and contacts to a group. Point to an account and select the **Add members to a group** command in the context menu or the **Action** menu, or click the **Add the selected objects to a group you specify** button on the toolbar. Then specify a group in the **Select Group** window.

If you initially select an OU, the system asks whether you want to add all users and contacts contained in this container to the specified group. This feature is very helpful for administering OUs.

Don't forget that to populate groups, you can also use the LDIFDE and CSVDE tools, as well as the AddUsers.exe utility. LDIFDE is also able to delete members from groups.

Adding Users and Groups to Domain

There are a few utilities (besides the batch import tools LDIFDE and CSVDE and custom scripts) that simplify the creation of a number of user accounts in the field or in test environments.

CreateUsers.vbs Script (RK)

This script can only create users. It operates with both the WinNT and LDAP provider. The following attributes are required (the minimal set of attributes):

- WinNT — *name*, and *password*
- LDAP — *cn*, *samAccountName*, and *password*

> **NOTE**
>
> You may use other attributes, too, but not *all*. Carefully test your command (and the input file, if present). Be sure that all specified attributes are consistent; otherwise, you could easily get an error message similar to:
>
> ```
> Error 0X80072035 occurred in settings properties for user cn=...
> ```
>
> This error (8245) means that "The server is unwilling to process the request." One of the possible sources of this error is the incorrect "naming" attributes: *cn*, *name*, *sn*, *distinguishedName*, etc. Don't forget to enclose any attributes' values containing spaces in double quotes.

Here is the simplest example of creating a user with CreateUsers.vbs:

createusers WinNT://W2KDOM **name:**user01 **password:**psw1

The script must output the following:

```
Working ...
Getting domain WinNT://W2KDOM...
Creating user user01
Succeeded in creating user user01 in W2KDOM.
```

To disable informative messages from the script, use the **/q** parameter.

New users will always be created in the *Users* container. You may want to move them to other containers (most probably, organizational units), but a better way is to use the "LDAP-version" of the CreateUsers.vbs, which "understands" the Active Directory structure:

createusers LDAP://OU=Staff,DC=w2k,DC=dom **cn:**"User User01"
↳ **samAccountName:**user-ldap01 **password:**psw1

Maybe the most intriguing issue is how to create a number of users *at once*. It's very easy. Create a file with the desired user properties and use the appropriate version of CreateUsers.vbs (WinNT or LDAP). For example, the following command will create users specified in a file in the Staff OU:

```
createusers LDAP://OU=Staff,DC=w2k,DC=dom /i:newUsers.txt
```

The file of descriptions may be similar to the following:

```
cn:"User01" samAccountName:user01 password:psw1
cn:"User02" samAccountName:user02 password:psw2
...
```

AddUsers.exe (RK)

AddUsers.exe has a few additional features in comparison to CreateUsers.vbs and CreateGroups.vbs. Besides adding users and groups to a domain, it allows you to:

- Dump account information (users and groups) to a file.
- Specify the control account-creation options. By default, a new user must change his or her password at logon.
- Delete users or groups. Account names can only be specified in the input file.
- Create an input file in a spreadsheet program, such as Microsoft Excel, and save it in comma-delimited format, which the tool can use. A separator character other than a comma can be specified.

One negative aspect of AddUsers.exe is that the tool doesn't "see" the Active Directory structure.

NOTE

Using AddUsers.exe, you can successfully *add* users to existing groups, despite the "Group already exists" error message. The groups may exist in any place in Active Directory, not only in the "default" *Users* container.

A sample dump file produced by AddUsers.exe is placed below (the attributes' names are in bold braces and are not really included in the file). Such a file can easily be imported to a spreadsheet.

```
[User]
{samAccountName, name, password, description, homeDrive,
homeDirectory, profilePath, scriptPath}
Administrator,,,Built-in account for administering the
↳ computer/domain,,,,
Guest,,,Built-in account for guest access to the computer/domain,,,,
jsmith,John Smith,,,W:,\\w2kdc4\UsersData\jsmith,
↳ \\w2kdc4\Profiles\jsmith,Users\Logons.vbs
...
[Global]
{samAccountName, description, member's account names...}
Domain Admins,Designated administrators of the domain,Administrator,
Domain Controllers,All domain controllers in the
↳ domain,W2KDC4$,W2KDC3$,
Domain Users,All domain users,Administrator,Guest,krbtgt,EAdm,
↳ w2kuser008,w2kuser009,w2kuser010,w2kuser011,w2kuser012,NT4DOM$,
↳ user025, user044,Staff-Adm,
...
[Local]
{samAccountName, description, member's account names...}
Administrators,Administrators have complete and unrestricted access to
↳ the computer/domain,W2KDOM\Administrator,W2KDOM\Enterprise
↳ Admins,W2KDOM\Domain Admins,NT4DOM\,
w2kLocalGroup,,**W2KDOM\w2kLocGrp**,W2KDOM\w2kuser009,W2KDOM\w2kuser010,W2
↳ KDOM\w2kuser011,W2KDOM\w2kuser012,
...
```

Notice in the last line that groups may contain other groups (a group name is shown in bold) including local groups (in native mode of a domain).

CAUTION!

It seems that this tool has problems with displaying membership in global and universal (placed in the [Global] section) groups. Test this in your environment before any real work!

As you can see, the dump file contains three sections: *User*, *Global*, and *Local*. The same format can be used for creating new users and groups. The irrelevant trailing commas, as well as unused sections, can be omitted in the input file. New groups may either be empty or contain the names of their members.

Publishing Folders and Printers

Active Directory considerably simplifies work with shared network resources in comparison to the traditional method of browsing domains. If a resource has been *published* in Active Directory, users can easily locate it (**Search | For Printers** command in the **Start** menu) and connect to it. Besides that, to simplify locating resources you may want to publish them all in one OU.

Publishing a folder or a printer in Active Directory is, in other words, creating a new directory object — *Shared Folder* or *Printer*, respectively.

Shared folders in Active Directory have a feature that helps users to search for information by its characteristics. Select a published folder from the **Active Directory Users and Computers** snap-in's tree pane, open its **Properties** window, and click **Keywords**. You can add words that are logically related to the folder's contents to the list. Then, if a user begins a search for shared folders in the **Find** window, he or she can specify keywords and find resources based on their contents rather than their names.

Printers on the Windows 2000 computers can be published only from a printer's **Properties** window (the **List in the Directory** flag on the **Sharing** tab).

By default, the local printer on a domain computer is not published during its installation if you don't share it. If a printer is installed as shared, it is immediately published in Active Directory in the computer's container (see *"Users, Groups, and Computers as Containers"* in *Chapter 4*). You can at any moment clear the **List in the Directory** flag, and the printer object will be deleted from Active Directory.

> **CAUTION!**
>
> When publishing a folder, you must be cautious, because the system won't verify the entered folder name, and you may run into an error, but only when opening the folder or mapping to it.
>
> If the RDN and NetBIOS names of a domain are different, you'll get this error — "The system cannot find the file specified" — when publishing a printer (see the *Microsoft Knowledge Base article Q255496*). To resolve the problem, you must install *Windows 2000 Service Pack 1*.

You can tune the process of publishing and pruning printers in the domain by using group policies (see the **Computer Configuration | Administrative Templates | Printers** node in the **Group Policy** snap-in).

Pubprn.vbs Script

You can execute the Pubprn.vbs script without parameters and get the help information. For example, the following command publishes the *HP6MP* printer connected to the *WKS10* computer in the *Office* OU of the *w2k.dom* domain:

```
pubprn \\wks10\hp6mp "LDAP://OU=office,DC=w2k,DC=dom"
```

The system verifies the printer name and the existence of the object that is specified by the LDAP name. If the printer has been published successfully, you'll get a message displaying the LDAP name of the printer in Active Directory.

Connecting to Shared Resources

Search operations are the preferred way for locating shared network resources in Windows 2000 domains. A user can easily and quickly find the necessary printer or shared folder and perform any operation available while browsing the domain tree.

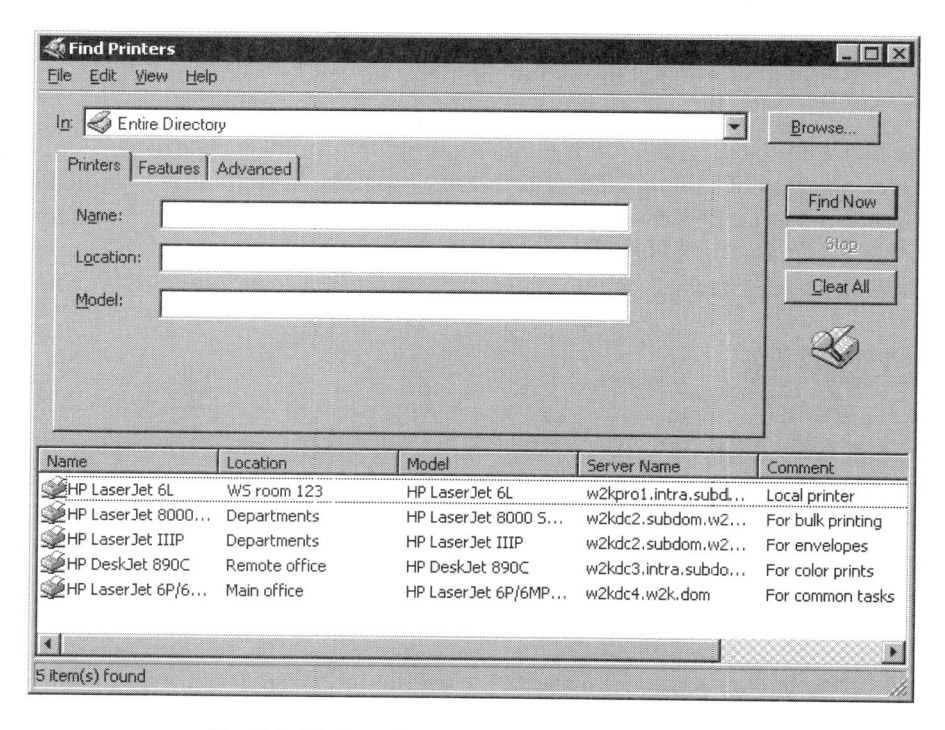

Fig. 5.2. Finding all printers in the enterprise (forest)

The scope of the search can vary from a specific container (OU) to a specific domain to the entire forest. (The **Entire Directory** option is equivalent to searching Global Catalog.) Fig. 5.2 contains an example of finding all printers in the forest. As you will notice from the **Server Name** column, the printers come from various domains. A user can point to an applicable printer and select the necessary operation from the context menu.

Users can carry out the following actions on the found shared folder: open, search the folder, map a network drive, and others.

Managing FSMO Roles in the Forest

Because the location of the Flexible Single Master Operation (FSMO) roles' masters is very important for proper functioning of a multi-domain forest, an administrator must know which domain controllers own the specific role(s) at any moment of the entire network's lifetime. Therefore, he or she must have facilities to easily find the role masters and to transfer a role from one DC to another. Moreover, it's necessary to have a way to *forcibly* transfer a role from a defunct DC. This process is called *"seizing of role"*.

Finding FSMO Role Owners

To find the owners of FSMO roles (operation masters), an administrator can use the "standard" administrative tools (see the previous chapter):

- The **Active Directory Users and Computers** snap-in displays the RID, PDC, and Infrastructure masters

- The **Active Directory Domains and Trusts** snap-in displays the Domain Naming master

- The **Active Directory Schema** snap-in displays the Schema master

This approach is, however, time-consuming, and it makes sense to use some "batch" tools or scripting. Some such tools are described below, and *Chapter 14, "Using ADSI for Administrative Tasks"*, contains additional information (see the "*How to Fink an FSMO Master?*" section and *Listing 14.18*).

Windows 2000 Domain Manager (NetDom.exe) (ST)

NetDom.exe (see *Chapter 9, "Manipulating Active Directory Objects"*) can display all operation masters in a specified domain. Use the following command syntax:

```
C:\>netdom QUERY /Domain:w2k.dom FSMO
```

DumpFSMOs.cmd (RK)

This command file is, in fact, a chain of instructions to the NTDSutil tool. (These instructions could also be entered manually.) The only mandatory parameter is the name of the DC from which the information is retrieved. A sample screen output is shown below (the utility's prompt is in bold):

```
C:\>dumpFSMOs w2kdc4.w2k.dom
ntdsutil: roles
fsmo maintenance: Connections
server connections: Connect to server w2kdc4.w2k.dom
Binding to w2kdc4.w2k.dom ...
Connected to w2kdc4.w2k.dom using credentials of locally logged on user
server connections: Quit
fsmo maintenance: select Operation Target
select operation target: List roles for connected server
Server "w2kdc4.w2k.dom" knows about 5 roles
Schema - CN=NTDS Settings,CN=W2KDC4,
    ↳ CN=Servers,CN=W2K-site,CN=Sites,CN=Configuration,DC=w2k,DC=dom
Domain - CN=NTDS Settings,CN=W2KDC4,
    ↳ CN=Servers,CN=W2K-site,CN=Sites,CN=Configuration,DC=w2k,DC=dom
PDC - CN=NTDS Settings,CN=W2KDC4,
    ↳ CN=Servers,CN=W2K-site,CN=Sites,CN=Configuration,DC=w2k,DC=dom
RID - CN=NTDS Settings,CN=W2KDC4,
    ↳ CN=Servers,CN=W2K-site,CN=Sites,CN=Configuration,DC=w2k,DC=dom
Infrastructure - CN=NTDS Settings,CN=W2KDC3,
    ↳ CN=Servers,CN=W2K-site,CN=Sites,CN=Configuration,DC=w2k,DC=dom
select operation target: Quit
fsmo maintenance: Quit
ntdsutil: Quit
Disconnecting from w2kdc4.w2k.dom ...
```

Active Directory Replication Monitor (ReplMon.exe) (ST)

All operation masters can be displayed with ReplMon.exe. Start the tool and add servers to the **Monitored Servers** list (tree). Select a DC from the tree pane, open the **Properties** window, and click the **FSMO Roles** tab. Fig. 5.3 shows a sample view of this tab.

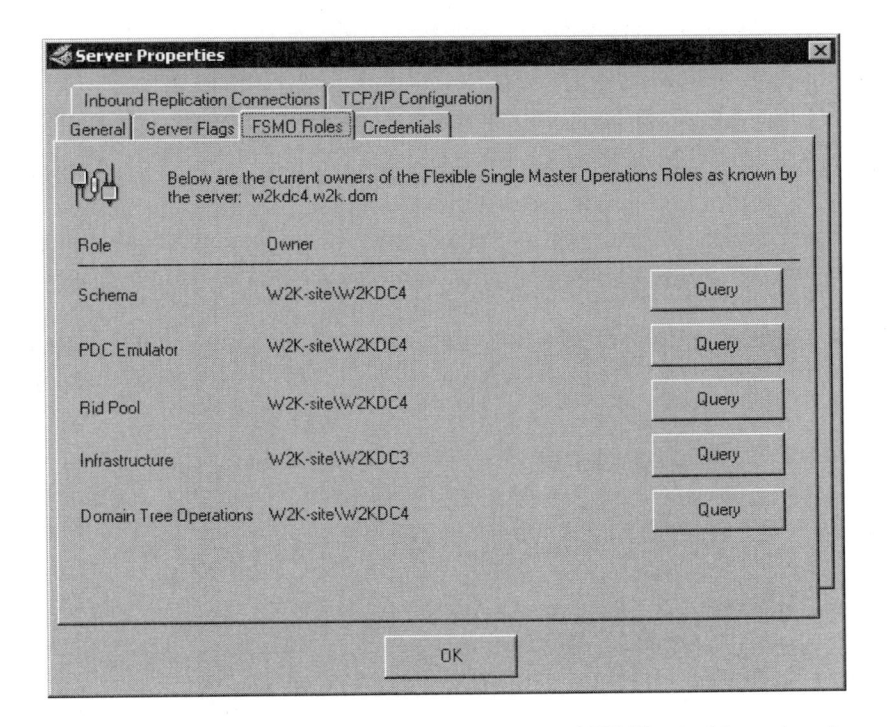

Fig. 5.3. Viewing all operation masters (the owners of FSMO roles) for a domain

From this window you can test any operation master by clicking **Query**. ReplMon answers with the following message: "Active Directory Replication Monitor was able/unable to resolve, connect, and bind to the server hosting this FSMO role."

> **NOTE**
> ReplMon is also able to display all Global Catalog servers in the enterprise.

Transferring and Seizing FSMO Roles

Usually, to transfer a FSMO role from one DC to another, the administrative snap-ins should be used. To seize a role, you must use the NTDSutil.exe.

> **NOTE**
>
> For additional information on the FSMO transfer and seizure process, you might be interested in *Microsoft Knowledge Base article Q223787*.

RID, PDC, and Infrastructure Operation Masters

You may for some reason (e. g. to maintain a DC want to transfer a FSMO role to another DC in the domain. In the **Active Directory Users and Computers** snap-in window you must first connect to the DC that is the potential operation master, point to the root node in the tree pane, and select the **Operation Masters** command in the context menu or in the **Action** menu. Click the appropriate tab: **RID**, **PDC**, or **Infrastructure**. You will see the current owner of the FSMO role and the potential master name. Click the **Change** button, and you'll get a new operation master.

Be careful when transferring the Infrastructure role. If there is more than one DC in the domain, make sure that a message similar to the following has not appeared in the Directory Service log on the new operation master:

```
Event Type: Error
Event Source:         NTDS General
Event Category:       Directory Access
Event ID:   1419
...
User:                 Everyone
Computer:   W2KDC4
Description:
This DC is both a Global Catalog and the Infrastructure Update master.
These two roles are incompatible.  If another machine exists in the
domain, it should be made the Infrastructure Update master.
The machine CN=NTDS Settings,CN=W2KDC2,CN=Servers,CN=W2K-
site,CN=Sites, CN=Configuration,DC=w2k,DC=dom is a good candidate
for this role. If all domain controllers in this domain are Global
Catalogs, then there are no Infrastructure Update tasks to complete,
and this message may be ignored.
```

Domain Naming Operation Master

The **Active Directory Domains and Trusts** snap-in allows you to transfer the *Naming master* FSMO role to any DC in the domain tree. This procedure is simple: connect to the DC that will be the role owner, point to the root node in the tree pane, and select the **Operations Master** command from the context menu. In the opened window, make sure that the names of the current master and future master are correct, click **Change**, and confirm the operation. Remember that only one server in the forest (enterprise) can perform the Naming master role, and this server must also be the Global Catalog server.

Schema Operation Master

The **Active Directory Schema** snap-in allows transfer of the *Schema Master* FSMO role to any DC in the forest. You should first connect to the potential master of the role, point to the root node in the tree pane, and select the **Operations Master** command from the context menu. After checking the DC name, click **Change**. Remember that only one server in the forest can perform the Schema Master role.

> **ATTENTION!**
>
> To modify the schema, you must first enable this operation (see *Chapter 4, "Domain Manipulation Tools"*). When you have transferred the Schema Master role to a DC, the flag **The Schema may be modified on this Domain Controller** remains set on the old schema master. This might not be in accordance with your desires, however.

NTDSutil

The NTDSutil can be used for transferring any FSMO role. This is the only tool that allows an administrator to forcibly assign a role to a DC. (It is assumed that the old owner of this role has been destroyed and cannot be repaired.). Using NTDSutil is discussed in detail in *Chapter 7, "Active Directory Diagnostics and Maintenance"*.

Refreshing Group Policy

When an administrator has changed a GPO, he or she may want to refresh group policy application to verify the effect of the new settings. (Certainly, it is possible to reboot the computer or make the user re-register to the domain. However, this is not always convenient.) To perform this task, it is possible to use the SecEdit.exe command-line utility.

The command syntax is very simple. To refresh the user policies, enter the following command:

`secedit /refreshPolicy user_policy`

The following command refreshes the computer policies:

`secedit /refreshPolicy machine_policy`

If you want to re-apply policies (GPOs), even if they haven't changed from the last time they were applied, add the `/enforce` parameter to the command. (Normally, GPOs are applied only once; unchanged GPOs are skipped.)

> **NOTE**
>
> You may want to change the default GPO refresh interval (90 minutes for normal computers, and 5 minutes for domain controllers), as well as the offset (30 minutes for normal computers, and 0 minutes for domain controllers). For that purpose, use group policies or modify the system registry. For additional information, see *Microsoft Knowledge Base article Q203607*.

Triggering Replication

An administrator has three tools that can be used to trigger Active Directory replication of either all directory partitions (contexts) or just a specified partition between a domain controller and one or all of its direct replication partners:

- The **Active Directory Sites and Services** snap-in
- RepAdmin
- ReplMon

As is usual for practically any administrative task, you can also use scripting (see example *in Chapter 14, "Using ADSI for Administrative Tasks"*).

> **NOTE**
>
> Remember that the "source" server (DC) always replicates its changes to the "target" server (DC). Usually, you first select the target, then the source.

The *Active Directory Sites and Services* snap-in

This snap-in allows an administrator to initiate replication of *all configured* directory partitions from each replication partner *separately*. Select a target DC from the **Servers** container of the applicable site and point to its **NTDS Settings** object. You can trigger replication *from* any server represented by a *Connection* object in the right pane (see example in Fig. 5.4). Select a connection and click **Replicate Now** in the context menu. You must wait until replication completes (with the "Active Directory has replicated the connections" message if successful).

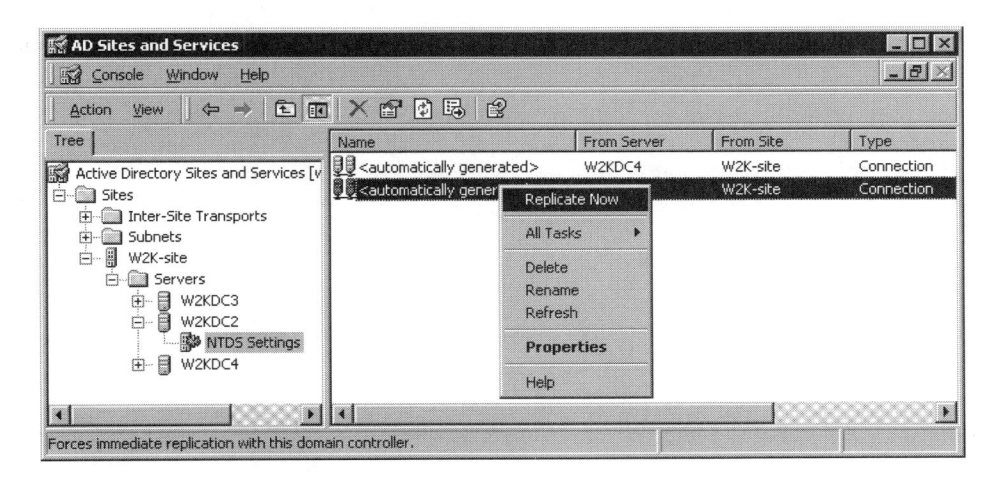

Fig. 5.4. Triggering replication from a direct partner

All directory partitions configured for that partner are replicated. You have no options to replicate only one partition.

Replication Diagnostics Tool (RepAdmin.exe) (ST)

With RepAdmin.exe, you replicate each directory partition separately, and from one or all sources. To trigger replication between the servers shown in Fig. 5.4, you can use the following command:

```
repadmin /syncall w2kdc4.w2k.dom DC=w2k,DC=dom,
```

where `w2kdc4.w2k.dom` is the server DNS name, and `DC=w2k,DC=dom` is the partition name (the domain naming partition in this case).

The difference between this command and the operation shown in Fig. 5.4 is the following:

- The command replicates only *one partition*, but from *all partners*
- In the snap-in window you replicate *all partitions*, but from *one partner* only

To force replication in the entire domain (forest), you might write similar commands for each DC and all directory partitions to a command file, which will serve to fulfill total replication in the domain.

> **CAUTION!**
>
> The `repadmin /syncall` *serverName* command replicates only one directory partition, and performing such a command is not enough to *fully* replicate the server specified.

The following command replicates *one partition* from *one partner* (specified by its GUID):

```
repadmin /sync DC=w2k,DC=dom
    w2kdc4.w2k.dom 0e5b9b82-4818-44a6-a8b9-0e51d2f6d97e
```

Normally, RepAdmin waits for replication to be completed. You can add the `/async` parameters to the command to start an operation and not wait for its finish.

RepAdmin is described in detail in *Chapter 8, "Network and Distributed Service"*.

Active Directory Replication Monitor (ReplMon.exe) (ST)

ReplMon.exe provides an administrator with the following replication modes (from the most "global" to more granular ones) for a server specified:

- Synchronize *each* directory partition with *all* servers (there are three additional options available with this mode)
- Synchronize *this* directory partition with *all* servers
- Synchronize *this* directory partition with *this* replication partner

You never need wait for a replication operation to complete, since all results of operations are written to the log files.

RepAdmin is described in detail in *Chapter 8, "Network and Distributed Service"*.

> **Additional Replication Tools**
>
> To force synchronization of replica sets managed by the **File Replication Service** (FRS), the contents of the SYSVOL volume for example, use the `ntfrsutl poll` command. See details in *Chapter 8, "Network and Distributed Services"*.
>
> To synchronize a Windows 2000-based server that owns the PDC Emulator FSMO role with **Backup Domain Controllers** (BDCs) in a mixed-mode domain, use the NLtest.exe tool. See the `/REPL`, `/SYNC`, `/PDC_QUERY`, and other parameters of this tool. The *LBridge.cmd* command file from the *Windows 2000 Server Resource Kit* should be used for copying files from the Windows 2000 System volume (SYSVOL) to the export directory on a Windows 4.0-based BDC.
>
> You can write custom **scripts** that will initiate replication events in accordance with your own strategy. See, for example, *Listing 14.15* in *Chapter 14, "Using ADSI for Administrative Tasks"*.

Delegating Administrative Control

The possibility of delegating all or a part of the administrative rights over an OU or a directory container to a group or a user is one of the most remarkable features of Windows 2000 domains that Active Directory realizes. Delegation of control is essentially the same thing as "wizard-aided" granting of permissions on Active Directory objects to a user or group. You can *manually* assign the permissions necessary for performing this administrative task to a user or group, but this process is considerably simplified thanks to the *Delegation of Control Wizard*. Delegating control is quite a simple operation, and problems are only possible when delegated tasks are being revoked from the user or group.

An administrator can delegate control (i. e. use the Delegation of Control Wizard rather than manually assigning permissions) for the following Active Directory objects (common administrative tasks are cited in parenthesis):

❑ In the **Active Directory Sites and Services** snap-in (Typical permissions are Full Control, Read/Write, Create/Delete All Child Objects, Read/Write All Properties.)

- *Sites* container
- *Inter-Site Transport* container

- *Subnets* container
- Site(s) (Manage Group Policy Links)
- *Server* container in site(s)

❑ In the **Active Directory Users and Computers** snap-in (The list of available permissions depends on the type of Active Directory container.)

- Entire domain (Join a computer to the domain; Manage Group Policy links)
- Organizational unit (Create, delete, and manage user account; Reset passwords on user accounts; Read all user information; Create, delete, and manage groups; Modify the membership of a group; and Manage Group Policy links)
- *Computers* container
- *ForeignSecurityPrincipals* container
- *System* container
- *Users* container

ATTENTION!

Remember that the *Authenticated Users* group (i. e. *any* logged on user) by default has the permission to add 10 users to a domain. This group has the permission to *Read All Properties* of a domain object; consequently, the group can read the value of the *ms-DS-MachineAccountQuota* attribute, which by default is equal to 10. (This value can be viewed or modified by using the **ADSI Edit** snap-in.) Draw your own conclusions. (You might wish to change this situation.)

To start the process of delegating control, run the appropriate snap-in, point to a Active Directory container, OU, or the domain itself in the tree pane, and select the **Delegate control** command in the context menu or **Action** menu. Depending on the container type, you can select a *common* task(s) or create a *custom* task. In the first case, you use a pre-defined set of permissions, while in the second case you select objects and permissions yourself, which allows you to be more specific in delegating the administrative rights.

Although it is very simple to *delegate* control, *revoking* administrative rights from a user or a group requires a bit more effort and clearer understanding of the process. You must turn on the *Advanced Features* mode (see the previous chapter), select the container over which control has been delegated, and open the **Security** tab in the container's **Properties** window. Then, find the permissions and access control settings for the user or the group, and delete them. By doing so, you are editing the ACL entries for a directory object. Delegation of control is done using the same process, but is simplified thanks to the wizard. Understanding this aspect will help you to easily and flexibly manipulate the directory objects and, as a result, to tune Active Directory accordingly to fit your tasks.

Look at Fig. 5.5. The Delegation of Control Wizard was executed, and the right of joining a computer to the domain was delegated to the *Admins* group. As a result, the *Create Computer Objects* permission was added to the access control list (ACL) of the domain container. You could manually perform the same operation, but the wizard helps to do this without error and frees you from knowing all the details of Active Directory object inheritance and permissions.

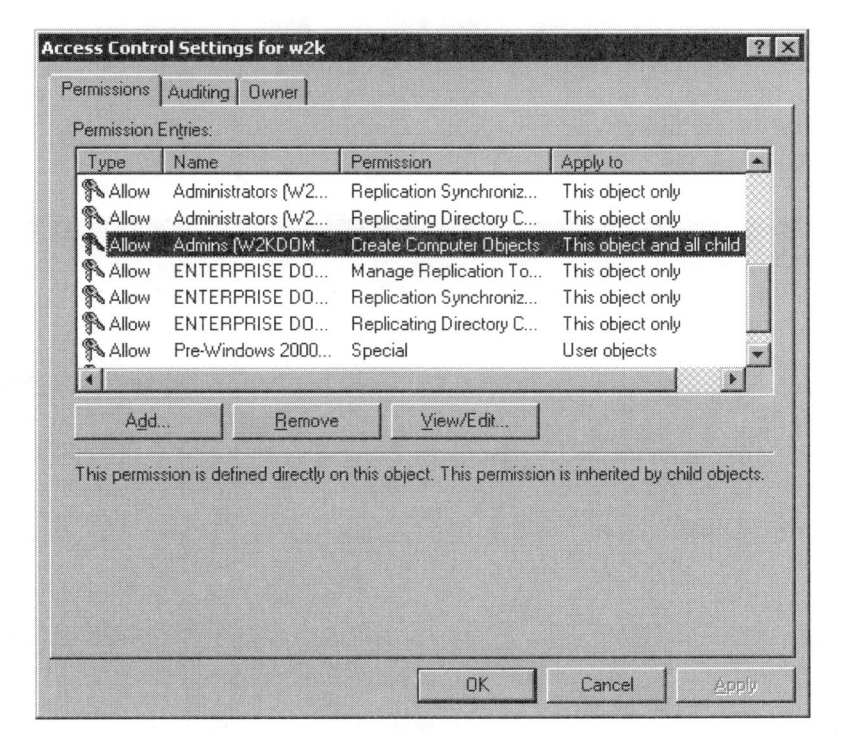

Fig. 5.5. The result of using the Delegation of Control Wizard: the highlighted permission allows the Admins group to join computers to the domain

Auditing Access to Active Directory Objects

In general, the procedure of enabling auditing consists of two steps. To audit access to Active Directory, you must:

1. Enable an appropriate auditing policy.
2. Define events to audit.

Auditing access to Active Directory objects relates to operations performed on the domain controller. Therefore, the most appropriate place to enable auditing is the *Default Domain Controllers Policy* (or another GPO linked to the *Domain Controller* OU). You may use the **Group Policy** snap-in linked to that GPO or the **Domain Controller Security Policy** snap-in. Select the node **Computer Configuration | Windows Settings | Security Setting | Local Policies | Audit Policy** and click twice on the *Audit directory service access* policy (Fig. 5.6). (Default setting for all audit policies — **No auditing**.) Then set the **Define these policy settings** flag and check the **Success** and/or **Failure** box.

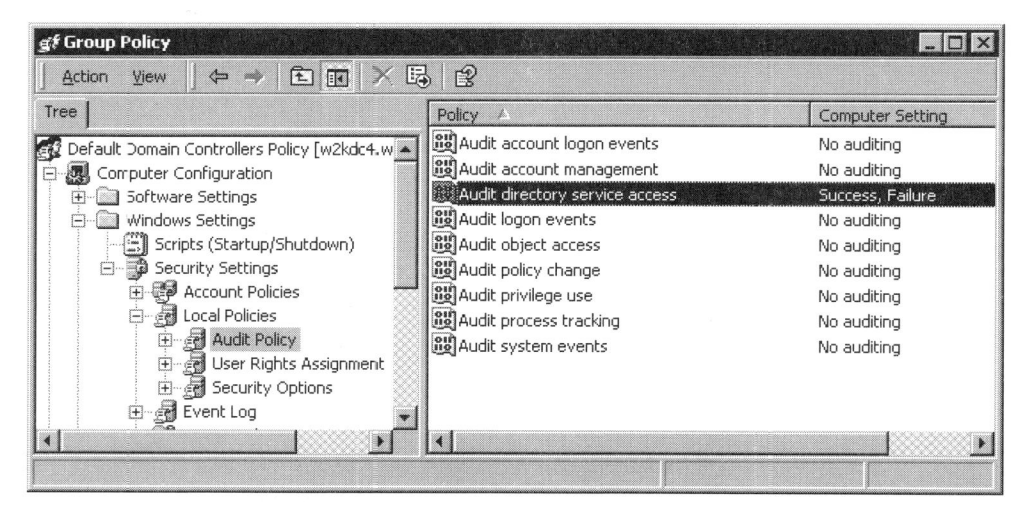

Fig. 5.6. Enabling auditing events related to access to Active Directory objects

Chapter 5: Common Administrative Tasks 149

ATTENTION!

No auditing and *Not defined* are not the same thing. When a policy is *Not defined*, you can define it on a lower level. If a policy is *No auditing*, it overwrites all possible down-level settings. The group policies for the Domain Controllers OU are applied last and have the highest priority. Therefore, the default audit parameters defined by these policies override any parameters assigned at other (higher) levels.

After the policy has been set, you can immediately apply it with the `secedit /refreshpolicy machine_policy` command.

For read operations, it is recommended to audit *failure* events, because a large number of *successful* event entries can quickly overflow the Security Log. The performance of domain controllers can also suffer. For write, create/delete, and other similar operations (that are much less frequent than read operations), it is possible to audit both *success* and *failure* events.

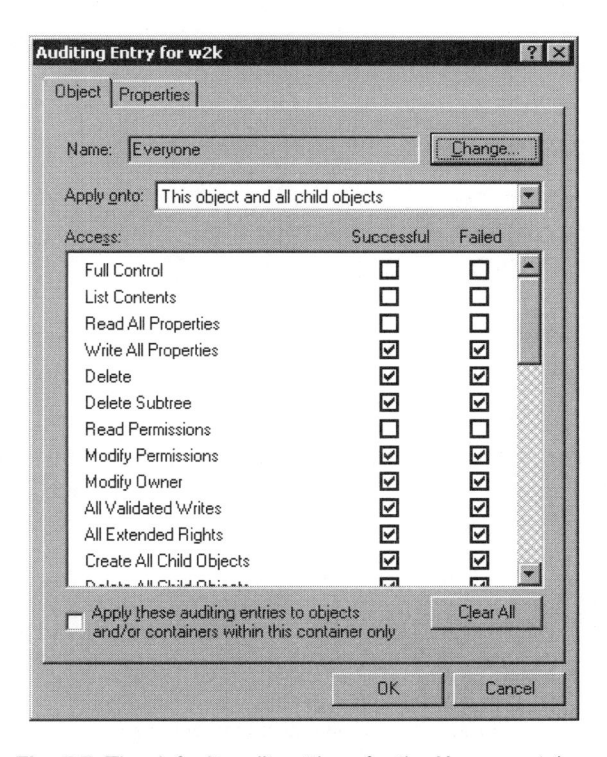

Fig. 5.7. The default audit settings for the Users container

By default, special access (successful and failed) to all objects in a domain is audited for the *Everyone* group (Fig. 5.7). All domain objects inherit this setting from the root domain container. Some containers have additional audit settings. All settings include auditing for "critical" operations, such as Write, Delete, Modify, and others. (Look up the entire list.) You can see all audit entries in an object's **Properties** window: open the **Security** tab, click **Advanced,** and open the **Auditing** tab. Then click **View/Edit** to view or change audit parameters. If you open the **Auditing** tab for a non-root directory object, you will notice that all checked boxes are grayed. This means that all parameters are inherited from the parent object. They cannot be directly modified, so you may need to address the parent or root object. If you check a free box, the system will create a new auditing entry and *add* it to the list.

> **CAUTION!**
>
> Because successful events are registered by default, you might get a huge number of entries in Event Viewer when working with auditing turned on. You therefore may wish to change the default settings when performing audit for a long time.

You can view all information on audit events in the Security Log of the Event Viewer. The source for these events is "Security", and the category is "Directory Service Access".

Recovering Active Directory

General Considerations

The standard Windows 2000 Backup program allows you to back up and restore both critical data and Active Directory. Operations with Active Directory can only be done *locally* for each domain controller. A backup operation is performed while a DC is online. To restore Active Directory on a DC, you must boot this DC into *Directory Service Restore Mode* (press <F8> at the computer startup).

System state

Backing up Active Directory is a part of the process of saving the *system state* of a DC. You cannot back up (or restore) individual items of the system state. On a member server or a workstation, the system state includes the following (Fig. 5.8):

❑ Boot Files

- COM+ Class Registration Database
- Registry

On a domain controller, two other items are added:

- Active Directory (the ntds.dit, edb.chk, edb*.log, and res1.log and res2.log files)
- Sys Vol (System Volume) (by default, the *%SystemRoot%*\SYSVOL\sysvol folder)

If the Certificate Services are installed on a server or DC, there is one more item:

- Certificate Server

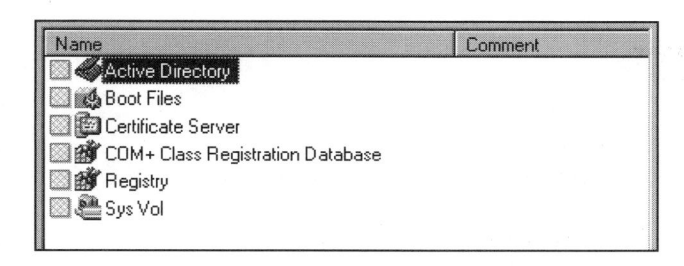

Fig. 5.8. System state of a domain controller

Schema

Modifications of the schema are irreversible, so you cannot restore an older version of the schema. Created attributes and classes cannot be deleted, and it is only possible to *deactivate* them.

Tombstones

A recovery plan should take into account the lifetime of the Active Directory *tombstones* (60 days, by default; minimal value is 2 days). This parameter is stored in the *tombstoneLifetime* attribute of a directory object named *CN=Directory Service,CN=Windows NT,CN=Service,CN=Configuration,DC=<ForestRootDomain>*. Tombstone is a deleted object that is maintained in Active Directory during its lifetime, before the system eventually destroys it. The age of the backup tape shouldn't exceed this time, otherwise the outdated data will be rejected.

Backing up Active Directory

To back up the system state, run the Backup utility by clicking **Start | Programs | Accessories | System Tools | Backup**. Click the **Backup** tab and check the **System State** box in the tree pane. (You can include some files in the backup as well.) Select backup media or file and click **Start Backup**. In the next window, click **Advanced**. The system state should always be saved as a *normal backup*. You may wish to clear the **Automatically backup System Protected Files with the System State** box set by default if you need a compact backup file without system files. Close the window and click **Start Backup** — the backup process will begin.

> **NOTE**
>
> Only the *full* backup will allow you to safely restore a crashed DC. It is possible to repair the system from the scratch in about 30-40 minutes. Restore the Windows 2000 Server image from a CD or network drive by using an image-duplicating tool like *Norton Ghost*. Boot the server, and restore the full backup file. You'll get a fully operational DC retaining its SID, GUID, and other necessary Active Directory parameters.

Restoring Active Directory

Restore is a more complicated process than back up. Primarily, you have two options:

- Reinstall the system on the damaged computer, promote it to a domain controller, and copy Active Directory information from other DCs through replication. You'll get an entirely new DC, and then will need to delete any references to the old DC from Active Directory.
- Restore Active Directory from backup media, retaining the DC identity.

There are three different methods of restoring the system state from backup media:

- Perform a **primary restore** when you have the only DC in the domain and want to rebuild this domain. A primary restore builds a new FRS database; therefore, the restored data will be replicated to other controllers in the domain.
- If there is at least one operational DC in the domain, perform a **non-authoritative restore**. The repaired DC will receive current data from other DCs through normal replication. This is the most used type of restore.
- If you want to restore inadvertently deleted Active Directory data, perform an **authoritative restore**. You cannot perform a true rollback, since authoritative

restore doesn't affect new changes made in the directory after the backup was created.

Remember that, in any case, Active Directory can be restored only when the server has been booted into the Directory Service Restore Mode.

Primary Restore

Run the Backup utility and open the **Restore** tab. Select the necessary media and check the **System State** box. Files should be restored to the **Original location**. Click **Start Restore** and select **Advanced** in the **Confirm Restore** window. Set the checkbox shown in Fig. 5.9, close the window, and begin restore.

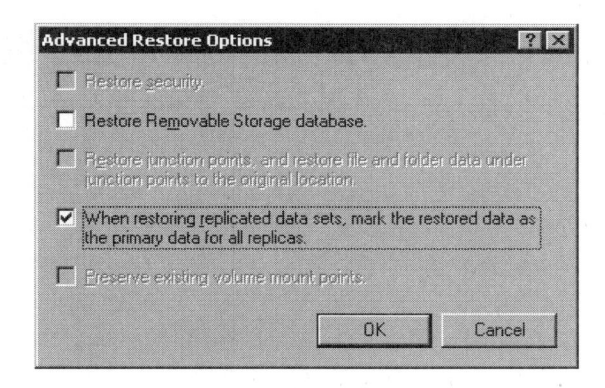

Fig. 5.9. This checkbox is only used for a primary restore

Non-authoritative Restore

A non-authoritative restore is performed as primary restore (described above); the difference is that you needn't select any non-default options. The restored DC will receive all changes from its replication partners.

Authoritative Restore

To perform authoritative restore, use the following steps:

❑ Run the Backup utility and restore the system state to an *alternative location*. The following folders appear in the specified folder or on the disk:

- Boot Files (ntdetect.com, ntldr)

- Registry (default, SAM, SECURITY, software, system, userdiff)
- Sys Vol (this folder reflects the structure of the SYSVOL volume)

❑ When the Backup utility completes its work (non-authoritative restore has been performed), it proposes that you restart the computer (Fig. 5.10). You must answer NO and close the program.

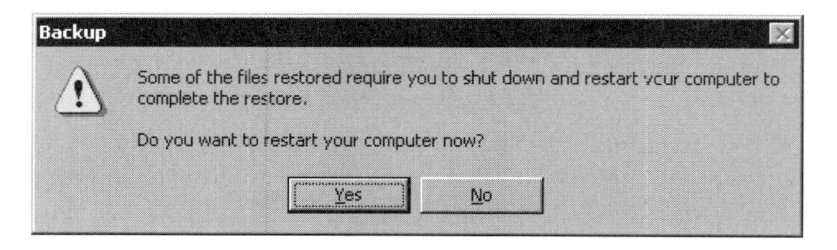

Fig. 5.10. Click **No** if you are performing an authoritative restore

❑ Run *NTDSutil.exe* from the command prompt. A sample dialog for the *authoritative restore* command is placed below:

```
C:\>ntdsutil
ntdsutil: authoritative restore
authoritative restore: restore subtree OU=Staff,DC=w2k,DC=dom

Opening DIT database... Done.

The current time is 09-21-00 17:35.49.
Most recent database update occured at 09-18-00 22:30.43.
Increasing attribute version numbers by 300000.

Counting records that need updating...
Records found: 0000000025
Done.

Found 25 records to update.
Updating records...
Records remaining: 0000000000
Done.
```

```
Successfully updated 25 records.
Authoritative Restore completed successfully.
authoritative restore: quit
ntdsutil: quit
```

- Reboot the computer into normal mode and wait until the SYSVOL volume is published (use the `net share` command to monitor this process).

- Copy the SYSVOL volume from the alternative location to the existing one. These changes of the SYSVOL volume will be the most recent and, therefore, will be replicated to other DCs as the authoritative data.

In the example shown, an OU object has been restored. You can mark an individual object, subtree, or entire directory partition as authoritative. This, however, doesn't extend to the Schema partition.

Notice the line in bold that indicates increment of the attribute version numbers, and two previous lines. The version numbers increase by 100,000 for each day after the original backup update. You can view changes of metadata by using ReplMon.exe. In our case, for example, the following command will be used:

repadmin /showmeta OU=Staff,DC=w2k,DC=dom w2kdc4.w2k.dom

By using this command on different DCs, you can verify that the authoritative restore was successful, and trace the replication's propagation.

If objects in your Active Directory installation have very low volatility, you may wish to override the default value of version increment. Use a command similar to the following:

restore subtree OU=Staff,DC=w2k,DC=dom **verinc** 1000

PART III

USING TOOLS AND UTILITIES

Chapter 6. General Characteristics and Purpose of System Tools

Chapter 7. Active Directory Diagnostics and Maintenance

Chapter 8. Network and Distributed Services

Chapter 9. Manipulating Active Directory Objects

Chapter 10. Migration Tools

Chapter 11. Security Tools

Chapter 12. Group Policy Tools

Chapter 6
General Characteristics and Purpose of System Tools

Long, long ago, in the time of mainframes and mini-computers, every system programmer knew that if the system was in a faulty state, it was time to run a test. Now, in the epoch of the PC and various GUI tools, system administrators have somewhat forgotten that certain handy and powerful diagnostics tools still exist. Thanks to these tools, you needn't rack your brains over the sources of these problems (i. e. you don't have to try to find the error source logically). You can quickly and easily get useful and extensive information that can be used for further analysis, or often even get a ready answer — the reason for the error — right away.

In this chapter, I'll try to classify and characterize various system tools shipped by Microsoft that help administrators manage and troubleshoot Active Directory services. The chapter should help you quickly find an appropriate tool for a specific task. In the following chapters, most of these tools are described in more detail. I didn't aim to provide comprehensive information on each parameter or option. (You can easily use the built-in help messages or HTML Help files, and obtain the list of all available keys.) I'll focus on the most interesting, useful, or non-evident features as well as examples of using these tools in real life.

Where Can You Find All These Tools?

Windows 2000 Support Tools

Some administrators forget or simply don't know that each Windows 2000 installation CD contains a pack of powerful tools named *Windows 2000 Support Tools*. This pack must be installed separately from the operation system. Run the Setup.exe file from the \SUPPORT\TOOLS folder, and install the pack on the hard disk. (The Windows 2000 Support Tools require about 20 MB of the hard disk space.) Then you'll be able to start tools from the **Start** menu or a command prompt.

Windows 2000 Resource Kit

The Windows 2000 Support Tools can be regarded as a subset of the *Windows 2000 Resource Kit*, a separately purchased product that contains hundreds of various utilities as well as comprehensive printed documentation. (There are two versions of the Kit: Server and Professional. Many of the tools described below are present in both versions.)

Chapter 6: General Characteristics and Purpose of System Tools 161

The Windows 2000 Resource Kit requires about 60 MB of the hard disk. The good news is that some very useful tools from this kit (and even complete sample chapters!) can be downloaded for free from the Microsoft web site (see *Appendixes*).

The Windows 2000 Server Resource Kit contains a collection of Visual Basic (VB) scripts called *Remote Administration Scripts*. Several scripts from this collection are mentioned in the tables below. If you are going to write your own scripts or applications, pay close attention to these scripts, since they will help you speed up the process of studying scripting basics (including ADSI programming concepts).

Classification by Purpose

First of all, you should become generally acquainted with the existing tools and the administrative tasks for which they are used. Look at Table 6.1. The tools from the *Windows 2000 Resource Kit* and *Windows 2000 Support Tools* packs listed in this table are divided into categories depending on the basic purpose of a tool. In some cases, the grouping of tools is rather voluntary, as some utilities can be used for different purposes.

Active Directory Migration Tool (ADMT) and AdsVw.exe (from the *Active Directory SDK*) can be downloaded for free from the Microsoft website, and are also included in the table. Every tool mentioned is characterized in Table 6.2.

Table 6.1. Windows 2000 Tools Sorted by Their Purpose

Administrative task	Tools to be used
Browsing and editing Active Directory objects	ADSIEdit.msc, Ldp.exe, AdsVw.exe, ModifyUsers.vbs
Querying Active Directory	Ldp.exe, Search.vbs, UserAccount.vbs, EnumProp.exe
Migration and restructure. Manipulating Active Directory objects	ADMT, MoveTree.exe, NetDom.exe, ClonePrincipal, AddUsers.exe, GrpCpy.exe
Bulk import/export	CSVDE.exe, LDIFDE.exe, AddUsers.exe, CreateUsers.vbs
Active Directory database diagnostics and maintenance	NTDSutil.exe
Diagnosis	NetDiag.exe, NSlookup.exe, DCdiag.exe, NLtest.exe, DNSCmd.exe, RPCPing

continues

Table 6.1 Continued

Administrative task	Tools to be used
Replication	RepAdmin.exe, ReplMon.exe, DsaStat.exe, NTFRSutl.exe
Active Directory security	ACLDiag.exe, DsACLs.exe, SDCheck.exe, KerbTray.exe, KList.exe
System objects (files, shares, registry, etc.) security	SIDWalker, SubInACL.exe, ADMT
Group Policies	GPOTool.exe, GPResult.exe

> **NOTE**
> Remember that Windows 2000 Server provides a few "traditional" utilities for administering Windows NT 4.0 domains: *Server Manager* (srvmgr.exe), *User Manager* (usrmgr.exe), and *System Policy Editor* (poledit.exe). The Windows 2000 Server Resource Kit also contains the *Domain Monitor* (dommon.exe). These are the updated versions that differ from their Windows NT 4.0 counterparts. This may be important in some cases.

Description of Selected Tools

Table 6.2 lists the file names of tools as well as their "official" names; a short description of the characteristics of each tool is also given. The table is sorted by the names of the files. (This is because it is the *filename* of a tool that you'll use most often.) Also, the name of the pack that contains the tool is specified, along with the chapter of this book that contains the most complete information about using the tool. (ST stands for the *Windows 2000 Support Tools*, RK means the *Windows 2000 Resource Kit*, and RAS is the abbreviation for *Remote Administration Scripts*. These marks are also present in the subtitles of the following chapters.)

Table 6.2. Selected Windows 2000 Tools and Their Purpose

Tool name	Contained in	Purpose	See chapter
ACLDiag.exe (ACL Diagnostics)	ST	View permissions (ACLs) on a directory object. Verify delegation of administrative control, and whether the object security settings correspond to the schema defaults	11

continues

Chapter 6: General Characteristics and Purpose of System Tools

Table 6.2 Continued

Tool name	Contained in	Purpose	See chapter
AddUsers.exe (Add Users)	RK	Output, create, and delete multiple user accounts. Add users to groups	5
ADSIEdit.msc (**ADSI Edit** snap-in) (GUI tool)	ST	View and modify Active Directory objects (including schema and configuration partitions). Set objects' ACLs	4
AdsVw.exe (Active Directory Browser) (GUI tool)	Active Directory SDK	Same as above, for both Windows 2000 and Windows NT domains (SAM database)	9
ClonePrincipal	ST	Create a copy of a user or group account in a different forest and retain user or group access rights to directory objects or shared resources. (Includes Clonepr.dll, Clonepr.vbs, Clonelg.vbs, Clonegg.vbs, Cloneggu.vbs, SIDHist.vbs tools)	10
CreateUsers.vbs	RK (RAS)	Create multiple user accounts in default or specified containers	5
CSVDE.exe (CSV Directory Exchange)	Sys	Export and import multiple directory objects using CSV file format	9
DCdiag.exe (Domain Controller Diagnostic Tool)	ST	Diagnose domain controller issues: connectivity, availability of the directory and other services, replication, etc.	7
DNSCmd.exe (DNS Server Troubleshooting Tool)	ST	Check and/or modify zones and resource records on a Windows 2000 DNS server. Manage the server configuration	3
DsACLs.exe	ST	View and/or modify permissions (ACLs) on directory objects. Restore default permissions	11
DsaStat.exe (DSA Statistics)	ST	Compare directory partitions on two different domain controllers and display statistics or comparisons of attributes. Global Catalog servers can also be checked	8
DumpFSMOs.cmd	RK	Display the FSMO roles known to the specified domain controller	5

continues

Table 6.2 Continued

Tool name	Contained in	Purpose	See chapter
EnumProp.exe	RK	Display some or all attributes (including GUIDs, SIDs, and security descriptor) of an Active Directory object specified by its distinguished name. (The LDAP provider is used)	—
GPOTool.exe (Group Policy Verification Tool)	RK	Test consistency of GPOs and check their replication in a domain	12
GPResult.exe (Group Policy Results)	RK	View group policy settings applied to a user and/or computer	12
GrpCpy.exe (GUI Tool)	RK	Copy users from one group to another in the same or another domain	—
KerbTray.exe (Kerberos Tray) (GUI tool)	RK	Display and purge all cached Kerberos tickets for authenticated services	14
KList.exe (Kerberos List)	RK	Same as above. Can purge only specified tickets	14
Ksetup.exe (Kerberos Setup)	ST	Configure Windows 2000 clients to use an MIT Kerberos server instead of a Windows 2000 domain	—
KTPass.exe (Kerberos Keytab Setup)	ST	Configure a non-Windows 2000 (UNIX) Kerberos service as a security principal in the Windows 2000 Active Directory	—
LDIFDE.exe	Sys	Export and import multiple directory objects using LDIF format. Modify attributes of objects	9
Ldp.exe (Active Directory Administration Tool) (GUI tool)	ST	Perform LDAP operations against any LDAP-compliant directory such as Active Directory	9
ModifyUsers.vbs	RK (RAS)	Modify specified attributes of multiple domain users. An input text file with defined values can be used	—
MoveTree.exe (Active Directory Object Manager)	ST	Move directory objects, such as user accounts, OUs, and universal groups from one domain to another in the same forest	10

continues

Table 6.2 Continued

Tool name	Contained in	Purpose	See chapter
NetDiag.exe (Network Connectivity Tester)	ST	Test various networking and connectivity issues (protocols, binding, DNS, WINS, and many others) on client computers	8
NetDom.exe (Windows 2000 Domain Manager)	ST	Manage and verify trusts and secure channels; join, move, and remove computer accounts	9
NLtest.exe	ST	List domain controllers for a domain, query for trusted domains, query and reset secure channels between domain computers, force replication to Windows NT 4.0 BDCs	8
NTDSutil.exe (Active Directory Diagnostic Tool)	Sys	Manage Active Directory database files, operations masters, orphaned domains and controllers. Perform authoritative restore	7
NTFRSutl.exe	RK	Manage the File Replication Service (including SYSVOL and DFS roots replication)	8
RepAdmin.exe (Replication Diagnostics Tool)	ST	Display replication partners, metadata and connections, force replication of directory partitions, trigger KCC	8
ReplMon.exe (Active Directory Replication Monitor) (GUI tool)	ST	Monitor and force replication, display replication metadata, topology, and domain controller information	8
RPingc.exe (GUI tool) and RPings.exe (RPC Ping: Connectivity Verification Tool)	RK	Test RPC connectivity between clients and RPC servers	8
SDCheck.exe (Security Descriptor Check Utility)	ST	Verify a directory object's ACL inheritance and replication of the security descriptor from one domain controller to another	11
Search.vbs	ST	Search for a object against an LDAP server	9

continues

Table 6.2 Continued

Tool name	Contained in	Purpose	See chapter
Security Administration tools (SIDWalker)	ST	Modify SIDs specified in the ACLs of files, shares, and registry keys. Grant access rights on objects to specified users and groups. (Include ShowAccs.exe, SIDWalk.exe, and SIDWalk.msc tools.)	—
SubInACL.exe	RK	Display security descriptors for files, registry keys, or services. Change security information such as owner of an object, domain name, or SID	—
UserAccount.vbs	RK (RAS)	Displays information on normal, locked out, and disabled user accounts in a domain	—

Chapter 7
Active Directory Diagnostics and Maintenance

The two system tools described in this chapter deal with domain controllers as the elements that form the distributed structure of Active Directory services. In order for the Active Directory system to function correctly as a whole, all of its components — the domain controllers — must be in good working order. Therefore, an administrator must have tools that can help him or her to test every DC. Besides which, an administrator must have repair tools for those emergency cases when the Active Directory database restoring, cleaning up, and other low-level operations are needed.

Domain Controller Diagnostic Tool (DCdiag.exe) (ST)

This utility represents a complex test (or more precisely — a set of specialized tests) that allows an administrator to quickly check the "health" of a DC and locate possible problems. DCdiag verifies serviceability of a DC, as well as its relations (connectivity, trusts, replication issues, etc.) with replication partners and other DCs. Thus the utility primarily checks Active Directory at a functional rather than a logical level (data consistency, semantic contents, etc.).

It is very useful (and recommended) to run DCdiag after each DC installation. It is fairly typical— especially in small networks — that an administrator will install Active Directory on the first DC in his or her network and consequently believe that the domain will automatically work correctly, since no faults or error messages were received. The problems usually begin when the administrator adds clients to the domain or installs the second DC (in the same or another domain). Apparently, the DC was configured incorrectly; very often this concerns DNS service (on a Windows 2000 Server or a third-party server.) In such a situation, DCdiag, in conjunction with NetDiag.exe, could resolve many potential problems from the beginning.

The DCdiag utility can generate a very generous output — especially with enterprise-wide tests, you should therefore use log files for successive analyzing the results. The diagnostic messages are quite informative and very often directly specify a problem, so you need only resolve it, without any further analysis on your part.

DCdiag is not well documented, and the built-in help (dcdiag /?) is the best description of all parameters. The *Windows 2000 Resource Kit* proposes much more information on how to use this utility. Let's discuss some of its more interesting features and examples of its use.

Chapter 7: Active Directory Diagnostics and Maintenance

NOTES

If you installed DCdiag.exe from the standard Windows 2000 distributive CD, download the newer version of the tool from http://www.microsoft.com/downloads/release.asp?ReleaseID=22939

You can run DCdiag from any network computer and test any DC in the forest. Some tests can be performed under a normal user account (*Replications*, *NetLogons*, and *ObjectsReplicated* can't), but to get the full functionality of DCdiag, you must either be logged on as an administrator (or even as an enterprise administrator) or provide an administrator's credentials in the command.

Standard Full Test

Let's look at what happens if DCdiag is passed successfully. You'll see from this output how the tests are structured and which tests DCdiag contains. The *Topology*, *CutoffServers*, and *OutboundSecureChannels* tests are omitted by default, and you must run them selectively.

DCdiag runs faster if you specify the DC's DNS name rather than its NetBIOS name. (If the DC name is omitted, your current logon server is implied.) The **/a** or **/e** parameters specified in a command allow you to run a selected test on every DC in a site or in the forest.

If you want to retrieve the maximum possible amount of information from DCdiag, use the **/v** (verbose) parameter with any test. There is also an undocumented parameter — **/d**, which is an equivalent to **/v**, and also produces plenty of information (pDsInfo) on your forest.

Here is the most common command for testing a DC:

```
dcdiag /s:w2kdc4.w2k.dom
```

The command's output will be similar to:

```
DC Diagnosis

Performing initial setup:
   Done gathering initial info.

Doing initial non skippeable tests
    Testing server: W2K-site\W2KDC4
       Starting test: Connectivity
          ......................... W2KDC4 passed test Connectivity
```

```
Doing primary tests
   Testing server: W2K-site\W2KDC4
      Starting test: Replications
         ......................... W2KDC4 passed test Replications
      Starting test: NCSecDesc
         ......................... W2KDC4 passed test NCSecDesc
      Starting test: NetLogons
         ......................... W2KDC4 passed test NetLogons
      Starting test: Advertising
         ......................... W2KDC4 passed test Advertising
      Starting test: KnowsOfRoleHolders
         ......................... W2KDC4 passed test
KnowsOfRoleHolders
      Starting test: RidManager
         ......................... W2KDC4 passed test RidManager
      Starting test: MachineAccount
         ......................... W2KDC4 passed test MachineAccount
      Starting test: Services
         ......................... W2KDC4 passed test Services
      Starting test: ObjectsReplicated
         ......................... W2KDC4 passed test
ObjectsReplicated
      Starting test: frssysvol
         ......................... W2KDC4 passed test frssysvol
      Starting test: kccevent
         ......................... W2KDC4 passed test kccevent
      Starting test: systemlog
         ......................... W2KDC4 passed test systemlog

   Running enterprise tests on : w2k.dom
      Starting test: Intersite
         ......................... w2k.dom passed test Intersite
      Starting test: FsmoCheck
         ......................... w2k.dom passed test FsmoCheck
```

The first two sections — *Initial setup* and *Non skippeable tests* — are always executed, if even you specify only one test. You may run the full test first to find a problem(s), but it's then advisable to run tests selectively in verbose mode to get a detailed diagnosis.

Error and diagnostic messages (in verbose mode) are very descriptive, and it is unnecessary to give many examples.

Checking Replication

DCdiag allows an administrator to resolve replication problems quite well. Let's discuss a simple scenario. A site contains 3 domain controllers, one of which is refusing to replicate with its partners. The following command will test all DCs and check replication issues on each DC:

dcdiag /s:w2kdc4.w2k.dom **/test**:Replications **/a /v**

The output of this command is following:

```
DC Diagnosis

Performing initial setup:
   * Connecting to directory service on server w2kdc4.w2k.dom.
   * Collecting site info.
   * Identifying all servers.
   * Found 3 DC(s). Testing 3 of them.
   Done gathering initial info.

Doing initial non skippeable tests
...
Doing primary tests
   Testing server: W2K-site\W2KDC4
      Starting test: Replications
         * Replications Check
         [Replications Check,W2KDC4] A recent replication attempt
failed:
            From W2KDC2 to W2KDC4
            Naming Context: CN=Schema,CN=Configuration,DC=w2k,DC=dom
            The replication generated an error (8456):
            The source server is currently rejecting replication
requests.
            The failure occurred at 2000-11-08 18:52.24.
            The last success occurred at 2000-11-08 18:50.52.
            1 failures have occurred since the last success.
            Replication has been explicitly disabled through the
server options.
   ...
                   ...................... W2KDC4 passed test Replications
   ...
      Testing server: W2K-site\W2KDC2
```

```
        Starting test: Replications
           * Replications Check
           [Replications Check,W2KDC2] Outbound replication is disabled.
           To correct, run "repadmin /options W2KDC2 -
DISABLE_OUTBOUND_REPL"
           ......................... W2KDC2 failed test Replications
...
    Testing server: W2K-site\W2KDC03
        Starting test: Replications
           * Replications Check
           Skipping server W2KDC2, because it has outbound replication
disabled
...
                ......................... W2KDC03 passed test Replications
...
```

As you can see from the test output, DCdiag provides comprehensive information about failed connections for each DC in the site.

Enterprise Tests

These tests check many elements that are vitally necessary in order for an enterprise (forest) to work: intersite links, bridgehead servers, FSMO role owners, etc.

It doesn't make sense to run the *Intersite* test on one DC only, so you must specify the /a (current site) or /e (entire enterprise) parameters.

Here is a snippet of the test output for 2 sites in the forest *w2.dom* (some lines are in bold for clarity):

```
Running enterprise tests on : w2k.dom
        Starting test: Intersite
           Doing intersite inbound replication test on site W2K-site:
                Locating & Contacting Intersite Topology Generator (ISTG)
...
                The ISTG for site W2K-site is: W2KDC4.
                Checking for down bridgeheads ...
                Bridgehead Remote-site\W2KDC2 is up and replicating
fine.
                Bridgehead W2K-site\W2KDC4 is up and replicating fine.
                Doing in depth site analysis ...
                All expected sites and bridgeheads are replicating into
site W2K-site.
```

Chapter 7: Active Directory Diagnostics and Maintenance

```
Doing intersite inbound replication test on site Remote-site:
      Locating & Contacting Intersite Topology Generator (ISTG)
...
      The ISTG for site Remote-site is: W2KDC2.
      Checking for down bridgeheads ...
         Bridghead W2K-site\W2KDC4 is up and replicating fine.
         Bridghead Remote-site\W2KDC2 is up and replicating fine.
      Doing in depth site analysis ...
         All expected sites and bridgeheads are replicating into site Remote-site.
      ......................... w2k.dom passed test Intersite
```

Active Directory Diagnostic Tool (NTDSutil.exe) (Sys)

This utility is automatically installed on every domain controller. One could hardly say that this tool is for everyday use, but every administrator must be familiar with its features since it is used in certain operations that are very important for Active Directory functioning, such as Active Directory restore, offline defragmentation, FSMO role manipulating, and so on.

Some commands in the NTDSutil's main menu can only be performed when the system is booted in the *Directory Services Restore Mode* (press <F8> at system startup). (If, nevertheless, you wish to enable them, set the environment variable **SAFEBOOT_OPTION=DSREPAIR**, and restart the utility. This is, however, not advisable, because conflicts with the running processes will not permit you to execute most of the available operations.) The following commands are prohibited when the Active Directory services are online:

❑ Authoritative restore

❑ Files

❑ Semantic database analysis

Commands used in NTDSutil are quite long, but the utility accepts truncated syntax (or you can easily copy-and-paste commands from the built-in help lines). For example, the command

connect to server *xxx*

could be shortened to

```
co t s xxx
```

Let's discuss the purpose and use of all NTDSutil's commands in the order in which the menus appear in the built-in help.

> **NOTES**
>
> For presentation purposes, the command's prompts in the given dialogs are shown in bold.
>
> The utility connects to DCs faster if you use the DNS names of domain controllers.

Authoritative Restore

This menu contains four commands that allow an administrator to perform authoritative restore of the entire Active Directory database or a selected subtree. The commands' syntax is very simple, and it is much more difficult to understand how *to use* these simple commands. Since using *Authoritative Restore* commands as well as selecting the proper values for the *verinc* parameter are closely linked to the entire process of backing up and restoring Active Directory, all of these commands are described in detail in *Chapter 5, "Common Administrative Tasks"*.

Domain Management

Creating a new domain requires more administrative power than does promoting a server to domain controller. You may wish to divide these tasks among different persons and not give full administrative rights to those personnel that are only allowed to create new DCs. There is an NTDSutil command that allows you to preliminarily create a new domain context in the existing forest, which could then be used by other administrators when adding DCs in that domain.

The following dialog shows how to create a new domain (*intra.subdom.w2k.dom*) in the existing forest (*w2k.dom*):

```
C:\>ntdsutil
ntdsutil: domain management
domain management: connections
server connections: connect to server w2kdc4.w2k.dom
Binding to w2kdc4.w2k.dom ...
```

Chapter 7: Active Directory Diagnostics and Maintenance

```
Connected to w2kdc4.w2k.dom using credentials of locally logged
on user
```
server connections: `quit`
domain management: `list`
```
Found 4 Naming Context(s)
0 - CN=Configuration,DC=w2k,DC=dom
1 - DC=w2k,DC=dom
2 - CN=Schema,CN=Configuration,DC=w2k,DC=dom
3 - DC=subdom,DC=w2k,DC=dom
```
domain management: `precreate DC=intra,DC=subdom,DC=w2k,DC=dom`
`w2kdc03.w2k.dom`
`adding object CN=intra,cn=Partitions,CN=Configuration,DC=w2k,DC=dom`
domain management: `list`
```
Found 5 Naming Context(s)
0 - CN=Configuration,DC=w2k,DC=dom
1 - DC=w2k,DC=dom
2 - CN=Schema,CN=Configuration,DC=w2k,DC=dom
3 - DC=subdom,DC=w2k,DC=dom
```
4 `- DC=intra,DC=subdom,DC=w2k,DC=dom`
domain management: `...`

As you may notice from the dialog, a new domain context has appeared after the command was executed.

Files: Managing AD Database Files

The commands in this menu allow you to perform the following operations:

- Retrieve information on the state of the Active Directory (Jet) database (the ntds.dit file) as well as the log files
- Move database and/or log files to another location
- Re-define paths for Active Directory files
- Perform database recovery and repair

> **ATTENTION!**
>
> You can move already installed Active Directory database and/or log files to another location (folder or disk), but it is *not possible* to change the SYSVOL's location without re-installing Active Directory on a domain controller.

Retrieving Information on Active Directory Files

The following command informs you about the size and location of all Active Directory database files. It is advisable to use the command (and thus verify the presence of the log files) after you've restored Active Directory or done maintenance operations (offline defragmentation, moving files, etc.).

```
file maintenance: info
Drive Information:
        C:\ FAT    (Fixed Drive  ) free(167.8 Mb) total(454.6 Mb)
...
        G:\ NTFS   (Fixed Drive  ) free(329.5 Mb) total(1.3 Gb)
        M:\ NTFS   (Network Drive) free(347.9 Mb) total(996.2 Mb)
...
DS Path Information:
        Database    : G:\WINNT\NTDS\ntds.dit - 16.1 Mb
        Backup dir  : G:\WINNT\NTDS\dsadata.bak
        Working dir : G:\WINNT\NTDS
        Log dir     : G:\WINNT\NTDS - 40.1 Mb total
                        res2.log - 10.0 Mb
                        res1.log - 10.0 Mb
                        ntds.pat - 16.0 Kb
                        edb00009.log - 10.0 Mb
                        edb.log - 10.0 Mb
```

Compressing the Database — Offline Defragmentation

Online defragmentation of the Active Directory database performed automatically at predefined intervals (by default, every 12 hours) does not reduce the physical size of the database file (ntds.dit). To compact this file, you need to perform *offline* defragmentation (in *Directory Services Restore Mode).* Offline defragmentation may be required when you delete a number of objects from a DC. For example, this is the case when a GC server loses this function and becomes a regular DC. The disk space saved in such a case may appear rather significant.

In general, the procedure of online defragmentation is as follows:

1. Boot the DC in restore mode

2. Start the defragmentation process — the new, compact version of the Active Directory database file is stored in an alternative (specified) location

Chapter 7: Active Directory Diagnostics and Maintenance 177

3. If defragmentation is successful, copy the compact file to its original location and delete old log files

This entire procedure is shown below. In this scenario, the database file is packed to a temporary G:\AD\Database folder, and all log files are stored in the default location — G:\WINNT\NTDS.

```
G:\>ntdsutil
ntdsutil: files
file maintenance: compact to G:\AD\Database
Opening database [Current].
Using Temporary Path: D:\
Executing Command: G:\WINNT\system32\esentutl.exe /d
"G:\WINNT\NTDS\ntds.dit" /8 /o /l"G:\WINNT\NT
DS" /s"G:\WINNT\NTDS" /t"G:\AD\Database\ntds.dit" /!10240 /p

Initiating DEFRAGMENTATION mode...
          Database: G:\WINNT\NTDS\ntds.dit
         Log files: G:\WINNT\NTDS
      System files: G:\WINNT\NTDS
    Temp. Database: G:\AD\Database\ntds.dit

                  Defragmentation Status ( % complete )

          0    10   20   30   40   50   60   70   80   90  100
          |----|----|----|----|----|----|----|----|----|----|
          ....................................................

Note:
   It is recommended that you immediately perform a full backup
   of this database. If you restore a backup made before the
   defragmentation, the database will be rolled back to the state
   it was in at the time of that backup.

Operation completed successfully in 28.861 seconds.

Spawned Process Exit code 0x0(0)

If compaction was successful you need to:
    copy "G:\AD\Database\ntds.dit" to "G:\WINNT\NTDS\ntds.dit"
    and delete the old log files:
      del G:\WINNT\NTDS\*.log
file maintenance:
```

Moving the Active Directory Database

You may wish to move Active Directory database files to another location due to the disk space limitations or disk reconfiguration. The procedure for moving the database file requires the following steps:

1. Backup Active Directory
2. Restart the DC and press <F8> at startup
3. Select Directory Services Restore Mode and boot the DC
4. Start NTDSutil from the command prompt and select the `files` command. You may run `info` to check the current locations of the Active Directory database files
5. Enter `move DB to [drive]:\[new folder]`. Run `info` to verify the new configuration
6. Quit NTDSutil and restart the DC in normal mode

The procedure for moving log files is similar to the one described above.

Database Integrity

The *Files* menu also contains three commands — *Recover*, *Integrity*, and *Repair* — that can be used to detect corruption of the Active Directory database (with respect to the ESENT database semantics) and to perform some operations for its recovery. (All of these commands require a lot of time to run; this primarily depends on the actual size of the database.) The Repair command shouldn't be run without first consulting with service personnel, since it can result in data losses. The Recover command should be run first, prior to the Integrity command. This command scans the log files and ensures that all transactions are committed. The Integrity command can then check the database file for low-level corruption. The command's output is similar to the following:

```
file maintenance: integrity
Opening database [Current].
Executing Command: G:\WINNT\system32\esentutl.exe /g
"G:\WINNT\NTDS\ntds.dit" /!10240 /8 /v /x /o

Initiating INTEGRITY mode...
        Database: G:\WINNT\NTDS\ntds.dit
```

Chapter 7: Active Directory Diagnostics and Maintenance

```
   Temp. Database: INTEG.EDB
got 515464 buffers
checking database header

checking database integrity
              Scanning Status   ( % complete )
           0    10   20   30   40   50   60   70   80   90   100
           |----|----|----|----|----|----|----|----|----|----|
              checking SystemRoot
              SystemRoot (OE)
              SystemRoot (AE)
         checking system table
...
         checking table "datatable" (6)
              checking data
...
...          checking index "LCL_ABVIEW_index00000419" (89)
              checking index "DNT_IsDeleted_Index" (88)
              checking index "INDEX_000901FD" (87)
...
              checking index "INDEX_00090092" (7)
              rebuilding and comparing indexes
         checking table "hiddentable" (16)
...
         checking table "link_table" (14)
...
              rebuilding and comparing indexes
...............
integrity check completed.
Operation completed successfully in 30.514 seconds.

Spawned Process Exit code 0x0(0)

If integrity was successful, it is recommended
 you run semantic database analysis to insure
 semantic database consistency as well.
```
file maintenance:

IP Deny List

To increase the security of a DC, an administrator can use the *IP Deny List* that is applied only to the *Default-Query Policy* object (see also the next section). This list contains IP addresses, from which a domain controller won't accept LDAP queries. The list entries can represent a single host or a subnet. For example, the command

```
Add 192.168.1.1 NODE
```

prevents a DC from accepting queries from the host with the address 192.168.1.1. The following command denies access from all hosts in a subnet with the address 192.168.1.0:

```
Add 192.168.1.0 255.255.255.0
```

LDAP policies

Let's discuss how NTDSutil allows an administrator to work with the *Default-Query Policy* object (see *Chapter 1, "Active Directory Concepts and Terminology"*) using the following example. Below, a dialog is shown that changes the *Initial Receive Timeout* from the default value of 120 to 30 (the changed value is put in bold italics).

```
ntdsutil: ldap policies
ldap policy: connections
server connections: connect to server w2kdc4.w2k.dom
Binding to w2kdc4.w2k.dom ...
Connected to w2kdc4.w2k.dom using credentials of locally logged on user
server connections: q
ldap policy: list
Supported Policies:
        MaxPoolThreads
        MaxDatagramRecv
        MaxReceiveBuffer
        InitRecvTimeout
        MaxConnections
        MaxConnIdleTime
        MaxActiveQueries
        MaxPageSize
        MaxQueryDuration
```

Chapter 7: Active Directory Diagnostics and Maintenance 181

```
            MaxTempTableSize
            MaxResultSetSize
            MaxNotificationPerConn
ldap policy: set InitRecvTimeout to 30
ldap policy: show values
Policy                              Current(New)

MaxPoolThreads                      4
MaxDatagramRecv                     1024
MaxReceiveBuffer                               10485760
InitRecvTimeout                     120(30)
MaxConnections                      5000
MaxConnIdleTime                     900
MaxActiveQueries                               20
MaxPageSize                         1000
MaxQueryDuration                               120
MaxTempTableSize                               10000
MaxResultSetSize                               262144
MaxNotificationPerConn                         5
ldap policy: commit changes
ldap policy: q
ntdsutil: q
Disconnecting from w2kdc4.w2k.dom ...
```

The *Windows 2000 Server Resource Kit* contains the ModifyLDAP.vbs script (which is included in the *Remote Administration Scripts*). This script allows an administrator to display policies, create new policies, and modify the existing ones, as well as assign policies to a DC or site. Here is the screen output for the LDAP Administrative limits of the *Default Query Policy*, which is installed and used (albeit not selected!) by default on all DCs:

```
modifyldap /P /O:"Default Query Policy"

LDAP Settings for Default Query Policy
MaxPageSize=1000
InitRecvTimeout=30
MaxReceiveBuffer=10485760
MaxDatagramRecv=1024
MaxPoolThreads=4
```

```
MaxResultSetSize=262144
MaxTempTableSize=10000
MaxQueryDuration=120
MaxNotificationPerConn=5
MaxActiveQueries=20
MaxConnIdleTime=900
MaxConnections=5000
```

NOTE

To select an existing LDAP policy, use the **Active Directory Sites and Services** snap-in. Point to the *NTDS Settings* object of the necessary DC and open the **Properties** window. Select a policy in the **Query Policy** list and click **Apply**.

Metadata Cleanup: Removing Orphaned Domains or Domain Controllers

Normally, the process of demoting a DC deletes the computer account and cleans up all metadata related to this DC from Active Directory. When the last DC in a domain is deleted, all cross-references (and other information about that domain) are also removed. There are, however, situations when a domain controller is decommissioned incorrectly (or failed and destroyed), and orphaned metadata remains in the directory. In such a case, you can remove information about the retired DC and/or domains by using NTDSutil. (You mustn't delete any information for *existing* domains and DCs!) In general, the procedure is the following:

1. Connect to a working DC that holds the information about orphaned metadata
2. Select an operation target (site, naming context, domain, and server). You may select one or more of these targets
3. Remove the necessary metadata

The following dialog illustrates how to remove a retired domain controller (*W2KDC3*) and a child domain (*intra.subdom.w2k.dom*) from the forest (*w2k.dom*). (In this example, the shortened command syntax is used; comments are in bold square brackets. You can also learn how to select an operation target, which is used in many commands.)

```
ntdsutil: m c
metadata cleanup: c
```

Chapter 7: Active Directory Diagnostics and Maintenance 183

```
server connections: co t s w2kdc4.w2k.dom
Binding to w2kdc4.w2k.dom …
Connected to w2kdc4.w2k.dom using credentials of locally logged on
user
server connections: q
metadata cleanup: s o t
select operation target: l si
Found 1 site(s)
0 - CN=W2K-site,CN=Sites,CN=Configuration,DC=w2k,DC=dom
select operation target: s si 0
Site - CN=W2K-site,CN=Sites,CN=Configuration,DC=w2k,DC=dom
No current domain
No current server
No current Naming Context
select operation target: l d
Found 3 domain(s)
0 - DC=w2k,DC=dom
1 - DC=subdom,DC=w2k,DC=dom
2 - DC=intra,DC=subdom,DC=w2k,DC=dom
select operation target: s d 2
Site - CN=W2K-site,CN=Sites,CN=Configuration,DC=w2k,DC=dom
Domain - DC=intra,DC=subdom,DC=w2k,DC=dom
No current server
No current Naming Context
select operation target: l se f d i s
Found 1 server(s)
0 - CN=W2KDC3,CN=Servers,CN=W2K-site,CN=Sites,CN=Configuration,
 ↳ DC=w2k,DC=dom
select operation target: s se 0
Site - CN=W2K-site,CN=Sites,CN=Configuration,DC=w2k,DC=dom
Domain - DC=intra,DC=subdom,DC=w2k,DC=dom
Server - CN=W2KDC3,CN=Servers,CN=W2K-site,CN=Sites,CN=Configuration,
 ↳ DC=w2k,DC=dom
        DSA object - CN=NTDS Settings,CN=W2KDC3,CN=Servers,
 ↳ CN=W2K-site,CN=Sites,CN=Configuration,DC=w2k,DC=dom
        DNS host name - w2kdc3.intra.subdom.w2k.dom
        Computer object - CN=W2KDC3,OU=Domain Controllers,
 ↳ DC=intra,DC=subdom,DC=w2k,DC=dom
No current Naming Context
select operation target: q
metadata cleanup: r s s
```

```
[The Server Remote Confirmation Dialog appears — you must click Yes.]
"CN=W2KDC3,CN=Servers,CN=W2K-site,CN=Sites,CN=Configuration,
 DC=w2k,DC=dom" removed from server "w2kdc4.w2k.dom"
metadata cleanup: r s d
[The Domain Remote Confirmation Dialog appears — you must click Yes.}
"DC=intra,DC=subdom,DC=w2k,DC=dom" removed from server
"w2kdc4.w2k.dom"
[Verifying that the operation has been done correctly:]
metadata cleanup: s o t
select operation target: l d
Found 2 domain(s)
0 - DC=w2k,DC=dom
1 - DC=subdom,DC=w2k,DC=dom
[Terminating the ntdsutil command:]
select operation target: q
metadata cleanup: q
ntdsutil: q
Disconnecting from w2kdc4.w2k.dom ...
```

Now the *intra.subdom.w2k.dom* domain has been deleted, and you can verify this by using the Event Viewer. The following information messages appear in the Directory Service log (the source is NTDS KCC):

```
The consistency checker deleted connection object... as the source
server to which it referred has been deleted.
The domain ... has been removed from the enterprise.
```

If there are other domains, a pair of messages similar to

```
The consistency checker has terminated change notification for the
following:
```

will appear for the Schema and Configuration name context.

ATTENTION!

You must also manually delete the corresponding entries from the DNS server.

To verify that the operation was successful, you may check the domain configuration by using the following tools: **Active Directory Domains and Trusts**, **ADSI Edit** (the **Configuration** container: the **Partitions** and **Sites | Servers** nodes), and **Active Directory Sites and Services** snap-ins. You may also run DCdiag (as well as `repadmin /showreps`) to ensure that there are no replication problems.

Roles: Managing FSMO Roles

NTDSutil allows an administrator to manipulate FSMO roles: to view and transfer them. See *Chapter 5, "Common Administrative Tasks"*, to learn how to dump all FSMO role owners. In this section, we'll discuss how to designate a DC as a role owner by using NTDSutil. You can:

- Seize role — this command designates the connected server as the specified role master. The command must be used only when the DC — the current master — has severely crashed and has been destroyed.

- Transfer role — this command "moves" the specified role from the current role holder to the connected server (DC). You can perform the same operation by using various administrative snap-ins (see *Chapter 4, "Domain Manipulation Tools"*). The NTDSutil.exe allows you to carry out the operation in batch mode (see *dumpFSMOs.cmd*).

Transferring a Role

If for some reason you can't (or don't want to) use the standard administrative snap-ins, you may use NTDSutil to transfer a role from its current owner to another DC. The most common steps are the following:

1. Connect to the potential role owner
2. Transfer a necessary role from the current owner to the selected server

> **NOTE**
> It is not advisable to *seize* a FSMO role if you can *transfer* this role. Seizing is used only when a FSMO role owner has failed and is unrecoverable.

In the following dialog, the Schema Master role is transferred to the *w2kdc2.subdom.w2k.dom* server. (This is an example! It is neither practical nor advisable to move the schema master role to a child domain.)

```
C:\>ntdsutil
ntdsutil: roles
fsmo maintenance: connections
server connections: connect to server w2kdc2.subdom.w2k.dom
Binding to w2kdc2.subdom.w2k.dom ...
```

```
Connected to w2kdc2.subdom.w2k.dom using credentials of locally logged
on user
```
server connections: `quit`

fsmo maintenance: `transfer schema master`

[The Role Transfer Confirmation Dialog **will appear** — **click** Yes.**]**

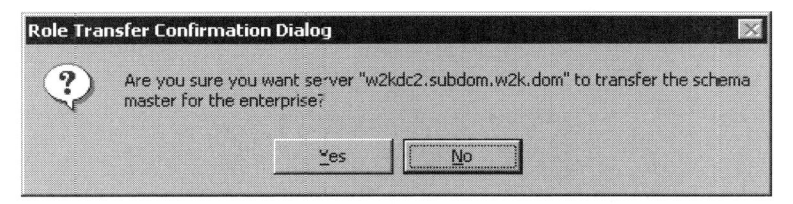

[Role Transfer Confirmation Dialog: Are you sure you want server "w2kdc2.subdom.w2k.dom" to transfer the schema master for the enterprise? Yes / No]

```
Server "w2kdc2.subdom.w2k.dom" knows about 5 roles
Schema - CN=NTDS Settings,CN=W2KDC2,CN=Servers,CN=Remote-site,
    CN=Sites,CN=Configuration,DC=w2k,DC=dom
Domain - CN=NTDS Settings,CN=W2KDC4,CN=Servers,CN=W2K-site,
    CN=Sites,CN=Configuration,DC=w2k,DC=dom
PDC - CN=NTDS Settings,CN=W2KDC2,CN=Servers,CN=Remote-site,
    CN=Sites,CN=Configuration,DC=w2k,DC=dom
RID - CN=NTDS Settings,CN=W2KDC2,CN=Servers,CN=Remote-site,
    CN=Sites,CN=Configuration,DC=w2k,DC=dom
Infrastructure - CN=NTDS Settings,CN=W2KDC2,CN=Servers,CN=Remote-site,
    CN=Sites,CN=Configuration,DC=w2k,DC=dom
```
fsmo maintenance: ...

> **NOTE**
>
> Notice that the same Configuration partition contains information about servers that may belong to different domains and sites.

Even if the connected DC already owns the specified role, the command dialog remains the same as shown above.

Seizing a Role

Suppose a DC that holds the Infrastructure FSMO role was destroyed, and you want to designate this role to another DC. The following dialog shows how to forcibly transfer the role to a new candidate (server *w2kdc4.w2k.dom*) (comments are in bold square brackets):

```
C:\>ntdsutil
ntdsutil: roles
```

Chapter 7: Active Directory Diagnostics and Maintenance

```
fsmo maintenance: connections
server connections: connect to server w2kdc4.w2k.dom
Binding to w2kdc4.w2k.dom ...
Connected to w2kdc4.w2k.dom using credentials of locally logged on
user
server connections: quit
fsmo maintenance: seize infrastructure master
```

[The Role Seizure Confirmation Dialog **appears** — **click** Yes.]

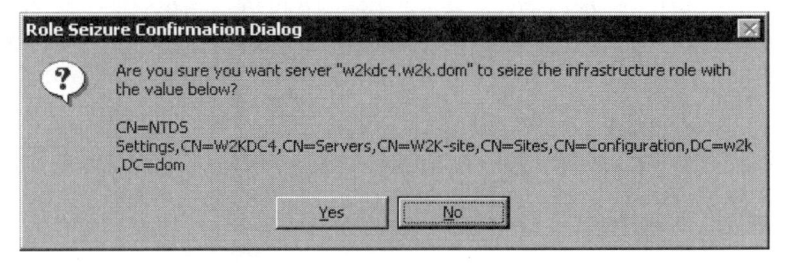

```
Attempting safe transfer of infrastructure FSMO before seizure.
```

[**The server tries to carry out the standard role transfer operation and fails. The same error message will appear every time you want to perform a role transfer operation while the current master is not operational.**]

```
ldap_modify_sW error 0x34(52 (Unavailable).
Ldap extended error message is 000020AF: SvcErr: DSID-03210194,
problem 5002 (UNAVAILABLE), data 1722
Win32 error returned is 0x20af(The requested FSMO operation failed.
The current FSMO holder could not be contacted.)
)
Depending on the error code this may indicate a connection,
ldap, or role transfer error.
Transfer of infrastructure FSMO failed, proceeding with seizure ...
```

[**The server successfully carries out the seize operation and reports the new information about role holders**]

```
Server "w2kdc4.w2k.dom" knows about 5 roles
...
```

Security Account Management

Since appearance of duplicated SIDs is possible (due to problems with the RID Master role owners), you may wish to verify a domain for conflicting SIDs. The commands in the *Security Account Management* menu will help you to solve this problem.

Semantic Database Analysis

The commands in this menu test the data with respect to Active Directory (not ESENT database!) semantics. The report generated (a file named dsdit.dmp.*nnn*) displays the number of active objects, including phantom and deleted records. The log file is placed in the current folder.

Notwithstanding the fact that Microsoft doesn't recommend that end users run semantic analysis commands themselves, it may be useful to check the database's integrity in some situations, and fix possible errors. (Be careful with the *Go Fixup* command, your data are at risk here!) For example, the following two successive commands have detected and fixed an error with a deleted reference object:

```
semantic checker: go
Fixup mode is turned off
Opening database [Current].....Done.

Getting record count...2857 records
Writing summary into log file dsdit.dmp.1
Records scanned:         2800
Processing records..
Error: Missing subrefs detected.
Done.
semantic checker: go fixup
Fixup mode is turned on
Opening database [Current].....Done.

Getting record count...2857 records
Writing summary into log file dsdit.dmp.2
Records scanned:         2800
Processing records..Done.
```

Chapter 8
Network and Distributed Services

All tools described in this chapter consider Active Directory as a distributed database that along with serving clients must support its own integrity and consistency. This global system task has different aspects, or problem areas, the most important of which are the following:

- Connectivity (including RPC connectivity) between domain controllers, and between a DC and a client
- Proper name resolving
- Mutual authentication (existence of secure channels, or trusts, between domains, domain controllers, and between a client and a DC)
- Synchronizing Active Directory replicas (all directory partitions including Global Catalog) stored on different domain controllers

As you can conclude from the list of problem areas, there are many sources of possible faults, which can prevent Active Directory services from working and responding to client queries properly. The tools described below help administrators to test Active Directory network infrastructure and monitor its state on different domain controllers.

NLtest.exe (ST)

The NLtest tool helps administrators to manage both native and mixed mode (with BDCs of earlier Windows NT versions) domains. It has a number of options including the following:

- Verifying and resetting secure channels
- Getting information on the network topology (list of DCs, selected site, domain trusts, etc.)
- Forcing synchronization with BDCs
- Forcing a shutdown on a computer and other options

NLtest is a very useful tool for troubleshooting authentication problems, since it allows you to test the trust relationships between every specific pair of computers (DC and DC, or DC and client) for which these trusts are defined.

> **NOTES**
>
> In most commands, it is preferable to specify *DNS* rather than NetBIOS names of Windows 2000-based computers.
>
> Some options of NLtest are similar to the options realized in the NetDom tool. (See *Chapter 9, "Manipulating Active Directory Objects"*.) You may choose which tool is the most appropriate for your specific tasks.

Verifying Secure Channels

First of all, you must not confuse transitive Windows 2000 trust relationships with non-transitive secure channels (trust links). (This was described in detail in *Chapter 1, "Active Directory Concepts and Terminology"*.) Although you can, for example, logon to a domain that belongs to *one* forest tree on a computer that has the account in *another* forest tree, this doesn't mean that domain controllers from the corresponding domains have *direct* trust relationships. (You *can*, however, manually establish such a relationship named *shortcut trust*. See *Chapter 3, "Deploying Active Directory"*.) That is why you can verify secure channels only directly between a child and its parent domain, or between tree root domains.

Normally, you should get the following result on every domain computer:

```
C:\>nltest /query
Flags: 0
Connection Status = 0 0x0 NERR_Success
The command completed successfully
```

This output means that the computer has been authenticated by a domain controller, and a secure channel exists between the client computer and a DC. If a user has been logged on locally, or for some reason a network logon has not been performed (DC not found, and so on), you'll get the following message:

```
Connection Status = 1311 0x51f ERROR_NO_LOGON_SERVERS
```

The following message indicates that the Netlogon service failed on start or doesn't run on the computer:

```
I_NetLogonControl failed: Status = 1717 0x6b5 RPC_S_UNKNOWN_IF
```

In that case you should open the **Services** snap-in and check the state of the service.

If the domain computer account was reset, NLtest responds with the message:

```
Connection Status = 5 0x5 ERROR_ACCESS_DENIED
```

If an administrator has disabled the domain computer account, NLtest reports:

```
Connection Status = 1737 0x6fb ERROR_NO_TRUST_SAM_ACCOUNT
```

If the account is enabled again, restart the Netlogon service on the computer or run the `nltest /sc_reset` command (see below).

To verify the secure channel or find the logon server, use the `nltest /sc_query` command, for example:

```
C:\>nltest /sc_query:w2k.dom
Flags: 30 HAS_IP HAS_TIMESERV
Trusted DC Name \\w2kdc4.w2k.dom
Trusted DC Connection Status Status = 0 0x0 NERR_Success
The command completed successfully
```

If the command responds

```
Connection Status = 1311 0x51f ERROR_NO_LOGON_SERVERS
```

you may try to log off and log on to the system, or to reset (re-establish) the secure channel by using the following command:

```
C:\>nltest /sc_reset:w2k.dom
```

If there are multiple DCs in the domain, the client computer will establish a secure channel with the DC that responds first.

NOTE

For verifying and resetting secure channels, it is also possible to use the `netdom /VERIFY` and `netdom /RESET` commands.

Now let's consider a scenario. You have two domains — a child and a parent — in the forest and want to test whether a DC *w2kdc4.w2k.dom* from the parent domain is authenticated by the child domain *subdom.w2k.dom*, i. e. whether the trust between domains is in a proper state. You use the following command, and for some reason it fails:

```
C:\>nltest /sc_query:subdom.w2k.dom /server:w2kdc4.w2k.dom
Flags: 0
Trusted DC Name
Trusted DC Connection Status Status = 1311 0x51f
ERROR_NO_LOGON_SERVERS
The command completed successfully
```

You could check this trust in another way. Run the **Active Directory Domain and Trusts** snap-in, open the **Properties** window for domain w2k.dom, and click the **Trusts** tab. Select the child domain subdom.w2k.dom in the **Domain trusted by this domain** list and click **Edit**, and then **Verify**. (An alternate way: run the **Active Directory Users and Computers** snap-in, point to the **System** container, and open the **Properties** window for the object subdom.w2k.dom of *Trusted Domain* type. Then click **Verify**.) The system will display a message window shown in Fig. 8.1. If you click **OK**, the system will try to reset the secure channel that failed.

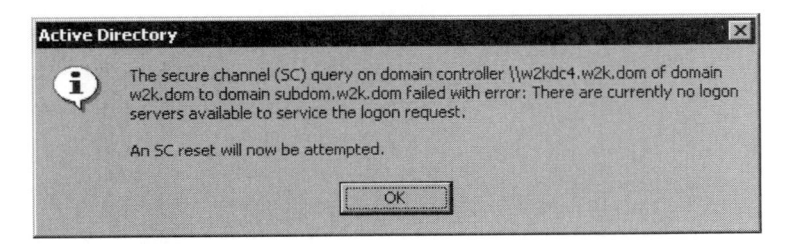

Fig. 8.1. This window informs you that the secure channel between two DCs in related domains is broken, but you can reset it

The following command will help you to repair the secure channel from the command prompt:

```
C:\>nltest /sc_reset:subdom.w2k.dom /server:w2kdc4.w2k.dom
Flags: 30 HAS_IP  HAS_TIMESERV
Trusted DC Name \\w2kdc2.subdom.w2k.dom
Trusted DC Connection Status Status = 0 0x0 NERR_Success
The command completed successfully
```

To troubleshoot authentication issues, you can test necessary domain controllers and clients in a similar manner and locate the source of problems.

Viewing Trusted Domains

Using NLtest, you can display all trust relationships established between the current domain and other domains in the same or in another forest. Verbose mode allows you to view domain SIDs and GUIDs. Look at a sample output:

```
C:\>nltest /trusted_domains /v
List of domain trusts:
    0: NT4DOM (NT 4) (Direct Outbound) (Direct Inbound)
```

```
        Dom Sid: S-1-5-21-1090471030-1714903380-1691616715
    1: SUBDOM subdom.w2k.dom (NT 5) (Forest: 2) (Direct Outbound)
(Direct Inbound)
        Dom Guid: 2a0a419f-0b2d-4e1a-958b-51ead1be3f0e
        Dom Sid: S-1-5-21-2523187317-3632519984-2123532372
    2: W2KDOM w2k.dom (NT 5) (Forest Tree Root) (Primary Domain)
(Native)
        Dom Guid: baf0baaf-5013-43d3-8fac-62cdbbcfa34a
        Dom Sid: S-1-5-21-2153319400-2659097208-1957364326
The command completed successfully
```

How should you analyze the displayed information? From this output you can conclude the following:

- ❑ A Window NT 4.0-based domain *NT4DOM* has explicit, two-way trusts with the current domain

- ❑ A Windows 2000-based domain *subdom.w2k.dom* is in mixed mode, and belongs to the same forest (`Forest: 2`) as the current domain

- ❑ The current (`Primary`) domain *w2k.dom* is in native mode, and is the forest root domain

Viewing Information on Network Topology

Information about which site (in a multiple site network) a client computer is connected to is not configured on that computer in any way. (The site is selected on the basis of client and subnet IP address data.) The following command will help you to find the site to which the local or remote computer has been connected after its logging on to the domain:

```
C:\>nltest /dsGetSite
W2K-site
The command completed successfully
```

(Add **/server:**<*computerName*> for a remote computer.)

Sometimes, a domain controller can serve more than one site. (If a new site has been created, but you didn't move a DC to that site, some DC from an existing site is selected to serve the new site. To increase network fault-tolerance, you can also intentionally configure a DC to serve a site when the domain controllers of that site are unavailable.) The following command lists all sites, which the DC can serve:

```
C:\>nltest /dsGetSiteCov /server:w2kdc4.w2k.dom
Remote-Site
W2K-site
The command completed successfully
```

(The **/server** parameter isn't required if the command is performed on a domain controller.)

Very often it is necessary to see the list of controllers configured for a domain. A command similar to the following allows you to view all DCs in a Windows 2000-based domain:

```
C:\>nltest /DClist:w2k.dom
Get list of DCs in domain 'w2k.dom' from '\\w2kdc4.w2k.dom'.
    w2kdc4.w2k.dom [PDC] [DS] Site: W2K-site
    w2kdc3.w2k.dom        [DS] Site: W2K-site
        nt4bdc2
The command completed successfully
```

Servers present in this list may be off-line! (Notice that the PDC is marked. To find the PDC, you can also use the nltest /DCname:*<NetBIOSDomainName>* command.) Notice also that a Windows 4.0-based BDC *nt4dc2* has no directory service and is not connected to the site topology.

To search a domain for a DC performing a specific role (PDC, Global Catalog, writable replica, etc.), use a command similar to the following (search for a GC server):

```
C:\>nltest /dsGetDC:subdom.w2k.dom /GC
            DC: \\w2kdc2.subdom.w2k.dom
       Address: \\192.168.0.2
      Dom Guid: 2a0a419f-0b2d-4e1a-958b-51ead1be3f0e
      Dom Name: subdom.w2k.dom
   Forest Name: w2k.dom
  Dc Site Name: W2K-site
 Our Site Name: W2K-site
         Flags: PDC GC DS LDAP KDC TIMESERV WRITABLE DNS_DC DNS_DOMAIN
DNS_FOREST CLOSE_SITE
The command completed successfully
```

You can add the **/FORCE** parameter, and the command will try to find another (different) DC with the specified property each time.

> **TIP**
>
> To find all GC servers in the forest, use ReplMon or query the DNS server for records in the `gc._msdcs.<forestDNSname>` subdomain, e. g.:
>
> ```
> C:\>nslookup gc._msdcs.w2k.dom
> Server:   w2kdc4.w2k.dom
> Address:  192.168.0.4
>
> Name:     gc._msdcs.w2k.dom
> Address:  192.168.0.3, 192.168.0.4
> ```

Note that all GC servers register their IP addresses in the same subdomain regardless of which domain they belong to, and you should always search for a GC server by specifying the DNS name of the forest root domain.

> **NOTE**
>
> For discovering domain controllers you can also use the `netdiag /test:DcList` and `netdiag /test:DsGetDc` commands.

Miscellaneous Options

Forcing Shutdown on a Remote Computer

You can use NLtest as an analog to the *Shutdown.exe* command (from the *Resource Kit*). The following command issues a warning message to the computer *w2kdc3.w2k.dom* and shuts it down in 60 seconds:

```
C:\>nltest /shutdown:"Administrative request for shutdown" 60
   /server:w2kdc3.w2k.dom
```

> **NOTE**
>
> In contrast to Shutdown.exe, NLtest cannot reboot the computer after shutdown.

Directory Time Conversion

Some attributes, e. g. *pwdLastSet*, *lastLogon*, or *badPasswordTime*, are stored in Active Directory as *Large Integers* (INTEGER8 format). NLtest can convert these values to a human-readable format. The conversion procedure is rather cumbersome, so you may prefer to use the `repadmin /showtime` command (see later in this chapter). Let's, for example, consider converting a time value *126191956001314960* obtained with Ldp.exe. Copy and paste the value in the *Calculator*, and convert it to hexadecimal format. The result will be 1C052EA56F85890. Enter `nltest /time`: at the command prompt and paste the hexadecimal value. Then you must highlight the eight rightmost digits and place them *before* the other digits. You should get the following result:

```
C:\>nltest /time:56F85890 1C052EA
56f85890 01c052ea = 11/20/2000 15:06:40
```

Notice that the command converts the entered value into *local time* rather than UTC.

Network Connectivity Tester (NetDiag.exe) (ST)

NetDiag is a powerful tool that can be used for diagnosing practically all network problems, from physical connectivity to name resolving and authentication. To see the complete list of NetDiag's options (tests), enter `netdiag /?` at the command prompt. You can run all tests, a selected test, or all tests excepting the specified ones. The test diagnosis messages are quite explanatory (especially in verbose and debug modes). You need to pay attention primarily to the strings [FATAL] and [WARNING]. All fatal problems must be fixed, or the system will not be able work properly. You need to analyze the warnings and find (and maybe repair) their causes. Sometimes, however, the warnings can be ignored.

Two options of NetDiag have already been discussed in *Chapter 3, "Deploying Active Directory"*. These tests can be useful for running before promoting a server to a DC or connecting a client computer (workstation or server) to a domain. In this chapter we'll consider a successful test run (the result output that you need to get for every domain computer to work properly) and fixing DNS issues.

> **NOTE**
>
> If you installed NetDiag from the standard Windows 2000 distributive CD, download the newer version of the tool from http://www.microsoft.com/downloads/release.asp?ReleaseID=22938.

Running Tests

Let's look at a sample test output that has been obtained by a domain administrator on a computer (*w2kpro1.w2k.dom*) that was successfully joined to a domain. (If a domain user runs NetDiag, the results will be slightly different.) Notice that the computer has no WINS settings. You may wish to compare this output with results obtained on your domain computers and analyze the differences. (Comments are given in bold brackets.)

```
C:\>netdiag
..................................

    Computer Name: W2KPRO1
    DNS Host Name: w2kpro1.w2k.dom
    System info : Windows 2000 Professional (Build 2195)
    Processor : x86 Family 5 Model 4 Stepping 3, GenuineIntel
    List of installed hotfixes :
        Q147222

Netcard queries test . . . . . . . : Passed

    Per interface results:          [All installed network adapters
                                     will be listed below.]

    Adapter : LAN1
        Netcard queries test . . . : Passed

        Host Name. . . . . . . . . : w2kpro1
        IP Address . . . . . . . . : 192.168.0.1    [Multiple IP
        addresses and other settings can be assigned to the same
        adapter. All will be displayed here.]
        Subnet Mask. . . . . . . . : 255.255.255.0
        Default Gateway. . . . . . : 192.168.0.4
        Dns Servers. . . . . . . . : 192.168.0.4

        AutoConfiguration results. . . . . . : Passed

        Default gateway test . . . : Passed    [This test can fail if
        there is no connectivity with other subnets and the default
        gateway is not configured.]
```

Chapter 8: Network and Distributed Services 199

```
        NetBT name test. . . . . . : Passed

        WINS service test. . . . . : Skipped
            There are no WINS servers configured for this interface.
```

Global results:

```
Domain membership test . . . . . . : Passed

NetBT transports test. . . . . . . : Passed
    List of NetBt transports currently configured:
        NetBT_Tcpip_{2B76E7F9-1DBA-433E-8144-E5BD86C6E71A}
    1 NetBt transport currently configured.
```
[This test is skipped if *NetBIOS over TCP/IP* is disabled.]

```
Autonet address test . . . . . . . : Passed

IP loopback ping test. . . . . . . : Passed

Default gateway test . . . . . . . : Passed

NetBT name test. . . . . . . . . . : Passed
```
[This test is skipped if *NetBIOS over TCP/IP* is disabled.]

```
Winsock test . . . . . . . . . . . : Passed

DNS test . . . . . . . . . . . . . : Passed
```
[On domain controllers the test should report the following:
```
DNS test . . . . . . . . . . . . . : Passed
    PASS - All the DNS entries for DC are registered on DNS server
'x.x.x.x'.
```
All warnings in this section must be carefully analyzed, since they can represent fatal errors. See also the note below.]

```
Redir and Browser test . . . . . . : Passed
    List of NetBt transports currently bound to the Redir
        NetBT_Tcpip_{2B76E7F9-1DBA-433E-8144-E5BD86C6E71A}
    The redir is bound to 1 NetBt transport.

    List of NetBt transports currently bound to the browser
        NetBT_Tcpip_{2B76E7F9-1DBA-433E-8144-E5BD86C6E71A}
    The browser is bound to 1 NetBt transport.
```
[This test is skipped if *NetBIOS over TCP/IP* is disabled.]

```
DC discovery test. . . . . . . . . . : Passed

DC list test . . . . . . . . . . . : Passed

Trust relationship test. . . . . . : Passed
    Secure channel for domain 'W2KDOM' is to '\\w2kdc4.w2k.dom'.
    [This test is skipped on the PDC Operations Master.]

Kerberos test. . . . . . . . . . . : Passed   [This test will be
skipped if the user is logged onto the computer locally.]

LDAP test. . . . . . . . . . . . : Passed
    [WARNING] Failed to query SPN registration on DC 'w2kdc4.w2k.dom'.
    [WARNING] Failed to query SPN registration on DC 'w2kdc3.w2k.dom'.
    [You can verify whether any problems really exist with LDAP by
    using the netdiag /test:LDAP /v command.]

Bindings test. . . . . . . . . . . : Passed

WAN configuration test . . . . . . : Skipped
    No active remote access connections.

Modem diagnostics test . . . . . . : Passed

IP Security test . . . . . . . . . : Passed
    IPSec policy service is active, but no policy is assigned.

The command completed successfully
```

ATTENTION!

On domain client computers, if the **Register this connection's addresses in DNS** box is not checked on the **DNS** tab in the **Advanced TCP/IP Settings** window, the DNS test can *pass*, even if there is no corresponding host record for a client on the DNS server.

Refreshing DNS Resource Records Registration (/fix)

If NetDiag detects that registration of some SRV records has failed for a domain controller, you can try to automatically fix the problem. Executing the `netdiag /fix` command yields the same result as restarting the Netlogon service. The command looks up all DNS records in the *%SystemRoot%*\system32\config\ netlogon.dns file and updates the corresponding records on the DNS server. When the command runs, strings similar to the following appear in the 'DNS test' section:

```
[FIX] re-register DC DNS entry '_ldap._tcp.w2k.dom.' on DNS server
'192.168.0.4' succeed.
```

The following message completes the fixing process:

```
FIX PASS - netdiag re-registered missing DNS entries for this DC
successfully on DNS server '192.168.0.4'.
```

You can analyze the command output to see which records were incorrect or absent. After NetDiag has tried to fix the DNS issues, run it once more to be sure that all the problems have been solved.

> **ATTENTION!**
>
> Remember that only the `ipconfig /registerdns` command re-registers the computer's A (host) record on the DNS server in both forward and reverse zones. The `netdiag /fix` command affects only SRV records.

> **ATTENTION!**
>
> Don't forget to clear the cache on the DNS server specified as primary after executing the `netdiag /fix` or `ipconfig /registerdns` commands! (If you don't, you must at least manually delete the records re-registered by these commands from the cache.) Even though the commands may have already updated the information in dynamic zones on the authoritative DNS server, the cache may still contain the old data for some records. As a result, it might seem that the problems still exist, since while testing, the commands use the cached responses from the primary DNS server. You may also need to clear the requester's (local) cache by using the **ipconfig /flushdns** command.

RPC Ping: RPC Connectivity Verification Tool (RK)

The RPC Ping tool verifies *remote procedure call* (RPC) connectivity on a network. The tool consists of the following components:

❏ A server, which echoes to clients and produces statistics

❏ A client, which connects, binds, and sends requests to the specific destination RPC server

The filenames of these components and the supported systems are listed in the table below.

Utility filename	Platforms supported
Server component	
Rpings.exe	Windows 2000 and Windows NT
Client component	
Rpingc.exe (32-bit version)	Windows 2000, Windows NT, Windows 9*x*/ME
Rpingc16.exe (16-bit version)	Windows 3.1*x*

Server Component (RPings.exe)

The server component performs only two RPC functions: *Echo* and *Stats*. You can run it with all available protocols or select only one protocol (**-p** parameter). If, for instance, only the TCP/IP protocol is installed on the server computer, RPings.exe displays the following messages while starting (the names of endpoints are shown in bold; these names later will be displayed by clients):

```
+endpoint \pipe\rping on protocol sequence ncacn_np is set for use.
 -cannot create endpoint 52 on ncacn_nb_nb
+endpoint rping on protocol sequence ncalrpc is set for use.
+endpoint 2256 on protocol sequence ncacn_ip_tcp is set for use.
+endpoint 53 on protocol sequence ncacn_nb_tcp is set for use.
 -protocol Sequence ncacn_spx not supported on this host
+endpoint 2256 on protocol sequence ncadg_ip_udp is set for use.
 -protocol Sequence ncadg_ipx not supported on this host
 -protocol Sequence ncacn_vns_spp not supported on this host

Enter '@q' to exit rpings.
```

Now the server is ready to respond to RPC requests (until you stop it), and can serve as many clients as you want.

Client Component (RPingc.exe)

The client component displays all information about the established RPC connection. It has two modes of operation:

❑ **Ping Only** (default) — can be one step or continuous (until you click **Stop**)

Chapter 8: Network and Distributed Services

- **Endpoint Search** — a one-time operation that allows you to find all available (responding) endpoints on the RPC server

> **NOTE**
> Notice that RPingc.exe doesn't appear on the task pad.

An example of the RPingc's window is shown in Fig. 8.2. (I'd recommend that you specify, in turn, both the DNS and NetBIOS names of a RPC server — the **Exchange Server** field. This is because the results may vary depending on the type of specified name and type of the selected operation.)

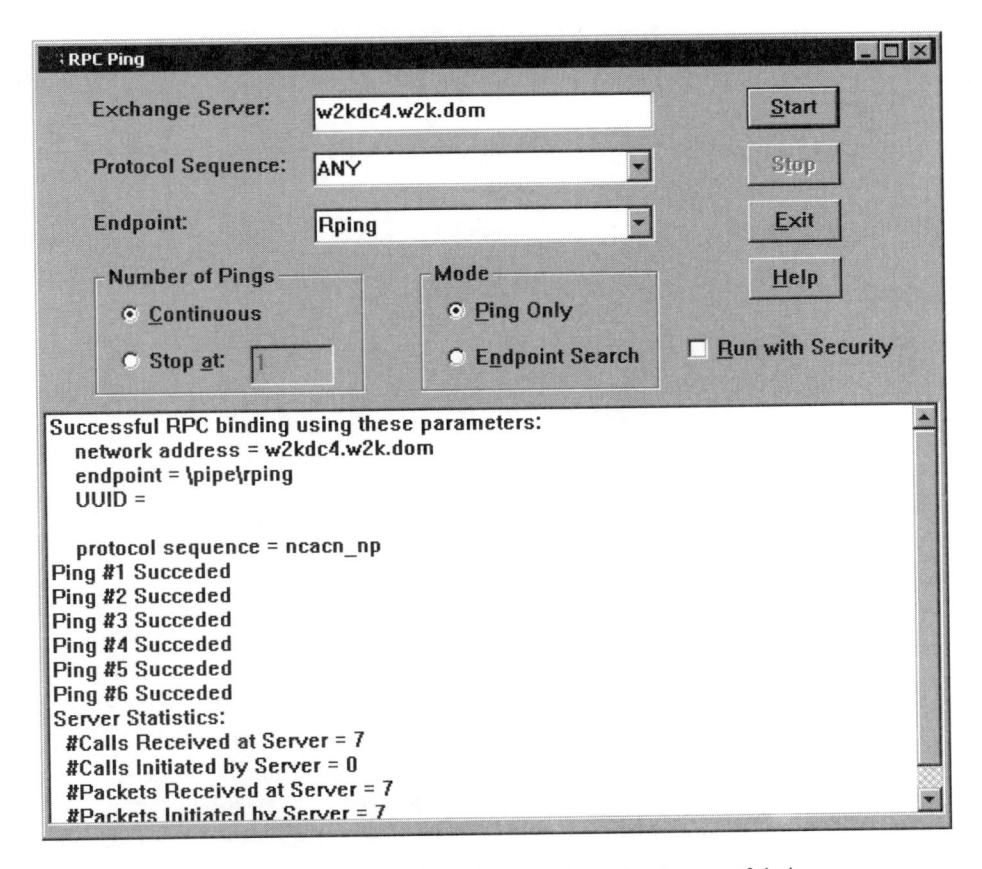

Fig. 8.2. This window contains the result of a few successful pings

A sample result of the *Endpoint Search* operation is shown below. (The settings **Protocol Sequence = ANY** and **Endpoint = Rping** were selected.)

```
Successful RPC binding using these parameters:
  network address = w2kdc4.w2k.dom
  endpoint = \pipe\rping
  UUID =

  protocol sequence = ncacn_np
...searching for uuids and endpoints...
FOUND: uuid for _Rping_ on w2kdc4.w2k.dom's protocol sequence:
ncacn_np
FOUND: endpoint for _Rping_ on w2kdc4.w2k.dom's protocol sequence:
ncacn_np
...
Endpoint Search done.
```

The displayed "FOUND:" strings depend on the types and number of endpoints created on the target computer by RPings.exe.

If a RPC Ping client cannot find the specified server or bind to it using the selected protocol sequence, the following string will appear after all diagnostic messages:

```
Endpoint Search failed to find anything.
```

Some problems cause the appearance of an error window(s), which may contain the return code and the "Unknown exception" message.

To verify authenticated RPCs, check the **Run with Security** box. Normally, this shouldn't affect the results of any operations.

NTFRSutl.exe (RK)

This command-line tool is practically undocumented. You can enter its name at the command prompt and get the list of parameters. This is all the information you have at your disposal. NTFRSutl produces a lot of rather cryptic data. Nevertheless, this tool may be very useful for monitoring, troubleshooting, and — to some extent — managing the File Replication Service (FRS) that replicates the System Volume (SYSVOL) information and Distributed File System (DFS) data. The tool can be run on a local as well as a remote DC. Let's consider some of NTFRSutl's parameters and their usage.

- `ntfrsutl ds` and `ntfrsutl sets` — these commands display the FRS configuration (replication partners, file filters, schedules, etc.). This information can be partially viewed in the **Active Directory Users and Computers** snap-in (see the **File Replication Service** node in the **System** container), and the objects of *FRS Subscriptions* type, which every domain controller has.

- `ntfrsutl stage` — this command displays the disk space used by replicated objects. Normally, when the configuration is stable, this space is 0 KB. Allocated space means that there are the data not yet replicated. The following two commands allow you to see which specific data are to be replicated.

- `ntfrsutl outlog` and `ntfrsutl inlog` — these commands normally display no data. If there are objects to be replicated, the logs contain information that can be useful to an administrator, such as an object file name, and date and time of changes.

- `ntfrsutl poll /now` — this command can override the current schedule and trigger replication of staging data between the current or any specified DC and its partners. Then, you can check logs or staging areas to make sure that all data were replicated.

DsaStat.exe (ST)

This tool allows an administrator to compare full directory replicas stored on different domain controllers, or compare a domain partition with the partial replica stored in Global Catalog. The comparison can be purely statistical or on a per-attribute content basis. The administrator can test either an entire directory partition or a subtree only. By default, all objects are compared, but it is possible to use a LDAP filter and choose only the necessary types of objects. Moreover, you can test either all or only selected attributes, or the attributes replicated to Global Catalog. Thus, DsaStat can serve as an instrument for verifying replication between domain controllers and actual information stored on a DC.

> **TIPS**
>
> Use the servers' DNS rather than NetBIOS names, and the tool will run faster.
>
> The tool may require quite a lot of time to run, and it is not easy to interrupt it. Besides, it produces significant network traffic. Therefore, plan its usage carefully.

Common Statistical Comparison

Let's first see how DsaStat compares directory replicas and produces the statistical data. In this mode the tool only counts the directory objects and displays totals. In the following example, the Configuration partition is verified on DCs from different domains. (If the -b parameter is omitted, all applicable partitions are compared.)

```
C:\>dsastat -s:w2kdc4.w2k.dom;w2kdc2.subdom.w2k.dom
 ↳ -b:CN=Configuration,DC=w2k,DC=dom
Stat-Only mode.
Unsorted mode.
Opening connections...
        w2kdc4.w2k.dom...success.
Connecting to w2kdc4.w2k.dom...
reading...
  **> ntMixedDomain = 0          [0—native mode]
reading...
  **> Options = 1                [1—Global Catalog server]
Setting server as [w2kdc4.w2k.dom] as server to read Config Info...
        w2kdc2.subdom.w2k.dom...success.
Connecting to w2kdc2.subdom.w2k.dom...
reading...
  **> ntMixedDomain = 1          [1—mixed mode]
reading...
  **> Options = 0                [0—"normal" server]
Generation Domain List on server w2kdc4.w2k.dom...
> Searching server for GC attribute partial set on property
attributeId.
> Searching server for GC attribute partial set on property
ldapDisplayName.
Retrieving statistics...
[The command can be cancelled only from this point and afterwards.]
Paged result search...
Paged result search...
  50 entries processed (7 msg queued, 0 obj stored, 0 obj deleted)...
...
2650 entries processed (7 msg queued, 0 obj stored, 0 obj deleted)...
...(Terminated query to w2kdc4.w2k.dom. <No result present in
message>)
...(Terminated query to w2kdc2.subdom.w2k.dom. <No result present in
message>)
```

Chapter 8: Network and Distributed Services

```
2700 entries processed (2 msg queued, 0 obj stored, 0 obj deleted)...

                      -=>>|*** DSA Diagnostics ***|<<=-
Objects per server:

Obj/Svr            w2kdc2.subdom.w2k.dom    w2kdc4.w2k.dom    Total

configuration                        1             1            2
container                           39            39           78
controlAccessRight                  48            48           96
crossRef                             6             6           12
crossRefContainer                    1             1            2
dHCPClass                            1             1            2
dSUISettings                        24            24           48
displaySpecifier                  1152          1152         2304
foreignSecurityPrincipal            16            16           32
infrastructureUpdate                 2             2            4
interSiteTransport                   2             2            4
interSiteTransportContainer          1             1            2
licensingSiteSettings                2             2            4
lostAndFound                         1             1            2
mSMQEnterpriseSettings               1             1            2
nTDSConnection                      20            20           40
nTDSDSA                              6             6           12
nTDSService                          1             1            2
nTDSSiteSettings                     2             2            4
pKICertificateTemplate              24            24           48
physicalLocation                     1             1            2
queryPolicy                          1             1            2
rRASAdministrationDictionary         1             1            2
server                               5             5           10
serversContainer                     2             2            4
site                                 2             2            4
siteLink                             1             1            2
sitesContainer                       1             1            2
subnet                               2             2            4
subnetContainer                      1             1            2
---
                                  1367          1367         2734

                        . . . . . . . . . . . .
```

```
Bytes per object:

configuration                      658
container                          10816
controlAccessRight                 19142
crossRef                           1692
crossRefContainer                  322
dHCPClass                          280
dSUISettings                       8400
displaySpecifier                   416448
foreignSecurityPrincipal           6056
infrastructureUpdate               572
interSiteTransport                 596
interSiteTransportContainer        408
licensingSiteSettings              830
lostAndFound                       334
mSMQEnterpriseSettings             350
nTDSConnection                     8036
nTDSDSA                            1944
nTDSService                        324
nTDSSiteSettings                   760
pKICertificateTemplate             18120
physicalLocation                   420
queryPolicy                        336
rRASAdministrationDictionary       398
server                             1462
serversContainer                   578
site                               548
siteLink                           312
sitesContainer                     288
subnet                             564
subnetContainer                    300
               . . . . . . . . . . . .
Bytes per server:
w2kdc2.subdom.w2k.dom              250647
w2kdc4.w2k.dom                     250647
               . . . . . . . . . . . .
Checking for missing replies...
```

```
            No missing replies!INFO: Server sizes are equal.
*** Identical Directory Information Trees ***
PASS               -=>> PASS <<=-
closing connections...
        w2kdc4.w2k.dom; w2kdc2.subdom.w2k.dom;
```

As you can see, the number of objects of each type is displayed, along with the total size of objects of a specific type.

Analyzing Differences between Partitions

Basically, there are three types of inconsistencies between directory replicas which DsaStat can detect. Let's consider these cases in examples. In each case, we'll compare the results of statistical and full-content comparisons for an object of OU type. For compactness, only the most interesting lines from the DsaStat's screen output are shown.

Different Attribute Values of the Same Object

If the values of one or more attributes of the same object are different on specified domain controllers, statistical comparison only counts total sizes and produces the following result:

```
Checking for missing replies...
       No missing replies!INFO: Server sizes are not equal (min=...,
max=...).
*** Identical Directory Information Trees ***
PASS              -=>> PASS <<=
```

You can conclude from such an output that the replicas differ, and nothing more.

Full-content comparison detects both the directory object (`CN=John Smith,...`) and the attribute name (`description`), for example:

```
FAIL  Value [0] of Attr[description] did not compare on dn
[<GUID=f905066ccb49e1439bc520f45c3b223f>;
<SID=010500000000000515000000e80b5980789a7e9e6602ab741e0c0000>;CN=John
Smith,OU=Staff,DC=w2k,DC=dom]
                     Servers [w2kdc4.w2k.dom]~[w2kdc3.w2k.dom]
FAIL   FAIL[1]: mismatch with current DIT image
...
Checking for missing replies...
```

```
        No missing replies!INFO: Server sizes are not equal (min=...,
max=...).
*** Different Directory Information Trees. 1 errors (see above). ***
FAIL             -=>> FAIL <<=-
```

Thus, you can see both the number of errors and their location.

Different Number of Attributes of the Same Object

If the replicas of the same object have different numbers of attributes, the statistical comparison, again, reports only that the replicas' sizes are not equal. Let's look at the results produced by full-content comparison. (Notice that the -t:FALSE parameter is used.)

```
C:\>dsastat -s:w2kdc4.w2k.dom;w2kdc3.w2k.dom -b:OU=Staff,DC=w2k,DC=dom
 -t:FALSE
Unsorted mode.
...
FAIL  AttrCount mismatch : Attrcount[9]@Server[w2kdc4.w2k.dom] !=
Attrcount[8]@Server[w2kdc3.w2k.dom]
for Dn
'<GUID=008805cd96c1664a35a6e10632d375ad>;OU=Staff,DC=w2k,DC=dom'
********** Dumping Attribute List **********
---------------> Server [w2kdc4.w2k.dom] <---------------
Attr[0] = description
Attr[1] = gPLink
Attr[2] = name
Attr[3] = nTSecurityDescriptor
Attr[4] = objectCategory
Attr[5] = objectClass
Attr[6] = ou
Attr[7] = replPropertyMetaData
Attr[8] = whenCreated
---------------> Server [w2kdc3.w2k.dom] <---------------
Attr[0] = gPLink
Attr[1] = name
Attr[2] = nTSecurityDescriptor
Attr[3] = objectCategory
Attr[4] = objectClass
Attr[5] = ou
```

```
Attr[6] = replPropertyMetaData
Attr[7] = whenCreated
FAIL  FAIL[1]: mismatch with current DIT image
...
Checking for missing replies...
        No missing replies!INFO: Server sizes are not equal
(min=11270, max=11292).
*** Different Directory Information Trees. 1 errors (see above). ***
FAIL              -=>> FAIL <<=-
```

As you can see, the tool displays the number of attributes for each object replica, shows the DN of the object, and then lists the attribute for each replica. The missing attribute is easily found.

Different Number of Objects

In the following example, the user *user01* has been deleted from the *Staff* OU on one domain controller, and the changes have not yet been replicated to another DC. In this case, both statistical and full-content comparisons report that the test has failed, and that there has been a "Server total object count mismatch". A full-content test, however, displays specific information about the error: the type and name of the missing object. Look at the following sample output:

```
...
Objects per server:

Obj/Svr               w2kdc3.w2k.dom  w2kdc4.w2k.dom  Total

computer                     1              1           2
contact                      1              1           2
group                        6              6          12
organizationalUnit           2              2           4
user                        15             14          29
volume                       3              3           6
---
                            28             27          55
FAIL  Server total object count mismatch
...
Bytes per server:

w2kdc3.w2k.dom                      11292
```

```
w2kdc4.w2k.dom                11072
                    . . . . . . . . . . . . . . .
Checking for missing replies...
Fail [2]: missing 1 replies for
'<GUID=e3806dfa0bb96e4e99aa47e6dbb26ad5>;<SID=010500000000000515
0000e80b5980789a7e9e6602ab743e0c0000>;CN=user01,OU=Staff,DC=w2k,DC=dom
'
INFO: Server sizes are not equal (min=11292, max=11072).
*** Different Directory Information Trees. 2 errors (see above). ***
FAIL                -=>> FAIL <<=-
```

Replication Diagnostics Tool (RepAdmin.exe) (ST)

RepAdmin is the only tool that allows an administrator to view and manage Active Directory replication topology from command prompt or batch files. This tool, coupled with DsaStat, helps to troubleshoot Active Directory consistency problems at a forest-wide level.

I'll consider some of the most frequently used options of this tool. Some of these options may seem to be too complicated. However, if you understand the Active Directory replication model well, you'll quickly learn how to use the tool in the most effective way.

> **NOTE**
>
> To use RepAdmin, you should be logged on to the network as a domain administrator. Some operations can only be performed on a domain controller rather than a client computer.

Monitoring Replication Topology

Triggering KCC

Normally, the Knowledge Consistency Checker periodically verifies and automatically rebuilds the replication topology. You may want to forcibly start this process after some topology changes (e. g. after deleting connections). Look at the example:

```
C:\>repadmin /kcc w2kdc4.w2k.dom
Consistency check on w2kdc4.w2k.dom successful.
```

Viewing Replication Partners (/showreps)

The first and most important step for managing replication is to enumerate partners (neighbors) which have connections to the specified DC, and then see the replication topology for each naming context. (This information is used with many other RepAdmin's parameters.) The following example was obtained for a forest that consists of two domains and two sites. The root domain *w2k.dom* is located in the *W2K-site* and contains two DCs (*W2KDC2 and W2KDC3*). The child domain *subdom.w2k.dom* is located in the *Remote-site* and has a single DC (*W2KDC2*). Let's see what kind of information RepAdmin displays for the specified DC. (In-line comments are in bold brackets.)

```
C:\>repadmin /showreps w2kdc4.w2k.dom
W2K-site\W2KDC4
DSA Options : IS_GC      [The specified DC is a Global Catalog server]
objectGuid  : 09317c0e-fb52-4a63-a9d0-8899068bc2a0  [By using this
GUID, you can bind to the DSA object named CN=NTDS Settings,CN=W2KDC4,
CN=Servers,CN=W2K-site,CN=Sites,CN=Configuration,DC=w2k,DC=dom.]
invocationID: c6357684-efca-441d-aa1b-fa5adbe75a02


==== INBOUND NEIGHBORS ======================================

CN=Schema,CN=Configuration,DC=w2k,DC=dom    [The Schema and
Configuration partitions are replicated among all DCs in the forest.]
    Remote-site\W2KDC2 via RPC
        objectGuid: 161d093e-426e-47cc-8da6-f40ce5bb7e10
        Last attempt @ 2000-10-22 17:26.53 was successful.
        [Last replication time and the result of this operation is
        displayed for each connection.]
    W2K-site\W2KDC3 via RPC
        objectGuid: a9d28d8e-e681-449f-b1be-38dadf6f4c06
        Last attempt @ 2000-10-22 18:18.23 was successful.

CN=Configuration,DC=w2k,DC=dom
    Remote-site\W2KDC2 via RPC
        objectGuid: 161d093e-426e-47cc-8da6-f40ce5bb7e10
        Last attempt @ 2000-10-22 17:26.53 was successful.
    W2K-site\W2KDC3 via RPC
```

```
                    objectGuid: a9d28d8e-e681-449f-b1be-38dadf6f4c06
                    Last attempt @ 2000-10-22 18:18.23 was successful.
    DC=w2k,DC=dom        [Domain partition is only replicated among DCs that
    serve the same domain.]
        W2K-site\W2KDC3 via RPC
                    objectGuid: a9d28d8e-e681-449f-b1be-38dadf6f4c06
                    Last attempt @ 2000-10-22 18:18.23 was successful.

    DC=subdom,DC=w2k,DC=dom    [This domain partition is also partially
    replicated to this DC, since it is a GC server.]
        Remote-site\W2KDC2 via RPC
                    objectGuid: 161d093e-426e-47cc-8da6-f40ce5bb7e10
                    Last attempt @ 2000-10-22 17:26.53 was successful.

    ==== OUTBOUND NEIGHBORS FOR CHANGE NOTIFICATIONS ============

    CN=Schema,CN=Configuration,DC=w2k,DC=dom
        W2K-site\W2KDC3 via RPC
                    objectGuid: a9d28d8e-e681-449f-b1be-38dadf6f4c06
        Remote-site\W2KDC2 via RPC
                    objectGuid: 161d093e-426e-47cc-8da6-f40ce5bb7e10

    CN=Configuration,DC=w2k,DC=dom
        W2K-site\W2KDC3 via RPC
                    objectGuid: a9d28d8e-e681-449f-b1be-38dadf6f4c06

    DC=w2k,DC=dom
        W2K-site\W2KDC3 via RPC
                    objectGuid: a9d28d8e-e681-449f-b1be-38dadf6f4c06
```

NOTE

In fact, the W2KDC4 and W2KDC2 domain controllers are connected by the IP transport (since the DCs are related to the different sites). However, both IP and RPC transports are displayed as "via RPC". The /showconn parameter (see below) displays more detailed information.

Verbose mode displays additional information, for example:

```
    ...
    CN=Schema,CN=Configuration,DC=w2k,DC=dom
        Remote-site\W2KDC2 via RPC
```

Chapter 8: Network and Distributed Services 215

```
        objectGuid: 161d093e-426e-47cc-8da6-f40ce5bb7e10
        Address: 161d093e-426e-47cc-8da6-f40ce5bb7e10._msdcs.w2k.dom
        ntdsDsa invocationId: 8ccaf13e-d8bf-4002-ae30-a7b2de062c2b
        WRITEABLE DO_SCHEDULED_SYNCS COMPRESS_CHANGES
    ↳ NO_CHANGE_NOTIFICATIONS
        USNs: 25321/OU, 25321/PU
        Last attempt @ 2000-10-28 20:08.56 was successful.
W2K-site\W2KDC3 via RPC
        objectGuid: a9d28d8e-e681-449f-b1be-38dadf6f4c06
        Address: a9d28d8e-e681-449f-b1be-38dadf6f4c06._msdcs.w2k.dom
        ntdsDsa invocationId: 7528dbeb-ddf7-45e6-9c8c-d67bb5ae89e6
        WRITEABLE SYNC_ON_STARTUP DO_SCHEDULED_SYNCS
        USNs: 51730/OU, 51730/PU
        Last attempt @ 2000-10-28 21:33.52 was successful.
...
```

Look at the highlighted flags from this output and notice the following:

- Both inter- and intra-site replications are scheduled (but these are the different schedules!)
- Intra-site replication is compressed
- There is no *change notification* between DCs related to different sites (this is the default state)
- DCs in the same site are synchronized on their startup

Viewing Connections with Replication Partners (/*showconn*)

To display the most comprehensive information on connections that have been established for a DC, use the /showconn parameter. You should specify the DNS name of the DC that will serve as the source of information, and the GUID (or the DSA's distinguished name) of the DC you are interested in. For example, the W2KDC4 domain controller from the sample configuration has two inbound connections:

```
C:\>repadmin /showconn w2kdc4.w2k.dom 09317c0e-fb52-4a63-a9d0-
8899068bc2a0
Show Connection Objects
```

```
<GUID=09317c0e-fb52-4a63-a9d0-8899068bc2a0>:
    W2KDC4\00cfca04-dcaf-4c92-b5bb-c634455d7d40
        enabledConnection: TRUE
        fromServer: W2K-site\W2KDC3
        TransportType: intrasite RPC
        options: isGenerated
         ReplicatesNC:
CN=Schema,CN=Configuration,DC=w2k,DC=dom
         Reason: RingTopology
         ReplicatesNC: DC=w2k,DC=dom
         Reason: RingTopology
         ReplicatesNC: CN=Configuration,DC=w2k,DC=dom
         Reason: RingTopology
        whenChanged: 20000705222131.0Z
        whenCreated: 20000705222028.0Z
    W2KDC4\8f4339b2-e731-4af5-9691-c159aaf2c349
        enabledConnection: TRUE
        fromServer: Remote-Site\W2KDC2
        TransportType: IP
        options: isGenerated overrideNotifyDefault
         ReplicatesNC: CN=Configuration,DC=w2k,DC=dom
         ReplicatesNC: DC=subdom,DC=w2k,DC=dom
        whenChanged: 20000705222028.0Z
        whenCreated: 20000705222028.0Z
```

Notice that two different transport types — one for intra-site and one for inter-site replication — are displayed.

Triggering Replication Events

By using RepAdmin, you can initiate replication events very flexibly. The following options are available:

- ❏ One directory partition is replicated from one DC to another
- ❏ One directory partition is replicated from all neighbors
- ❏ A cross-site replication of a directory partition can be performed
- ❏ Replication can be switched from pull mode to push mode

Let's consider them in detail.

Replication between Two Neighbors

To perform the most atomic replication operation, you must specify a directory context, the DNS name of the target server, and the GUID of the source server (from which the changes are copied). For example, to replicate the domain partition, use a command similar to:

```
C:\>repadmin /sync DC=w2k,DC=dom w2kdc4.w2k.dom a9d28d8e-e681-449f-b1be-38dadf6f4c06
Sync from a9d28d8e-e681-449f-b1be-38dadf6f4c06 to w2kdc4.w2k.dom completed successfully.
```

You must wait until the operation completes. Or you can start the operation synchronically and check the replication queue to see whether the operation has completed. To trigger a full replication, you can, for example, use the following command:

```
C:\>repadmin /sync DC=w2k,DC=dom w2kdc4.w2k.dom a9d28d8e-e681-449f-b1be-38dadf6f4c06 /full /async
Successfully enqueued sync from a9d28d8e-e681-449f-b1be-38dadf6f4c06 to w2kdc4.w2k.dom.
```

Then, to monitor the operation, use the command

```
C:\>repadmin /queue
```

Here is a sample output:

```
Queue contains 1 items.
Current task began executing at 2000-10-28 22:12.35.
Task has been executing for 0 minutes, 3 seconds.

[353] Enqueued 2000-10-28 22:12.35 at priority 90
    SYNC FROM SOURCE
    NC DC=w2k,DC=dom
    DSA W2K-site\W2KDC3
    DSA objectGuid a9d28d8e-e681-449f-b1be-38dadf6f4c06
    DSA transport addr a9d28d8e-e681-449f-b1be-38dadf6f4c06._msdcs.w2k.dom
    ASYNCHRONOUS_OPERATION WRITEABLE FULL
```

Replication from All Partners

The /syncall parameter can be used to synchronize a directory partition between a DC and *all* its partners. Sometimes, the command fails. Look, for example, at the following output produced by a command:

```
C:\>repadmin /syncall w2kdc4.w2k.dom DC=w2k,DC=dom
```

```
CALLBACK MESSAGE: Win32 error 1722 contacting server (network error):
    161d093e-426e-47cc-8da6-f40ce5bb7e10._msdcs.w2k.dom
CALLBACK MESSAGE: The following replication is in progress:
    From: a9d28d8e-e681-449f-b1be-38dadf6f4c06._msdcs.w2k.dom
    To  : 09317c0e-fb52-4a63-a9d0-8899068bc2a0._msdcs.w2k.dom
CALLBACK MESSAGE: The following replication completed successfully:
    From: a9d28d8e-e681-449f-b1be-38dadf6f4c06._msdcs.w2k.dom
    To  : 09317c0e-fb52-4a63-a9d0-8899068bc2a0._msdcs.w2k.dom
CALLBACK MESSAGE: SyncAll Finished.

SyncAll reported the following errors:
Win32 error 1722 contacting server (network error):
    161d093e-426e-47cc-8da6-f40ce5bb7e10._msdcs.w2k.dom
```

The error reported means that "The RPC server is unavailable." You can get a text description of a message by running RepAdmin with the /showmsg parameter and specifying the error code (see below).

The command, when run, displays all partners' names, and if successful reports that

```
SyncAll terminated with no errors.
```

ATTENTION!

If you don't specify a naming context in the repadmin /syncall command, only the Configuration partition is replicated.

Use the repadmin /syncall /h command to see help information for additional parameters, two of which are especially important:

- /e — enables cross-site replication. You can see the difference if, for example, you try to synchronize the Configuration partition by using a command with this parameter, and then without it.

- /P — reverses the direction of replication. When this parameter is used, the changes are propagated from the specified server to all partners (vice versa by default).

Failed Replications

If a replication partner is not available, or a network connection doesn't work, the scheduled replications periodically fail. The following command allows you to see the statistics on failed replications:

```
C:\>repadmin /failcache w2kdc4.w2k.dom
```

Chapter 8: Network and Distributed Services

```
==== KCC DSA CONNECTION FAILURES ============================
(none)

==== KCC DSA LINK FAILURES ===================================
    Remote-site\W2KDC2
        objectGuid: 161d093e-426e-47cc-8da6-f40ce5bb7e10
        2 consecutive failures since 2000-10-22 18:32.57.
    W2K-site\W2KDC3
        objectGuid: a9d28d8e-e681-449f-b1be-38dadf6f4c06
        No failures.
```

Viewing Directory Changes

RepAdmin has a few options that can be used for testing the actual state of domain controllers. You can easily determine whether changes were made on a DC, and whether directory partitions are synchronized on different DCs.

Is the Server up to Date?

Suppose we want to determine whether the domain partition (*DC=w2k,DC=dom*) is synchronized on two domain controllers — *W2KDC4* and *W2KDC3*. We first need to find the highest USN on the first server. Use the following command:

```
C:\>repadmin /showvector DC=w2k,DC=dom w2kdc4.w2k.dom
W2K-site\W2KDC4                             @ USN 43490
1ee17992-dea9-423d-9693-3864297217f8        @ USN 4870
W2K-site\W2KDC3                             @ USN 51877
b6b967e6-ba90-4eb3-abbf-b20cc31460b3        @ USN 7541
W2K-site\W2KDC4                             @ USN 122618
d24ccd55-52e2-44c6-a11e-d227b2634754        @ USN 5097
```

Then we must check the value known to the second server. We should specify: the invocationID of the first server (see description of the /showreps parameter above), the USN, and the DNS name of either DC:

```
C:\>repadmin /propcheck DC=w2k,DC=dom c6357684-efca-441d-aa1b-
fa5adbe75a02 122618 w2kdc4.w2k.dom
W2K-site\W2KDC4: yes (USN 122618)
W2K-site\W2KDC3: ** NO! ** (USN 122593)
```

As you can see, the second server holds an older USN. If we run the command again after replicating changes from W2KDC4 to W2KDC3, the result should be the following:

```
G:\>repadmin /propcheck DC=w2k,DC=dom c6357684-efca-441d-aa1b-
fa5adbe75a02 122618 w2kdc4.w2k.dom
W2K-site\W2KDC4: yes (JSN 122618)
W2K-site\W2KDC3: yes (JSN 122618)
```

Displaying Replication Metadata

By seeing replication metadata for a directory object, you can check consistency between different replicas — compare attribute versions and USN numbers on different domain controllers. Also, you can see on which DC ("originating DSA") the attributes were changed last time. The following example shows metadata for an OU object. (The output is compressed horizontally to fit the page.)

```
C:\>repadmin /showmeta OU=Staff,DC=w2k,DC=dom w2kdc4.w2k.dom

13 entries.

Loc.USN     Originating DSA   Org.USN    Org.Time/Date       Ver Attribute
=======     ===============   =======    =============       === =========
   4300     W2K-site\W2KDC4      4300    2000-09-03 20:28.12   1 objectClass
  56898     W2K-site\W2KDC3      4306    2000-12-10 19:50.43   2 c
 122308     W2K-site\W2KDC4    122308    2001-01-28 20:42.22   5 ou
  56898     W2K-site\W2KDC3      4306    2000-12-10 19:50.43   3 description
   4300     W2K-site\W2KDC4      4300    2000-09-03 20:28.12   1
    instanceType
   4300     W2K-site\W2KDC4      4300    2000-09-03 20:28.12   1 whenCreated
  56898     W2K-site\W2KDC3      4306    2000-12-10 19:50.43   2 co
 118271     W2K-site\W2KDC4    118271    2001-01-27 17:09.08  86
    nTSecurityDescriptor
 122308     W2K-site\W2KDC4    122308    2001-01-28 20:42.22   5 name
  56398     W2K-site\W2KDC3      4306    2000-12-10 19:50.43   2 countryCode
   4300     W2K-site\W2KDC4      4300    2000-09-03 20:28.12   1
    objectCategory
  48227     W2K-site\W2KDC4     48227    2000-11-24 18:32.22   4 gPLink
  24638     W2K-site\W2KDC4     24638    2000-10-07 12:14.55   1 gPOptions
```

This output is easier to analyze when compared to the metadata information produced by the Ldp.exe tool (see Fig. 9.15 in *Chapter 9, "Manipulating Active*

Directory Objects"). As you can see, the attribute names are displayed here in text format.

> **NOTE**
>
> If an authoritative restore is performed on a DC, the attribute version numbers will have large values, since by default versions are increased by 100,000 for each "normal" restore operation (i. e. if the `verinc` parameter is not used).

Registering Changes Made on a Specific DC

It is possible to register all of the changes made on a specific domain controller since defined time. The following command analyzes the current state of the domain partition and writes the result to a file:

```
C:\>repadmin /getchanges DC=w2k,DC=dom w2kdc3.w2k.dom /cookie:log1.txt
Using cookie from file log1.txt (228 bytes)

==== SOURCE DSA: w2kdc3.w2k.dom ====

No changes.
New cookie written to file log1.txt (228 bytes)
```

After some time elapses, you can re-run the command:

```
C:\>repadmin /getchanges DC=w2k,DC=dom w2kdc3.w2k.dom /cookie:log1.txt
Using cookie from file log1.txt (228 bytes)

==== SOURCE DSA: w2kdc3.w2k.dom ====

Objects returned: 3
(0) modify CN=Backup Operators,CN=Builtin,DC=w2k,DC=dom
        1> objectGUID: 200f9656-d18d-47f4-ab38-c31fd1d4e19a
        1> instanceType: 4
(1) modify CN=John Smith,OU=STAFF,DC=w2k,DC=dom
        1> objectGUID: 6c0605f9-49cb-43e1-9bc5-20f45c3b223f
        1> instanceType: 4
        1> nTSecurityDescriptor: <1516 byte blob>
        1> userPrincipalName: jsmith@w2k
(2) delete OU=Ouname\
```

```
DEL:ce5ee5d8-7bd5-47fa-ba40-ad34fe4f45e0,CN=Deleted
Objects,DC=w2k,DC=dom
        1> parentGUID: 8f627029-b7ec-4610-94d5-c62c727b7e85
        1> objectGUID: ce5ee5d8-7bd5-47fa-ba40-ad34fe4f45e0
        1> instanceType: 4
        1> isDeleted: TRUE
        1> name: Ouname
DEL:ce5ee5d8-7bd5-47fa-ba40-ad34fe4f45e0
New cookie written to file log1.txt (228 bytes)
```

As you can see, two objects have been modified, and one object has been deleted. The time stamp is renewed, and only new changes will be registered from that moment.

The same information will be displayed if you run the command

```
C:\>repadmin /getchanges DC=w2k,DC=dom w2kdc4.w2k.dom a9d28d8e-e681-
449f-b1be-38dadf6f4c06
```

Notice that the command contains the domain partition name, the DNS name of a replication partner, and the GUID of the initial domain controller (w2kdc3.w2k.dom). This command displays changes made before the replication is performed and two directory replicas are synchronized.

Comparing Information on Different Domain Controllers

The command that compares the partition replicas stored on different servers must contain the DNS name of a "reference" server and the GUID of a "source" server. All changes made in the source server will be registered. As a matter of fact, this command performs the same job as the DsaStat tool does. The output shown below was obtained at the time of adding 1000 new users to the server W2KDC3.

```
C:\>repadmin /getchanges DC=w2k,DC=dom w2kdc4.w2k.dom a9d28d8e-e681-
449f-b1be-38dadf6f4c06 /statistics
Building starting position from destination server w2kdc4.w2k.dom

Source Neighbor:
DC=w2k,DC=dom
    W2K-site\W2KDC3 via RPC
        objectGuid: a9d28d8e-e681-449f-b1be-38dadf6f4c06
        Address: a9d28d8e-e681-449f-b1be-38dadf6f4c06._msdcs.w2k.dom
        ntdsDsa invocationId: 7528dbeb-ddf7-45e6-9c8c-d67bb5ae89e6
```

Chapter 8: Network and Distributed Services

```
            WRITEABLE SYNC_ON_STARTUP DO_SCHEDULED_SYNCS
            USNs: 45417/OU, 45417/PU
            Last attempt @ 2000-10-28 16:48.51 was successful.

Destination's Up To Dateness Vector:
09317c0e-fb52-4a63-a9d0-8899068bc2a0 @ USN 43490
1ee17992-dea9-423d-9693-3864297217f8 @ USN 4870
7528dbeb-ddf7-45e6-9c8c-d67bb5ae89e6 @ USN 45417
b6b967e6-ba90-4eb3-abbf-b20cc31460b3 @ USN 7541
c6357684-efca-441d-aa1b-fa5adbe75a02 @ USN 119925
d24ccd55-52e2-44c6-a11e-d227b2634754 @ USN 5097

== SOURCE DSA: a9d28d8e-e681-449f-b1be-38dadf6f4c06._msdcs.w2k.dom ==

*********Cumulative packet totals********
Packets:                 1
Objects:                 100
Object Additions:        100
Object Modifications:    0
Object Deletions:        0
Object Moves:            0
Attributes:              1691
Values:                  1989
Dn-valued Attributes:    100
MaxDnVals on any attr:1
#dnvals 1-250   251-500 501-750 751-1000       1001+
add     100     0       0       0       0
mod     0       0       0       0       0
**************************************************
...
...
*********Grand total********
Packets:                 6
Objects:                 585
Object Additions:        582
Object Modifications:    3
Object Deletions:        0
Object Moves:            0
Attributes:              9894
Values:                  11638
```

```
Dn-valued Attributes: 582
MaxDnVals on any attr:1
    #dnvals  1-250    251-500  501-750  751-1000    1001+
    add      582      0        0        0           0
    mod      0        0        0        0           0
****************************************************
```

If both replicas are synchronized, the command reports

`No changes.`

Auxiliary Options

Setting DSA Options

Each Directory System Agent (DSA) is represented in Active Directory by an object of the *nTDSDSA* class named *CN=NTDS Settings* that belongs to the appropriate server object in the *Configuration* partition. (You can view the attributes of DSA objects with the **ADSI Edit** snap-in.) DSA objects have the *options* attribute, which significantly affects their state and behavior. An administrator can set the value of this attribute by using RepAdmin with an undocumented parameter **/options**. Let's discuss a few examples.

The following command detects that the specified domain controller is a Global Catalog server:

```
C:\>repadmin /options w2kdc4.w2k.dom
Current options: IS_GC
```

The *options* attribute is equal to 1 in this case. You can set the IS_GC flag to promote a DC to GC server. Usually, this operation is performed in the **Active Directory Sites and Services** snap-in.

The following two parameters allow you to "isolate" a DC from its replication partners for troubleshooting or some other purpose. The next example shows that replication *from* the specified DC (outbound replication) is disabled:

```
C:\>repadmin /options w2kdc2.subdom.w2k.dom
Current options: DISABLE_OUTBOUND_REPL
```

The *options* attribute is equal to 4 (hex) in that case.

The state of inbound replication (from partners *to* a specified DC) is determined by the *DISABLE_INBOUND_REPL* flag. (This flag corresponds to an *options* attribute value equal to 2.) You can set both flags and totally disable replication for the DC.

To set a flag, specify it with a "+" (plus) sign. To clear a flag, use "−" (minus). For example, the following command clears the flag and re-enables outbound replication from the DC:

```
C:\>repadmin /options w2kdc2.subdom.w2k.dom -DISABLE_OUTBOUND_REPL
Current options: DISABLE_OUTBOUND_REPL
New options    : (none)
```

Every "disable replication" operation is registered in the *Directory Service* log (Event ID 1113, 1114, 1115, and 1116). Look at two following examples:

```
Event Type: Warning
Event Source:      NTDS General
Event Category:    Replication
Event ID:   1115
...
Computer:   W2KDC4
Description:
Outbound replication is disabled.
```

When replication is enabled, an informational event is also registered:

```
Event Type: Information
Event Source:      NTDS General
Event Category:    Replication
Event ID:   1114
...
Computer:   W2KDC4
Description:
Inbound replication is re-enabled.
```

Converting Directory Time (*/showtime*)

RepAdmin can convert time values stored in Active Directory into a readable format. (See also NLtest description at the beginning of this chapter). Let's convert the same value *126191956001314960*. Enter `repadmin /showtime` at the command prompt, and paste the value in. Erase the seven rightmost digits and press <Enter>. The result should be the following:

```
C:\>repadmin /showtime 12619195600
```

```
12619195600 = 0x2f029a4d0 = 00-11-20 12:06.40 UTC = 2000-11-20
06:06.40 local
```

You may notice that both UTC and local time are displayed.

Displaying Error Description (/showmsg)

RepAdmin.exe has an option that will help you in writing and debugging ADSI scripts and application and analyzing event logs, as well as in many other cases. You can use this utility rather than searching the documentation for information on each error. The utility provides many more options than the `net helpmsg` command does. RepAdmin.exe can display error text for both Win32 error codes (including errors for ADSI 2.5) and generic COM error codes.

You can specify an error code in either form: as a long integer (e. g. **-2147016684**) or a hexadecimal value (e. g. **0x80072014**; the **0x** prefix is mandatory, don't forget to add this prefix if you have copied a code from the Event Viewer). Short integers, such as **8453**, are also acceptable. Here is an example of using this parameter:

```
C:\repadmin /showmsg 0x80072014
-2147016684 = 0x80072014 = "The requested operation did not satisfy
one or more constraints associated with the class of the object."
```

Active Directory Replication Monitor (ReplMon.exe) (ST)

Active Directory Replication Monitor is a GUI tool that is exclusively intended for monitoring and managing all kinds of replication in Windows 2000-based domains. By using this tool, you can monitor and register all replication events, force replication, start generating replication topology, view Global Catalog and bridgehead servers, and view trusts and replication metadata for an Active Directory object. The list of options could be continued. The tool has a simple and friendly user interface.

Preparation Steps

After the tool's start-up, you should create a list of monitored servers. This might be a tiresome operation, but you only need to perform it once. When all necessary servers have been added to ReplMon, save the current configuration by clicking **Save Monitored List As** in the **File** menu. The next time the tool is running,

Chapter 8: Network and Distributed Services

choose the **Open Script** command and load the necessary configuration. A sample screen of the ReplMon's main window is shown in Fig. 8.3.

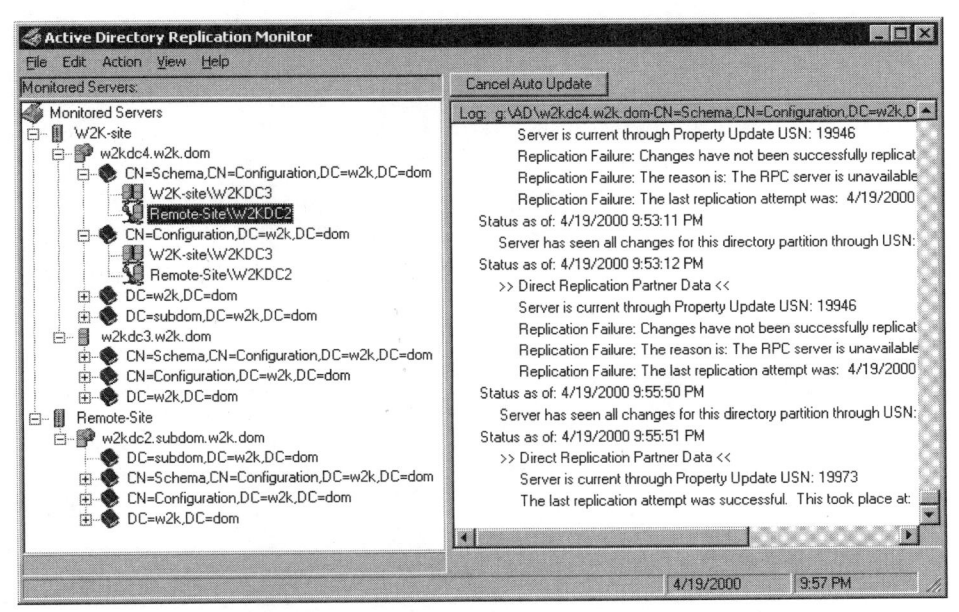

Fig. 8.3. The main window of ReplMon, where you can browse the domain tree and see log files for selected domain partition and replication partner

ReplMon uses various icons to represent a monitored server and its replication partners, which helps an administrator to easily determine replication status. The meanings of icons are described in the table below.

Icon	Description
	Directory partition that has replication problems
	Bridgehead server
	Global Catalog server
	Direct replication partner that has encountered replication problems
	Successfully replicated direct replication partner
	Transitive replication partner

Log Files

By default, ReplMon writes all *Replication Status Logs* to the **My Documents** folder of the current logged on user. The log name combines the domain controller's DNS name, directory partition name and a replication partner down-level name. You can assign a different location if you like. Click **Options** in the **View** menu, check the **Default Path for Replication Status Logs** box, and enter the necessary path. (To troubleshoot replication problems, you can also enable debug logging, allowing ReplMon to register every performed operation.) ReplMon updates the Replication Status Logs at its start-up, and you can specify a time interval for automatic updating. If you do so, all replication activity for monitored servers will be registered in the logs.

Managing Replication

By using ReplMon, you can initiate any replication events possible for the selected domain controller. Most operations are started through the context menu of the selected DC. These operations are quite simple to learn, and all the tool's features are visible in the menu.

ReplMon has a very useful feature that allows you to view performance data normally available through the **Performance** snap-in. (See the "Monitoring Replication" section in *Chapter 2, "Configuring and Troubleshooting Windows 2000-based Domains"*.) First, open the **Performance** snap-in and choose the counters you are interested in. Then start ReplMon, click **Options** in the **View** menu, and select the **Status Logging** tab. Check the **Performance Statistics** box, click **Add,** and enter the counter name. Repeat this step if necessary. Now you can select a DC and choose the **Show Current Performance Data** command from the context menu. Note that this option only works with domain controllers from the same site.

Chapter 9
Manipulating Active Directory Objects

Finding Objects in Active Directory

Since Active Directory may consist of a huge number of directory objects, and may also have a complex structure of domains, it's necessary to have the ability to quickly locate or pick out the desired objects. You may use the following tools for that purpose:

- **Active Directory Users and Computers** snap-in — This snap-in has a filter option that allows you to narrow the scope of viewed objects. The *Find* option allows you to locate and select objects for manipulating in the domains as well as in the entire forest (since it is able to work with Global Catalog.) (The snap-in was discussed in *Chapter 4, "Domain Manipulation Tools".*)
- Search.vbs — A script from the *Support Tools* pack. Can search only in one domain, and works only with the LDAP provider.
- AdsVw.exe and Ldp.exe — These powerful tools allow you to compose complex queries and apply them as to a domain as well as to the entire forest. AdsVw.exe can open a number of query windows simultaneously. (Both of these tools are described later in this chapter.)

Active Directory Search Tool (Search.vbs) (ST)

The *Search.vbs* script is a simple, handy tool that allows you to retrieve the attributes of the specified objects. By default, the script displays the *AdsPaths* of the children of the object specified by its distinguished name. These children may be of any type.

Administrators or any users may use the script on any Windows platform, provided that the Windows Scripting Host (WSH) is installed. This is a unique feature, since the other search tools require Windows 2000.

> **CAUTION!**
>
> The *Search.vbs* script doesn't display certain object attributes, such as *objectGUID*, *objectSID*, *lastLogon* (these are attributes of "complex" types, such as OctetString, LargeInteger, etc.), and some others. What's worse, the script has an internal bug, which sometimes produces an erroneous output when such attributes are included in the returned parameters list (for instance, search for a user's *objectSID*, *lastLogon*, and *cn* attributes).

Analyzing the listing of the script will help you to better understand the methods of retrieving data of various types (see also *Chapter 13, "Active Directory Service Interfaces (ADSI)"*) while composing your own scripts.

Output Data Format

The script outputs the found data as a sequence of lines in the following format:

```
attributeName object# [=] propertyValue
```

If the script cannot *display* a property value, it outputs only the first two components, e. g. "objectSid 1". If a property has an *empty* value or is *not defined*, the "=" character is added, e. g. "description 1 =".

A pair of examples of using Search.vbs are presented below.

Example 1. Searching for an Object Using Its GUID

Suppose you want to verify whether a known GUID really belongs to a directory object, or you want to check the name of this object. You may use the following command:

```
search "LDAP://<GUID=ac8a4d9c59d0b54782ebb14b8989e57e>" /S:Base
```

The resulting output will be similar to:

```
<LDAP://<GUID=ac8a4d9c59d0b54782ebb14b8989e57e>>;(ObjectCategory=*);ADsPath;Base
Finished the query.
Found 1 objects.
ADsPath 1 = LDAP://OU=ADMINs,DC=w2k,DC=dom
```

You may also widen the scope of the search (i. e. select the /S:oneLevel or /S:subTree parameter), or specify display of additional attributes.

> **NOTE**
>
> If the object's name is all you want to know, you may also use the *Guid2obj.exe* utility from the *Windows 2000 Resource Kit*. You provide the object GUID as a parameter, and the tool retrieves the distinguished name of the object from the nearest global catalog server.

Example 2. Finding All Policies in a Domain

Sometimes, it's necessary to know what policies (GPOs) exist in a domain, and which names they go by in administrative snap-ins. You could look up the value of the *displayName* attribute for each policy object in the CN=Policies,CN=System subtree of a domain container. But a much faster way is to use Search.vbs. The query might look like this :

```
search "LDAP://DC=w2k,DC=dom" /C:(objectClass=GroupPolicyContainer)
    /S:subtree /P:cn,displayName
```

Resulting output:

```
<LDAP://DC=w2k,DC=dom>;((objectClass=GroupPolicyContainer));
cn,displayName;subtree
Finished the query.
Found 5 objects.
cn 1 = {31B2F340-016D-11D2-945F-00C04FB984F9}
displayName 1 = Default Domain Policy
cn 2 = {6AC1786C-016F-11D2-945F-00C04fB984F9}
displayName 2 = Default Domain Controllers Policy
cn 3 = {2EE56B2E-0CDD-4527-AD6C-57C4B4855691}
displayName 3 = W2k-Site's GPO
cn 4 = {C176B4F5-C854-4D68-B147-6A246D3A6473}
displayName 4 = COMPs OU's GPO
cn 5 = {478374B0-9857-4A3E-B06B-A7C839F05155}
displayName 5 = ADMINs OU's GPO
```

As you can see, there are three additional GPOs (one for site and two for OUs) in the domain, besides the default ones.

Browsing and Editing Active Directory Objects

There are three basic "standard" tools that can be used for browsing Active Directory and for editing the properties of directory objects:

- ❑ **ADSI Edit** snap-in — from the *Support Tools* or *Windows 2000 Administration Tools* packs. This snap-in was discussed in *Chapter 4, "Domain Manipulation Tools"*. It doesn't display all directory objects and attributes, but has a simple user interface and a flexible mechanism of custom query views. It provides you with access to all Active Directory partitions, as well as Global Catalog and the standard way of working with permissions on objects. Works with the *LDAP protocol* only.

- Active Directory Browser (ADsVw.exe) — from the *Windows Active Directory Software Development Kit* (SDK). The only tool able to use both the *LDAP* and *WinNT protocols*. It therefore allows you to simultaneously work with Windows 2000 domains and with Windows NT domains. It isn't well documented and requires a good understanding of Active Directory. Works with security descriptors.

- Active Directory Administration Tool (Ldp.exe) — from the *Support Tools*. The most sophisticated tool for manipulating directory objects using the *LDAP protocol*. It requires a profound knowledge of LDAP basics (naming, queries, etc.) as well as Active Directory architecture. Works with security descriptors and Active Directory replication metadata.

These utilities can be regarded as a "mandatory" tool set for troubleshooting various directory problems, and especially for composing your own administrative scripts or designing Active Directory-oriented applications.

NOTES

Unfortunately, among the mentioned tools, only the **ADSI Edit** snap-in works correctly with Unicode names of objects. The limitations of the other two tools are discussed below in the appropriate sections.

If you need to work with objects' GUIDs (the *objectGUID* attribute), use Ldp.exe, since the other two tools (AdsVw.exe and ADSI Edit) display a GUID as a binary value (octet string), which cannot be used for binding, referring, etc.

Active Directory Browser (AdsVw.exe) (AD SDK)

The Active Directory Browser is included in the Active Directory SDK (also known as ADSI SDK) that can only be downloaded from Microsoft web site (see links in *Appendixes*).

The main peculiarity of the Active Directory Browser is its ability to work both with Windows NT 4.0 and Windows 2000 domains (see Fig. 9.1 and Fig. 9.2). Moreover, it is the only browsing tool that has multiple-document interface

(MDI), which allows you to open separate windows for different objects or queries, organize them in the main window, and, therefore, simultaneously work with many directory objects, either in the same domain or in a few domains.

Regretfully, this tool is not documented. That's why I'll describe some basic features in more detail, since many of the tool's options are not particularly obvious.

> **NOTE**
>
> AdsVw.exe displays a Unicode name as a sequence of the "?" (question) characters. If the LDAP provider is used, distinguished names as well as RDNs with Unicode coding are also displayed as strings of question marks.

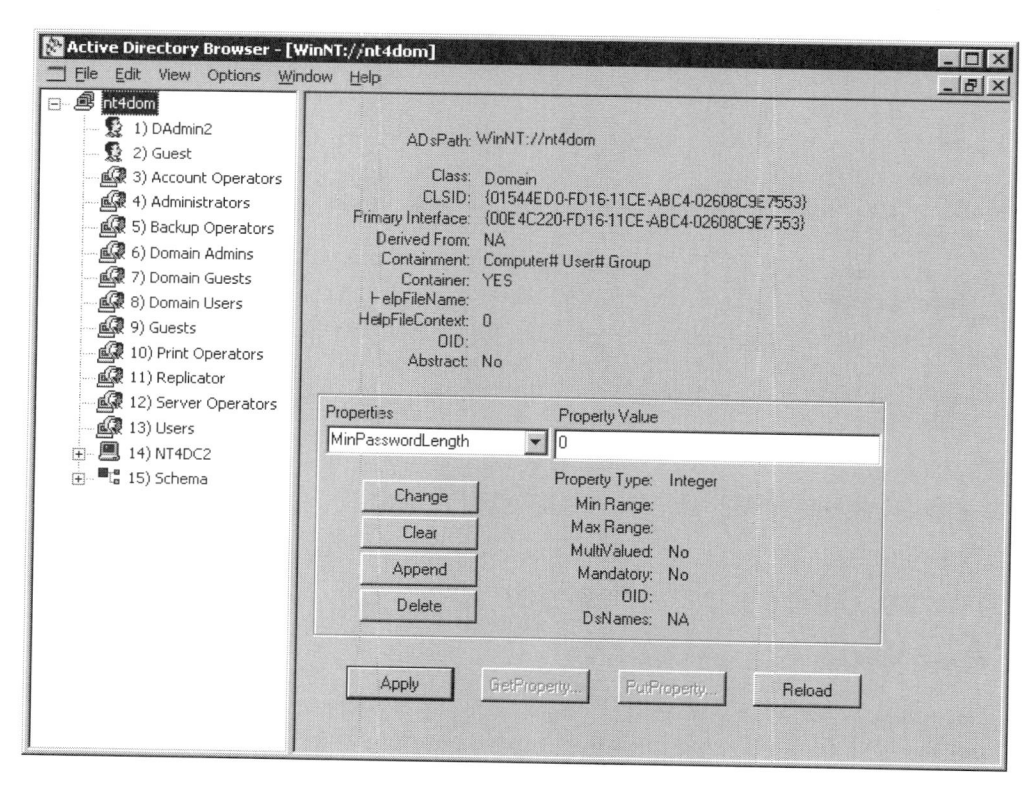

Fig. 9.1. Browsing the linear namespace of the directory objects of a Windows NT 4.0 domain

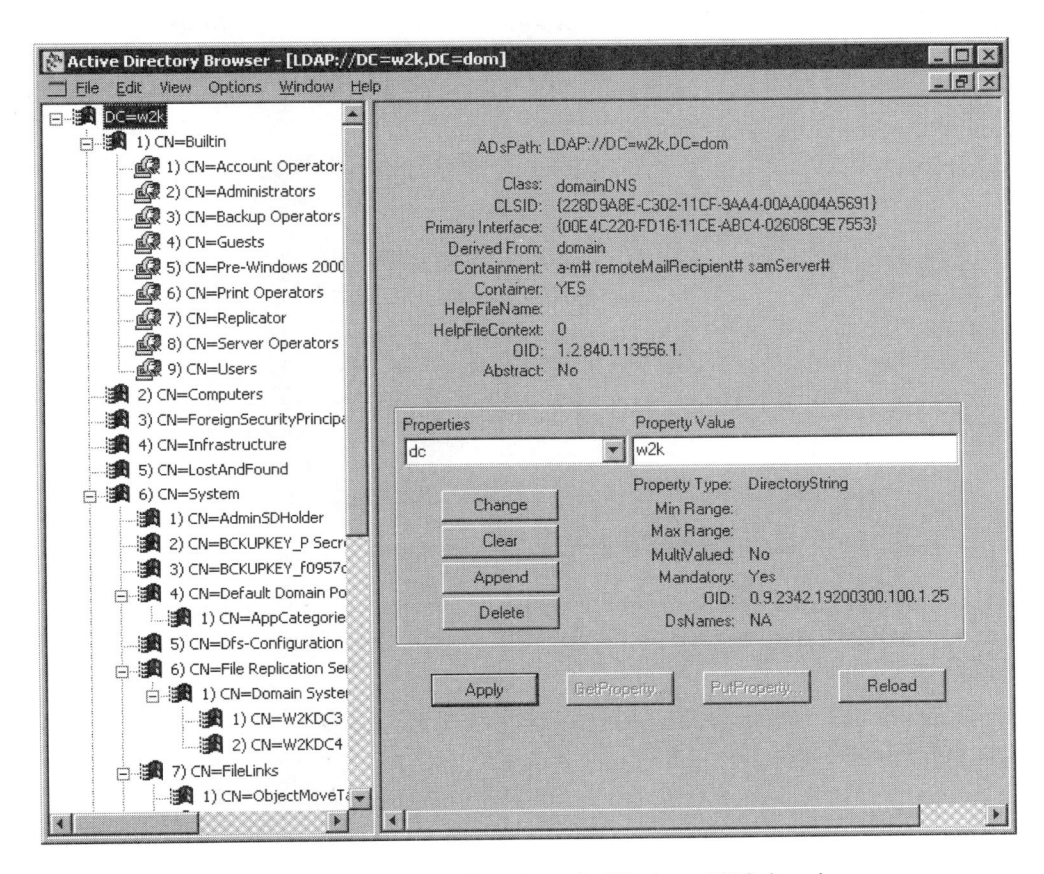

Chapter 9: Manipulating Active Directory Objects 235

Fig. 9.2. Browsing the object tree of a Windows 2000 domain

The tool provides child windows of two types:

❑ **ObjectViewer** — A two-pane window, in which you can navigate the object tree and view/edit their values (see Fig. 9.1 and Fig. 9.2). If the current user doesn't have permissions to access a property, the "???" string is displayed instead of the property's value.

❑ **Query** — A table form (see Fig. 9.5) that consists of the selected attributes for the objects found in accordance with the specified query string (an LDAP filter).

To open a new *browsing window*, press the <Ctrl>+<N> keys, select **ObjectViewer** in the opened window, and fill in the **Enter ADs path** field (Fig. 9.3). (Remember that you can include the name of a specific server in the directory path.)

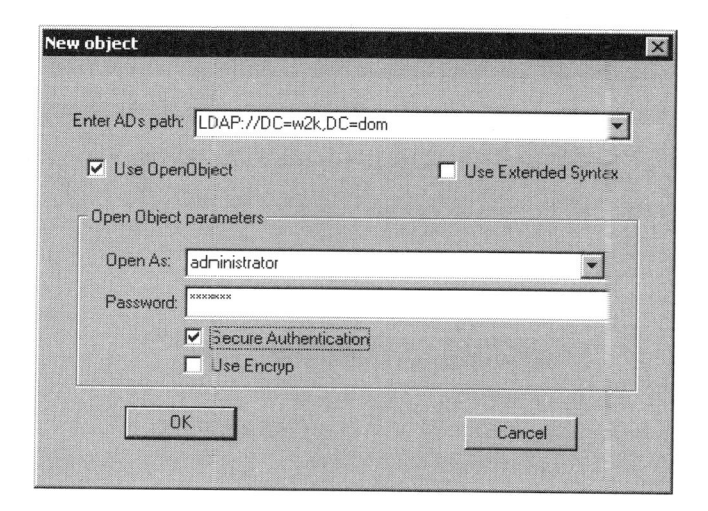

Fig. 9.3. Basic information for a new browsing session

To use credentials different from the ones of the last connected user, check the **Use OpenObject** and **Secure Authentication** boxes, and fill in the **Open As** and **Password** fields.

Some attributes, such as *primaryGroupToken*, can be viewed only if you check the **Use Extended Syntax** box.

> **NOTE**
>
> The mandatory attributes of an object are shown first in the **Properties** list (see Fig. 9.1 and Fig. 9.2) and are followed by the optional attributes in alphabetical order.

The results of a *query* are shown in Fig. 9.5. To start a query, press the <Ctrl>+<N> keys, select **Query** in the opened window, and fill in *all* fields in the **Edit Query** window (Fig. 9.4). All attribute names must be explicitly specified. Click **OK**. You may leave empty all fields in the next window, **Set Search Preferences**. (You'll better understand the meaning of the parameters presented in this window if you read the section about the Ldp.exe tool later in this chapter, and about LDAP queries in *Chapter 13, "Active Directory Service Interfaces (ADSI)".*)

> **NOTE**
>
> You may use the privileges of the currently logged user when browsing directory objects (using either protocol), but you must *always* provide valid credentials while creating a

new query. Otherwise the query will be unauthenticated (and therefore *very* restricted), and the result set will most probably be empty.

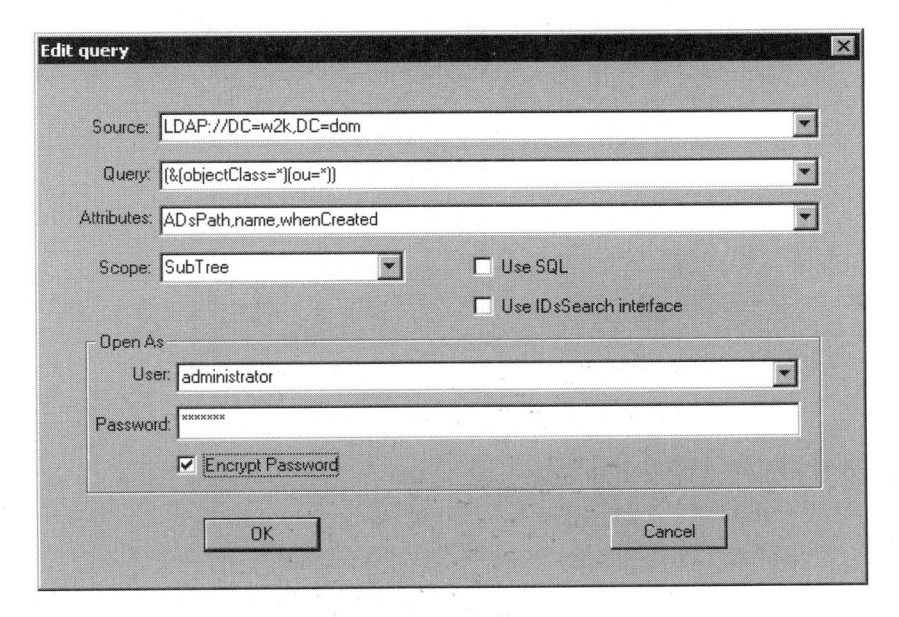

Fig. 9.4. Preparing a sample query: finding all OUs in the domain

The window with the result set for the sample query is shown in Fig. 9.5.

Fig. 9.5. A sample query

If the result set doesn't fit in the window, you must scroll down all lines to see the entire set for the first time.

Active Directory Administration Tool (Ldp.exe) (ST)

Active Directory Administration Tool (Ldp.exe) is a GUI tool, which allows you to query, browse, and modify LDAP-compliant directories via the LDAP protocol. The tool allows an administrator to access information that cannot be derived from other tools, as well as to compose sophisticated and powerful queries with varying scopes.

NOTE

In the tree view, Ldp.exe fails to display the directory objects whose distinguished names are Unicode-coded. All Unicode values of attributes are displayed in string format in the form of `<ldp: Binary blob>`.

Connecting and Binding

To work with an LDAP server, two primary operations — connecting and binding — must be performed. (Connectionless operations and operations without binding (authenticating) are extremely restricted.) The information necessary for both operations is shown in Fig. 9.6.

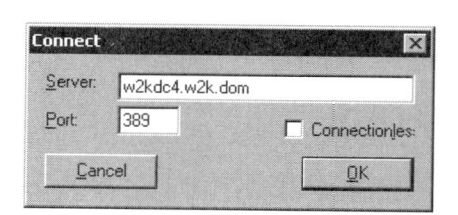

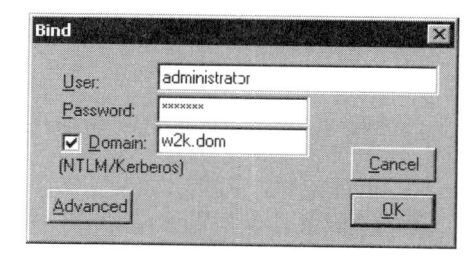

Fig. 9.6. Connecting and binding to a LDAP server

The **Server** field in the **Connect** window can contain a server's DNS name or IP address as well as a domain DNS name. By default, port 389 is used for the LDAP protocol, and port 3268 is designated for Global Catalog. If you leave the **Server** field blank in a Windows 2000 environment, a connection is made to your logon DC (LOGONSERVER). (To work with Ldp.exe in a Windows 2000 environment, you must be logged on to a forest.) If the User and Password fields are left blank, the credentials of the user who is currently logged on are used.

If the connection is successful, the information about the *RootDSE* object is displayed. After binding, you can make queries and/or browse the object tree (click **Tree** in the **View** menu) (Fig. 9.7).

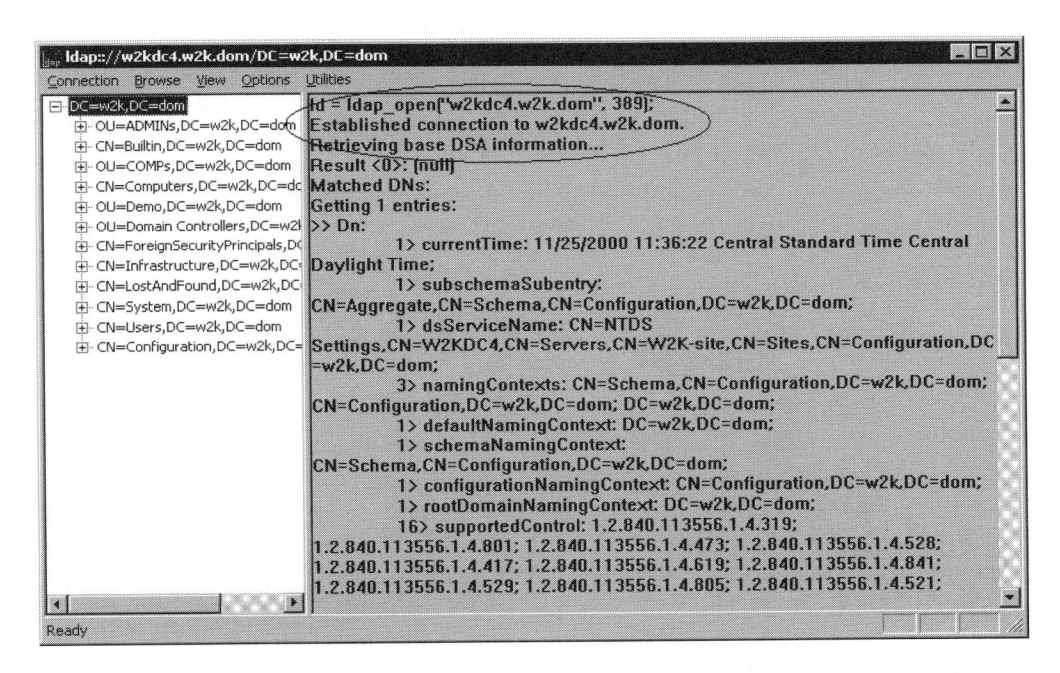

Fig. 9.7. Connecting to a Windows 2000 domain controller and viewing the object tree of the domain

As shown in Fig. 9.7, the tool's window is divided into two panes: the tree pane (left) and the result pane (right). To explode a node in the object tree, simply click twice on it. Which objects are displayed in the result pane depends on the privileges of the user whose credentials you entered while binding to the server.

General Options

The tool's basic options are defined in the **General Options** window. To open it, click **General** in the **Options** menu (Fig. 9.8).

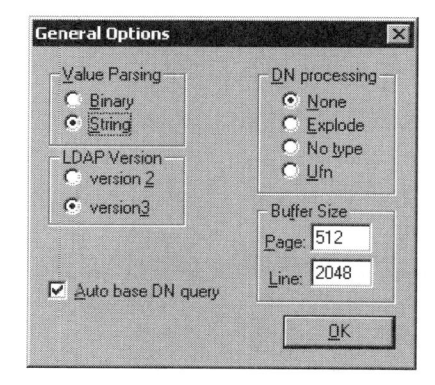

Fig. 9.8. Default general options

Value Parsing

In some specific cases you may want the values of found attributes to be displayed in binary format. Select the **Binary** switch and, instead of the default string representation of an attribute, you'll get its "low-level" value. For instance, the string format may look like:

```
1> whenCreated: 8/28/2000 8:37:43 Central Standard Time Central
Daylight Time;)
```

The binary format will be:

```
1> whenCreated:
    32 30 30 30 30 38 32 38 31 33 33 37 34 33 2e 30    20000828133743.0
    5a                                                  Z
```

LDAP Version

You can select the version of LDAP protocol only before the connection is made. After this, both switches in the **LDAP Version** group are grayed.

Auto Base DN Query

Checking this box enables display of the RootDSE information when connecting to a LDAP server. Also, if this box is checked, the domain context name is automatically used as the base DN when the tree view is selected. Otherwise, you must always specify a DN.

DN Processing

In the **DN Processing** group you can indicate how the tool will display the distinguished names of the objects found. All options are listed below with sample strings:

- **None** (default)

    ```
    >> Dn: CN=Administrator,OU=ADMINs,DC=w2k,DC=dom

    >> Dn: CN=Administrator,CN=Certificate Templates,CN=Public Key
    Services,CN=Services,CN=Configuration,DC=w2k,DC=dom
    ```

- **Explode**

    ```
    >> Dn: CN=Administrator; OU=ADMINs; DC=w2k; DC=dom;
    >> Dn: CN=Administrator; CN=Certificate Templates; CN=Public Key
    Services; CN=Services; CN=Configuration; DC=w2k; DC=dom;
    ```

- **No type**

    ```
    >> Dn: Administrator; ADMINs; w2k; dom;
    >> Dn: Administrator; Certificate Templates; Public Key Services;
    Services; Configuration; w2k; dom;
    ```

- **Ufn**

    ```
    >> Dn: CN=Administrator, OU=ADMINs, DC=w2k, DC=dom
    >> Dn: CN=Administrator, CN=CertificateTemplates,
    CN=PublicKeyServices, CN=Services, CN=Configuration, DC=w2k, DC=dom
    ```

Notice that in the last case there are no spaces in RDNs.

Buffer Size

The **Page** parameter sets the number of rows displayed in the result pane before wrapping begins. Don't forget that you cannot have more rows in a query than the *MaxPageSize* value in the query policy permits.

The **Line** parameter sets the maximum number of characters displayed per line. Lines whose length exceeds this value are truncated.

Referrals and Their Effect on Search Results

In practice, referrals are very important in search operations, as they may greatly influence the results. The **Chase referrals** box in the **Search Options** window (see

Fig. 9.11, left) determines whether or not the server generates LDAP referrals when trying to find an object. (By default, the box is not checked, since this improves the performance of the search.) However, in some cases checking this box may result in an error:

```
Error: Search: Referral. <10>
Result <10>: 0000202B: RefErr: ...
```

Some other scenarios in which you may get a result that you don't expect are also possible. Therefore, it is necessary to carefully select the status of this checkbox. Let's discuss the issue using two examples.

Suppose you are logged onto a computer that is joined to a child domain, and want to search the parent domain (or a domain from another domain tree) by entering its DN as the base of the search. You must either make an LDAP connection to a DC in the parent domain or enable *chasing referrals*. (Otherwise, the referral error will be reported.) Why referrals should help in such a situation will be clear a bit later. (Maybe you already understand what happens.)

Let's go to the second example. Suppose, for instance, you are searching for referrals objects or DSA objects in your own domain. The `(objectClass=crossRef)` or `(cn=NTDS Settings)` filter strings, respectively, can be used for this purpose. The domain DN is specified as the base of the search.

Without the **Chase referrals** box checked, you'll get an empty result set. Maybe you have forgotten, or didn't know to begin with, that required objects are contained in the *Configuration* namespace (directory partition). Besides, remember that the search is only performed in one namespace unless you enable generating referrals. The above-described search operation will be successful if you have done one of the following: either directly specified the appropriate name context as the base of the search, or enabled generation of referrals.

If the **Chase referrals** box is checked, the search is performed:

❑ within *all* partitions stored on a server

❑ within the domain partitions of *all child* domains, to which the referrals are directed

Turning to the first example, it is clear now that if a server finds an object that refers to another domain and cannot (is not allowed to) connect to the server that stores the corresponding partition, it generates a referral error message.

> **NOTE**
> The problem of cross-domain (cross-partition, and cross-tree) searching can also be resolved by using a connection over the Global Catalog (3268) port. It might even be a more appropriate way. Don't forget, however, that not all attributes are replicated to GC.

Paged Search

Sometimes, a requested server can return a number of rows that exceed the *MaxPageSize* value. (Do not confuse the number of rows returned by a server on a request and the number of rows that the tool can display in the result pane — the **Page** parameter.) The following error will be reported:

```
Error: Search: Size Limit Exceeded. <4>
Result <4>: [null]
```

In such a case it is necessary to use paging search results. You can request the results in pages of a specific size. Open the **Search Options** window (see Fig. 9.11) and select the **Paged** switch in the **Search Call Type** group. The **Page size** value defines the length of page. Now you'll get the results of a search operation in 16-row pages (by default):

```
Result <0>:
Matched DNs:
Getting 16 entries:
...
   -=>> 'Run' for more, 'Close' to abandon <<=-
```

You can continue searching by clicking **Run,** or can terminate the operation at any moment. When paging is used, you needn't worry about how long the result of a search is.

Saving Results

To clear the result pane before a new operation, click **New** in the **Connection** menu. Any information displayed in this pane can be copied-and-pasted.

At any moment you may save the contents of the result pane by selecting **Save** or **Save As** from the **Connection** menu. (You needn't close the **Search** window.) The latter option always asks you for a file name. The former option allows you to save information in the current output file, and asks for a file name only after the tool starts or the **New** command has been performed.

The Forest View

You may look up all domains and DCs in the forest in tree form. Click **Enterprise Configuration** in the **View** menu. In the opened window, click **Refresh**. After some time, the actual configuration of your enterprise will be displayed in the window (Fig. 9.9). You can get the configuration only after binding to a server.

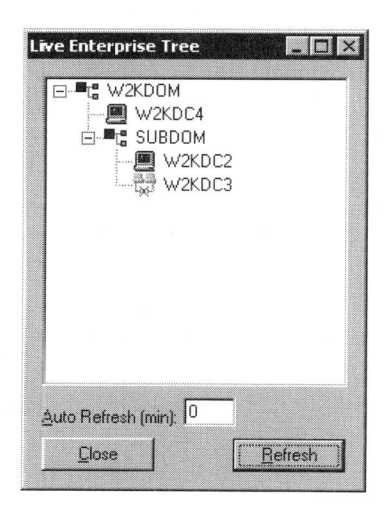

Fig. 9.9. In this window, you can see the entire domain structure (the forest) and the state of all DCs

As Fig. 9.9 shows, two DCs (W2KDC4, W2KDC2) in the forest are online, and one DC (W2KDC3) is offline. Knowing the real state of your network will help you to select servers for connecting and making queries.

Searching

For clarity and simplicity, we'll discuss the process of finding objects in Active Directory using two particular scenarios.

> **NOTE**
>
> Don't forget that every DC in a domain stores three Active Directory partitions (see the RootDSE object's information when a connection is made). Although these partitions have contiguous DNS names — and this may seem a little confusing — they are absolutely different namespaces when it comes to performing a search.

Example 1. Finding the Deleted Objects

Deleted Active Directory objects (so called *tombstones*) are stored in the *Deleted Objects* container for a preconfigured period of time, and then permanently purged by the garbage collection. This container cannot be viewed by using standard snap-ins. The *Show Deleted Object* control (controlType = 1.2.840.113556.1.4.417) and search command allow you to retrieve the tombstones. (You must have administrative privileges.)

Start Ldp.exe and carry out the following operations:

1. Connect to a DC, and bind using the credentials of an administrator.
2. Click **Search** in the **Browse** menu, and enter the distinguished name of the domain and the filter string (**isDeleted=***). Select the **Subtree** switch and click **Options** (Fig. 9.10).

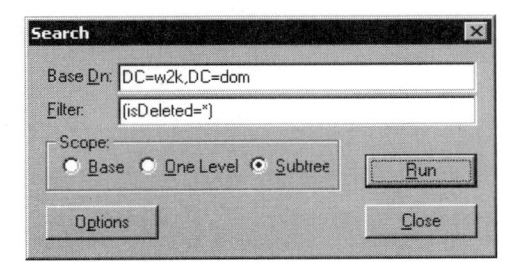

Fig. 9.10. Primary search parameters

3. Click **Extended** in the **Search Call Type** group, and enter the attributes of the deleted objects that you wish to view (see Fig. 9.11, left). (You may also need to increase the default **Timeout (s)** from 0 to a bigger number. The value can be determined by experimenting.) Click **Controls**.

> **NOTE**
>
> If you receive the following error massage, increase the timeout value:
> ```
> Error: Search: Timeout. <85>
> Error<94>: ldap_parse_result failed: No result present in message
> Getting 0 entries:
> ```

4. Enter the type of the control in the **Object Identifier** field, and click **Check in**.

> **NOTE**
>
> You may combine a number of various controls.

5. Select **Server** from the **Control Type** group (see Fig. 9.11, right).

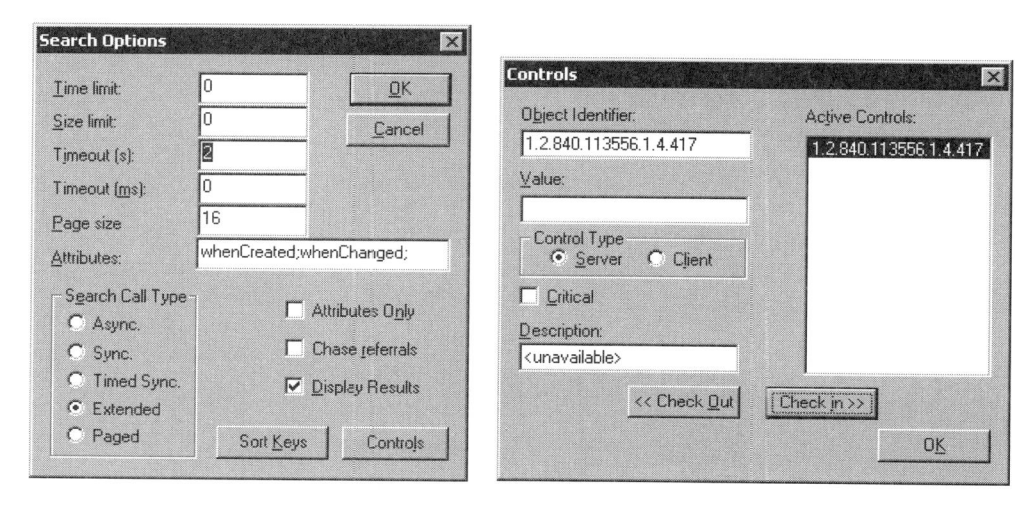

Fig. 9.11. Configuring the search options for deleted objects

6. Close the **Controls** and **Search Options** windows.
7. Click **Run** and execute the search.

Example 2. Searching for Object GUIDs

As you know, the name (e. g. the *cn* attribute) of a directory object can be changed by a *rename object* operation. If, for instance, an application uses the name for referring to the object, it will "lose" this object after its renaming. The more appropriate way is to use the object GUID, which remains the same throughout the entire lifetime of the object.

The question is thus how to find the object GUID? You might search for the object and enter the *objectGUID* attribute in the **Search Options** window. However, it is possible to immediately get the GUID of each object found in a search operation. You need to perform a search using the *Return Extended Distinguished Names* LDAP control (controlType = 1.2.840.113556.1.4.529).

Chapter 9: Manipulating Active Directory Objects 247

> **NOTE**
> It is possible to get an objectGUID by using ADSI Edit. However, it may be inconvenient, since the *objectGUID* attribute (as well as *objectSid*) is in *OctetString* format (e. g. "0xaf 0xba 0xf0 0xba ..." — 16 bytes in all). You cannot directly substitute such a string in a search or bind command.

The GUID search preparation steps are similar to the ones for deleted objects described above. Let's find the GUIDs of the OUs that are contained in a domain. Enter the following information:

- **Base DN** — domain DN
- **Filter** — `(ou=*)`
- **One Level** scope
- **Attributes** — `ADsPath`
- **Active Controls** — 1.2.840.113556.1.4.529

You'll get a list of OUs in a format similar to the following:

```
Dn: <GUID=0855ae368790cb4b8726cf37cb2222a5>;OU=Domain Controllers,
    DC=w2k,DC=dom
```

The new component (marked here in bold) appears in the distinguished name. The found GUID can be verified by using Search.vbs (see *"Searching for an Object using its GUID"* at the beginning of this chapter), or you may use the entire string (between and including the angle brackets) in a script in a bind operation.

Updating Attributes

The LDAP update operations are the following: Add, Modify, Modify RDN, and Delete. On the one hand (regarding the user interface), they are quite simple and obvious; on the other hand, they require a profound understanding of Active Directory architecture (particularly the schema, classes, and attributes). That is why other tools, such as the administrative snap-ins (**ADSI Edit**, **Active Directory Users and Computers**, and so on), are more convenient for modifying Active Directory objects. I'll show in an example just the most common steps when using Ldp.exe for this purpose.

> **NOTE**
> The *Modify RDN* operation is equivalent to renaming or moving an object.

Modifying an Attribute

Let's change a user's UPN. First, click **Modify** in the **Browse** menu. In the opened window, enter the DN of the user, the attribute name, and its new value. Then select **Replace** from the **Operation** group (because the attribute already exists), and click **Enter** to add the data to the **Entry List**. No checks are performed at this time, so be careful. You may correct the entered data by clicking **Edit** (and then editing the information) or **Remove**. A sample window is shown in Fig. 9.12.

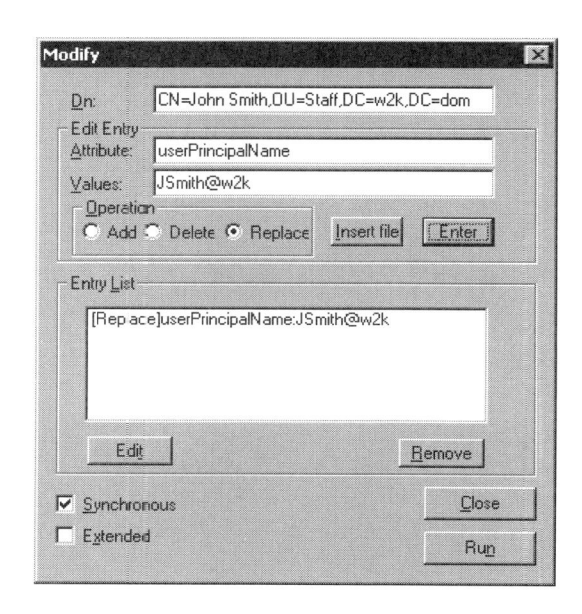

Fig. 9.12. The information necessary to change the UPN of a user

When all is ready, click **Run**. The server will verify all entered data (syntax rules, acceptable values, etc.) and perform the operation if all requirements have been met. The result message may be similar to the following:

```
***Call Modify...
ldap_modify_s(ld, 'CN=John Smith,OU=Stuff,DC=w2k,DC=dom',[1] attrs);
Modified "CN=John Smith,OU=Stuff,DC=w2k,DC=dom".
```

If an error arises at some step of executing an operation, the tool reports an error message, which depends on the kind of error (such as a syntax error in the entered data, or an error with the directory database, etc.). The message contains a description of the error.

For example:

```
***Call Modify...
ldap_modify_s(ld, 'CN=John Smith,OU=Stuff,DC=w2k,DC=dom',[1] attrs);
Error: Modify: No Such Object. <32>
Unwilling To Perform. <53>
```

Deleting Objects

The delete operation is also fairly obvious and simple. However, a problem may arise when you want to delete an object that has child object(s), for example, an OU with user accounts. The following error may be reported:

```
Error: Delete: Not allowed on Non-leaf. <66>
```

To perform such an operation, you must use the *Tree Delete* LDAP control (controlType = 1.2.840.113556.1.4.805). This control allows you to delete an entire subtree, provided that you have sufficient permissions.

To delete a non-leaf object (i. e. a container):

1. Add the *Tree Delete* control to the list of active controls.

2. Click **Delete** in the **Browse** menu.

3. In the Delete window, enter the distinguished name of the container and check the Extended box. (An example window is shown in Fig. 9.13.)

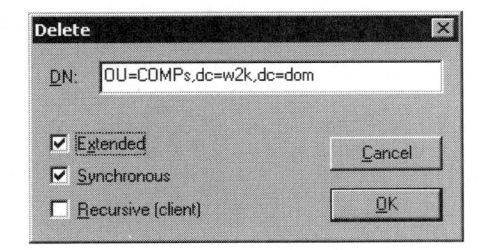

Fig. 9.13. Deleting a *non-empty* container (an OU in this case)

4. Click **OK**.

CAUTION!

Be extremely careful when deleting an entire container! No warnings are generated.

> **NOTE**
>
> To view and activate/deactivate the controls, you can at any moment open the **Controls** window by clicking **Controls** in the **Options** menu.

Viewing the Security Descriptors

Ldp.exe allows you to view the security descriptor for any directory object. This feature is intended for solving problems related to the accounts' permissions on directory objects (e. g. when moving the security principals to another domain).

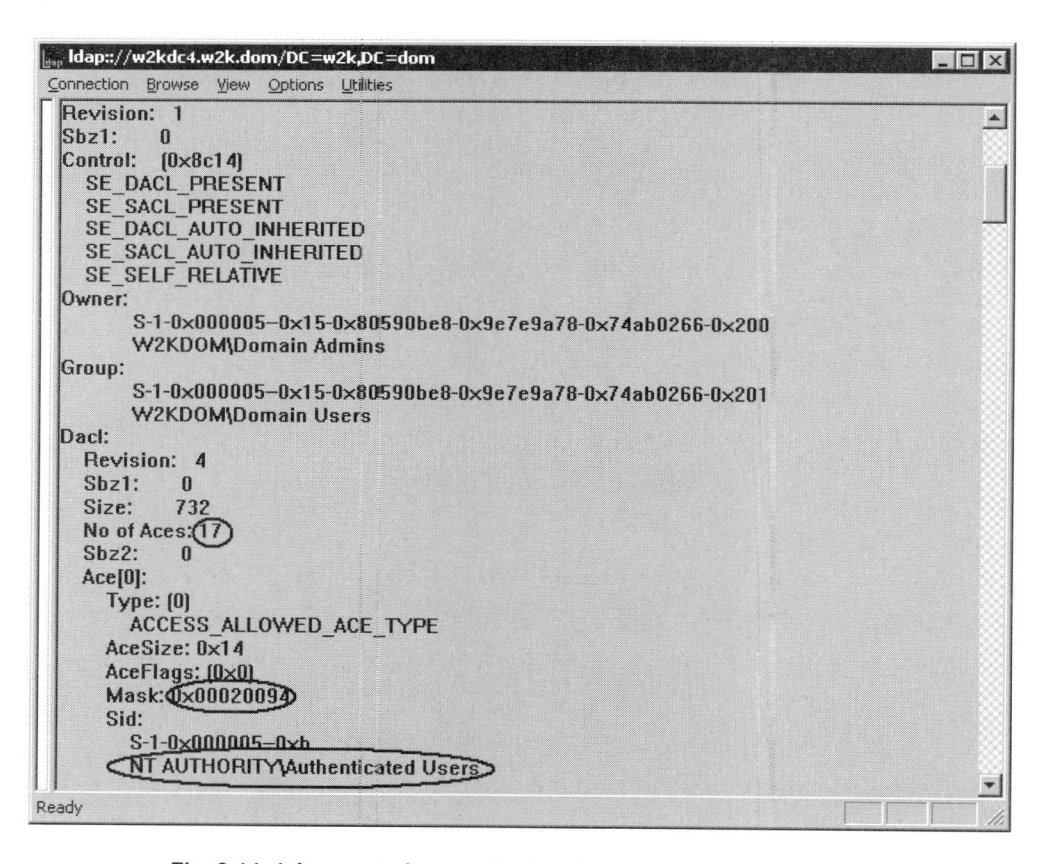

Fig. 9.14. A fragment of a security descriptor shown by using Ldp.exe

It is especially useful when you are debugging scripts or applications that work with security descriptors (see *Chapter 13, "Active Directory Service Interfaces (ADSI)"* and *Chapter 14, "Using ADSI for Administrative Tasks"*). Using this feature requires a good understanding of the Active Directory security model (access control lists (ACL) and access control elements (ACE), their inheritance, etc.).

To view the security descriptor for a directory object, select the **Security | Security Descriptor** command from the **Browse** menu and specify the distinguished name of the object. If you want to see the directly specified or inherited audit settings (the system ACLs) on this object, check the **SACL** box. A sample output produced by this command is shown in Fig. 9.14. The command also displays the descriptor in the SDDL (Security Descriptor Definition Language) string format (not shown in the figure).

As Fig. 9.14 shows, you can see all the information about the descriptor (some of its elements are circled in the figure). That information includes, in particular, the control flags, the owner of the object, the number of ACEs, and elements of each ACE, such as the ACE's type, the access mask, and the name and SID of the security principal that was granted this right. You can retrieve all described information from a descriptor by using a script (*Chapter 14, "Using ADSI for Administrative Tasks"*, contains an example of such a script). You can also programmatically manipulate the ACEs, i. e. grant or revoke rights on directory objects.

Viewing Replication Metadata

Ldp.exe can display the directory object's metadata information (the *replPropertyMetaData* attribute) that is used in replication. You can also view this information by using the RepAdmin.exe command with the `/showmeta` parameter (see *Chapter 8, "Network and Distributed Services"*).

To view the metadata for an object, select the **Replication | View Metadata** command from the **Browse** menu and enter the object's distinguished name. A sample output is presented in Fig. 9.15.

When troubleshooting replication issues, you can connect to various domain controllers and compare the metadata for the stored replicas of the desired object.

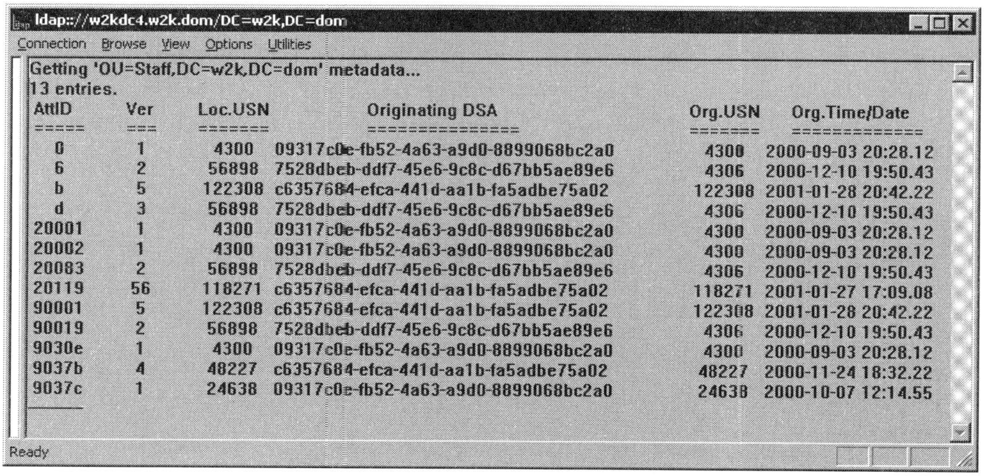
ldap://w2kdc4.w2k.dom/DC=w2k,DC=dom

Connection Browse View Options Utilities

Getting 'OU=Staff,DC=w2k,DC=dom' metadata...
13 entries.

AttID	Ver	Loc.USN	Originating DSA	Org.USN	Org.Time/Date
0	1	4300	09317c0e-fb52-4a63-a9d0-8899068bc2a0	4300	2000-09-03 20:28.12
6	2	56898	7528dbeb-ddf7-45e6-9c8c-d67bb5ae89e6	4306	2000-12-10 19:50.43
b	5	122308	c6357684-efca-441d-aa1b-fa5adbe75a02	122308	2001-01-28 20:42.22
d	3	56898	7528dbeb-ddf7-45e6-9c8c-d67bb5ae89e6	4306	2000-12-10 19:50.43
20001	1	4300	09317c0e-fb52-4a63-a9d0-8899068bc2a0	4300	2000-09-03 20:28.12
20002	1	4300	09317c0e-fb52-4a63-a9d0-8899068bc2a0	4300	2000-09-03 20:28.12
20083	2	56898	7528dbeb-ddf7-45e6-9c8c-d67bb5ae89e6	4306	2000-12-10 19:50.43
20119	56	118271	c6357684-efca-441d-aa1b-fa5adbe75a02	118271	2001-01-27 17:09.08
90001	5	122308	c6357684-efca-441d-aa1b-fa5adbe75a02	122308	2001-01-28 20:42.22
90019	2	56898	7528dbeb-ddf7-45e6-9c8c-d67bb5ae89e6	4306	2000-12-10 19:50.43
9030e	1	4300	09317c0e-fb52-4a63-a9d0-8899068bc2a0	4300	2000-09-03 20:28.12
9037b	4	48227	c6357684-efca-441d-aa1b-fa5adbe75a02	48227	2000-11-24 18:32.22
9037c	1	24638	09317c0e-fb52-4a63-a9d0-8899068bc2a0	24638	2000-10-07 12:14.55

Ready

Fig. 9.15. Viewing the replication metadata for a directory object

Importing, Exporting, and Batch Modifying Directory Objects

By default, every Windows 2000-based domain controller has two utilities installed — LDIF Directory Exchange (LDIFDE.exe) and CSV Directory Exchange (CSVDE.exe) — that are primarily intended for bulk operations. You can use these utilities to:

- ❑ Export Active Directory information to a text file (in LDIF or CSV format) that can be easily viewed or/and edited. The retrieved information can be used for:
  - composing documentation on directory objects
  - performing bulk editing operations that cannot be done using the standard administrative snap-ins
  - creating templates for new users (if the standard option of copying user accounts is not convenient for you)
  - migrating directory objects between domains into the same or another domain forest
  - backing up the existing domain configuration (for safety or for re-installation of domain controllers)

- Import Active Directory information from a file. This means creating new objects or modifying the attributes of existing ones in batch mode. Besides the already mentioned export operations that imply import — bulk editing, migrating, backing up, and creating user templates — the import into Active Directory can be carried out for:
  - deploying a pre-configured domain configuration (by the way, import is performed when a domain controller is promoted — the CSVDE utility is used for creating the "default" Active Directory structure)
  - deploying Active Directory-oriented applications (extending the schema is also possible)

> **NOTE**
>
> Normally, the standard *Backup* utility is used for backing up and restoring Active Directory. But in some cases, export/import may be a preferable choice.

You can select *either* of these utilities for your tasks, provided that you keep in mind the two main differences between LDIFDE and CSVDE for a user:

- Data format — LDIFDE uses files that respond to the LDIF standard, whereas CSVDE supports the CSV format (see the appropriate section on each tool)
- Possible operations — CSVDE can only export and import (create) data; LDIFDE also allows you to modify attributes and delete objects

The book contains a few examples of using LDIFDE and CSVDE. These examples can be run with either utility, depending on your specific requirements.

All of the tasks listed can also be fulfilled (and often, more effectively!) with custom ADSI scripts. Knowing the possibilities and restrictions of all the tools permits you to save time and select the appropriate tool for a specific task.

Basic information on the LDIFDE and CSVDE utilities is contained in the Help system (search for "Importing and exporting directory information"). (The -u parameter is missing in the Help!) You can also run the utilities without parameters and get the help information.

> **ERROR LOGS**
>
> Both utilities create an error log file (csvde.err or ldif.err) and a log for completed operations (csvde.log or ldif.log). By default, these files are stored in the current folder, and the logs' location is configured.

Parameters

Table 9.1 lists some of the most frequently used parameters of both utilities — LDIFDE and CSVDE.

Table 9.1. Some Parameters of the LDIFDE and CSVDE Utilities

Parameter	Description and comments	Meaning (or value) if the parameter is omitted (default)
Common parameters		
-f	Input or output filename. `-f con` can be used for output to the console. Required parameter	No
-s	DC name	The name of the DC to which the user is currently logged on
-t	Port number. The Global Catalog port (3268) can also be used	389 (LDAP)
-u	Use Unicode format	ANSI format is used
Parameters for Export operations		
-d	Search base	Domain naming context
-c	Replace all occurrences of `string 1` with `string 2`. Very helpful for copying data from one domain to another	No
-r	Search filter	`(objectClass=*)`
-p	Search scope	Subtree
-l	Selection. A list of attributes. `"1.1"` or empty string can be used with the meaning of "no attributes returned" (if you need only a list of objects)	All attributes
Parameters for Import operations		
-i	Specifies import mode	Export mode
-k	Skip errors. If some objects were successfully imported to the directory and others weren't, you may correct errors in the import file and continue its processing	No

Chapter 9: Manipulating Active Directory Objects 255

> **NOTE**
> Don't forget about the omitted parameters (which have the default values), or you may obtain an undesirable or unpredictable result. Compare, for example, the cases when you want to export OU objects only and when you need to export an entire OU subtree (default).

Exporting and Re-Importing Objects

Export operations are usually successful. (The worst-case scenario is that the export file doesn't contain all the objects you expect it should contain.) You need only take into consideration the following: when you specify a list of attributes (by using the -l parameter) in the export command, LDIFDE and CSVDE don't include any information about non-defined attributes in the output file. Therefore, you might need to manually include the attributes' names (if you need them) in the import file and assign the appropriate values.

> **NOTES**
> It is not possible to export security descriptors (or group policies — for domains and/or OUs). Also be careful about the built-in and default groups, such as *Domain Users*. In the exported file, you may see a list of members different from the one that the **Active Directory Users and Computers snap-in** displays.
>
> The (givenName=*) filter allows you to choose only accounts of newly created users, with the exception of built-in accounts. Built-in users (administrator, guest, etc.) don't have *given names*.
>
> When exporting information from Global Catalog (using the 3268 port), don't forget that GC contains a restricted set of attributes. For example, 40-50 attributes (a very modest value, since the minimum is about 32 attributes and possible maximum is about two hundred) are exported for a user object by default. When GC is used, only 25-30 attributes are exported.

The number and type of the objects exported depend on a combination of the search base and the LDAP filter (described in detail in *Chapter 13, "Active Directory Service Interfaces (ADSI)"*). You can export either a single directory object or all Active Directory objects. The choice of the appropriate search base and filter is not a challenge unless you don't use both or you've forgotten about the default values. The following two commands might seem equivalent since both export a computer account (provided that the computer's *cn* attribute has a unique value in the domain):

```
ldifde -f Export.ldf -d "CN=Comp1,OU=STAFF,DC=w2k,DC=dom"
ldifde -f Export.ldf -r "(&(objectCategory=computer)(cn=Comp1))"
```

In fact, the first command can export a few objects, and the second exports strictly one object. In both cases the omitted -p parameter (the scope of the search) means that the search will be conducted in the subtree. Since the computer object is a container and can have child objects, the first command exports the entire "family". The second command finds the specified computer in the domain and exports it alone (since there is no computer with such a name in the domain).

After a little practice with search base and filters you'll learn how to most effectively and precisely select only the necessary objects from Active Directory. (See more examples of command string below in this chapter.)

> **NOTE**
>
> I prefer to specify *objectCategory* in filters rather than *objectClass*. Both attributes are replicated in Global Catalog. However, the former attribute is indexed, and the latter is not. As a result, the filters with objectCategory work faster.
>
> There is, however, a pitfall in such an approach. "objectCategory=Person" defines users as well as contacts. Consequently, you need to add the *objectClass* attribute in the filter.

Errors are more common when import is performed. There are three main sources of errors:

- Read-only attributes, which only the system can change. A typical error message: 'Unwilling To Perform. The server side error is "Access to the attribute is not permitted because the attribute is owned by the Security Accounts Manager (SAM)."' You cannot include such attributes as *objectSid*, *objectGUID*, etc, in the import files and must always use the -m parameter while exporting objects if a successive import is planned. When the -m parameter is specified, all of the SAM attributes are ignored (see also "*Working with User Objects*" later in this chapter).

- Mandatory attributes that are missing. Refer to Table 9.2 to see which attributes must be defined in import files when new directory objects are created. The *objectSid* attribute is shown in bold to remind you that, notwithstanding the fact that it is a mandatory attribute, it mustn't be used in import.

Chapter 9: Manipulating Active Directory Objects 257

Table 9.2. Some Important Object Classes and Their Mandatory Attributes

Object class (category)	Mandatory attributes
computer (Computer)	cn, instanceType, objectCategory, objectClass, **objectSid**, sAMAccountName
group (Group)	cn, groupType, instanceType, objectCategory, objectClass, **objectSid**, sAMAccountName
organizationalUnit (Organizational-Unit)	instanceType, objectCategory, objectClass, ou
printQueue (Print-Queue)	cn, instanceType, objectCategory, objectClass, printerName, serverName, shortServerName, uNCName, versionNumber
user (Person)	cn, instanceType, objectCategory, objectClass, **objectSid**, sAMAccountName
volume (Volume)	cn, instanceType, objectCategory, objectClass, uNCName

❑ Violations of the syntax rules, inconsistency of attribute values, values of wrong types, or values out of range. For example, using the -c parameter may result in incorrect values of naming attributes (see later in the chapter). If you are creating new objects from scratch, verify carefully the attribute types and values, and refer to the abstract schema and schema container if needed (see also the schema description in *Chapter 13, "Active Directory Service Interfaces (ADSI)"*).

When directory objects are copied (exported and imported) from one domain to another, it is helpful to use the -c parameter.

Unicode Support

LDFIDE and CSVDE have some problems with supporting Unicode (localized string values). You should take this into consideration if non-ANSI values are stored in your Active Directory. Test your installation before starting the bulk import/export operations. Since such values aren't written in the output file in plain text format, it is hard to edit them. Encoding restrictions of the utilities are listed below.

LDIFDE

❑ Unless the -u parameter is specified, LDIFDE exports the Unicode values as Base64-encoded (e. g., `sn:: 0J/QtdGC0YDQvtCy`). (Notice that the colon character is doubled in such lines. Binary values are always encoded.) If the Unicode characters are included in the distinguished name of a directory object, the entire line (dn) name is coded. You can safely re-import all these values.

- LDIFDE *accepts* the Unicode values in an input file if this file is saved as Unicode-encoded. Use common format with *one* colon!

CSVDE

- Unless the -u parameter is specified, CSVDE fails if Unicode characters are included in the distinguished name of a directory object. However, it always accepts the Unicode values in other attributes. Error message:

  ```
  Error writing to file. This error happens when the entry cannot be
  written, it can be caused by writing a Unicode value to a non-unicode
  file.
  ```

- Regardless of the presence of the -u parameter, CSVDE exports the Unicode (and binary) values (except for dn) in the following format: X'8c39...c3bc'. You can safely re-import these values.

- CSVDE *accepts* the Unicode values in an input file (in usual format) if this file is saved as Unicode-encoded.

LDIFDE Utility (Sys)

LDIFDE, a command-line utility that is installed by default on every DC, can be used for adding, modifying, renaming, and deleting directory objects. This utility uses LDAP Data Interchange Format (LDIF) — an Internet standard that defines a file format to perform batch operations for LDAP-accessible directories. LDIFDE is also a preferred tool for extending the Active Directory schema.

Examples of LDIF files are shown below. LDIFDE can be run on any Windows 2000-based client, provided you have supplied appropriate domain credentials.

Working with User Objects

Table 9.3 is a snippet of an export file and lists all attributes of an exported user object in LDIF format. Notice attributes in bold face, which are *not exported* when the -m parameter is specified, and shouldn't be imported. Notice also that the *objectGUID* and *objectSid* are exported as binary values (this is marked with a double colon). A few additional remarks are placed at the end of the table. These are

Chapter 9: Manipulating Active Directory Objects

not *all* of the possible attributes, only a typical minimal set. The names of some attributes as they are presented in the **Active Directory Users and Computers** snap-in's UI are specified in bold square brackets. The relative DN (RDN) is also specified, although it isn't presented in the UI and cannot be directly modified.

Table 9.3. Influence of *-m* Parameter on the Resulting Attribute List

Exported attributes and their values
dn: CN=John Smith,OU=STAFF,DC=w2k,DC=dom
changetype: add
memberOf: CN=Server Operators,CN=Builtin,DC=w2k,DC=dom
memberOf: CN=Account Operators,CN=Builtin,DC=w2k,DC=dom
accountExpires: 9223372036854775807
badPasswordTime: 0
badPwdCount: 0
**cn: John Smith
codePage: 0
countryCode: 0
displayName: John Smith   **[Display name]**
distinguishedName: CN=John Smith,OU=STAFF,DC=w2k,DC=dom
givenName: John   **[First name]**
homeDirectory: \\w2kdc4\UsersData\jsmith
homeDrive: W:
**instanceType: 4
lastLogoff: 0
lastLogon: 0
logonCount: 0
name: John Smith   **[RDN]**
**objectCategory: CN=Person,CN=Schema,CN=Configuration,DC=w2k,DC=dom
*objectClass: user
objectGUID:: +QUGbMtJ4UObxSD0...

continues

Table 9.3 Continued

Exported attributes and their values
objectSid:: AQUAAAAAAAUVAAAA6...
primaryGroupID: 513
profilePath: \\w2kdc\Profiles\jsmith
pwdLastSet: 126205092770106560
*sAMAccountName: jsmith
sAMAccountType: 805306368
scriptPath: Users\Logons.vbs
sn: Smith   [Last Name]
***userAccountControl: 512
userPrincipalName: jsmith@w2k
† uSNChanged: 54011
† uSNCreated: 54007
† whenChanged: 20001205170117.0Z
† whenCreated: 20001205170115.0Z

* — these attributes *are required* for importing (creating) objects. To create a new user, it is sufficient to specify the *objectClass* and *sAMAccountName* attributes. Other objects will require some additional attributes (see Table 9.2).

** — these attributes are mandatory for a user object, but are *not* required for an import operation because the system itself creates the corresponding values.

*** — if this string is included in an import file, the new user will have to change his or her password at first logon; otherwise the new account will be disabled.

† — these attributes are exported, too, with the **-m** parameter, but it makes absolutely no sense to *import* them.

Here is a sample command string that allows you to export the specified attributes of all users (except for built-in accounts) from your current domain:

```
ldifde -f ExportedUSERs.ldf
    -r "(&(objectCategory=Person)(objectClass=User)(givenName=*))"
    -l "cn,givenName,objectClass,sAMAccountName"
```

Working with Container Objects (Domains and OUs)

When working with container objects, you must always remember that the combination of the search base and the LDAP filter defines the result of the operation: either you export only container objects of the specified type, or you export an entire container.

Compare, for example, following two commands. The first command exports all OU objects from the current domain (remember default values for the omitted -l, -d, and -p parameters):

```
ldifde -f ExportedOUs.ldf -r "objectCategory=OrganizationalUnit" -v
```

The second command exports an entire subtree, i. e. all objects (of any type), from the specified OU:

```
ldifde -f ExportedOU.ldf -d "OU=Staff,DC=w2k,DC=dom" -v
```

Extending the Schema

Ldp.exe is the tool recommended by Microsoft for extending the schema (however, using CSVDE is also possible). (The requirements on the schema extension are described in *Chapter 13, "Active Directory Service Interfaces (ADSI)"*. Remember that you must generate the base OID for your own attributes and classes before starting a similar command. The following is an example of an LDIF import file, which creates a string attribute with *stringAttribute* LDAP display name:

```
dn: CN=String Attribute,CN=Schema,CN=Configuration,DC=w2k,DC=dom
changetype: add
attributeID: 1.2.840.113556.1.4.7000.233.....1
attributeSyntax: 2.5.5.12
cn: String Attribute
isSingleValued: TRUE
objectCategory: CN=Attribute-Schema,CN=Schema,CN=Configuration,
 ↳ DC=w2k,DC=dom
objectClass: attributeSchema
oMSyntax: 64
```

The successful command output is similar to the following (`w2kdc4.w2k.dom` is the name of the DC that is the schema master):

```
ldifde -i -f AddStrAttr.ldf
Connecting to "w2kdc4.w2k.dom"
```

```
Logging in as current user using SSPI
Importing directory from file "AddStrAttr.ldf"
Loading entries..
1 entry modified successfully.

The command has completed successfully
```

Modifying Attribute Values. Deleting Objects

Only the LDIFDE utility can be used for batch modifying Active Directory objects. To change (or set) one or more attribute values of an object (or a number of objects) use the following procedure:

1. Export the necessary object(s) to a file. Use the appropriate filters. You may export all attributes or specific ones only. This step is optional — you may create the import file manually.

2. Edit the export file. Delete the entries for unnecessary (unchanged) attributes. Change *changetype* from `add` to `modify`. Replace each attribute entry with the following lines:

   ```
   replace: <attributeName>
   <attributeName>: <newValue>
   ```

If the second line is omitted, the attribute value is cleared. The "-" (minus) character must follow the lines for *each* attribute (including the last one). An empty line must precede *each* attribute's distinguished name (excluding the first one). Let's illustrate these requirements with an example. The sample import file is used for modifying attributes of two user objects (the comments in bold square brackets aren't really included in the file!):

```
dn: CN=user3,OU=Staff,DC=w2k,DC=dom
changetype: modify
replace: description
description: A test user
-
replace: scriptPath
scriptPath: Users\Logons.vbs
-
    [This empty line is mandatory]
dn: CN=user4,OU=Staff,DC=w2k,DC=dom
```

```
changetype: modify
replace: description
description: A user
```
− [All "-" characters are mandatory]

3. Import the edited file. The import is performed until the first error, but you can safely repeat it as many times as you wish while correcting errors.

By modifying attribute values, you can also change membership in (a) group(s). To add a user to a group use lines similar to the following:

```
dn: CN=GroupName,OU=Staff,DC=w2k,DC=dom
changetype: modify
replace: member
member: CN=user2,OU=Staff,DC=w2k,DC=dom
```

> **NOTE**
>
> If LDIFDE.exe doesn't meet your specific needs, write a custom script (see *Chapter 14, "Using ADSI for Administrative Tasks"*). This won't take more time than editing a file if you are familiar with ADSI scripting. However, the scripts are much more flexible, as well as reusable. For example, say you need to re-do the export and/or edit the import file each time when a user is added (deleted), while the *same* script can modify the specified attributes for any number of users in a container.

To delete a *leaf* object, it is sufficient to include the following two lines into the import file:

```
dn: CN=user2,OU=Staff,DC=w2k,DC=dom
changetype: delete
```

You *cannot* delete a container if it has child objects. The LDAP protocol is for the most part able to delete a subtree (see the Ldp.exe tool description earlier in this chapter), but LDIFDE doesn't allow you to perform such an operation.

CSVDE Utility (Sys)

CSVDE uses Comma-Separated Value (CSV) file format (with a .csv extension). Files in this format can easily be viewed (imported) or prepared (edited and exported) by using various applications, including Microsoft Excel. The first line in such files contains the names of attributes, separated by the comma. The next lines contain the values of attributes, one line per object. An example of such a file is shown below.

Working with Unicode Values

Let's discuss the problem of Unicode support in an example with the CSVDE utility. The following command exports the minimal set of OUs' attributes that allow you to import the OU structure to another domain:

```
csvde -f ExportedOUs.csv -r "(objectCategory=OrganizationalUnit)"
↳ -l "objectClass,ou" -v -u
```

NOTE

If *all* attributes are exported (no -l parameter used), add the -m parameter to the command.

On the screen, the command produces an output (thanks to the verbose mode) similar to the following:

```
Connecting to "(null)"
Logging in as current user using SSPI
Exporting directory to file ExportedOUs.csv
Searching for entries...
Writing out entries
Exporting entry: "OU=Domain Controllers,DC=w2k,DC=dom"
Exporting entry: "OU=STAFF,DC=w2k,DC=dom"
...
Exporting entry: "OU=Персонал,OU=HQ,DC=w2k,DC=dom"

Export Completed. Post-processing in progress...
7 entries exported
The command has completed successfully
```

Notice the Unicode string in an OU name ("OU=Персонал,..."). If the -u parameter has not been specified, the command results in an error (which is also written to the csv.err file):

```
Error writing to file. This error happens when the entry cannot be
written, it can be caused by writing a Unicode value to a non-unicode
file. An error has occurred in the program
```

Here is the exported CSV-file produced by the command (the first line contains the attributes' names):

```
DN,objectClass,ou
"OU=Domain Controllers,DC=w2k,DC=dom",organizationalUnit,Domain
↳ Controllers
```

```
"OU=STAFF,DC=w2k,DC=dom",organizationalUnit,STAFF
...
"OU=Персонал,OU=HQ,DC=w2k,DC=dom",organizationalUnit,X'd09fd0b5d180d18
↳ 1d0bed0bdd0b0d0bb'
```

Notice that the last line contains a coded value for the *ou* attribute.

> **CAUTION!**
>
> If you create an import file with Unicode values from scratch, don't forget to save it in Unicode format (not in ANSI) and use the **-u** parameter when importing the file.

Exporting Information for Successive Import

As already has been said, some attributes presented or incorrectly (inconsistently) specified in an import file may cause an error. Here are two frequently encountered errors that are reported on in import operations:

```
Add error on line 2: Unwilling To Perform
The server side error is "The modification was not permitted for
security reasons."
0 entries modified successfully.
An error has occurred in the program
```

The following error specifies that you want to import an attribute(s) that only the system can change:

```
Add error on line 3: Constraint Violation
The server side error is "Access to the attribute is not permitted
because the attribute is owned by the Security Accounts Manager
(SAM)."
```

If you encounter such an error, use the **-m** parameter for export, and if the error still exists, verify the import file for consistency. Try to get rid of "unnecessary" attributes when doing export. Let's look at a situation where you yourself produce a critical error by using the **-c** parameter.

The scenario is the following. Suppose that you want to copy an entire OU from one domain (w2k.dom) to another (subdom.w2k.dom) and rename the OU at the same time. You use the **-c** OU=Personnel OU=Staff,DC=subdom parameter to change the source DN "OU=Personnel,DC=w2k,DC=dom" to the destination

DN "OU=Staff,DC=subdom,DC=w2k,DC=dom". The problem is that the *ou* attribute isn't changed by such a replace operation, and remains the same. As a result, an inconsistency in the *dn* and *ou* attributes has appeared. You can resolve the problem either by changing the -c parameter or by omitting the *ou* attribute when doing export. The *sIDHistory* attribute presented in the import file will also prevent you from successfully importing. The following command meets all requirements and may perform the desired action:

```
csvde -f Subtree.csv -d OU=Personnel,DC=w2k,DC=dom
      -c OU=Personnel OU=Staff,DC=subdom -o ou,sidhistory -m -v
```

If the copying OU contains computer accounts, you can copy them by using the following command (or add the *primaryGroupID* attribute in the list of omitted attributes in the previous command):

```
csvde -f Comp.csv -d OU=Personnel,DC=w2k,DC=dom
      -r "objectCategory=Computer" -c OU=Personnel OU=Staff,DC=subdom
      -o primaryGroupID -m -v
```

CAUTION!

Note that the *memberOf* attribute is not exported, so you may need to verify (and reestablish) all group memberships of the imported accounts. To add users to (a) group(s), you can also use the *AddUsers.exe* command from *Windows 2000 Resource Kit* (see Chapter 5, "Common Administrative Tasks").

Windows 2000 Domain Manager (NetDom.exe) (ST)

Windows 2000 Domain Manager is a command-line tool that has some unique features, such as moving computer accounts between domains, as well as joining computers to a domain. The tool allows you to:

❑ Retrieve diverse information about domains

❑ Add, join, and move computers to a domain (these operations are "OU-aware"), as well as remove computers from a domain

❑ Reset and verify the computer secure channels

❑ Verify, establish, reset, break, and change domain trusts (including Kerberos trusts)

Chapter 9: Manipulating Active Directory Objects

> **NOTE**
> Be careful, the documentation on this tool is rather inconsistent. There are quite a few divergences between parameters' description in the Support Tools Help and in built-in help.

Let's discuss some interesting features of NetDom.exe on examples. To see detailed information on how an operation is performed, you may use the **/Verbose** parameter with any command. Many tool's commands accept the DNS name of computers and domains, but sometimes the NetBIOS names are preferable.

Querying Domains

NetDom.exe is one of the tools that allow you to view FSMO roles' owners in the forest. For example, the following command shows that the server W2KDC2 holds all roles in its domain, whereas all forest-wide roles are owned by the server W2KDC4 in the root domain:

```
netdom QUERY /D:subdom.w2k.dom FSMO
Schema owner                w2kdc4.w2k.dom
Domain role owner           w2kdc4.w2k.dom
PDC role                    w2kdc2.subdom.w2k.dom
RID pool manager            w2kdc2.subdom.w2k.dom
Infrastructure owner        w2kdc2.subdom.w2k.dom
The command completed successfully.
```

The following command displays all domains that have direct trusts with the specified domain (the trusts may be also verified by using the `netdom TRUST` command; see later):

```
netdom QUERY /D:w2k.dom TRUST /Direct
Direction  Trusted\Trusting domain          Trust type
=========  =======================          ==========
  <->           NT4DOM                       Downlevel
  <->           subdom.w2k.dom               Uplevel
The command completed successfully.
```

The `netdom QUERY` command can also verify and/or reset (the /Reset parameter) domain trusts. The following command checks trusts between the parent (current) domain and a child (the command is run in the parent domain; the credentials of the child's administrator must be provided):

```
netdom QUERY /D:subdom.w2k.dom TRUST /UD:administrator /PD:* /Verify
Type the password associated with the domain user:
Direction  Trusted\Trusting domain       Via domain             Status
=========  =======================       ==========             ======
<->        w2k.dom                                              Verified
The command completed successfully.
```

When you delegate control over some OUs to a user (`jsmith` is our example), you might want to verify all administrative power of that user (you must know the user password). The following command may help you to do this task:

```
netdom QUERY /D:w2k.dom OU /UD:jsmith /PD:*
Type the password associated with the domain user:
List of Organizational Units within which the specified user can create a
machine account:
OU=STAFF,DC=w2k,DC=dom
OU=Sales,OU=Marketing,DC=w2k,DC=dom
The command completed successfully.
```

Compare this output with the results received for an administrative account.

Managing Computer Accounts

The command shown below creates a computer account in the domain (but doesn't *join* a computer to the domain). Note that you can specify a target OU for that account. Remember that if you are working on a computer and join it to a domain using a newly created account, this account by default is added to the *Computer* container. You may use the command for pre-creating accounts in the necessary OUs (domains) before actually joining the computers to the forest.

```
netdom ADD compName /D:w2k.dom /OU:OU=Staff,DC=w2k,DC=dom
The command completed successfully.
```

NetDom.exe can be used for migrating computer accounts from Windows NT resource domains to a Windows 2000 domain or between Windows 2000 domains. All commands — ADD, JOIN, MOVE, and REMOVE — are "OU-aware", so you can manipulate accounts according to the OU structure of your domains.

To move a computer (compName in the example) from the current domain to a destination domain (you must be logged on to the current domain as an administrator and provide an administrator's credentials in the destination domain), use a command similar to:

```
netdom MOVE compName /D:subdom.w2k.dom
    /OU:OU=Personal,DC=subdom,DC=w2k,DC=dom /UO:adminName /PO:*
```

NOTE

The computer being moved must be online and accessible, otherwise the command generates the "The network path was not found" error.

Verifying and Resetting Secure Channels

NetDom.exe can verify and reset the secure channels that exist between each computer in a domain and a domain controller. To verify that the computer W2KPRO1 has the actual secure channel with its domain W2KDOM, it's possible to use the following command (the command's output is also shown):

```
netdom VERIFY w2kpro1.w2k.dom /D:w2k.dom
The secure channel from W2KPRO1.W2K.DOM to the domain W2K.DOM has been
verified.  The connection is with the machine \\W2KDC4.W2K.DOM.
The command completed successfully.
```

The same operation can also be done by using the NLtest tool:

```
nltest /sc_query:w2k.dom /server:w2kpro1.w2k.dom
```

To reset the broken secure channel, use the command

```
netdom RESET w2kpro1.w2k.dom /D:w2k.dom
The secure channel from W2KPRO1.W2K.DOM to the domain W2K.DOM has been
reset.  The connection is with the machine \\W2KDC4.W2K.DOM.
The command completed successfully.
```

The NLtest tool can also be used for that purpose:

```
nltest /sc_reset:w2k.dom /server:w2kpro1.w2k.dom
```

Managing Domain Trusts

NetDom.exe allows you to verify domain (including Kerberos v5 authentication protocol) trusts issues. For example, the following command checks the Kerberos trusts between two domains in the forest (both domain administrators' credentials must be specified!):

```
netdom TRUST subdom.w2k.dom /D:w2k.dom /Kerberos /UD:administrator
     /PD:* /UO:administrator /PO:* /Verify
Type the password associated with the domain user:
Type the password associated with the object user:
The trust between subdom.w2k.dom and w2k.dom has been successfully
verified
The command completed successfully.
```

To reset domain trusts, enter the command:

```
netdom TRUST subdom.w2k.dom /D:w2k.dom /UD:administrator /PD:*
     /UO:administrator /PO:* /Reset
```

The successful output should be similar to:

```
Resetting the trust passwords between subdom.w2k.dom and w2k.dom
The trust between subdom.w2k.dom and w2k.dom
has been successfully reset and verified
The command completed successfully.
```

If trust relationship issues exist, you can try to isolate the problem and use the `netdom VERIFY` or `nltest /sc_query` commands to check trusts between pairs of domain controllers.

> **NOTE**
>
> For verifying and resetting trusts, the **Active Directory Domains and Trusts** snap-in (see *Chapter 4, "Domain Manipulation Tools"*) can also be used.

NetDom.exe allows you to remove a non-existing ("dead") domain (including cross reference and trusted domain objects), which doesn't contain domain controllers. The `netdom TRUST /Remove /Force` command is used for that purpose.

Chapter 10
Migration Tools

Moving Active Directory objects *within* a domain is a rather simple operation. You only need to open the **Active Directory Users and Computers** snap-in, point to the object, and select a target container for the Move operation. Moving objects *between* domains is a more complicated task requiring specific tools. When the domains belong to different forests, then you should talk about *migrating* rather than *moving* objects.

This chapter describes two utilities — *MoveTree* and *ClonePrincipal* — that allow an administrator to reconfigure domains, or migrate users and groups from one forest (or a Windows NT 4.0-based domain) to another. The main difference between these utilities is that MoveTree operates only in intra-forest scenarios, and ClonePrincipal provides inter-forest operations only. Besides, MoveTree destroys the source object (assigning its GUID to the new object), and ClonePrincipal creates a copy of the object, leaving the source intact.

Adventures of the *ObjectSID* Attribute

Changing an Active Directory object's domain membership results in the changing of the object security identifier (SID). Windows 2000-based native mode domains have a mechanism permitting users and security principals to retain access to network resources after they are moved to other location in the domain structure. Let's discuss this mechanism in an example using ClonePrincipal.

Every security principal object in native-mode domains has the multi-valued *sIDHistory* attribute. This attribute, as well as the object SID (the *objectSid* attribute), is used in the object's access token for granting access to network resources. If any SID value is presented in the ACL of a network resource, the object is granted access to this resource (provided that the granted access permission is *Allow* rather than *Deny*). This process is outlined in Fig. 10.1.

After either ClonePrincipal or MoveTree creates a new object, it adds the source object's SID value to the new object's *sIDHistory* list. As a result, the new object will have access to all resources available to the source object (Fig. 10.2).

In addition, the *sIDHistory* list of the source object — if the list is not empty — is added to the *sIDHistory* of the target object.

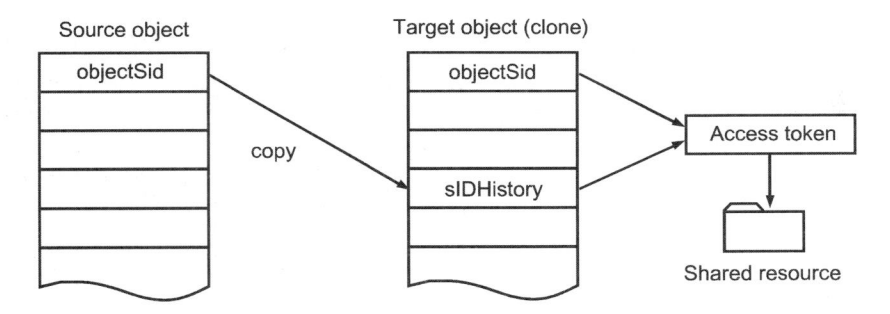

Fig. 10.1. The *sIDHistory* attribute allows the new object to retain the access permissions granted to the source object

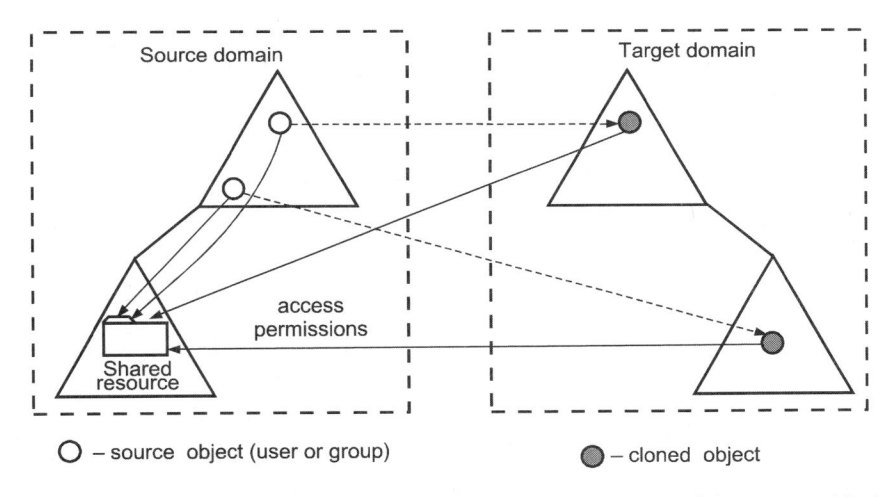

Fig. 10.2. The cloned (or moved) object inherits the access rights of the source object

Active Directory Object Manager (MoveTree.exe) (ST)

MoveTree is the main tool (and the only one, if you exclude the Active Directory Migration Tool) that allows administrators to reconstruct Windows 2000-based domains that belong to the same forest. This tool can move both single Active Directory objects and entire containers (OU) from one domain to another. The following objects are supported:

❑ Users (the passwords are preserved)

- *Empty* local and domain global groups
- Universal groups (all members are preserved)
- Organizational units (with contents)

You cannot use MoveTree for moving computer accounts, system objects, or domain controllers.

> **NOTE**
>
> If you prefer GUI tools, try the Active Directory Migration Tool (ADMT), which has many additional options when compared to MoveTree, albeit is not scriptable.

> **IMPORTANT!**
>
> The documentation on MoveTree in *Windows 2000 Support Tools Help* omits the most important restriction of the tool: the *target* domain must be in *native* mode. Only native-mode domains support the *sIDHistory* attribute (updateable by the tool) for the security principals. You may not consider this fact a limitation, but don't forget about it while working with mixed mode domains!

The syntax of MoveTree is quite simple: you must specify the source and destination of an operation, as well as the operation's type. Practically all parameters are mandatory. MoveTree has two "modes":

- The test mode that checks many conditions without moving any object
- The working mode that initiates the move operation

Moving an OU Subtree

Moving OUs with all their child objects is arguably the most attractive feature of MoveTree. You must take into consideration the fact that when an OU is moved, it retains all links with Group Policy Objects (GPOs) assigned to this OU. It is necessary to re-create these GPOs in the new domain, and break the links with GPOs from the old domain.

Suppose, for example, we'd like to move the *Personnel* OU from the *w2k.dom* domain to the *subdom.w2k.dom* domain and rename it *Staff* OU. You must have administrative rights in the source domain, and may need to provide administrative credentials in the destination domain. The following "text mode" command checks whether this operation will be correct:

```
C:\>movetree /check /s w2kdc4.w2k.dom /d w2kdc2.subdom.w2k.dom
```
- **/sdn** OU=Personnel,DC=w2k,DC=dom
- **/ddn** OU=Staff,DC=subdom,DC=w2k,DC=dom
- **/u** W2KDOM\administrator **/p** *

Notice that the destination OU name differs from the source OU name. Suppose you got the following messages:

```
MOVETREE PRE-CHECK FINISHED.
MOVETREE DETECTED THERE ARE SOME OBJECTS CAN NOT BE MOVED.
PLEASE CLEAN THEM UP FIRST BEFORE TRYING TO START THE MOVE TREE OPERATION.
READ movetree.chk FOR DETAILS.
```

The *movetree.chk* file (in the same folder in which the command has been executed) always contains the diagnostics messages for each step of the command execution (successful operations have the "0x0" code). This file is generated for each check or successful move operation. (You may also specify the **/verbose** parameter with the command, and all detailed diagnostics will be displayed on the console.) You can easily locate the problem and source of an error (marked here in bold), for example:

```
ReturnCode: 0x0 The operation completed successfully. MoveTree check
destination RDN conflict for object: OU=Personnel,DC=w2k,DC=dom

ReturnCode: 0x0 The operation completed successfully. MoveTree cross
domain move check for object: OU=Personnel,DC=w2k,DC=dom
...
```
ReturnCode: 0x212d `Can't move objects with memberships across domain boundaries as once moved, this would violate the membership conditions of the account group.  Remove the object from any account group memberships and retry. MoveTree cross domain move check` **for object:** `CN=user048,OU=Personnel,DC=w2k,DC=dom`
...

> **NOTE**
>
> You'll get the *0x212d* error if you try to move a computer account (a single account or an account included in an OU). Use NetDom or ADMT for that purpose.

If you delete the reported user object (cn=user048) from any security group (excluding the primary group — *Domain Users*) and repeat the command, you'll get the following result:

```
MOVETREE PRE-CHECK FINISHED.
MOVETREE IS READY TO START THE MOVE OPERATION.

MOVETREE FINISHED SUCCESSFULLY.
```

This means that the command has found no errors, and the move operation has a chance to succeed. Now you can complete the move operation by replacing the /check parameter with either the /startnocheck or /start parameter. All diagnostics are always written to the *movetree.log* file located in the current folder.

ATTENTION!

The "test mode" (with the /check parameter) doesn't guarantee that the operation won't fail. For example, the following error ("Insufficient access rights to perform the operation") may appear only in the "working mode":

```
MOVETREE FAILED. 0x2098
READ movetree.err FOR DETAILS.
```

NOTE

After moving directory objects, force replication, or wait until replication is complete. The Infrastructure operations master and Global Catalog must be updated. Otherwise, some changes in the domains may not be "understood" in the forest.

Moving User and Group Accounts

The destination container must already exist before a user or group account is moved. The object can be renamed when moving, you only need to specify the appropriate distinguished names with the /sdn and /ddn parameters.

Local and global groups must be empty when moved. (Only universal groups retain all their members when moved.) Otherwise, a message similar to the following appears in the movetree.chk file:

```
ReturnCode: 0x2133 Cross-domain move of resource groups is not
allowed. MoveTree cross domain move check for object:
CN=LocalGroup,OU=Personnel,DC=w2k,DC=dom
```

Cloning Security Principals (ClonePrincipal) (ST)

ClonePrincipal is not really a utility or command, but a set of scripts that allows administrators to perform *inter-forest* migration, primarily to incrementally migrate (copy) accounts from an existing Windows NT 4.0-based domain to a new Windows 2000 domain. (In contrast to MoveTree, ClonePrincipal doesn't affect the source objects.) ClonePrincipal can also be used for reorganizing Windows 2000-based forests. This tool and its GUI counterpart — the Active Directory Migration Tool (ADMT) — are the only facilities used for upgrading existing Windows NT 4.0-based domains in cases when users preserve continuous access to network shared resource and administrators can fulfill fallback in an emergency.

> **NOTE**
> ADMT is a more powerful tool than ClonePrincipal. ADMT has many additional features, for example, it also supports *intra-forest* operations, and can migrate user profiles, computers, and trusts. ClonePrincipal and ADMT have quite a few similar features. However, they differ internally, and Microsoft doesn't recommend mixing these tools for migration operations. If you learn ClonePrincipal's basics (especially the environmental requirements and mechanism of SID migration), you'll be able to master ADMT without problems.

Well-known SIDs and RIDs

Let's first clarify some terms used below.

A unique *Security Identifier* (SID) of a security principal (i. e. user, computer, or group account) is used to grant the principal access to shared network resources. The SID is composed of two parts: the unique "domain part", which is the same for all principals of the domain where they reside, and *Relative Identifier* (RID), which uniquely identifies the principal in the domain.

An account with a *well-known RID* has an SID composed of an RID that is identical in every domain, and a "domain part" that is unique for each domain. Such an account can only be cloned onto an account with the same RID. Here are accounts with well-known RIDs:

- Administrator
- Guest

- Domain Users
- Domain Admins
- Domain Guests

An account with a *well-known SID* cannot be cloned, since its SID is identical in every domain. (Therefore, it doesn't make sense to copy an account whose SID already exists in the target domain.) Here are accounts with well-known SIDs:

- Users
- Administrators
- Guests
- Account Operators
- Backup Operators
- Print Operators
- Server Operators
- Power Users
- Replicator

Supported Object Types

With ClonePrincipal, you can clone the following objects:

- User accounts
- Security group accounts:
    - Local groups
    - Global groups
    - Domain local groups (Windows 2000 native mode only)
    - Universal groups (Windows 2000 native mode only)

ClonePrincipal *doesn't* support the following objects:

- Computer accounts (workstations or domain controllers)
- Inter-domain trusts
- Accounts with well-known SIDs (for example, Administrators, or Users local groups)

ClonePrincipal Components

ClonePrincipal consists of the following files:

- Clonepr.dll — a COM server that implements all functions
- Clonepr.vbs — the script that clones a *single* security principal (user account; global, universal, local, or domain local group), creating the target principal if necessary
- Clonelg.vbs — the script that clones *all* local (except built-in) or domain local groups in a domain
- Clonegg.vbs — the script that clones *all* global and universal groups in a domain
- Cloneggu.vbs — this script clones *all* users and global groups (users, global groups, and universal groups accounts) in a domain, including well-known global groups such as Domain Admins, Domain Users, and Domain Guests
- SIDHist.vbs — the script that copies (adds) the value of the *objectSid* attribute of a source principal to the *sIDHistory* attribute of a target principal

Using all these scripts is discussed below.

Configuring Migration Environment

One of the most important requirements for ClonePrincipal (as well as for ADMT) to work well is the proper configuration of both source and target domains. If you are also planning to use (test) ADMT, see also the *additional* requirements below. ClonePrincipal will fail if any of the requirements are omitted.

Here are some general considerations:

- If ClonePrincipal was installed separately from the *Support Tools*, make sure that the Clonepr.dll is registered on the target DC
- All ClonePrincipal scripts must be run on the PDC Emulator (the FSMO role master) of the target domain
- You must log on to the DC as a member of the *Domain Admins* group of the target domain

Registry Settings (*TcpipClientSupport*)

In the source domain running Windows NT 4.0 (with Service Pack 4 or later) or Windows 2000, create the registry REG_DWORD:0x1 value named *TcpipClientSupport* on the PDC (or PDC Emulator) under the following subkey:

```
HKEY_LOCAL_MACHINE\SYSTEM\CurrentControlSet\Control\Lsa
```

Reboot the PDC.

Audit Settings

It is necessary to set auditing, both in the source and target domains. Use the procedure described below.

For Windows 2000 domains (both the source and target):

1. Open the Group Policy Object (GPO) for the *Domain Controller* OU. (Use either the **Domain Controller Security Policy** or the **Active Directory Users and Computers** snap-in.)

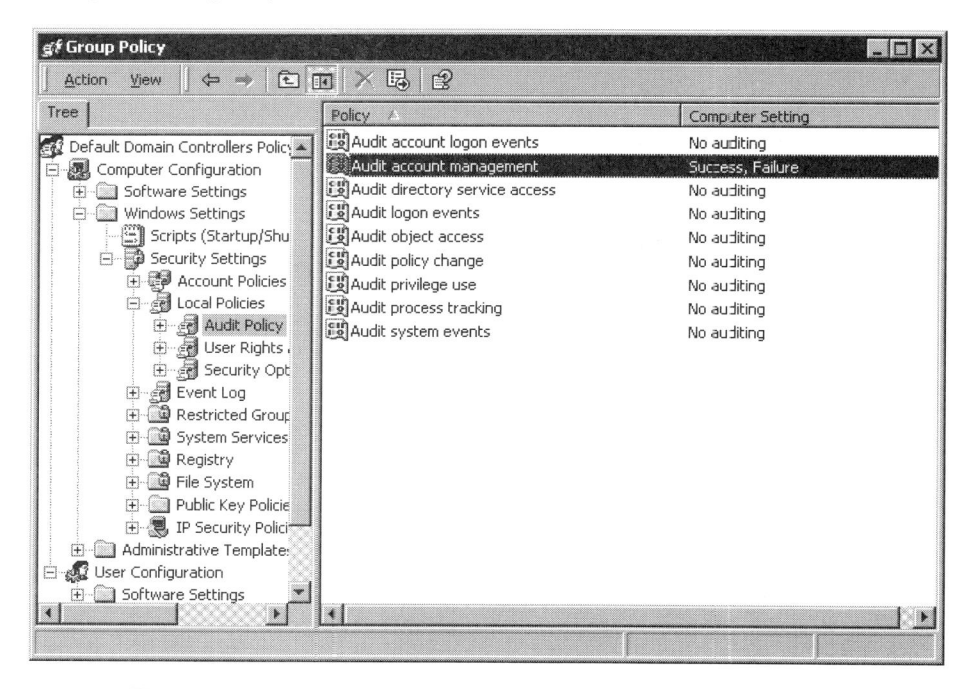

Fig. 10.3. Setting audit on the Windows 2000-based domain controllers

2. Open the **Security Settings | Local Policies | Audit Policy** node.

3. Double-click the **Audit account management** policy and check both the **Success** and **Failure** boxes. Click **OK**. A sample screen is shown in Fig. 10.3. Refresh the computer policy or wait for updates to take place.

For a Windows NT 4.0-based source domain:

1. In User Manager for Domains, click **Audit** in the **Policies** menu.

2. Select **Audit These Events** and check the **Success** and **Failure** boxes for **User and Group Management** (Fig. 10.4).

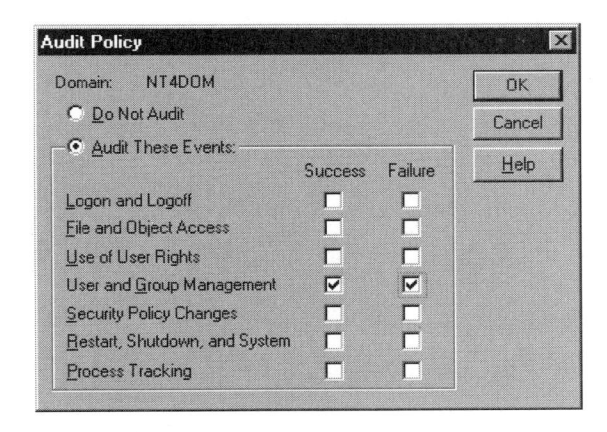

Fig. 10.4. Setting audit on a Windows NT 4.0-based domain controller

Creating the Audit Group

In either Windows NT 4.0- or Windows 2000-based *source* domain, you must create a special group that is used for auditing cloning operations. The name of the group is composed of the source domain NetBIOS (pre-Windows 2000) name appended with three dollar signs, for example, NT4DOM$$$.

Trusts

Establish a *bi-directional* trust between the source and target domains (i. e. the source domain must trust the target domain, and vice versa.) (For details, see "Establishing Trusts" in *Chapter 3, "Deploying Active Directory"*.) Before that, make sure that name resolving is working properly in your configuration. You must be able successfully ping the target DC from the source DC by the NetBIOS (pre-Windows 2000) name, and vice versa.

Configuring Groups

To run ClonePrincipal successfully, you must have the appropriate administrative rights: add the *Domain Admins* global group from the target domain to the *Administrators* local group in the source domain.

Additional Requirements for ADMT

In *addition* to the considerations and necessary procedures described above, you must carry out the following operations:

❑ Add the *Domain Admins* global group from the source domain to the *Administrators* local group in the target domain.

❑ Add the *Domain Admins* global group from the source domain to each migrated computer's *Administrators* local group. The same is applicable to each computer on which security is translated.

❑ Make sure that administrative shares exist on the target DC as well as on each computer you migrate.

Cloning Users

Even if the source domain is Windows 2000-based, ClonePrincipal does not treat the user properties inherent to Active Directory. Only the following Windows NT 4.0 properties are copied from the source object to the target object:

❑ General properties:

- *Full name*
- *Description*
- Account flags (such as *Account Expires*, *Logon Hours*, *Logon To*, and others)

❑ Profile properties:

- User profile (*Profile path* and *Logon script*)
- Home directory (*Local path*, *Connect* drive and location)

Chapter 10: Migration Tools   283

- Dial-in properties
- File and Print for NetWare properties
- Terminal Server Properties

The following flags are set for the existing or cloned (newly created) user account:

- **User must change password at next logon**
- **Account is disabled**

The following flags are cleared:

- **User cannot change password**
- **Password never expires**

The user password is set to empty (null).

By default, the cloned user becomes a member of the *Domain Users* group. The user's group memberships are retained in the target domain if the target global and/or universal groups are clones of the source groups in which the source user is a member. That is, if both user and global (universal) group accounts are copied (Cloneggu.vbs is used), the groups can retain all their members (if *all* of them are cloned).

Cloning Groups

When cloning global groups, you must consider the fact that the Cloneggu.vbs and Clonegg.vbs scripts copy accounts with well-known RIDs, and will fail if you specify a target container (the **/dstOU** parameter) different from the default *User* container where these accounts reside. You cannot, for example, perform such a command without a fatal error:

```
cloneggu /srcDC:nt4dc2 /srcDom:nt4dom
         /dstDC:w2kdc4 /dstDom:w2k.dom /dstOU:OU=Staff,DC=w2k,DC=dom
```

You have three following options:

1. Specify the Users container as the target OU, for example, **/dstOU**:CN=Users,DC=w2k,DC=dom.

2. Copy all accounts with well-known RIDs (Administrator, Guest, Domain Admins, etc.) to the target OU.

3. Do not clone (i. e. ignore) the accounts with well-known RIDs. Open the Cloneggu.vbs or Clonegg.vbs script in a text editor, find the code shown below, and uncomment the specified statements:

```
'To Stop Cloning Well Known Sids Uncomment 4 lines below
'  if HasWellKnownRid(sidString) then
'     ShouldCloneObject = False
'     exit function
'  end if
```

4. In this case, the target "well-known" accounts will lose access to those network resources, which contain the source "well-known" accounts in their ACLs (since the *sIDHistory* attribute of these target accounts will not be updated). You may manually update the ACLs of the appropriate shared resources, or copy the SIDs from the source accounts to the target ones by using SIDHist.vbs.

ClonePrincipal Samples

Let's now consider some examples of using ClonePrincipal. Each parameter of all ClonePrincipal scripts is mandatory. You can view the parameter list for every script by entering the script name and question mark at the command prompt.

Cloning SID (*SIDHist.vbs*)

Normally, the SIDHist.vbs is executed by other ClonePrincipal scripts. However, you can run it manually to accomplish some specific tasks. You may want, for example, grant the Domain Admins group in the target domain the right to access network resources available to the same group from the source domain.

> **NOTE**
>
> You can monitor all changes of the *sIDHistory* attribute with Ldp.exe. AdsVw.exe allows you to view the *objectSid* attribute (in hexadecimal byte format) on the source Windows NT-based DC. To see this attribute in the same format on the destination DC, you can also use the **ADSI Edit** snap-in.

The following script adds the *objectSid* attribute on the *nt4user1* from the *nt4dom* domain to the *sIDHistory* attribute of the *w2kuser1* user from the *w2k.dom* domain:

```
C:\>sidhist /srcDC:nt4dc2 /srcDom:nt4dom /srcSAM:nt4user1
       /dstDC:w2kdc4 /dstDom:w2k.dom /dstSAM:w2kuser1
```

As a result, the w2kuser1 user will have the same resource access rights as the nt4user1 user.

You can perform this operation only for *one* selected account in the target domain. Otherwise, the script will fail with the following error:

```
Connected
Error 0x8007215B occurred.
Error Description: Failed to add the source SID to the destination
object's SID history. The error was: "The source object's SID already
exists in destination forest."
Error HelpContext: 0
Error HelpFile     :
Error Source       : DSUtils.ClonePrincipal.1
```

If the operation is successful, the resulting output is very simple:

```
C:\>sidhist /srcDC:nt4dc2 /srcDom:nt4dom /srcSAM:nt4user1
↳ /dstDC:w2kdc4 /dstDom:w2k.dom /dstSAM:w2kuser1

Connected
Success
```

After the above-mentioned command has been executed, the following message appears in the Security Log on the destination DC:

```
Event Type: Success Audit
Event Source:         Security
Event Category:       Account Management
Event ID:   669
...
Computer:   W2KDC4
Description:
```

Add SID History:

```
    Source Account Name:  NT4DOM\nt4user1
    Source Account ID:    W2KDOM\w2kuser1
    Target Account Name:  w2kuser1
    Target Domain: W2KDOM
    Target Account ID:    W2KDOM\w2kuser1
    Caller User Name:     administrator
    Caller Domain: W2KDOM
    Caller Logon ID:      (0x0,0x193AE)
    Privileges:     -
```

Cloning a User (*ClonePr.vbs*)

The following script clones a user from a Windows NT domain to a Windows 2000 domain, where the user is placed into the specified organizational unit. This container must exist before the script is executed. (Note that the user can already exist on the target DC.)

```
C:\>clonepr /srcDC:nt4dc2 /srcDom:nt4dom /srcSAM:nt4user1
    /dstDC:w2kdc4 /dstDom:w2k.dom /dstSAM:ntUser1
    /dstDN:CN=user1,OU=Staff,DC=w2k,DC=dom

Connected to source and destination domain controllers
Bound to source User nt4user1
Destination object ntUser1 not found (by SAM name) path used:
WinNT://w2k.dom/w2kdc4/ntUser1
Destination DN found
Setting properties for target user CN=user1
Downlevel properties set.
Fixing group memberships for user CN=user1
   Found global group WinNT://nt4dom/nt4dc2/Domain Users
   Skipping WinNT://nt4dom/nt4dc2/Domain Users -- not cloned yet
User's Group memberships restored.
User changes commited.
Adding SID for source User nt4user1 to SID history of target user
CN=user1
SID history set successfully.
nt4user1 cloned successfully.
1 object(s) cloned
```

Two events are registered in the Security Log on the target DC: Event ID 642 (User Account Changed) and Event ID 669 (Add SID History). Thus, you can trace all clone operations performed in the domain.

Finding Groups of a Specific Type

When cloning groups, you may need to view the list of already copied groups and monitor the process of migration. There is a trick that allows you to find *only* the groups of a specific type located in any container in the object tree.

You need to use LDAP search and the LDAP_MATCHING_RULE_BIT_AND matching rule control in the search filter. (For details, search for the "query filter" string in the *Active Directory SDK*.) For example, the following command displays the *ADsPath* property of all universal groups that exist in the domain:

```
search "LDAP://DC=w2k,DC=dom"
 ↳ /C:"groupType:1.2.840.113556.1.4.803:=2147483656" /S:subtree
```

This search filter can also be used in other tools, such as Ldp.exe. The filter's values for various group types are listed in the table below. (Only the decimal values are used. Notice also the minus sign in the last table row.)

Group type	Hexadecimal value	Decimal filter value
Built-in and Domain local	0x80000004	2147483652
Global	0x80000002	2147483650
Universal	0x80000008	2147483656
Built-in only	0x7FFFFFFB	-2147483643

Chapter 11
Security Tools

This chapter describes the tools related to Active Directory security, and primarily to permissions on directory objects. These tools allow an administrator to perform the following tasks:

- View and/or modify permissions (the ACL lists) on directory objects (ACLDiag, DsACLs) and verify delegation of administrative tasks
- Verify inheritance of ACLs at different levels of the directory object hierarchy and replication of ACLs between domain controllers (SDCheck)
- Verify Kerberos authentication (KerbTray, KList)

ACL Diagnostics (ACLDiag.exe) (ST)

Most often, an administrator views and modifies the security setting (the ACL lists) on Active Directory objects by using the **Security** tab of the object's **Properties** window. This window can be opened from an appropriate administrative snap-in. However, it is sometimes more convenient to analyze the ACL lists in a "plain text" form. The ACLDiag tool allows an administrator to view all the information about a directory object's security settings. Any user can run ACLDiag, but the tool's output will depend on the user's rights to view that (or some other) object.

The ACLDiag's options are discussed below in examples. (You might prefer to use the DsACLs tool discussed later; it doesn't have some of the features that ACLDiag does, but it allows ACL modifications and seems to be more reliable.)

> **NOTE**
>
> It's necessary to note that the tool requires quite a long time to run, especially when the /geteffective parameter is specified and produces an output that usually should be redirected to a file.

Viewing All Permissions

ACLDiag can display (in a readable or tab-delimited form) all directly defined or inherited permissions on an object, as well as the audit settings. The tool's output is structured in such a way that helps an administrator analyze information. Essentially, the tool has two subtests: *Security Diagnosis* (you may skip this by using the /skip parameter) and *Effective Rights Diagnosis* (see later). Let's see, for example,

Chapter 11: Security Tools 291

in which form ACLDiag displays permissions for an OU. (For clarity, the output section's titles are in bold.)

```
C:\>acldiag "OU=Staff,DC=w2k,DC=dom"
```
Security Diagnosis for OU=Staff,DC=w2k,DC=dom
Description
    Owner: W2KDOM\Domain Admins

    Permissions effective on the object:
        Allow NT AUTHORITY\Authenticated Users   Read all properties
        Allow NT AUTHORITY\Authenticated Users   List contents
        Allow NT AUTHORITY\Authenticated Users   List object
        Allow W2KDOM\Domain Admins   Create all subobjects
        Allow W2KDOM\Domain Admins   Delete all subobjects
...

Permissions inherited by subobjects:
    Inherit to All Subobjects:
        Allow BUILTIN\Administrators   Create all subobjects
        (Inherited permission from DC=w2k,DC=dom)
        Allow BUILTIN\Administrators   Read all properties
        (Inherited permission from DC=w2k,DC=dom)
...
    Inherit to Group objects only:
...
    Inherit to User objects only:
...
    Inherit to Computer objects only:
...

Auditing effective on this object:
        Audit Successful and Failed Create all subobjects attempts by \Everyone
        Audit Successful and Failed Delete all subobjects attempts by \Everyone
...

Auditing inherited to subobjects:
    Inherit to All Subobjects:
        Audit Successful and Failed Create all subobjects attempts by \Everyone
        Audit Successful and Failed Delete all subobjects attempts by \Everyone
...

Viewing the Effective Rights

To see the effective rights for all or some users or groups, use the /geteffective parameter. For example, the following command displays rights on an OU for all users and groups. If the rights are not defined for a user or group, the corresponding output section will be empty. As you can see, detailed information on each attribute's permissions is given.

```
C:\>acldiag "OU=Staff,DC=w2k,DC=dom" /geteffective:* /skip
Security Diagnosis for OU=Staff,DC=w2k,DC=dom

Effective Rights Diagnosis

W2KDOM\Domain Admins:
          Can Modify Membership (via W2KDOM\Domain Admins
membership)
          All control accesses for class Organizational Unit (via
W2KDOM\Domain Admins membership)
          Can List object (via W2KDOM\Domain Admins membership)
...
    Can read the following properties
          Read flags (via W2KDOM\Domain Admins membership)
          Read replUpToDateVector (via W2KDOM\Domain Admins
membership)
...
    Can write the following properties
          Write subClassOf (via W2KDOM\Domain Admins membership)
          Write mayContain (via W2KDOM\Domain Admins membership)
...
jsmith@w2k.dom:
Staff-Adm@w2k.dom:
W2KDOM\Enterprise Admins:
          Can Modify Membership
          All control accesses for class Organizational Unit
          Can List object
          Can List contents
...
    Can read the following properties
          Read flags
          Read replUpToDateVector
...
```

```
Can write the following properties
        Write subClassOf
        Write mayContain
...
```

Verifying Delegation of Control

ACLDiag allows an administrator to check out whether the *Delegation of Control Wizard* was run for an object, and whether or not this wizard was run successfully. Let's consider an example. In the following scenario, two users — *jsmith@w2k.dom* and *Staff-Adm@w2k.dom* — have received specific administrative rights over the *Staff* OU. (Remember that there are *six* common administrative tasks for OU objects.) By using a command similar to the following, you can easily determine who has the delegated rights and which rights these are:

```
C:\>acldiag "OU=Staff,DC=w2k,DC=dom" /chkdeleg /skip
Security Diagnosis for OU=Staff,DC=w2k,DC=dom


Delegation Template Diagnosis:
        Create, delete, and manage user accounts allowed to Staff-Adm@w2k.dom
                Status: OK
                Applies on this object: YES
                Inherited from parent: NO

        Reset passwords on user accounts allowed to jsmith@w2k.dom
                Status: OK
                Applies on this object: YES
                Inherited from parent: NO

        Read all user information
                Status: NOT PRESENT

        Create, delete and manage groups allowed to Staff-Adm@w2k.dom
                Status: MISCONFIGURED
                Applies on this object: YES
                Inherited from parent: NO
```

```
    Modify the membership of a group
            Status: NOT PRESENT
    Manage Group Policy links allowed to Staff-Adm@w2k.dom
            Status: OK
            Applies on this object: YES
            Inherited from parent: NO
```

Notice that if a common task has not been delegated, the tool reports `Status` as `NOT PRESENT`. As you can see, one task's status is `MISCONFIGURED`. (In this case one of the ACEs composing that administrative task was deleted.) Although the documentation on ACLDiag declares that the `/fixdeleg` parameter should repair that issue, it doesn't seem to work like that, and you should run the Delegation of Control Wizard again. You may also run the DsACLs.exe utility with the `/s` parameter (see below), which resets all permissions on the object to schema defaults. (Use this option with caution! See below "Restoring Security Settings" in this chapter.)

Comparing with Schema Default Permissions

To verify whether an object retains all the permissions that were set at the object's creation, use a command similar the following:

```
C:\>acldiag "OU=Staff,DC=w2k,DC=dom" /schema /skip
Security Diagnosis for OU=Staff,DC=w2k,DC=dom

Schema Defaults Diagnosis
        Schema defaults: Present
        Obtained         : At CREATION
```

In this case, the tool reports that the object's permissions are unchanged since its creation. If some permission has been removed, the tool displays the message

```
Schema defaults: Partial
```

To see the default (schema) permissions on a directory object, you should refer to the schema partition. Use a command similar to the following (for OU):

```
C:\>acldiag "CN=Organizational-Unit,CN=Schema,CN=Configuration,
↳ DC=w2k,DC=dom"
```

DsACLs.exe (ST)

As opposed to ACLDiag, the DsACLs command-line tool allows an administrator to both view and *modify* the ACL lists of directory objects, i.e. to fulfil all operations available on the **Security** tab in the object's **Properties** window. (For directory objects, DsACLs does a job similar to what the CACLs.exe utility does for file system objects.) Modifying security descriptors may require a good understanding of Active Directory objects' security model, especially inheritance of permissions.

DsACLs is quite well documented, so I'll consider only a few examples.

> **NOTE**
> The DsACLs' parameters are case sensitive and all letters must be upper case.

Viewing Security Settings

You can analyze the following screen output and decide which tool — DsACLs or ACLDiag — is more convenient for you to view security descriptors of directory objects. (The former command works faster, but is not as comprehensive as the latter. Notice, for example, the lines related to the *Domain Admins* group in both command's output. Maybe you yourself want to select an object and compare the *full* outputs.) When the /A parameter is specified, the owner and auditing information is also displayed. In the audit list, "all" means that an audit is performed for both *Successful* and *Failed* events.

```
C:\>dsacls OU=Staff,DC=w2k,DC=dom /A
Owner: W2KDOM\Domain Admins
Group: W2KDOM\Domain Users

Audit list:
Effective Permissions on this object are:
   All     Everyone  SPECIAL ACCESS    <Inherited from parent>
                     DELETE
                     WRITE PERMISSIONS
...
Permissions inherited to subobjects are:
Inherited to all subobjects
   All     Everyone  SPECIAL ACCESS    <Inherited from parent>
```

```
                         DELETE
                         WRITE PERMISSIONS
...
Access list:
Effective Permissions on this object are:
Allow NT AUTHORITY\Authenticated Users       SPECIAL ACCESS
                                             READ PERMISSONS
                                             LIST CONTENTS
                                             READ PROPERTY
Allow W2KDOM\Domain Admins                   FULL CONTROL
Allow NT AUTHORITY\SYSTEM                    FULL CONTROL
Allow BUILTIN\Administrators                 SPECIAL ACCESS
<Inherited from parent>
                                             DELETE
                                             READ PERMISSONS
                                             WRITE PERMISSIONS
...
Permissions inherited to subobjects are:
Inherited to all subobjects
Allow BUILTIN\Administrators                 SPECIAL ACCESS
<Inherited from parent>
                                             DELETE
                                             READ PERMISSONS
...
Inherited to user
...
Inherited to group
...
The command completed successfully
```

Granting and Removing Permissions

Let's now consider a couple of examples of modifying security descriptors. The first command grants the user *jsmith@w2k.dom* the *Generic Read* right (List Contents, Read All Properties, and Read Permissions) for the *Staff* OU:

   dsacls OU=Staff,DC=w2k,DC=dom **/G** jsmith@w2k.dom:GR

You may verify the result of the operation with all possible (and already mentioned) means.

The second command prevents the user from reading two properties of the OU object:

```
dsacls OU=Staff,DC=w2k,DC=dom /D jsmith@w2k.dom:RP;gPLink
    ↳ jsmith@w2k.dom:RP;gPOptions
```

ATTENTION!

The attribute names in the last command are case sensitive. You can specify any applicable number of attributes in the same command.

Restoring Security Settings

For various reasons you may want to return an object's security settings to their initial state. The default settings for an object class are defined in the Active Directory schema. (Besides, the settings inherited from the parents are also applied to the object.) For example, the following command restores defaults for an OU:

```
C:\>dsacls OU=Staff,DC=w2k,DC=dom /S
```

(You can also use the /T parameter and restore the defaults on the entire tree of objects.)

Be cautious; this operation deletes the audit settings from the object. The command

```
C:\>dsacls OU=Staff,DC=w2k,DC=dom /A
```

will display the following message:

```
Audit list:
{This object is protected from inheriting permissions from the parent}
THERE ARE NO ACCESS CONTROL ENTRIES
...
```

To restore the default audit settings, open the object's Properties window (in the **Active Directory Users and Computers** or **ADSI Edit** snap-in), click the **Security** tab, and then **Advanced**. In the **Auditing** tab in the **Access Control Settings** window, check the **Allow inheritable auditing entries from parent to propagate to this object** box, and click **Apply**. Click **OK** in the warning window and close all opened windows. If the operation was successful, the `acldiag <objectName> /schema /skip` command will report the following:

```
Schema Defaults Diagnosis
      Schema defaults: Present
      Obtained           : At CREATION
```

> **CAUTION!**
>
> If you don't restore the audit settings after the `dsacls /S` command, the ACLDiag command with the `/chkdeleg` or `/schema` parameters will fail.

Security Descriptor Check Utility (SDCheck.exe) (ST)

The SDCheck command-line tool is primarily intended to help administrators verify and monitor the following issues related to directory objects' security descriptors:

- ❑ Propagation of inherited ACLs for a specified directory object
- ❑ Replication of ACLs between different domain controllers

Let's consider how to manage the listed tasks in the following sample output. In this scenario we test the ACLs of a user object (*user2@w2k.dom*) that belongs to a nested OU. (A domain controller must be also specified in the command.) Some lines, as well as the comments placed in the text below these lines, are shown in bold.

```
C:\>sdcheck w2kdc4.w2k.dom user2@w2k.dom

Microsoft(R) Windows (R) 2000 Operating System
Security Descriptor Check Utility - build(2160)

Input:   user2@w2k.dom
Object:  CN=User02,OU=Inside,OU=Staff,DC=w2k,DC=dom
Domain:  w2k.dom
Domain:  DC=w2k,DC=dom
Server:  w2kdc4.w2k.dom

*** Warning: No values returned for dSCorePropagationData on
DC=w2k,DC=dom

Object:   CN=User02,OU=Inside,OU=Staff,DC=w2k,DC=dom
Classes:  top person organizationalPerson user
SD:       1124 bytes
Metadata: 12/21/2000 20:21:38 @ w2kdc3.w2k.dom ver: 300002
```
[By viewing metadata, an administrator can monitor the replication of the changed security descriptor. Notice that the version number is different, and that the changes have been originated by another DC. To view the replication metadata, you can also use the *repadmin /showmeta* command.]

Chapter 11: Security Tools 299

```
History:    12/28/2000 01:23:50 flags(0x1) SD propagation
            12/28/2000 02:04:51 flags(0x1) SD propagation
            12/28/2000 02:47:53 flags(0x1) SD propagation
            12/28/2000 03:05:14 flags(0x1) SD propagation

Object:     OU=Inside,OU=Staff,DC=w2k,DC=dom
Classes:    top organizationalUnit
SD:         536 bytes
Metadata:   12/21/2000 20:11:38 @ w2kdc4.w2k.dom ver: 300001
History:    12/28/2000 01:23:50 flags(0x1) SD propagation
            12/28/2000 02:04:51 flags(0x1) SD propagation
            12/28/2000 02:47:53 flags(0x1) SD propagation
            12/28/2000 03:05:14 flags(0x1) SD propagation

Object:     OU=Staff,DC=w2k,DC=dom
Classes:    top organizationalUnit
SD:         536 bytes
Metadata:   12/28/2000 03:05:14 @ w2kdc4.w2k.dom ver: 300019
History:    12/28/2000 02:04:51 flags(0x1) SD propagation
            12/28/2000 02:26:37 flags(0x1) SD propagation
            12/28/2000 02:42:04 flags(0x1) SD propagation
            12/28/2000 03:05:14 flags(0x1) SD propagation
```

[Notice that the last lines in the history are the same for all three objects. This means that a change of the security descriptor at the *Staff* OU level has been successfully propagated to the user object level. If the time values are different, the inheritance might be blocked and this fact should be tested.]

```
Object:     DC=w2k,DC=dom
Classes:    top domain domainDNS
SD:         612 bytes
Metadata:   12/22/2000 17:17:35 @ w2kdc4.w2k.dom ver: 400006
```

Checking ACL inheritance ... [This test will display the ACL inheritance errors at any level if such an error is found.]
```
    Parent: 3 - DC=w2k,DC=dom
    Child:  2 - OU=Staff,DC=w2k,DC=dom

Checking ACL inheritance ...
    Parent: 2 - OU=Staff,DC=w2k,DC=dom
    Child:  1 - OU=Inside,OU=Staff,DC=w2k,DC=dom
```

```
Checking ACL inheritance ...
    Parent: 1 - OU=Inside,OU=Staff,DC=w2k,DC=dom
    Child:  0 - CN=User02,OU=Inside,OU=Staff,DC=w2k,DC=dom
```

The shown output is an example of a successful test.

To verify the "continuity" of the inherited ACLs, use the **-debug** parameter. Suppose, in our example, that propagation of ACLs is blocked at the *Inside* OU level. This means that the **Allow inheritable permissions from parent to propagate to this object** checkbox is cleared on the **Security** tab in the Inside's **Properties** window. You can quickly diagnose this fact by using the command

```
C:\>sdcheck w2kdc4.w2k.dom user2@w2k.dom -debug
```

At a specific moment, the tool outputs a warning:

```
Checking ACL inheritance ...
    Parent: 2 - OU=Staff,DC=w2k,DC=dom
    Child:  1 - OU=Inside,OU=Staff,DC=w2k,DC=dom
*** Warning: Child has SE_DACL_PROTECTED set, therefore doesn't
inherit - skipping test
...
```

If the ACL inheritance is not blocked, the test will run without any warnings.

Kerberos Tray (KerbTray.exe) (RK)

The *Kerberos Tray* tool lists all cached Kerberos tickets and allows you to view the tickets' properties and purge them. This information may help in resolving problems with authentication and access to network resources. (If a Windows 2000-based computer has not obtained the initial ticket-granting-ticket (TGT) from a Kerberos Distribution Center (KCC) during the first user's logon onto the domain, or if the cached tickets have expired and haven't been renewed, the computer won't be able to authenticate to resources.)

The tool starts in minimized mode, and you can find its icon on the system tray (in the right bottom corner of the screen). If you move the mouse cursor over the icon, the time left on the initial TGT will be displayed (Fig. 11.1).

If you double-click the icon or select the **List Tickets** command from the context menu, the main tool's window will appear (Fig. 11.2). It displays all cached Kerberos tickets acquired at/since the first user's logon.

Fig. 11.1. Kerberos Tray displays the time left on the initial TGT before it expires (left); the tool's context menu (right) allows you to select an operation

The **Purge Tickets** command clears the entire ticket cache (it thus differs from the *Kerberos List* tool, which is able to delete tickets selectively). No warnings are issued before clearing the cache, so be cautious! While the cache is empty, you may be prevented from authenticating to resources, and logoff and logon will be required.

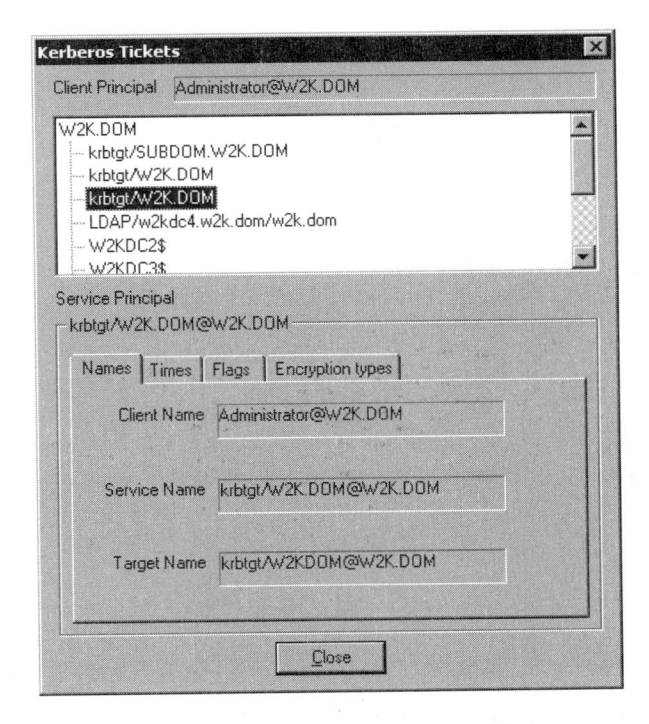

Fig. 11.2. You can see in this window the information about all cached tickets and their properties

> **NOTE**
>
> The utility's window is not updateable. Therefore, if you believe that the new tickets might appear (while connecting to a new resource or new services), close the window and open it again.

Let's discuss the main ticket's properties, which are displayed by the tool.

- The **Client Principal** field contains the name of the current logon account. If the ticket cache is empty, this field displays the "No network credentials" message.

- All tickets obtained since logon are listed in the scrolling window. The properties of the selected ticket are displayed on the tabs below.

- The strings below the scrolling list contain the name of a security principal for the selected ticket. If the ticket time is over, the "Expired" string is displayed and no properties are shown on the tabs.

- The **Names** tab contains:
  - **Client Name** — requestor of the ticket. In most cases (while accessing resources in the current domain) this is the same name that is displayed in the **Client Principal** field.
  - **Service Name** — the security principal (account) name for the service. The *samAccountName* attribute of the account's directory object stores this name.
  - **Target** Name — one of the service names that are contained in the multi-valued *servicePrincipalName* attribute of the computer's directory object. This is the service name the ticket has been obtained for.

- The time when the ticket was obtained (**Start time**) and its expiration time (**End time**) are shown on the **Time** tab. Interpretation of the **Flags** tab requires a more profound understanding of Kerberos protocol. The **Initial** flag is set only for the ticket that was obtained without the TGT.

Kerberos List (KList.exe) (RK)

This command-line tool has practically the same possibilities and features as the *Kerberos tray* tool described earlier. The tool has the following commands:

- `klist tgt` — displays the initial TGT
- `klist tickets` — lists all cached tickets (see the example below)

❑ **klist purge** — allows you to delete a specific ticket in a dialog. An example of such a dialog is shown below:

```
C:\>klist purge
Cached Tickets: (4)

    Server: krbtgt/SUBDOM.W2K.DOM@W2K.DOM
        KerbTicket Encryption Type: RSADSI RC4-HMAC(NT)
        End Time: 12/18/2000 2:32:53
        Renew Time: 12/24/2000 16:32:53

Purge? (y/n) : y
        Deleting ticket:
            ServerName = krbtgt/SUBDOM.W2K.DOM (cb=42)
            RealmName  = W2K.DOM (cb=14)
Submit Buffer size = 84
        Ticket purged!
```

You must answer "yes" or "no" for each ticket.

If the client has no cached tickets, the tool returns the "Cached Tickets: (0)" message.

Chapter 12
Group Policy Tools

There are only two tools — GPResult and GPOTool — that can help an administrator troubleshoot group policies by analyzing the effect that a group policy object (GPO) produces on a computer and/or user, and by verifying the "health" of GPOs and their replication between domain controllers in a domain.

Group Policy Results (GPResult.exe) (RK)

GPResult is a very powerful, and at the same time, simple instrument that allows an administrator to manage and troubleshoot issues related to *Change and Configuration Management* and realized through group policies (registry and software setting, disk quotas, folder redirection, IP security, and scripts). The tool's screen output may be enormous and laden with details. (As a rule, you should redirect it to a file for successive analysis, or use the `more` pipe.) This shouldn't frighten you too much, since the tool is pretty well documented, and its results are, in fact, quite simple to interpret.

GPResult can only be run on the current computer for the currently logged-on user. (You cannot use the *RunAs* command with GPResult.) You can also run GPResult on a remote computer by using a *telnet* session.

> **NOTES**
>
> If a GPO is created and linked to a container, but not yet configured (i. e. has the version 0:0; see the *GPOTool*'s description below), it will be "invisible" to GPResult, even if the group policies linked to that container must affect (directly or by inheritance) the user or computer.
>
> In the tool's output, date and time lines may be displayed incorrectly for some locales.
>
> You can download a free copy of GPResult.exe from Microsoft website.

General Structure of the Tests

The best way to get acquainted with GPResult is to view a brief description of sample output from the tool. Let's first look at the general structure of the test. GPResult displays the following information:

- Date and time when the test was run
- Information on the operating system where the test was run

- Information on the *user* who has run the test (this information is omitted if the /c parameter is specified)
  - Date and time when the user policy was last applied
  - Settings received by the user
- Information for the *computer* where the test was run (this information is omitted if the /u parameter is specified)
  - Date and time when the computer policy was last applied
  - Setting received by the computer

The tool has three operational modes:

- **Normal** — Displays general information only. You may use this mode to verify whether or not the user or computer has received settings from a particular GPO that you are interested in, or to find out which GPOs affect the user or computer.
- **Verbose** — The main mode for viewing detailed information.
- **Super-verbose** — A special mode that should only be used when an administrator needs the following information: the binary values of registry settings, the list of applications that are present in the **Add/Remove Programs** window (as according to the documentation claims; I personally couldn't get this information), and version numbers of both of GPO's parts (the Active Directory and SYSVOL parts).

Description of Tests

Let's discuss an example output, which GPResult has produced in verbose mode. The comments divide the output into logical sections. For presentation purposes, some lines and words are shown in bold. Comments in bold square brackets have also been inserted.

```
C:\>gpresult /v
Microsoft (R) Windows (R) 2000 Operating System Group Policy Result
tool
Copyright (C) Microsoft Corp. 1981-1999
```

The date when the test was run:

```
Created on Tuesday, December 12, 2000 at 10:31:11 PM
```

The system information:

```
Operating System Information:

Operating System Type:         Domain Controller
Operating System Version: 5.0.2195
Terminal Server Mode:          None
```

The common information for the user account:

User Group Policy results for:
CN=Jessica,OU=Sales,OU=Marketing,DC=w2k,DC=dom

```
Domain Name:        W2KDOM
Domain Type:        Windows 2000
Site Name:          W2K-site

Roaming profile: (None)
Local profile:   E:\Documents and Settings\jessica
```

The user is a member of the following security groups:
```
W2KDOM\Domain Users
\Everyone
BUILTIN\Pre-Windows 2000 Compatible Access
BUILTIN\Users
W2KDOM\W2kUNI
\LOCAL
NT AUTHORITY\INTERACTIVE
NT AUTHORITY\Authenticated Users
```

The user has the following security privileges:
```
Bypass traverse checking
Add workstations to domain          [Remember that by default
a "normal" user has the right to add up to 10 clients to the
domain!]
```

The last time group policies were applied to the user:

```
Last time Group Policy was applied: Tuesday, December 12, 2000 at
10:29:10 PM
Group Policy was applied from: w2kdc4.w2k.dom
```

Below, all settings (divided by type: *Registry*, *Folder Redirection*, etc.) that the user was received are listed in detail (the given sample output doesn't contain *all* possi-

Chapter 12: Group Policy Tools 309

ble settings). The following information is displayed for each GPO: the friendly and GUID names of a GPO, and the distinguished name of the container to which it is linked.

```
The user received "Registry" settings from these GPOs:

    MARKETING's GPO
        Revision Number:  5
        Unique Name:      {1D6C9700-CBC3-4BC3-A3BE-6A3E3D3D3772}
        Domain Name:      w2k.dom
        Linked to:        Organizational Unit
                             ↳ (OU=Marketing,DC=w2k,DC=dom)

    SALES' GPO
        Revision Number:  3
        Unique Name:      {C3A33B77-388B-4C89-AF3B-CA18B8AEBE4F}
        Domain Name:      w2k.dom
        Linked to:        Organizational Unit
                             ↳ (OU=Sales,OU=Marketing,DC=w2k,DC=dom)
```

The following descriptions allow an administrator to easily determine exactly which settings the user has received from each GPO. The policies' names settled in the **Group Policy** snap-in are specified in square brackets.

```
    The following settings were applied from: MARKETING's GPO

        KeyName:
    Software\Microsoft\Windows\CurrentVersion\Policies\Explorer
        ValueName: NoSMHelp    [Remove Help menu from Start Menu]
        ValueType: REG_DWORD
        Value:     0x00000001

        KeyName:
    Software\Microsoft\Windows\CurrentVersion\Policies\Explorer
        ValueName: NoNetworkConnections  [Remove Network &
                                    Dial-in Connections from Start Menu]
        ValueType: REG_DWORD
        Value:     0x00000001

    The following settings were applied from: SALES' GPO

        KeyName:
    Software\Microsoft\Windows\CurrentVersion\Policies\Explorer
```

```
            ValueName: NoRecentDocsMenu    [Remove Documents menu
                                             from Start Menu]
            ValueType: REG_DWORD
            Value:     0xC0000001

            KeyName:
            Software\Microscft\Windows\CurrentVersion\Policies\Explorer
            ValueName: NoControlPanel     [Disable Control Panel]
            ValueType: REG_DWORD
            Value:     0x00000001
```

The scripts defined are followed below. Notice that if the script is located in the default folder (...*policyGUIDName*\USER\Scripts\Logon), only the script's name is displayed. However, if a script is stored in a shared folder, you can specify a UNC name for that script.

```
The user received "Scripts" settings from these GPOs:

    W2k-Site's GPO
        Revision Number:   14
        Unique Name:       {2EE56B2E-0CDD-4527-AD6C-57C4B4855691}
        Domain Name:       w2k.dom
        Linked to:         Site (CN=W2K-site,CN=Sites,
                               ↳ CN=Configuration,DC=w2k,DC=dom)

    Logon scripts specified in:  W2k-Site's GPO
        Logon.vbs
```

The information for the computer account is structured in the same way as for the user: general description — time — settings. Notice that the user account is located in one domain (*W2KDOM*), but the computer account belongs to another domain (*SUBDOM*). Therefore, the user and computer get policies from different domain controllers. However, since both domains are placed in the same site (*W2K-Site*), both the user and computer receive the settings from a GPO linked to that site. The *Local Group Policy* and *Default Domain Policy* GPOs provide the default computer settings for domain controllers.

```
    Computer Group Policy results for:

    CN=W2KDC2,OU=Domain Controllers,DC=subdom,DC=w2k,DC=dom

    Domain Name:            SUBDOM
    Domain Type:            Windows 2000
    Site Name:              W2K-site
```

Chapter 12: Group Policy Tools

The computer is a member of the following security groups:

```
BUILTIN\Administrators
\Everyone
BUILTIN\Pre-Windows 2000 Compatible Access
BUILTIN\Users
SUBDOM\W2KDC2$
SUBDOM\Domain Controllers
NT AUTHORITY\ENTERPRISE DOMAIN CONTROLLERS
NT AUTHORITY\NETWORK
NT AUTHORITY\Authenticated Users
```

###
Last time Group Policy was applied: Tuesday, December 12, 2000 at 10:30:54 PM
Group Policy was applied from: **w2kdc2.subdom.w2k.dom**

===
The computer received "Registry" settings from these GPOs:

Local Group Policy
```
    Revision Number:    2
    Unique Name:        Local Group Policy
    Domain Name:
    Linked to:          Local computer
```

W2k-Site's GPO
```
    Revision Number:    14
    Unique Name:        {2EE56B2E-0CDD-4527-AD6C-57C4B4855691}
    Domain Name:        w2k.dom
    Linked to:          Site (CN=W2K-site,CN=Sites,
                           ↳ CN=Configuration,DC=w2k,DC=dom)
```

Default Domain Policy
```
    Revision Number:    7
    Unique Name:        {31B2F340-016D-11D2-945F-00C04FB984F9}
    Domain Name:        subdom.w2k.dom
    Linked to:          Domain (DC=subdom,DC=w2k,DC=dom)
```

The following settings were applied from: Local Group Policy

```
    KeyName:    Software\Policies\Microsoft\SystemCertificates\EFS
    ValueName: EFSBlob
```

```
        ValueType: REG_BINARY
        Value:     Binary data.  Use the /S switch to display.

    KeyName:
Software\Policies\Microsoft\SystemCertificates\EFS\Certificates\
56F9BB1F2DBE48432512773AC638193BD9786DA4
        ValueName: Blob
        ValueType: REG_BINARY
        Value:     Binary data.  Use the /S switch to display.

    KeyName:
Software\Policies\Microsoft\SystemCertificates\EFS\CRLs
        ValueName:
        ValueType: REG_NONE
        Value:     This key contains no values
```

The following settings were applied from: W2k-Site's GPO

```
    KeyName:
Software\Microsoft\Windows\CurrentVersion\Policies\Explorer
        ValueName: NoWelcomeScreen
        ValueType: REG_DWORD
        Value:     0x00000001
```

The following settings were applied from: Default Domain Policy

```
    KeyName:   Software\Policies\Microsoft\SystemCertificates\EFS
        ValueName: EFSBlob
        ValueType: REG_BINARY
        Value:     Binary data.  Use the /S switch to display.

    KeyName:
Software\Policies\Microsoft\SystemCertificates\EFS\Certificates\
92D8718A86AFB763DD2823BB1182D4DD8EA6C8E0
        ValueName: Blob
        ValueType: REG_BINARY
        Value:     Binary data.  Use the /S switch to display.

    KeyName:
Software\Policies\Microsoft\SystemCertificates\EFS\CRLs
        ValueName:
        ValueType: REG_NONE
        Value:     This key contains no values
```

Chapter 12: Group Policy Tools

```
    KeyName:
Software\Policies\Microsoft\SystemCertificates\EFS\CTLs
    ValueName:
    ValueType: REG_NONE
    Value:     This key contains no values
```

===
The computer received "Scripts" settings from these GPOs:

W2k-Site's GPO
```
    Revision Number: 16
    Unique Name:     {2EE56B2E-0CDD-4527-AD6C-57C4B4855691}
    Domain Name:     w2k.dom
    Linked to:       Site (CN=W2K-site,CN=Sites,
                          ↳ CN=Configuration,DC=w2k,DC=dom)
```

Startup scripts specified in: W2k-Site's GPO
```
    Up.vbs
```

===
The computer received "Security" settings from these GPOs:

W2k-Site's GPO
```
    Revision Number: 14
    Unique Name:     {2EE56B2E-0CDD-4527-AD6C-57C4B4855691}
    Domain Name:     W2K.DOM
    Linked to:       Site (CN=W2K-site,CN=Sites,
                          ↳ CN=Configuration,DC=w2k,DC=dom)
```

Default Domain Policy
```
    Revision Number: 7
    Unique Name:     {31B2F340-016D-11D2-945F-00C04FB984F9}
    Domain Name:     SUBDOM.W2K.DOM
    Linked to:       Domain (DC=subdom,DC=w2k,DC=dom)
```

Default Domain Controllers Policy
```
    Revision Number: 6
    Unique Name:     {6AC1786C-016F-11D2-945F-00C04fB984F9}
    Domain Name:     SUBDOM.W2K.DOM
    Linked to:       Organizational Unit
              ↳ (OU=Domain Controllers,DC=subdom,DC=w2k,DC=dom)
```

Run the Security Configuration Editor for more information.

```
============================================================
The computer received "EFS recovery" settings from these GPOs:

    Local Group Policy
        Revision Number: 2
        Unique Name:       Local Group Policy
        Domain Name:
        Linked to:         Local computer

    Default Domain Policy
        Revision Number: 7
        Unique Name:       {31B2F340-016D-11D2-945F-00C04FB984F9}
        Domain Name:       subdom.w2k.dom
        Linked to:         Domain (DC=subdom,DC=w2k,DC=dom)

    Additional information is not available for this type of policy
setting.
```

You can find additional information on GPResult in the supplied HTML Help file or in the *Windows 2000 Resource Kit Tools* documentation.

Group Policy Verification Tool (GPOTool.exe) (RK)

Group Policy Verification Tool allows you to:

- ❏ Check the internal consistency of the specified or all group policy objects that are stored on the selected domain controller or all DCs. These DCs can be located in the current or specified domain. The tool verifies both the directory service and SYSVOL parts of each GPO.

- ❏ Check replication of GPOs by comparing replicas (instances) of each GPO on different domain controllers.

The tool can be run with any credentials on any domain computer.

NOTES

The *policy* and *group policy object* (GPO) terms are used as synonyms in this section. Remember that each GPO has a *directory service part* that is stored in Active Directory and a *SYSVOL part* that is stored in the system volume on the disk.

The `/new` and `/del` parameters described in the *Windows 2000 Resource Kit* are not realized in the released version of the tool.

You can download a free copy of GPOToole.exe from Microsoft website.

General Tests

By default, *all* policies on *all* domain controllers in the user's domain are tested. If some DCs are off-line at the time, their names are not listed in the "Available DCs" section (they will be shown as "down" only in verbose mode). Here is an example of the tool's resulting output:

```
C:\>gpotool
Validating DCs...
Available DCs:
w2kdc4.w2k.dom
w2kdc3.w2k.dom
Searching for policies...
Found 7 policies
=============================================================
Policy {1D6C9700-CBC3-4BC3-A3BE-6A3E3D3D3772}
Policy OK
=============================================================
Policy {2EE56B2E-0CDD-4527-AD6C-57C4B4855691}
Policy OK
...

Policies OK
```

If a corrupted policy is found, it is displayed in *verbose* mode (see below) and the "Errors found" line appears at the end of the tool's output.

> **NOTE**
>
> A unique name is displayed for each policy (and extension) in the tool's output. This name is the policy's *cn* attribute rather than the GUID of the object that stores the directory part of the policy in Active Directory. (The braces are included in the policy name.) Remember that you can bind to a directory object only by using its GUID or distinguished name, not a "naming" attribute (*cn*, *displayName*, etc.).

It is possible to specify a testing domain different from the user's logon domain by using the /domain parameter. Also, you can specify one or more domain controllers that will be tested with the /dc parameter. To test only one or a certain number of policies, use the /gpo parameter with the policies' unique names (*cn*) or *friendly* names (see below). Note that all names must be specified without spaces.

Detailed Information about the Policies

More detailed information can be obtained from the tool by using the /verbose parameter. Since the output can be very large, redirect it into a file for subsequent lookup. An example of the resulting output in verbose mode is shown below (the comments are in bold square brackets).

```
C:\>gpotool /verbose
Domain: w2k.dom
Validating DCs...
w2kdc4.w2k.dom: OK
w2kdc3.w2k.dom: down              [one DC in the domain is down]
Available DCs:
w2kdc4.w2k.dom
Searching for policies...
Found 7 policies
============================================================
Policy {1D6C9700-CBC3-4BC3-A3BE-6A3E3D3D3772}
Policy OK
Details:
------------------------------------------------------------
DC: w2kdc4.w2k.dom                [information on the policy is
                                  displayed individually for each DC that stores this policy]
Friendly name: MARKETING's GPO    [this is the value of the
                                  displayName attribute of the policy's object in Active Directory]
Created: 12/17/2000 5:17:39 PM
Changed: 12/17/2000 5:36:32 PM
DS version:      3(user) 0(machine)
Sysvol version: 3(user) 0(machine) [SYSVOL versions must correspond
                                   to directory service versions]
Flags: 0                          [see Notes below]
```

```
User extensions: [{25537BA6-77A8-11D2-9B6C-0000F8080861}
{88E729D6-BDC1-11D1-BD2A-00C04FB9603F}][{35378EAC-683F-11D2-A89A-
00C04FBBCFA2}{0F6B957E-509E-11D1-A7CC-0000F87571E3}]          [The
extension name is enclosed in square brackets. Here are two extension
names displayed]
Machine extensions: not found
Functionality version: 2                    [must be 2 or higher]
------------------------------------------------------------
============================================================
Policy {2EE56B2E-0CDD-4527-AD6C-57C4B4855691}
Policy OK
Details:
------------------------------------------------------------
DC: w2kdc4.w2k.dom
Friendly name: W2k-Site's GPO
Created: 10/29/2000 4:08:54 PM
Changed: 12/17/2000 6:12:48 PM
DS version:      12(user) 14(machine)   [see Notes below]
Sysvol version: 12(user) 14(machine)
Flags: 0
User extensions:
Machine extensions: [{35378EAC-683F-11D2-A89A-00C04FBBCFA2}
{0F6B957D-509E-11D1-A7CC-0000F87571E3}][{827D319E-6EAC-11D2-A4EA-
00C04F79F83A}{803E14A0-B4FB-11D0-A0D0-00A0C90F574B}]
Functionality version: 2
------------------------------------------------------------
… … …
------------------------------------------------------------
Policies OK
```

> **NOTES**
>
> You can disable the unused parts of a GPO — Computer Configuration and User Configuration — in its **Properties** window. `Flags: 1` corresponds to a disabled User Configuration, and `Flags: 2` corresponds to a disabled Computer Configuration.
>
> Version numbers 0:0 correspond to a new GPO that may even be linked to a container, but is not configured yet.
>
> GUIDs for client-side extensions are listed in the article Q216357 in the Microsoft Knowledge Base. For example, GUID 827D319E-6EAC-11D2-A4EA-00C04F79F83A belongs to the *Security* component, and GUID 25537BA6-77A8-11D2-9B6C-0000F8080861 is as-

signed to the *Folder Redirection* component. These and other GUIDs are the same in each Windows 2000 system.

Note that this output doesn't contain any information on policies' options (whether a policy is disabled or not) and on the state of inheritance (blocking and overriding). Also, you cannot see whether the policy is linked to a container or not.

To obtain information on one policy or on a number of them, use the /gpo parameter. If the policy unique name is used, the command will look similar to this:

```
gpotool /gpo:{C3A33B77-388B-4C89-AF3B-CA18B8AEBE4F}
```

If you know the friendly name of the policy, use it. For example, the command

```
gpotool /gpo:COMPs OU's GPO
```

can be used for the policy with the name

```
Friendly name: COMPs OU's GPO
```

Several policy names — if specified — are separated by commas; spaces between names are not allowed.

Corrupted Policies

The tool returns quite informative messages on the corrupted GPOs, you can therefore precisely locate a problem and find the missed components of the failed GPO. Look below at a few examples of error messages.

The following message indicates that a replication problem existed, and that two replicas of a GPO on different domain controllers are not consistent:

```
Error: w2kdc4.w2k.dom - w2kdc3.w2k.dom sysvol mismatch
```

The next message indicates that a SYSVOL part of a GPO is not full (the gpt.ini file is missing):

```
Error: Cannot access \\w2kdc4\sysvol\w2k.dom\policies\
{C3A33B77-388B-4C89-AF3B-CA18B8AEBE4F}\gpt.ini, error 2
```

Here is an example of problems with the information stored in Active Directory (notice the strings in bold italic):

```
Error: Property versionNumber not found on w2kdc4
Error: Version mismatch on w2kdc4, DS=not found, sysvol=65536
Details:
------------------------------------------------------------
```

```
DC: w2kdc4
Friendly name: SALES' GPO
Created: 12/17/2000 5:18:08 PM
Changed: 12/18/2000 11:27:20 AM
DS version: not found
Sysvol version: 1(user) 0(machine)
Flags: 0
User extensions: [{35378EAC-683F-11D2-A89A-00C04FBBCFA2}{0F63957E-
509E-11D1-A7CC-0000F87571E3}]
Machine extensions: not found
Functionality version: 2
-----------------------------------------------------------
Errors found
```

You can manually correct such an error by using the **ADSI Edit** tool and setting the specified attribute (versionNumber) to the necessary value (65536).

PART IV

PROGRAM ACCESS TO ACTIVE DIRECTORY

Chapter 13. Active Directory Service Interfaces (ADSI)

Chapter 14. Using ADSI for Administrative Tasks

Chapter 13
Active Directory Service Interfaces (ADSI)

The last two chapters of this book are intended for those administrators who want to learn how to use scripting methods for managing various directories, primarily Windows NT 4.0 and Windows 2000 domains. Two of Microsoft products — Active Directory Service Interfaces (ADSI) and Windows Script Host (WSH) — allow administrators to implement a uniform approach to managing various platforms and program products. I'll consider only a small part of this challenging problem area, and try to describe how to use ADSI for managing Windows NT 4.0- and Windows 2000-based directories (i. e. NTDS and Active Directory). The Visual Basic and VBScript programming languages were selected for examples, since Basic is a popular, simple, and compact language for illustrating ADSI programming. I don't like to recite documentation or overload the book with reference information. (You can find and print out the necessary files yourself.) Rather, I'd like to consider some ADSI essentials and pitfalls that can be dangerous for beginners, and illustrate the basic programming methods with simple but practical scripts and applications. (Most of them illustrate a few methods at the same time.) I'd strongly recommend you to download the Active Directory SDK (also known as ADSI SDK) from Microsoft website, or use the online MSDN library. (See links in *Appendix A*.) You will need to have at hand many reference tables, and definitions of interfaces and their methods and properties, constants, error codes, etc.

ADSI as an Administrative Tool

ADSI is very valuable facility for administrators, since ADSI is quite easy to learn and use, and can significantly help in performing bulk or routine operations. For example, you can write an export/import tool specific to your domain configuration, or a specialized migration utility.

For an administrator, ADSI has two distinct advantages:

❑ ADSI can communicate with a number of platforms and products, including the following:

- LDAP-compliant servers, such as Windows 2000 Active Directory and Exchange 5.*x*

- Windows NT 4.0 Primary and Backup Domain Controllers

- Internet Information Services (IIS)

- Novell Directory Services (NDS) servers (4.*x* and higher)

- Novell NetWare Servers (3.*x*)

- ADSI supports many automation-compliant languages like Visual Basic, VBScript or JScript, and Perl; full-fledged languages, such as C/C++ are also supported — and uses the *same* component object model (COM). Scripting languages doesn't require a lot of time spent learning them beforehand; you can combine or modify a few existing scripts, and quickly construct a working, individual tool.

To work with ADSI, it is very helpful to have at hand some administrative tools, such as the Ldp.exe and AdsVw.exe utilities, and the **ADSI Edit** and **Active Directory Schema** snap-ins. These tools will allow you to control the results obtained from the developed scripts or applications, monitor the Active Directory state and values of object attributes, and do a lot of work, without which your programming efforts would not be very effective.

Remote Administration Scripts

The *Windows 2000 Server Resource Kit* contains a collection of scripts called *Remote Administration Scripts*. You can use them not only for performing various administrative tasks, but as a "cookbook", too, while learning ADSI basics and creating your own scripts. All scripts are located in the Ras.cab file on the *Windows 2000 Resource Kit* CD and installed to the same folder as all Resource Kit tools.

Windows Script Host (WSH)

Windows Script Host is a framework to run scripts written in VBScript or JScript. WSH is a standard component of Windows 2000 and Windows 98/ME, and can be installed under Windows 95 and Windows NT. Therefore, administrators can run the *same* scripts on *all* of the mentioned platforms. The latest WSH version (5.5) can be downloaded for free from Microsoft website. (See links in *Appendix A*.)

Don't forget that WSH can be used for managing various system components, not only Active Directory (however, these topics are beyond the scope of this book).

Informal View of the ADSI Architecture

For a beginner, the main challenge in studying ADSI is arguably the great number of exposed interfaces (over 50), which, in turn, have many methods and properties. If, however, one understands the ADSI essentials and certain restrictions, it is easy to begin using ADSI, and then gradually study new interfaces and advanced programming topics.

Attributes and Properties

Let's outline the problem in general terms. All you need to do is to select a directory object — a user, group, computer, or some other item — and perform some action over it.

Hereafter, the terms *attribute* and *property* are used as synonyms. *Attribute* is an element of an object stored in Active Directory, while *property* relates to an ADSI object represented programmatically. You can find mapping between ADSI properties and Active Directory attributes in the Active Directory SDK.

ADSI System Providers

Any directory object exists in a *namespace* that is specific to each directory type. (The hierarchical structure of Active Directory evidently differs from flat Windows NT domains.) Besides, a user in a Windows NT 4.0 domain has attributes different from attributes available for a user in Active Directory. Therefore, ADSI has a specific *system provider* (or simply *provider*) for every supported directory type. Here are four main ADSI providers:

Provider name	Directory	DLL name(s)
WinNT:	Windows NT 4.0 domains	adsnt.dll
LDAP:	LDAP servers (Exchange 5.x and Active Directory)	adsldp.dll, adsldpc.dll, and adsmsext.dll
NDS:	Novell Directory Services (NDS)	adsnds.dll
NWCOMPAT:	Novell NetWare bindary (3.x)	adsnw.dll

(The names of providers are case sensitive!)

The following script lists all providers installed in a system:

```
'Dim objRoot, objChild 'As IADs
Set objRoot = GetObject("ADs:")
For Each objChild In objRoot
  WScript.Echo objChild.Name
Next
```

When selecting a system provider, you define both the naming conventions for a directory object and the ADSI program representation of this object.

Interfaces and Methods

A programmer can access the ADSI objects which correspond to the directory objects via COM *interfaces*, or, more precisely, through *methods* and *properties* of these interfaces. Therefore, the selected interface determines what operations can be done over the object, or which information can be retrieved/set. (Compare, for instance, the methods and properties lists of the *IADs* and *IADsUser* interfaces.) Some interfaces are supported by each provider, and some interfaces can be supported by only one provider. For example, Table 13.1 lists some basic ADSI objects for the LDAP provider, together with the ADSI interfaces. (You can also find a similar table for the WinNT provider.)

Table 13.1. Basic ADSI Objects and Corresponding Interfaces Supported by the LDAP Provider

ADSI Object	Supported interfaces
General object (user, computer, group, etc.)	IADs
	IADsContainer
	IDirectoryObject
	IDirectorySearch
	IADsPropertyList
	IADsObjectOptions
	IADsDeleteOps
Group account	IADsGroup
	IADsExtension
Organizational unit	IADsOU
	IADsExtension
Print queue	IADsPrintQueue
	IADsPrintQueueOperations
	IADsExtension
User account	IADsUser
	IADsExtension

In Table 13.1, you can see that every ADSI object implements two or more interfaces. *This means that you can call any method of any implemented interface, and the object exposes all properties defined in these interfaces.* This table must serve as a starting point for selecting interfaces, or for understanding methods and properties that ADSI provide for a directory object. You needn't learn all or most of interfaces (especially at the beginning). Quite a few interfaces, called *core* interfaces, can cover most of your needs. (See the table in *Appendix B*. These interfaces are shown in bold.) The *IADs* and *IADsContainer* interfaces provide access to practically any directory object, and allow you to perform a number of manipulations with objects — create, delete, rename, enumerate, and so on. The *IADsOpenDSObject* interface allows for specifying alternative credentials when binding to an object. (See *Chapter 14, "Using ADSI for Administrative Tasks"* for examples.)

As you can see from the table of the supported interfaces (*Appendix B*), the WinNT provider doesn't support, for example, OU objects, and the LDAP provider doesn't support file shares or services. So, you shouldn't be under the impression that either the LDAP or WinNT provider is better than the other. Certainly, only the LDAP protocol can provide full value access to Active Directory. Nevertheless, there are operations that can only be performed via the WinNT provider, and situations where this provider produces a more compact code.

For a programmer, selecting a provider and interface for a directory object is, therefore, a crucial operation that determines the methods and properties that will be accessible later. The ADSI SDK help file contains lists of interfaces and properties supported by each provider, and you can print out the necessary tables. If you solidly understand all the stated considerations, you'll have no problems declaring variables or calling object's methods.

The *ADsSystemInfo* Interface

There is a very useful interface available only under Windows 2000 and not mentioned in the ADSI documentation (see updated documentation in the *Platform SDK*). It allows you to retrieve current domain information. Look at the following code snippet:

```
Dim objSysInfo As ADSystemInfo
Set objSysInfo = CreateObject("ADSystemInfo")
Debug.Print objSysInfo.ComputerName
Debug.Print objSysInfo.DomainDNSName
Debug.Print objSysInfo.ForestDNSName
```

```
Debug.Print objSysInfo.IsNativeMode
Debug.Print objSysInfo.SiteName
Debug.Print objSysInfo.UserName
```

The last statement displays the name of current logged on user.

Basic ADSI Programming

In every script or application, the programmer needs to select an object and perform some action over it. To implement these general tasks, ADSI provides operations of the following types:

- Binding to an object and authenticating in Active Directory. Before any operation begins, the programmer selects an object, or *binds* to the object using either current user credentials (recommended) or a specified one.

- Accessing the object's attributes. Depending on the ADSI object's declaration and methods implemented by the object, you can retrieve values of object's attributes.

- Enumerating objects. There are a few programming methods that allow you to obtain a set of objects (users, computers, groups, etc.) — or to *enumerate* objects — selected on a specific criterion. You won't know the number of objects beforehand. (You can see a few examples of enumerating in the next chapter.) It is possible to enumerate:

    - child objects of a container (*Listing 14.7*)
    - members of a group (section "*Manipulating Group Memberships*")
    - all objects of a specific type in a container (this is called *filtering*) (*Listing 14.6*)

- Manipulating the object. The object can be created, moved to another container or domain, or deleted.

- Querying a Directory. ADSI provides search access via an ADO *read-only* interface.

- Managing security descriptors. ADSI can manipulate permissions on various objects, including Active Directory objects, files, etc.

- Managing the schema. The schema can be changed or extended. Schema extension is the process of adding new attributes or classes to the schema.

The next chapter contains examples illustrating all the listed operations.

Reading Object Properties

The Active Directory objects have three types of properties that are stored and accessed differently. Beginners sometimes forget this fact, which often results in errors.

Replicated properties stored in Active Directory

Most properties are stored in Active Directory (such as *cn*, *description*, *objectGUID*, etc.) and replicated between all domain controllers within a domain. Some of them are indexed, and some are replicated to Global Catalog. (Including an indexed property in a query improves the performance of the query.)

To read properties, use the obj.*Get* method or *IADsProperty** methods. Use the obj.*Put* method for updating these properties.

Non-replicated properties stored locally on a DC

Some properties (*lastLogon*, *lastLogoff*, *badPwdCount*, etc.) are not replicated between domain controllers. To determine the last logon time of a user, you need to read the *lastLogon* property for the user at every domain controller in the domain, and compare the values. These properties can be retrieved in the usual way.

Constructed (operational) properties

There are a few properties (such as *primaryGroupToken*, *ADsPath*, *distinguishedName*, *canonicalName*, etc.) that Active Directory uses for itself. These properties are not stored in the directory, but calculated by the DC. (Note that *ADsPath* and *distinguishedName* are not defined in the schema.) These properties may require an obj.*GetInfoEx* call to retrieve them (use the obj.*PutInfoEx* method for updating these properties):

```
obj.GetInfoEx Array("canonicalName"), 0
WScript.Echo obj.Get("canonicalName")
```

Searching Active Directory

ADSI provides search operations via ActiveX Data Objects (ADO). There are two syntaxes used by ADSI in a query statement:

- LDAP dialect consists of the base DN, search filter (according to RFC 1960), list of attributes, and search scope
- SQL dialect is similar to the *SELECT* statement from standard SQL language

Chapter 13: Active Directory Service Interfaces (ADSI)

> **ATTENTION!**
>
> ADSI has *read-only* access to OLE DB interfaces. If you need to change a found object after a search operation, bind *directly* to this object and modify its attributes.

The following application finds all groups in the domain and displays their *ADsPath*. Both LDAP and SQL dialects can be used in this example. It also illustrates how to navigate the resulting record set.

Listing 13.1. ADOQuery.bas — Searching for Groups in an Entire Domain (*w2k.dom*)

```
Option Explicit
Dim objConnection As Connection
Dim objCommand As Command
Dim objRSet As Recordset
Dim i As Integer

' Opening a connection:
Set objConnection = CreateObject("ADODB.Connection")
objConnection.Provider = "ADsDSOObject"

' Preparing the command:
Set objCommand = CreateObject("ADODB.Command")
objConnection.Open "Active Directory Provider"
Set objCommand.ActiveConnection = objConnection

' To find all groups in the forest, you must specify
' the "GC:" namespace instead of "LDAP:" for both dialects.
' The LDAP dialect:
objCommand.CommandText = _
"<LDAP://DC=w2k,DC=dom>;(objectCategory=group);ADsPath"
' The search scope can be defined directly in the command string
'    objCommand.CommandText = _
'    "<LDAP://DC=w2k,DC=dom>;(objectCategory=group);ADsPath;subtree"

' The SQL dialect allows you to sort (notice the ORDER BY clause)
' the record set by some attribute:
' objCommand.CommandText = "SELECT ALL ADsPath FROM
```

continues

Listing 13.1 Continued

```
    '  ↳  'LDAP://DC=w2k,DC=dom' WHERE objectCategory='group'
    '  ↳  ORDER BY name"


    ' The search scope can be defined here or directly in the string
    ' assigned to the CommandText property (above):
    objCommand.Properties("SearchScope") = ADS_SCOPE_SUBTREE   '=2
            'This constant is defined in the ADS_SCOPEENUM enumeration
    objCommand.Properties("Page Size") = 1000
    ' Many other Command Properties can be set here. For details, search
    ' for the "Searching Properties" string in the Active Directory SDK
    ' documentation:
    'objCommand.Properties("Timeout") = 30       'seconds

    ' Executing the prepared query:
    Set objRSet = objCommand.Execute
    Debug.Print "Ready... (Total) " + CStr(objRSet.RecordCount)

    If objRSet.RecordCount = 0 Then
      Debug.Print "No records found!"
      Exit Sub
    End If

    ' Displaying the record set
    objRSet.MoveFirst
    While Not objRSet.EOF
      ' This code must be modified to work with multi-valued properties!
      For i = 0 To objRSet.Fields.Count - 1
        Debug.Print objRSet.Fields(i).Name + " = " + _
                    objRSet.Fields(i).Value
      Next
      objRSet.MoveNext
    Wend

    Set objConnection = Nothing
    Set objCommand = Nothing
    Set objRSet = Nothing
    Debug.Print "End."
```

> **IMPORTANT!**
>
> The number of rows returned from a normal (non-paged) search operation is limited by the *MaxPageSize* parameter (by default, 1000) of *Default Query Policy* (see *Index* for details). (This is also applicable to other search tools, such as Ldp.exe or Search.vbs.) If you *explicitly* specify the "Page Size" parameter in your script or program, a paged search is performed, and you can retrieve any number of rows.

Active Directory Schema

Even if you are an administrator rather than a professional programmer, you may still need to know the basics of the Active Directory schema. For example, using various administrative tools (such as Ldp.exe or **ADSI Edit**) for troubleshooting or tuning Active Directory may require knowing about attribute syntax, the values range, etc. Besides, the schema is the source of such valuable information as whether an attribute is indexed or replicated to Global Catalog, as well as other information. Understandably, if you want to *modify* or *extend* the schema, knowing its essentials is essential. (Extending the schema is the same as creating new attributes and classes.) Extending the schema is not a very sophisticated process, and even a non-programmer can manage it. It is necessary (and enough) to know only some basic rules and requirements.

> **NOTE**
>
> You can view a lot of information about the schema, including descriptions of all attributes and classes, on the web page http://msdn.microsoft.com/certification/schema/.

The Abstract Schema

All definitions of a forest's classes and attributes (the *classSchema* and *attributeSchema* objects) are located in the Schema partition. This partition also contains an object of the *subSchema* class. This object, named *Aggregate*, is known as the *abstract schema*.

The abstract schema contains an "extract" from class and attribute definitions. It provides a simple and efficient mechanism for retrieving frequently used information about classes and attributes, such as the optional and mandatory attributes of an object class, or the value range of a numeric attribute.

Listing 14.1 in the next chapter presents a program that reads the abstract schema. The listing also contains samples of information that can be obtained.

Extending the Schema

When extending the schema, you must specify a unique Object Identifier (OID) for every new attribute or class. A *base OID* for your organization can be requested from an International Standards Organization (ISO) Name Registration Authority, or obtained by using a command-line utility, *OID Generator* (OidGen.exe), that is included in the *Windows 2000 Server Resource Kit*. This utility generates two base OIDs: one for attributes and one for classes. You should run it *only once*. (Don't use different root OIDs in the same Active Directory installation.) New OIDs for your attributes and classes are generated by adding "suffixes" (i. e. the unique numbers separated by a period from the base part) to the appropriate base OID. It is your responsibility to manage these suffixes.

See examples of creating a new attribute and class in the next chapter (*Listings 14.21* and *14.22*).

> **CAUTION!**
> It is not possible to delete an attribute or class. You can only *deactivate* it in the **Active Directory Schema** snap-in.

> **NOTE**
> You may wonder how to create a UI for custom classes and attributes, or how to add new tabs to existing administrative snap-ins for editing new attributes. This is a rather sophisticated topic, which requires, in addition, using non-scripting programming languages, such as C/C++. See the "*Extending the User Interface for Directory Objects*" section in the Active Directory SDK Help, or search for the "display specifier" string on Microsoft website. You may also wish to look up one of the "Step-by-Step" articles related to this topic while you're there.

Creating a New Attribute

When creating an attribute, you must define the following properties of a new *attributeSchema* object:

❑ *attributeID* (OID)

- Naming properties — *cn*, *lDAPDisplayName*
- Syntax properties: *attributeSyntax*, *oMSyntax* (see *Table 13.2* below)
- *isSingleValued*

The *schemaIDGUID* and *adminDisplayName* properties are generated by the system, if omitted (the last one is copied from the *cn* property). If the *searchFlags* and *isMemberOfPartialAttributeSet* properties are not defined, the new attribute is neither indexed nor replicated to Global Catalog.

Optional properties: *rangeLower*, *rangeUpper*, *linkID*, *adminDescription*. (I'd recommend that you always define the last property, since this is very useful information for browsing the schema.)

Creating a New Class

When creating a class, you must define the following properties of a new *classSchema* object:

- *governsID* (OID)
- Classes from which the new class inherits — *subClassOf*
- *objectClassCategory* (structural, auxiliary, or abstract) (Remember that only structural classes can be instantiated in the directory)
- Naming properties — *cn*, *lDAPDisplayName*
- Mandatory and/or optional attributes of the new class — *mustContain*, *systemMustContain*, *mayContain*, *systemMayContain*
- Possible parents (if, for example, you specify "organizationalUnit", the instances of the new class will only be created in OUs) — *possSuperiors*, *systemPossSuperiors*

The *schemaIDGUID* and *adminDisplayName* properties are generated by the system, if omitted (the last one is copied from the *cn* property). By default, the naming attribute for the new class is *CN*. The *rDnAttId* property can define a different value (but this is discouraged).

Optional properties: *auxiliaryClass, systemAuxiliaryClass, defaultSecurityDescriptor, adminDescription*. (I'd recommend that you always define the last property.) The *defaultHidingValue* property of the new class (TRUE, by default) specifies that new instances of this class will be hidden from the **Active Directory Users and Computers** snap-in and the Windows shell. This means that the *showInAdvancedViewOnly* attribute of new instances will be set to TRUE.

Naming Attributes and Classes

Microsoft recommends using some naming conventions for new Active Directory attributes and classes. You should also explicitly specify the *lDAPDisplayName* for all custom attributes and classes. Meeting the conventions ensures the consistency of names used by different software vendors, convenient browsing of the schema, and the possibility of using documentation programs (see later).

According to these recommendations, the Common-Name must consist of the following sections:

- DNS domain name of the company
- Four-digit year indicating when the DNS name was registered
- Product name unique in the company
- Attribute or class description

Each section in the name begins with an upper-case letter and is separated by a hyphen.

To derive the LDAP-Display-Name from a Common-Name, use the following rules:

- Make the first character lowercase
- Capitalize the first character immediately following each hyphen
- Remove all hyphens except those immediately following the company and product components of the name.

Here are a few examples of names:

Common-Name (*cn*)	LDAP-Display-Name (*lDAPDisplayName*)
Microsoft-Com-1999-DS-Consistency-GUID	microsoftCom1999-DS-ConsistencyGUID
Microsoft-Com-1999-RRAS-Attribute	microsoftCom1999-RRAS-Attribute
MyCorp-Com-2000-TEST-User-ID	myCorpCom2000-TEST-UserID

For development or testing purposes, you may also add a version suffix to the *cn* and *lDAPDisplayName* attributes.

Syntaxes of Active Directory Attributes

Table 13.2 contains a list of some frequently used attribute syntaxes. The *Name* column contains two syntax names: the first name is used in the **ADSI Edit** snap-in, the second one (in parenthesis) is used in the **Active Directory Schema** snap-in. The *Description* column also contains examples of Active Directory attributes that have the given syntax.

Table 13.2. Some Basic Syntaxes of Active Directory Attributes

Name	oMSyntax	attributeSyntax	Description
Boolean (Boolean)	1	2.5.5.8	Boolean (*isDeleted*, *isMemberOfPartialAttributeSet*)
Integer (Integer)	2	2.5.5.9	32-bit integer (*flags*, *groupType*, *primaryGroupID*, *rangeLower*, *rangeUpper*, *userAccountControl*)
INTEGER8 (Large Integer)	65	2.5.5.16	64-bit integer (*accountExpires*, *lastLogon*, *maxPwdAge*, *uSNCreated*, *uSNChanged*)
OctetString (Octet String)	4	2.5.5.10	Array of bytes (*objectGuid*). Use OctetString to store binary data
ObjectSecurityDescriptor (NT Security Descriptor)	66	2.5.5.15	Octet string containing a security descriptor (*nTSecurityDescriptor*)
DN (Distinguished Name)	127	2.5.5.1	String containing a distinguished name (DN) (*member*, *memberOf*, *objectCategory*).
			Active Directory automatically keeps up-to-date distinguished names stored in strings of this syntax, i. e. if the object referenced by the distinguished name is renamed or moved, Active Directory tracks all changes. Consider, for example, the relationships of a group and its members. If a user is renamed, it doesn't lose the group membership
DirectoryString (Unicode String)	64	2.5.5.12	String: Unicode, case-insensitive (*description*, *displayName*, *name*, *sn*, *location*)

continues

Table 13.2 Continued

Name	oMSyntax	attributeSyntax	Description
GeneralizedTime (Generalized Time)	24	2.5.5.11	Generalized-Time is time string format (*whenCreated*, *whenChanged*). For example: 12/11/2000 10:34:28 AM
OID (Object Identifier)	6	2.5.5.2	String for containing OIDs (*objectClass*). The OID is a string containing digits (0-9) and decimal points (.)
Sid (SID)	4	2.5.5.17	Octet string containing a security identifier (SID) (*objectSid*, *sIDHistory*). Use this syntax to store SID values only

Useful Tools for Working with the Schema

SchemaDiff.vbs Script

The *Windows 2000 Server Resource Kit* (the *Remote Administration Scripts* section) contains the *SchemaDiff.vbs* script, which allows an administrator to compare the schema of two different forests. This script checks the schema version number, the number of classes, the mandatory and optional attributes for each class, and the syntax and range for each attribute. You can also use the script as an example of manipulations with schema objects when composing your own scripts or learning ADSI programming basics.

SchemaDoc Program

The *Schema Documentation Program* (SchemaDoc.exe) is used to document the schema extensions made in your Active Directory installation. The program copies the information from the classes and attributes into an XML-file. To use SchemaDoc, it is necessary to comply with Microsoft recommendations on attribute and class names, i. e. use the same prefix on all created names. SchemaDoc will search Active Directory based on this prefix.

You can download the program and documentation (140 Kbytes) by using the link: http://www.microsoft.com/TechNet/win2000/schema.asp.

IADsTools ActiveX DLL

The *Windows 2000 Support Tools* (see *Chapter 6, "General Characteristics and Purpose of System Tools"*) contain a COM object named *IADsTools* that is used by Active Directory Replication Monitor (ReplMon.exe). You can call its functions from a custom script or application. IADsTools can be regarded as a high-level framework of basic ADSI interfaces. The supplied iadstools.doc file provides a description of all calling functions. *Appendix C* contains the complete list of these functions. A few examples of using IADsTools will be discussed in the next chapter.

IADsTools are installed as a part of the Support Tools, but can be distributed separately. Copy the iadstools.dll file from the "\Program Files\Support Tools" folder to the *%SystemRoot%* folder (or to any different folder) on a target computer, and run the `regsvr32 iadstools.dll` command from the command prompt on that computer.

By default, all the IADsTools' errors are recorded to the Application Log (Source: `IADsTools`; Category: `None`; Event ID: `1`).

Using Visual Basic and VBScript

Visual Basic is a powerful interactive environment that can be used for developing both applications and scripts. You can first design and debug Visual Basic applications, and then transform them into scripts in VBScript. These language versions have some differences, but they can be easily eliminated.

You need to add references to the appropriate Active Directory libraries to Visual Basic projects. Click **References** in the **Project** menu and check the **Active DS Type Library** box in the **Available References** list. If you use the *ADSI Resource Kit*, you also need to add the appropriate DLLs (such as ADsSecurity.dll or ADsError.dll) to the project's references. (Don't forget to register these DLLs: enter `regsvr32 <DLLName>.dll` at the command prompt.) To use ADSI search via ADO, add the *Microsoft ActiveX Data Objects 2.5 Library* to the references as well.

The standard Visual Basic feature — *Code completion assistant* — significantly helps beginners to study ADSI. You need not remember all of the methods and properties of an ADSI interface, since the assistant will display them for each declared variable (Fig. 13.1).

```
Dim objChild As (IADs)

ADsPath = "LDAP://DC=w2k,DC=dom"
Set objContainer = GetObject(ADsPath)

For Each objChild In objContainer
    Debug.Print objChild.|
Next

End Sub
```

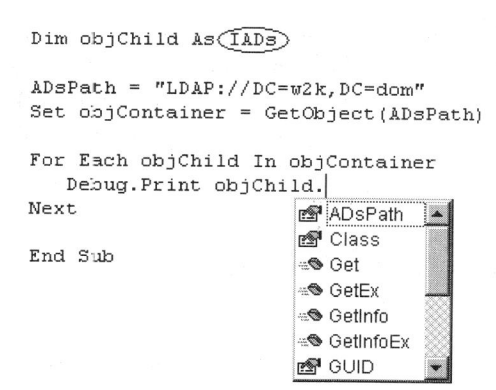

ADsPath
Class
Get
GetEx
GetInfo
GetInfoEx
GUID

Fig. 13.1. Code completion assistant will help you to correctly select a method according to the object's definition

There is, however, a pitfall here. Remember that an ADSI object can implement several interfaces at once, so you can call methods of *all* these interfaces and access *all* their properties. Code completion assistant, however, only displays information about the interface that is used in a variable declaration. Therefore, the other interfaces will be accessible, but not "visible".

In Visual Basic, you should carefully select variable declarations. Consider, for example, the following program that enumerates all child objects in an OU:

```
Dim ADsPath As String
Dim objContainer As IADsContainer
Dim objChild As IADs

ADsPath = "LDAP://OU=Staff,DC=w2k,DC=dom"
Set objContainer = GetObject(ADsPath)

For Each objChild In objContainer
    Debug.Print objChild.Name + " ---> " + objChild.Class
Next
```

Suppose you wish to view all users in this OU and use the following declaration

```
Dim objChild As IADsUser
```

instead of

```
Dim objChild As IADs
```

The program will work fine if the OU only contains user objects. However, you'll get the error "Type mismatch" if there are objects of other types in this OU. In this case you must use a more "universal" interface — *IADs*. VBScript would not impose such a problem, since all its variables always have one fundamental data type, *Variant*.

Converting a Visual Basic Program to a Script

To transform a Visual Basic program into a script in VBScript, it is sufficient to perform the following operations over the program code:

- Delete the `Sub` and `End Sub` statements
- In variable declarations (the `Dim` statements), delete all substrings beginning with (and including) the "As" keyword
- Replace the `Debug.Print` statement (or a similar one) with `WScript.Echo`

Certainly, a reverse conversion is also possible.

Debugging Scripts

The simplest tool for debugging scripts written on VBScript or JScript is the *Microsoft Script Debugger*. You can install it by using the Add/Remove Programs applet in the Control Panel and starting the Windows Component Wizard. The installed tool can then be found in the **Accessories** group.

To start a debug session, use a command similar to the following (the script name must include an extension):

```
cscript Enumerating.vbs //X
```

The debugger starts and the script code is displayed in the debugger window, in which you can:

- Start the script by pressing the <F5> key.
- Point to the code line(s), toggle breakpoint(s) (<F9> key), and run the code between them.
- View and modify the values of variables. Select the **Command Window** from the **View** menu (see below).

❑ Stop debugging. The debugging session terminates, and you can only save the modified text or immediately exit the debugger.

> **NOTE**
>
> You cannot actually change the script code in the debugger window. All changes to the code require restarting the debug session.

A sample debugging session is shown in Fig. 13.2. The presenting code is used for enumerating objects in the specified container, i. e. the code has a loop. Let's discuss some details of working with the command window.

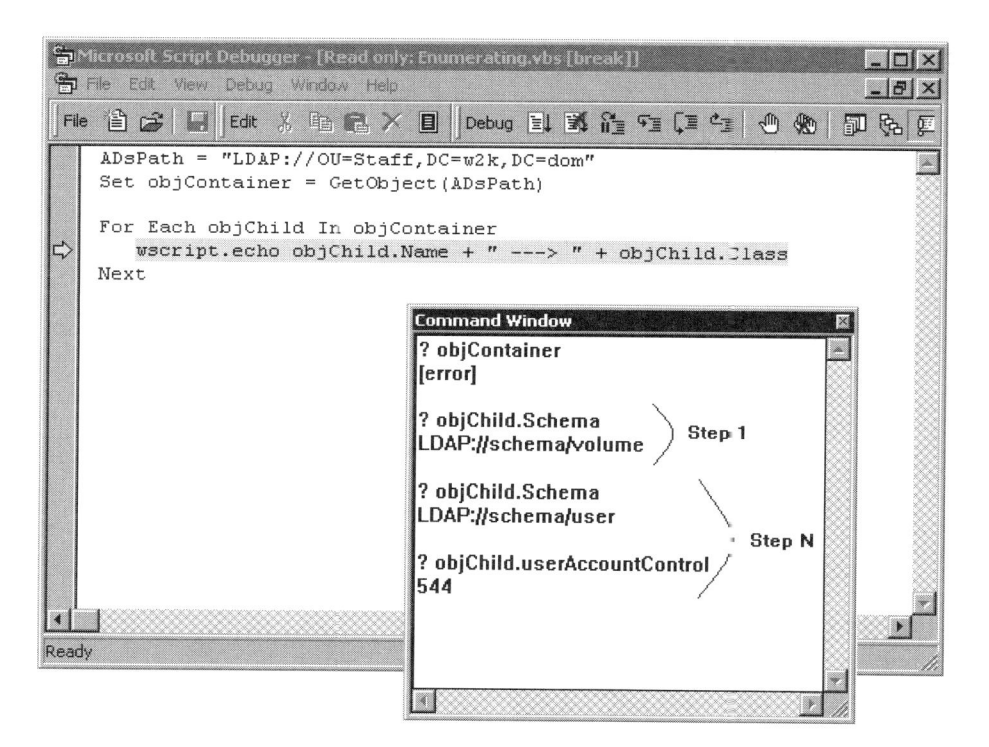

Fig. 13.2. Viewing the current values of variables in a script debugging session

The first request for a value for the object (*objContainer*) was unsuccessful in this example, since the debugger cannot display the entire object. Step 1 shows that we can view the current value of *any* valid property of the specified object. In successive loops, we can trace the same property or select others (Step N). Note that the character case in the names of objects and properties doesn't matter. It is possible at any moment to view and modify all objects already created. For instance, while debugging the presented code we can use the `? objContainer.Parent` command and get the parent name of the specified container.

To change a value, enter an assignment statement in the command window. In our example, we could enter the following string after executing the first line of the code:

```
ADsPath = "LDAP://DC=w2k,DC=dom"
```

After this modification we'll get the list of child objects that relate to the domain container rather than to the *Staff* OU, as was initially specified.

Certainly, debugging in such environment as Visual Basic has many more possibilities and features in comparison to the Script Debugger.

ADSI Error Codes

You have two options for interpreting error in ADSI scripts or applications:

❑ Find "Win32 Error Codes for ADSI 2.5" in Active Directory SDK or MSDN (see links in *Appendix A*).

❑ Use the `repadmin /showmsg <errCode>` command (see detailed information in *Chapter 8, "Network and Distributed Services"*).

Chapter 14
Using ADSI
for Administrative Tasks

This chapter contains a lot of examples that will illustrate some basic ADSI programming principles and at the same time be useful to an administrator. You can easily extend functions of every script to meet your specific tasks. Look up all examples, since many scripts illustrate programming methods useful in various scenarios that are different from main purpose of these scripts. You can combine elements of the scripts and thus quickly start composing your own scripts or applications without thorough familiarity with all ADSI interfaces and techniques.

All proposed examples are written in either VBScript or Visual Basic languages. You can quickly translate them into another language, for example, JavaScript or Perl. The rules of converting a VBScript script into a Visual Basic application and vice versa were dealt with in the previous chapter.

This chapter covers using ADSI only. Remember, however, that you can also use scripts for managing many other components of Windows systems (including Windows NT and Windows 9x/ME), and the WinNT provider can be used for managing both Windows NT and Windows 2000 domains.

Object Names Used in This Chapter

All scripts and programs discussed below have been debugged in a test environment. You must replace the string values in the listings with the values relevant to your network environment. Here are some "tunable" parameters:

- DC=w2k,DC=dom — the distinguished name of forest root domain *w2k.dom* (which has a child domain *subdom.w2k.dom*)
- W2KDOM — the NetBIOS (pre-Windows 2000) name of the domain
- W2K-site — name of the site where domain w2k.dom is located
- W2KDC4 — the NetBIOS (pre-Windows 2000) name of the domain controller *w2kdc4.w2k.dom*
- Staff — a sample organizational unit (OU)
- administrator — a SAM account name with administrative privileges
- psw — a password

NOTE

If two or more lines in the scripts or programs presented in this chapter are split with this symbol ↳ (due to limitations on the page width), they must be treated as a single line (statement).

Reading Information from Active Directory

Retrieving information from Active Directory is, maybe, one of the most important operations. (Writing data into Active Directory or modifying attributes of Active Directory objects is not a challenge if you know the type of these data (i. e. attribute syntax rules) and are familiar with methods of access to data of such a type.) You can certainly use any standard tools and administrative snap-ins discussed earlier in this book to get information; however, custom scripts allow you to save a lot of time on routine operations or combine data in the way most convenient for you. Here are topics that the following scripts aim to demonstrate:

- Which data can be valuable for administrators
- Where these data are located
- How to retrieve data of frequently used types

Saving Results to a Disk File. Reading the Abstract Schema

Before we begin discussing various ADSI scripts, I'd like to show how to save results for successive analysis. As an example, I'll use a script that produces about two thousand lines in total. The following script reads all information about attributes and classes represented in the Active Directory schema (in a particular installation) and simultaneously displays results on the screen and writes them to a file. You can insert statements (only four in total!) similar to the bold ones into any script, and save the obtained results if necessary.

All attributes of the abstract schema used — *attributeTypes*, *extendedAttributeInfo*, *objectClasses*, and *extendedClassInfo* — are multi-valued. Thus, this script is also an example of reading properties that may have more than one value.

Listing 14.1. AbstrSchema.bas — Writing the Definitions of Active Directory Attributes and Classes to a File

```
Option Explicit
Dim objSchema As IADsContainer
Dim attr, x As Variant
Dim i As Integer
Dim myFile As Variant
Dim objFSO As Variant

Set objSchema = _
GetObject("LDAP://CN=Aggregate,CN=Schema,CN=Configuration,DC=w2k,
    ↳ DC=dom")
objSchema.GetInfo
Set objFSO = CreateObject("Scripting.FileSystemObject")
' Specify your own file name. An existing file will be re-written!
Set myFile = objFSO.CreateTextFile("C:\Abstract Schema.txt", True)

i = 1
' Reading attributes represented in the schema.
' Here is a sample output string (parentheses are included):
'    ( 2.5.4.3 NAME 'cn' SYNTAX '1.3.6.1.4.1.1466.115.121.1.15'
    ↳ SINGLE-VALUE )
' All Microsoft attribute IDs begin with the prefix
"1.2.840.113556.1".
attr = objSchema.attributeTypes
For Each x In attr
  ' Debug.Print CStr(i) + ". " + x
  myFile.WriteLine CStr(i) + ". " + x
  i = i + 1
Next
Debug.Print " Attributes (TOTAL) " + CStr(i - 1)

i = 1
' Reading additional information about attributes.
' Here is a sample output string:
'    ( 2.5.4.3 NAME 'cn' RANGE-LOWER '1' RANGE-UPPER '64'
    ↳ PROPERTY-GUID '3F7996BFE60DD011A28500AA003049E2'
    ↳ PROPERTY-SET-GUID '54018DE4F8BCD111870200C04FB96050' INDEXED )
```

continues

Listing 14.1 Continued

```
attr = objSchema.extendedAttributeInfo
For Each x In attr
  ' Debug.Print CStr(i) + ". " + x
  myFile.WriteLine CStr(i) + ". " + x
  i = i + 1
Next

i = 1
' Reading attributes represented in the schema.
' Output strings are similar to the following:
'    ( 2.5.20.1 NAME 'subSchema' SUP top STRUCTURAL MAY
     ⮡ (extendedClassInfo
     ⮡ $ extendedAttributeInfo $ dITContentRules $ attributeTypes
     ⮡ $ objectClasses $ modifyTimeStamp ) )
' Keep in mind that each class also inherits the attribute list of its
' parent class!
attr = objSchema.objectClasses
For Each x In attr
  ' Debug.Print CStr(i) + ". " + x
  myFile.WriteLine CStr(i) + ". " + x
  i = i + 1
Next
Debug.Print " Classes (TOTAL) " + CStr(i - 1)

i = 1
' Reading additional information about classes, for example:
'    ( 2.5.20.1 NAME 'subSchema'
     ⮡ CLASS-GUID '61328B5A8DC3D111BBC90080C76670C0' )
attr = objSchema.extendedClassInfo
For Each x In attr
  ' Debug.Print CStr(i) + ". " + x
  myFile.WriteLine CStr(i) + ". " + x
  i = i + 1
Next

myFile.Close
Set objSchema = Nothing
```

continues

Listing 14.1 Continued

```
Set attr = Nothing
Set x = Nothing
Set objFSO = Nothing
Set myFile = Nothing
```

Retrieving Information from a RootDSE

From the following script you can learn how to access the RootDSE object and use two popular interfaces, namely, *IADsPropertyList* and *IADsPropertyEntry*. RootDSE is the main source of information about names of Active Directory partitions and Directory Service Agents. (See *Chapter 1, "Active Directory Concepts and Terminology"* for detailed information on RootDSE.)

This script can also serve as an example of handling ADSI errors.

Listing 14.2. getRootDSE.vbs — Reading the Attributes of a RootDSE Object

```
Option Explicit
Dim objRootDSE 'As IADsPropertyList
Dim objProperty 'As IADsPropertyEntry
Dim i 'As Integer
Dim intCount 'As Integer

On Error Resume Next
' Serverless binding is preferable.
Set objRootDSE = GetObject("LDAP://RootDSE")
' In some cases you may need to bind to a specific DC:
'Set objobjRootDSE =
GetObject("LDAP://w2kdc2.subdom.w2k.dom/objRootDSE")
' Catching possible errors:
If Hex(Err.Number) = "8007203A" Then
    WScript.Echo "ERROR_DS_SERVER_DOWN (" & Hex(Err.Number) & ")"
    WScript.Quit
ElseIf Hex(Err.Number) <> 0 Then
    WScript.Echo "Error", Hex(Err.Number)
```

continues

Listing 14.2 Continued

```
    WScript.Quit
End If

objRootDSE.GetInfo
WScript.Echo "*** RootDSE object on " + objRootDSE.Get("dnsHostName") _
            + " ***" + vbCrLf
intCount = objRootDSE.PropertyCount
For i = 0 To intCount - 1
    Set objProperty = objRootDSE.Item(i)
    WScript.Echo CStr(i + 1) + ") " + objProperty.Name
Next
WScript.Echo "-----------------------------------"

WScript.Echo " DSA name: " + objRootDSE.dsServiceName
' Names of Active Directory partitions must be always obtained
' from the RootDSE object only:
WScript.Echo " Domain partition:        " + _
            objRootDSE.Get("defaultNamingContext")
WScript.Echo " Schema partition:        " + _
            objRootDSE.Get("schemaNamingContext")
WScript.Echo " Configuration partition: " + _
            objRootDSE.Get("configurationNamingContext")

WScript.Echo " Highest USN: " + objRootDSE.Get("highestCommittedUSN")
WScript.Echo " Is synchronized?      " + _
            objRootDSE.Get("isSynchronized")
WScript.Echo " Is a Global Catalog? " + _
            objRootDSE.Get("isGlobalCatalogReady")

Set objRootDSE = Nothing
Set objProperty = Nothing
```

The highest USN committed by the server is one of the basic parameters used for troubleshooting Active Directory replication. Besides, if you register the USN at a specific moment of time, you'll be able to determine which objects have been modified since then, for instance, by using a simple command similar to the following:

```
search "LDAP://DC=w2k,DC=dom" /C:"uSNChanged>=123456" /S:subtree
```

The *isSynchronized* attribute indicates whether the DC has replicated all directory partitions after its promotion. Don't mix this initial replication with a normal scheduled one.

Remember that the *isGlobalCatalogReady* attribute is TRUE only when the DC has successfully completed its promotion to a GC server. Don't expect that it will be immediately set once you have designated (manually or programmatically) this DC as a GC server.

Retrieving the Actual Attribute List

Here is another example of using the *IADsPropertyList* and *IADsPropertyEntry* interfaces with various providers as well as with Global Catalog. By using this code, you can compare the directory object's attribute lists received from different providers and/or see the attributes replicated to Global Catalog. Only defined attributes (i.e. those that have values) are included in the list. You can also view the type of each attribute that is defined in the *ADSTYPE* enumeration.

Listing 14.3. Prop-of-User.bas — Retrieving the Attribute List of a Directory Object

```
Option Explicit

Dim objAD As IADsPropertyList
Dim objProp As IADsPropertyEntry
Dim iCount As Integer
Dim i As Integer

' Select the necessary binding string:
Set objAD = GetObject("LDAP://CN=John Smith,OU=Staff,DC=w2k,DC=dom")
'***** Binding to Global Catalog:
'Set objAD = GetObject("GC://CN=John Smith,OU=Staff,DC=w2k,DC=dom")
'***** Binding to a user or group with use of the WinNT provider:
'Set objAD = GetObject("WinNT://W2KDOM/jsmith,user")
'Set objAD = GetObject("WinNT://W2KDOM,domain")
'Set objAD = GetObject("WinNT://W2KDOM/Domain Users,group")
objAD.GetInfo

Debug.Print "Attributes of", objAD.ADsPath
```

continues

Listing 14.3 Continued

```
iCount = objAD.PropertyCount
Debug.Print "   Total # " + CStr(iCount)
For i = 0 To iCount - 1
   Set objProp = objAD.Item(i)
   Debug.Print CStr(i + 1) + ") " + objProp.Name + _
               " (type " + CStr(objProp.ADsType) + ")"
Next

Set objAD = Nothing
Set objProp = Nothing
```

Retrieving Characteristics of an Object Class from the Schema

You may want to get complete information about a directory object, i.e. an object class. These data are stored in the *Schema* partition, and there is a special interface named *IADsClass* that allows for retrieval of these data. A few methods of this interface are represented in the following program.

Listing 14.4. attrsOfClass.bas — Getting Common Information and the List of Possible Attributes for a Directory Class

```
Option Explicit

Dim strPath As String
Dim objADs As IADs
Dim objClass As IADsClass
Dim varAttr As Variant
Dim arr As Variant
Dim n As Integer

' A user account has been specified here;
' you can specify any directory object:
strPath = "LDAP://CN=John Smith,OU=Staff,DC=w2k,DC=dom"
```

continues

Listing 14.4 Continued

```
' Connecting to the directory object specified in the path
Set objADs = GetObject(strPath)
Debug.Print "Schema path: '" + objADs.Schema & "' for " + strPath
Debug.Print "Object class: '" + objADs.Class + "'" + vbCrLf
Debug.Print "=== The properties of the class ==="

' Retrieving the information about the class - binding to the schema.
' You could omit the previous statements and directly specify the name
' of the necessary object class, for example "LDAP://schema/user".
Set objClass = GetObject(objADs.Schema)
Debug.Print "Is abstract class? " + CStr(objClass.Abstract)
Debug.Print "ADsPath: " + objClass.ADsPath
Debug.Print "Is container? " + CStr(objClass.Container)
If objClass.Container Then
  Debug.Print "  May contain:"
  ' The list of object classes that the selected class can contain:
  arr = objClass.Containment
  On Error Resume Next
  If Len(arr) = 0 Then
    For Each varAttr In arr
       Debug.Print "   - " + varAttr
    Next
  Else
      Debug.Print "   - " + objClass.Containment
  End If
End If
Debug.Print "Derived from: " + objClass.DerivedFrom
Debug.Print "Naming: " + objClass.NamingProperties
Debug.Print "Class OID: " + objClass.OID
Debug.Print "Possible superiors:"
arr = objClass.PossibleSuperiors
On Error Resume Next
If Len(arr) = 0 Then
  For Each varAttr In arr
    Debug.Print " - " + varAttr
  Next
```

continues

Listing 14.4 Continued

```
Else
   Debug.Print " - " + objClass.PossibleSuperiors
End If

Debug.Print vbCrLf + "=== Attributes ==="
Debug.Print "MUST have:"         ' The list of mandatory attributes
n = 0
For Each varAttr In objClass.MandatoryProperties
   Debug.Print " :: " + varAttr
   n = n + 1
Next
Debug.Print "(TOTAL): " + CStr(n)
Debug.Print

Debug.Print "MAY have:"          ' The list of optional attributes
n = 0
For Each varAttr In objClass.OptionalProperties
   Debug.Print " :: " + varAttr
   n = n + 1
Next
Debug.Print "(TOTAL): " + CStr(n)

Set objADs = Nothing
Set objClass = Nothing
```

Reading Properties of Different Types

Some problems may arise when attempting to display the values of certain properties. This is often due to selection of an inappropriate format. The following example program displays some property types. Some types, such as *Large Integer*, *NT Security Descriptor*, or *Octet String* (for example, the *objectSid* property), require special conversion procedures. Notice the obj.*Guid* method inherited from the *IADs* interface. It produces a string that can be used for binding to the object (in format "LDAP://GUID=xxxx>"); however, this string is not applicable for Search.vbs or Guid2obj.exe tools.

Data types are defined in the *ADSTYPE* enumeration.

Listing 14.5. getProps.vbs — Retrieving the Property List of an User Object

```
Option Explicit
Dim objPropList As IADsPropertyList
Dim objPropEntry As IADsPropertyEntry
Dim objVar As Variant
Dim i As Integer
Dim iCount As Integer

' You can select any directory object; a user account, for example:
Set objPropList = _
        GetObject("LDAP://CN=John Smith,OU=Staff,DC=w2k,DC=dom")
objPropList.GetInfo

iCount = objPropList.PropertyCount
Debug.Print "***** Total " + CStr(iCount) + " attributes defined for " _
        + objPropList.ADsPath + " *****"
Debug.Print "GUID: " + objPropList.Guid

For i = 0 To iCount - 1
  Set objPropEntry = objPropList.Item(i)  'or = objPropList.Next
  Debug.Print objPropEntry.Name + " (" + _
  CStr(objPropEntry.ADsType) + ")"
  Select Case objPropEntry.ADsType
    Case 1   'ADSTYPE_DN_STRING
      For Each objVar In objPropEntry.Values
        Debug.Print "   Value: " + objVar.DNString
      Next

    Case 3   'ADSTYPE_CASE_IGNORE_STRING
      For Each objVar In objPropEntry.Values
        Debug.Print "   Value: " + objVar.CaseIgnoreString
      Next

    Case 7   'ADSTYPE_INTEGER
      For Each objVar In objPropEntry.Values
        Debug.Print "   Value: " + CStr(objVar.Integer)
      Next
```

continues

Listing 14.5 Continued

```
      Case 8   'ADSTYPE_OCTET_STRING
         Debug.Print "    =Octet String="

      Case 9   'ADSTYPE_UTC_TIME
         For Each objVar In objPropEntry.Values
            Debug.Print "    Value: " + CStr(objVar.UTCTime)
         Next

      Case 10  'ADSTYPE_LARGE_INTEGER
         Debug.Print "    =Large Integer="     ' Object doesn't support this
                                               ' property or method

      Case 25  'ADSTYPE_NT_SECURITY_DESCRIPTOR
         Debug.Print "    =Security Descriptor="    ' Object doesn't
         'support this property or method

      Case Else
         Debug.Print "    Value hasn't been converted."
   End Select
Next

Set objPropList = Nothing
Set objPropEntry = Nothing
Set objVar = Nothing
```

Searching Active Directory for Objects

The following two small programs demonstrate various ways to treat directory objects of the same type (enumerating objects). Generally, the most preferable way is the following: use ActiveX Data Objects (ADO) for access to Active Directory, find the applicable objects, bind to them, and carry out modifications. (Remember that access through ADO is read-only!) Nevertheless, it is also possible to filter or enumerate child objects located in containers. Let's discuss what facts must be taken into consideration.

The flat WinNT namespace can have advantages if you need to find similar objects in an entire domain. However, you won't be able to determine locations of found objects in the OU structure.

Listing 14.6. FilterInNT.bas — Using a Filter and the WinNT Provider

```
Option Explicit
Dim objAD As IADsContainer
Dim obj As IADs


Set objAD = GetObject("WinNT://W2KDOM,domain")
' You can also bind to a computer object
' Set objAD = GetObject("WinNT://w2kdc4,computer")


' Using the LDAP provider is not effective since you cannot filter
' objects in the nested containers. WinNT namespace is flat,
' and all objects are "visible" at one level.
' Set objAD = GetObject("LDAP://DC=w2k,DC=dom") - such a binding
' will allow you to find groups at the domain level only.
objAD.Filter = Array("group")

For Each obj In objAD
   Debug.Print obj.name + " ..... " + obj.ADsPath
Next

Set objAD = Nothing
Set obj = Nothing
```

> **NOTE**
>
> You can specify any object classes (*user*, *organizationalUnit*, *volume*, etc.) in the filers.

The following program enumerates all children of both the domain object and nested containers. Thus, all objects of specified type can be found, and the directory path to each object reflects its location in the entire domain namespace. This script, however, works slower than the previous one does.

Listing 14.7. FilterInLDAP.bas — Using Recursion and the LDAP Provider

```
Option Explicit
Dim objAD As IADsContainer
Dim obj As IADs

   Set objAD = GetObject("LDAP://DC=w2k,DC=dom")
   Call getGroups(objAD)

End Sub

Sub getGroups(objRoot)
   Dim obj As IADs

   For Each obj In objRoot
      If obj.Class = "group" Then
         Debug.Print obj.name + " ..... " + obj.ADsPath
      End If
      If obj.Class = "organizationalUnit" Or obj.Class = "container" Then
         Call getGroups(obj)
      End If
   Next
End Sub
```

Manipulating User Objects

This section describes some typical manipulations with the most frequently used directory objects — user accounts. I'd once again recommend you to print out all documentation on the user object (methods and properties supported by various system providers, relevant enumerations, etc.) to keep it on hand.

Creating a User Account

Creating a user is basically a very simple operation. You need only consider some details, which different providers will determine. In general, the procedure is the same for both WinNT and LDAP providers: you bind to a container object and use the *IADsContainer.Create* method for creating a new object of the specified type. However if the WinNT provider is used, you must bind to a domain, and the new account will appear in the default container — *Users*. By using the LDAP provider, you can bind to any container or OU and create an account there. Look at the following code snippets:

WinNT provider:

```
Set objDomain = GetObject("WinNT://W2KDOM")
Set objUser = objDomain.Create("user", "JSmith")
objUser.SetInfo
```

LDAP provider:

```
Set objOU = GetObject("LDAP://OU=Staff,DC=w2k,DC=dom")
Set objUser = objOU.Create("user", "cn=John Smith")
objUser.Put "samAccountName", "JSmith"
'Additional (non-default) property definitions go here, e.g.:
'   objAD.FirstName = "John"
'   objAD.LastName = "Smith"
'   objAD.UserPrincipalName = "JSmith@w2k.dom"
' You can set the password only after creating the user account
objUser.SetInfo
```

In both cases, a user account with the *minimal* number of defined attributes is created. (See also "Creating Multiple Objects" below.) See Table 14.1 for the differences between these cases.

Chapter 14: Using ADSI for Administrative Tasks

Table 14.1. The Default Values of User Attributes

Property	Value	
	LDAP provider	WinNT provider
Account Disabled	TRUE	FALSE
Account Never Expires	TRUE	TRUE
CN (common name)	Must be specified explicitly	SAM Account Name
First Name (givenName)	Empty	Empty
Full Name	Empty	SAM Account Name
Group	Domain User	Domain User
Last Name (sn)	Empty	Empty
Password	Empty	Empty
Password Never Expires	FALSE	FALSE
Profile	Empty	Empty
SamAccountName	Must be specified explicitly	Must be specified explicitly
User Cannot Change Password	FALSE	FALSE
User Must Change Password	TRUE	TRUE
User Principal Name (UPN)	Empty	Empty

Resetting the Password

To set or change the password of a user account, you need to use the special methods — *SetPassword* and *ChangePassword* — of the *IADsUser* interface. The following script sets a new password for a user and forces the user to change it at the first logon to the system.

Listing 14.8. setPassword.vbs — Resetting User Password

```
Dim strPath 'As String
Dim objUser 'As IADsUser
```

continues

Listing 14.8 Continued

```
'strPath = "WinNT://w2kdc4/JSmith"
strPath = "LDAP://CN=John Smith,OU=Staff,DC=w2k,DC=dom"

' Connect to the directory object specified in the path
Set objUser = GetObject(strPath)
objUser.SetPassword "newPsw"
' User must change the password
objUser.Put "pwdLastSet", 0

' The following statements are used with the WinNT provider
'objUser.SetPassword "newPsw"
' User must change the password
'objUser.Put "PasswordExpired", CLng(1)

On Error Resume Next
objUser.SetInfo
WScript.Echo "Error: " + Hex(Err.Number)

Set objUser = Nothing
```

Disabling Accounts

You can disable or enable a user or computer account by binding to an object using the *IADsUser* interface, and calling the IADsUser.*AccountDisabled* method. Look at the following example script:

Listing 14.9. disableAccount.vbs — Disabling an Account

```
Dim objAccount 'As IADsUser
' Set objAccount = GetObject("WinNT://W2KDOM/JSmith") - for users only
' The LDAP provider allows you to disable both user and computer
' accounts:
' Set objAccount = _
'       GetObject("LDAP://CN=John Smith,OU=Staff,DC=w2k,DC=dom")
```

continues

Listing 14.9 Continued

```
Set objAccount = GetObject("LDAP://CN=W2KPRO1,OU=Staff,DC=w2k,DC=dom")
objAccount.AccountDisabled = True
objAccount.SetInfo
Set objAccount = Nothing
```

Manipulating Group Memberships

The *IADsUser* and *IADsGroup* interfaces have some useful methods that are designated for enumerating groups and users. Certainly, you could directly access the appropriate properties — *memberOf* for user objects, and *member* for group objects — that are responsible for the membership information. However, it is much more convenient to use the access methods, especially when modifying memberships.

Which Groups Does a User Belong to?

The *Groups* method of the IADsUser interface allows you to enumerate all groups that a user belongs to. Here is a code snippet that displays the names of the groups:

```
Dim objUser as IADsUser
Dim x As Variant

Set objUser = GetObject("LDAP://CN=John Smith,OU=Staff,DC=w2k,DC=dom")
For Each x In objUser.Groups
   Debug.Print x.ADsPath, x.Name, x.distinguishedName
Next
```

(`ADsPath` can be used for successive direct binding to a group.)

Otherwise, you can directly read the value of the *memberOf* property and use the following statements, instead of the last three statements shown above:

```
'Dim arrGroups As Variant
arrGroups = objUser.Get("memberOf")
For Each x In arrGroups
   Debug.Print x
Next
```

> **ATTENTION!**
>
> By using the *Groups* method or reading the *memberOf* property, you cannot display a user's primary group, i. e. the *Domain Users* group (by default). (By default, the primary group for computer accounts is *Domain Computers*, and for DCs — *Domain Controllers*.) To see an account's primary group, bind to that account and use the *Get* method: `object.Get("primaryGroupID")`.

Who are the Members of a Group?

By using the *Members* method of the IADsGroup interface, you can list all members — users or another groups — of the specified group. Here is a sample code snippet:

```
Dim objGroup As IADsGroup
Dim x As Variant

Set objGroup = GetObject("LDAP://CN=LocalGrp,OU=Staff,DC=w2k,DC=dom")
For Each x In objGroup.Members
   Debug.Print x.Class, x.Name, x.ADsPath, x.distinguishedName
Next
```

How to Add a Member to a Group?

Only one statement (shown in bold) is enough to add an account (user, computer, or group) to an existing group. Look at the following code:

```
Dim objGroup As IADsGroup
Set objGroup = GetObject("LDAP://CN=LocalGrp,OU=Staff,DC=w2k,DC=dom")
objGroup.Add ("LDAP://CN=John Smith,OU=Staff,DC=w2k,DC=dom")
objGroup.SetInfo
```

Creating Multiple Objects

For experimental purposes, or to evaluate the query performance of your server configuration under a stress, you may want to create a large number of directory objects of some type (usually user, computer, or group accounts). The following script will help you to manage this task. You can modify it to fit your domain environment as well as to meet your requirements of number and type of objects.

Listing 14.10. new1000.vbs — Creating Multiple Objects in Active Directory

```
Option Explicit
Dim strPath As String
Dim objAD As IADs
Dim objContainer As IADsContainer
Dim n As Integer
Dim nMax As Integer
Dim strName As String

nMax = 1000     ' The number of new objects
strPath = "LDAP://OU=Staff,DC=w2k,DC=dom"    ' any container you want
'***** For the WinNT provider:
' strPath = "WinNT://W2KDOM,domain"
' The accounts are created in the Users container

Debug.Print "Connecting to " + strPath
Set objContainer = GetObject(strPath)

For n = 1 To nMax
   strName = "user" + String(3 - Len(CStr(n)), "0") + CStr(n)
   '***** For the LDAP provider:
   Set objAD = objContainer.Create("user", CStr("CN=" & strName))
   ' or Set objAD = objContainer.Create("group", CStr("CN=" & strName))
   objAD.Put CStr("sAMAccountName"), CStr(strName)
   ' Statements for defining other properties can be placed here.

   ' The following four statements are necessary to immediately
   ' enable the new accounts:
   '   objAD.SetInfo
   '   strPath = objAD.ADsPath     'binding to the user object
   '   Set objAD = GetObject(strPath)
   '   objAD.AccountDisabled = False
   ' Now, you can also set a password:
   '   objAD.SetPassword "psw"

   '***** For the WinNT provider:
   '   Set objAD = objContainer.Create("user", strName)
```

continues

Listing 14.10 Continued

```
    ' The account will be enabled at once, and you can immediately
    ' set the password:
    '    objAD.SetPassword "psw"
    ' The WinNT provider only makes a very restricted set of user
    ' properties available, including PasswordAge, PasswordExpired,
    ' UserFlags, and a few others.
    objAD.SetInfo

    Debug.Print "User " + strName
Next

Debug.Print CStr(nMax) + " objects have been created "
Set objAD = Nothing
Set objContainer = Nothing
```

Reconstructing an Object Tree

By using ADSI, you can programmatically reconfigure your domain structure: move, delete, and rename objects. Don't forget that this opportunity doesn't extend to built-in and system objects.

Moving and Renaming Objects

Moving and renaming an object is essentially the same operation. You simply specify *different* source and target containers for a move operation, and the *same* container for a rename operation. While moving, an object can retain or change its name. The following script moves a user from one OU to another. The *IADsContainer.MoveHere* method is used.

> **IMPORTANT!**
>
> The source and destination containers can be located in *different* domains in the same forest. Thus, it is possible to perform inter-domain move operations. You need only take into account possible authentication issues.

Listing 14.11. moveObject.vbs — Moving or Renaming a Directory Object

```
Dim strOldContainerPath, strNewContainerPath, strOldObjName, _
    strNewObjName 'As String
Dim objCont 'As IADsContainer
Dim objObject 'As IADs

' If strNewContainerPath is equal to strOldContainerPath,
' then a renaming operation is performed, if not, a moving one is
' performed.
strOldContainerPath = "OU=Inside,OU=Personal,DC=w2k,DC=dom"
strNewContainerPath = "OU=Staff,DC=w2k,DC=dom"

' If strNewObjName is equal to strOldObjName, the object is moved
' to a new container, retaining its name
strOldObjName = "CN=John Smith"
strNewObjName = "CN=John Smith New"

Set objCont = GetObject("LDAP://" + strNewContainerPath)
Set objObject = objCont.MoveHere("LDAP://" + _
          strOldObjName + "," + strOldContainerPath, strNewObjName)

Set objCont = Nothing
Set objObject = Nothing
```

Deleting Objects

There are two options for deleting a directory object: use the *Delete* method of the *IADsContainer* interface, or use a special interface named *IADsDeleteOps*.

To delete an object in the first case, you need to bind to the object's parent container and call the *Delete* method. This method is applicable for leaf objects only (i. e. the object must not have child objects). If you try to delete a non-leaf object, you get the error 2147016683 (0x80072015), which means "The directory service can perform the requested operation only on a leaf object."

By using the *IADsDeleteOps* interface, you can delete an *entire* container with all child objects. (Be careful, since this is a crucial operation. You may want to verify first whether an object has children.) Look at the following two scripts.

Listing 14.12. deleteObject.vbs — Deleting a User (a leaf object)

```
Dim objCont 'As IADsContainer

Set objCont = GetObject("LDAP://OU=Staff,DC=w2k,DC=dom")
Call objCont.Delete("user", "CN=Manager")

Set objCont = Nothing
```

Listing 14.13. deleteContainer.vbs — Deleting an Entire Container

```
Dim objCont 'As IADsDeleteOps

Set objCont = GetObject("LDAP://OU=Staff,DC=w2k,DC=dom")
Call objCont.DeleteObject(0)

Set objCont = Nothing
```

Designating a Global Catalog Server

The following script checks whether the specified DC is a GC server and changes, if it is so instructed, the status of the DC.

Listing 14.14. SetGC.vbs — Designating a DC as a Global Catalog Server

```
Option Explicit
Dim strDSSettings, strServerDN 'As String
Dim objRootDSE 'As IADs
Dim objDsService 'As IADs
Dim objComp 'As IADs
Dim iFlag 'As Integer

' Binding to the RootDSE on a specific server
Set objRootDSE = GetObject("LDAP://w2kdc4.w2k.dom/RootDSE")
```

continues

Listing 14.14 Continued

```
' *** Getting the Directory Service Settings ***
strDSSettings = objRootDSE.Get("dsServiceName")
WScript.Echo "NTDS Settings:", strDSSettings
Set objDsService = GetObject("LDAP://" & strDSSettings)

' ----- Getting the distinguished name of the server
strServerDN = objRootDSE.Get("serverName")
WScript.Echo "Server Name:", strServerDN
Set objComp = GetObject("LDAP://" & strServerDN)

On Error Resume Next
iFlag = objDsService.Get("options")
If Hex(Err.Number) = "8000500D" Then
  WScript.Echo "PROPERTY_NOT_FOUND"
  WScript.Echo objComp.Get("name"), "is not a GC server"
  WScript.Quit
End If

WScript.Echo "Current flag value is", iFlag
' Uncomment necessary statements to change status of the server
If (iFlag And 1) Then
  ' Revoke the GC server role
  ' objDsService.Put "options", iFlag Xor 1     'clear the flag
  ' objDsService.SetInfo
  ' WScript.Echo objComp.Get("name") + " is no longer a GC server"
Else

  ' WScript.Echo objComp.Get("name") + " will be advertised
              ↳ as a GC server"
  ' objDsService.Put "options", iFlag Xor 1     'set the flag
  ' objDsService.SetInfo
End If

Set objRootDSE = Nothing
Set objDsService = Nothing
Set objComp = Nothing
```

How to Find an FSMO Master?

There are five FSMO roles, and there are five Active Directory objects that "know" about names of the operations masters. You can easily find them by using *Ldp.exe*. Make a synchronous search with the following parameters:

- **Base DN** — the forest root distinguished name
- **Filter** — `fSMORoleOwner=*`
- **Scope** — Subtree
- **Attributes** — `objectClass`
- Chase referrals

The results — the distinguished names of the objects as well as their type — must be similar to the ones shown in Table 14.2.

> **NOTE**
>
> It is possible to use other tools, or to retrieve this information programmatically, for example, by making a search using ADO queries. (Specify the filter and an object class shown in Table 14.2.) You can also simply display data on the screen or use them in your scripts or programs.

Table 14.2. Active Directory Objects that Hold Information about the FSMO Masters

Object's distinguished name	objectClass
PDC FSMO master	
DC=w2k,DC=dom	domainDNS
RID FSMO master	
CN=RID Manager$,CN=System,DC=w2k,DC=dom	rIDManager
Infrastructure FSMO master	
CN=Infrastructure,DC=w2k,DC=dom	infrastructureUpdate
Domain Naming FSMO master	
CN=Partitions,CN=Configuration,DC=w2k,DC=dom	crossRefContainer
Schema FSMO master	
CN=Schema,CN=Configuration,DC=w2k,DC=dom	dMD

The *fSMORoleOwner* attribute (syntax *DN*) of each found object holds the distinguished name of the DSA (an object of the *nTDSDSA* class) that owns the appropriate FSMO role. Here is an example of such a name (the elements that will retain their names in your Active Directory installation are in bold):

CN=NTDS Settings, CN=W2KDC4, **CN=Servers**, CN=W2K-site, **CN=Sites**,
↳ **CN=Configuration**, DC=w2k, DC=dom

You can bind to a specific DSA and ask for its parent object (by using the *Parent* method) — this will be the name of the server that masters the appropriate FSMO role.

Using IADsTools

The IADsTools DLL contains over 180 functions (see the full list in *Appendix C*) that help administrators to perform various tasks, from retrieving some configuration data to triggering replication of a directory partition. This facility is not supported, so you may refrain from using some function if you encounter problems.

I'll only consider a few examples of using IADsTools for scripting administrative tasks. You can easily expand the basic approach to other functions.

Initiating Replication

To force replication that meets certain specific requirements, it is possible to write a batch file that uses the RepAdmin utility. IADsTools allow you to write a more customizable script that will perform the same task and, maybe, some others. The following example illustrates how to initiate replication of a directory partition (shown in bold) between two domain controllers.

Listing 14.15. initReplication.vbs — Replicating the *Configuration* Partition from One DC to Another

```
Dim objDLL 'As Object
Dim intResult 'As Long
Dim strDestDC, strSrcDC 'As String

strDestDC = "w2kdc4.w2k.dom"
strSrcDC = "w2kdc3.w2k.dom"
```

continues

Listing 14.15 Continued

```
Set objDLL = CreateObject("IADsTools.DCFunctions")
' Initiate inter-domain replication of the configuration container
intResult = objDLL.ReplicaSync(CStr(strDestDC), _
CStr("CN=Configuration,DC=w2k,DC=dom"), CStr(strSrcDC))
If intResult = 0 Then
  MsgBox "Replication" + vbCrLf + " FROM " + strSrcDC + vbCrLf + _
         " TO " + strDestDC + vbCrLf + _
         "has been completed SUCCESSFULLY."
Else
  MsgBox "Replication FAILED!"
End If
```

Note that the script will wait until the replication process is completed.

Triggering Knowledge Consistency Checker (KCC)

To manually start the topology generation on a specific DC, open the **Active Directory Sites and Services** snap-in, select the **NTDS Settings** object for a server, open the context menu, and click **Check Replication Topology** in the **All Tasks** submenu. The following script will also accomplish the same thing:

Listing 14.16. triggerKCC.vbs — Manually Triggering the Knowledge Consistency Checker (KCC)

```
Set comDLL=CreateObject("IADsTools.DCFunctions")
intResult=comDLL.TriggerKCC("W2KDC4")
If intResult=0 then MsgBox "KCC has been triggered successfully." _
   else MsgBox "Failed"
```

Viewing the Flags of a Domain Controller

IADsTools have many functions that allow administrators to gather information about the Active Directory configuration. For example, here is a script that displays

Chapter 14: Using ADSI for Administrative Tasks 373

the flags, i. e. the functional roles, of a specified DC. You can get the same information by entering `nltest /dsGetDC:<domainName>` at the command prompt. (For additional information on NLtest see *Chapter 8, "Network and Distributed Services"*).

Listing 14.17. getDcInfo.vbs — Getting a Domain Controller's Flags

```
Dim strDomainName 'As String
Dim strDCName 'As String
Dim objDLL 'As Object
Dim intReturn 'As Long
Dim strFlags 'As String

strDomainName = InputBox("Domain:", "Enter the name of a domain", _
                                    "w2k.dom")
strDCName = InputBox("Domain controller:", "Enter the name of a DC", _
                                    "w2kdc4.w2k.dom")
Set objDLL = CreateObject("IADsTools.DCFunctions")
On Error Resume Next
intReturn = objDLL.DsGetDcName(CStr(strDomainName), CStr(strDCName))
If intReturn <> 0 Then
  WScript.Echo "Error # " + Hex(Err.Number)
Else
  strFlags = Replace(objDLL.ReturnedFlags, vbCr, vbCrLf + vbTab)

  WScript.Echo "Flags for server " + objDLL.DCName + ":"
  WScript.Echo vbTab + strFlags
End If
```

Here is a sample output of this script:

```
Flags for server w2kdc4.w2k.dom:
        DS_PDC_FLAG
        DS_GC_FLAG
        DS_DS_FLAG
        DS_KDC_FLAG
        DS_TIMESERV_FLAG
        DS_CLOSEST_FLAG
        DS_WRITABLE_FLAG
        DS_PING_FLAGS
```

```
DS_DNS_CONTROLLER_FLAG
DS_DNS_DOMAIN_FLAG
DS_DNS_FOREST_FLAG
```

Finding FSMO Role Owners

IADsTools have certain methods that return the names of FSMO masters. You need only one statement per FSMO master. In the following script, the domain and DC names are "hardwired" into the script, but you may want to enter them interactively (as in the previous example).

Listing 14.18. getFSMOs.vbs — Asking a DC for the Known FSMO Role Owners

```
Dim strDomainName 'As String
Dim strDcName 'As String
Dim objDLL 'As Object

strDcName = "w2kdc2.subdom.w2k.dom"    'any DC name
strDomainName = "w2k.dom"              'forest root domain
Set objDLL = CreateObject("IADsTools.DCFunctions")

WScript.Echo "Schema Master:          ", _
                        objDLL.GetSchemaFSMO(CStr(strDcName))
WScript.Echo "Domain naming Master: ", _
                        objDLL.GetDomainNamingFSMO(CStr(strDcName))
WScript.Echo "PDC Master:             ", _
    objDLL.GetPdcFSMO(CStr(strDcName), CStr(strDomainName))
WScript.Echo "Infrastructure Master:", _
    objDLL.GetInfrastructureFSMO(CStr(strDcName), CStr(strDomainName))
WScript.Echo "RID Master:             ", _
    objDLL.GetRidPoolFSMO(CStr(strDcName), CStr(strDomainName))
```

This script produces an output similar to the following (the "Site\Server" format is used):

```
Schema Master:         W2K-site\W2KDC4
Domain naming Master:  W2K-site\W2KDC4
```

```
PDC Master:              Remote-Site\W2KDC2
Infrastructure Master:   Remote-Site\W2KDC2
RID Master:              Remote-Site\W2KDC2
```

From this output you can see that the server W2KDC2 (W2K-site) owns tree FSMO roles in its own domain, while the server W2KDC4 (Remote-Site) owns two forest-wide FSMO roles.

Various Operations

The following program contains a few more very different examples of using IADsTools functions. Some screen outputs are placed below.

Listing 14.19. iADsTools.bas — Various Examples of Using the IADsTools ActiveX Object

```
Option Explicit
Dim comDLL As Object
Dim i, intResult As Integer

Set comDLL = CreateObject("IADsTools.DCFunctions")

'***** Displaying some metadata information for a directory object
'       stored on the specified DC:
intResult = comDLL.GetMetaData("w2kdc4.w2k.dom", _
                       "CN=Sites,CN=Configuration,DC=w2k,DC=dom")
Debug.Print "Attribute  *  Local USN  *  Version"
For i = 1 To intResult
   Debug.Print comDLL.MetaDataName(i) + ": " + _
            CStr(comDLL.MetaDataLocalUSN(i)) + " " + _
            CStr(comDLL.MetaDataVersionNumber(i))
Next

'***** Sending a message to a network computer (w2kpro1.w2k.dom):
intResult = comDLL.NetSendMessage("w2kpro1.w2k.dom", _
         "Domain Administrator", "W2KDC4 will be rebooted in 30 sec!")
```

continues

Listing 14.19 Continued

```
'***** Enumerating all GC servers advertised in the forest:
intResult = comDLL.GetGCList("w2kdc4.w2k.dom")
Debug.Print "GC servers (total): " + CStr(intResult)
For i = 1 To intResult
    Debug.Print comDLL.GCName(i)
Next
```

Here is a sample output of metadata for a directory object:

```
Attribute     *   Local USN   *   Version
objectClass: 1165 1
cn: 150104 2
instanceType: 150105 100001
whenCreated: 150105 100001
isDeleted: 150105 100000
showInAdvancedViewOnly: 150105 100001
nTSecurityDescriptor: 150105 100001
name: 150104 100001
systemFlags: 150105 100001
objectCategory: 150105 100001
```

You can obtain these data by using the Ldp.exe tool and the `repadmin / showmeta` command.

IADsTools provide a very easy way to find all GC servers in the enterprise. The example script produces a result similar to the following:

```
GC servers (total): 2
W2KDC2
W2KDC4
```

Manipulating Security Descriptors

Working with security descriptors of Active Directory objects is an advanced programming topic that requires a good understanding of the Active Directory access-control model. However, administrators can easily use some operations that deal

Chapter 14: Using ADSI for Administrative Tasks 377

with reading and/or settings permissions on Active Directory objects. ADSI 2.5 contains tree interfaces that help to perform these tasks:

- *IADsSecurityDescriptor* provides access to the common properties of a directory object's security descriptor, such as the owner of the object, the meaning of the descriptor, etc.

- *IADsAccessControlList* allows for managing the object's Discretionary Access Control List (DACL) that contains the Access Control Entries (ACEs). System ACL (SACL), which controls audit settings, is also supported.

- *IADsAccessControlEntry* manages individual ACEs.

When programmatically setting permissions, you should reference the enumerations shown in the table below. These enumerations contain all necessary constants that must be set in the new Access Control Element (ACE).

Property	Enumeration
AccessMask	ADS_RIGHTS_ENUM
AceFlags	ADS_ACEFLAG_ENUM
AceType	ADS_ACETYPE_ENUM

The following program adds a new ACE that allows the user *W2KDOM\Jessica* to read properties (permissions *List Contents*, *Read All Properties*, and *Read Permissions*) of the *Staff* OU directory object. It also displays all permissions set on this object.

With minimal changes, you can use this program with NTFS File, Registry, Exchange Directory, or Active Directory objects if you install the *ADsSecurity* DLL from the *Active Directory SDK Resource Kit*. Notice the comments marked with symbol $. (You may also want to learn the example located in the \ResourceKit\ADsSecurity\File folder.)

Listing 14.20. addSecDescr.bas — Viewing and Modifying the Security Descriptor of an Object

---

```
Option Explicit
Dim objObject As IADs                       '$ New ADsSecurity
Dim objSD As IADsSecurityDescriptor
Dim objPropEntry As IADsAccessControlEntry
```

continues

Listing 14.20 Continued

```
Dim objDACL As IADsAccessControlList
'Dim objSACL As IADsAccessControlList    'System ACL
Dim i As Integer

' Binding to an Active Directory object:
Set objObject = GetObject("LDAP://OU=Staff,DC=w2k,DC=dom")
objObject.GetInfo
'$ Delete the two previous statements if ADsSecurity is used.
'$ For VBScript you must also add the following statement:
'$    objPropList = CreateObject("ADsSecurity")
'$ Reading the object's security descriptor directly:
'$ (from an Active Directory object)
'$ Set objSD = _
'$ objPropList.GetSecurityDescriptor("LDAP://OU=Staff,DC=w2k,DC=dom")
'$ (from a file)
'$ Set objSD = _
'$ objPropList.GetSecurityDescriptor("FILE://C:\text.txt")

' Retrieving the security descriptor and some its properties:
Set objSD = objObject.Get("ntSecurityDescriptor") '$ delete this
                            '$ statement if ADsSecurity is used
Debug.Print "========================================================"
Debug.Print "Control", objSD.Control, Hex(objSD.Control) + "(Hex)"
Debug.Print "Group", objSD.Group
Debug.Print "Owner", objSD.Owner
Set objDACL = objSD.DiscretionaryAcl
'Set objSACL = objSD.SystemAcl

'***** Creating a new ACE
Set objPropEntry = CreateObject("AccessControlEntry")

'***** Defining properties of the ACE
' The permissions are granted to the user:
objPropEntry.Trustee = 'W2KDOM\Jessica"
```

continues

Listing 14.20 Continued

```
' Which permissions are granted (0xF01FF = Full control):
objPropEntry.AccessMask = ADS_RIGHT_GENERIC_READ 'ADS_RIGHTS_ENUM

' Defining objects to which the permissions are applied:
'    ADS_ACEFLAG_NO_PROPAGATE_INHERIT_ACE = This object only (Default)
'    ADS_ACEFLAG_INHERIT_ACE = This object and all child objects
objPropEntry.AceFlags = ADS_ACEFLAG_INHERIT_ACE 'ADS_ACEFLAG_ENUM

' Granting or denying (ADS_ACETYPE_ACCESS_DENIED) access rights:
objPropEntry.AceType = ADS_ACETYPE_ACCESS_ALLOWED 'ADS_ACETYPE_ENUM

'***** Modifying the ACL and assigning it to the security descriptor
objDACL.AddAce objPropEntry
objSD.DiscretionaryAcl = objDACL
On Error Resume Next
objObject.Put "ntSecurityDescriptor", Array(objSD)   '$ if ADsSecurity
   '$ is used, replace this statement with the following one:
   '$   objObject.SetSecurityDescriptor objSD
objObject.SetInfo     '$ delete this statement if ADsSecurity is used
If Err.Number = 0 Then
   MsgBox "ACE has been successfully added!", , "Modify permissions"
Else
   MsgBox "Error (Hex): " + Hex(Err.Number), , "Modify permissions"
   Exit Sub
End If

'***** Reading current ACL
objObject.GetInfo
Debug.Print objDACL.AceCount    'Total number of the ACEs

i = 1
For Each objPropEntry In objDACL    'Displaying some ACE's properties
   Debug.Print CStr(i) + ") "; objPropEntry.Trustee
   Debug.Print "   Mask (Hex) " + Hex(objPropEntry.AccessMask)
```

continues

Listing 14.20 Continued

```
    Debug.Print "   Flags (Hex) " + Hex(objPropEntry.AceFlags)
    Debug.Print "   Type", objPropEntry.AceType
    i = i + 1
Next

Set objObject = Nothing
Set objPropEntry = Nothing
Set objSD = Nothing
Set objDACL = Nothing
```

The program presented will display the permissions on the directory object in the following form:

```
1) NT AUTHORITY\Authenticated Users
   Mask (Hex)   20094
   Flags (Hex)  0
   Type 0
2) W2KDOM\Domain Admins
   Mask (Hex)   F01FF
   Flags (Hex)  0
   Type 0
3) W2KDOM\jsmith
   Mask (Hex)   20014
   Flags (Hex)  0
   Type 0
...
14) W2KDOM\Jessica
    Mask (Hex)   80000000
    Flags (Hex)  2
    Type         0
```

ATTENTION!

If you use ADsSecurity.dll from a Visual Basic application, don't forget to register the DLL and add to the project a reference to the *ADsSecurity 2.5 Type Library*.

> **IMPORTANT!**
>
> By using ADsSecurity.dll, you can manipulate permissions on the file system as well as other objects. However, in the current version of ADSI it is not possible to control access to file or print *shares*.

Extending Schema

Before extending the schema, open the **Active Directory Schema** snap-in, point to the root of the tree in the **Tree** pane, and click **Operations Master** in the context menu. Make sure that **The Schema may be modified on this Domain Controller** box is checked. If this box is cleared, you'll get the LDAP_UNWILLING_TO_PERFORM error. You can verify the correctness of the created attributes and classes by using either the **Active Directory Schema** or **ADSI Edit** snap-ins. Don't forget to reload or refresh the schema if these tools were opened before a creation operation.

> **NOTE**
>
> Remember that on its starting the **Active Directory Schema** snap-in always connects to the Schema FSMO operation master.

To better understand the entire mechanism of extending the schema and its requirements and restrictions, you may first create a sample attribute or class interactively, by using the features of the **Active Directory Schema** snap-in (see *Chapter 4, "Domain Manipulation Tools"*). It is possible also to use the **ADSI Edit** snap-in, but this tool is not as straightforward as the aforementioned snap-in.

Creating a New Attribute

The following script creates a new string attribute. All defined properties except *adminDescription* are mandatory.

Listing 14.21. newAttribute.vbs — Creating a New String Attribute in the Schema

```
Dim objSchema 'As IADsContainer
Dim root, objNewAttr 'As IADs
Dim str1 'As String
```

continues

Listing 14.21 Continued

```
Set root = GetObject("LDAP://RootDSE")
root.GetInfo
str1 = root.Get("schemaNamingContext")
' Binding to the Schema on the Schema Master:
Set objSchema = GetObject("LDAP://" + str1)
objSchema.GetInfo

' Creating an attribute object
Set objNewAttr = objSchema.Create("attributeSchema", _
                                 "cn=MyCorp-TEST-StringAttribute")
objNewAttr.Put "cn", "MyCorp-TEST-StringAttribute"
objNewAttr.Put "lDAPDisplayName", "myCorp-TEST-StringAttribute"
objNewAttr.Put "attributeID", "1.2.840.113556.1.4.7000. ... .1"
objNewAttr.Put "attributeSyntax", "2.5.5.12"
objNewAttr.Put "oMSyntax", 64
objNewAttr.Put "isSingleValued", True
objNewAttr.Put "adminDescription", "My-Test-Attribute"

On Error Resume Next
' Committing the changes:
objNewAttr.SetInfo
If Hex(Err.Number) = 0 Then
   WScript.Echo "The attribute has been successfully created!"
ElseIf Hex(Err.Number) = "80072035" Then
   WScript.Echo "Error (LDAP_UNWILLING_TO_PERFORM)"
ElseIf Hex(Err.Number) = "80071392" Then
   WScript.Echo "Error (LDAP_ALREADY_EXIST)"
Else
   WScript.Echo "Error:" + Hex(Err.Number)
End If

Set objSchema = Nothing
Set IADsContainer = Nothing
Set objNewAttr = Nothing
```

Using the Created Attribute

When a new attribute has been created, how do you use it? To do so, you must perform one more step in extending the schema: add the new attribute to an existing class. (It can be either a standard or newly created class.) The **Active Directory Schema** snap-in is the best tool for this purpose.

1. Open the **Class** folder in the snap-in's window and find the class you want to extend. Suppose we choose the *user* class.

2. Open the **Properties** window and select the **Attributes** tab (Fig. 14.1).

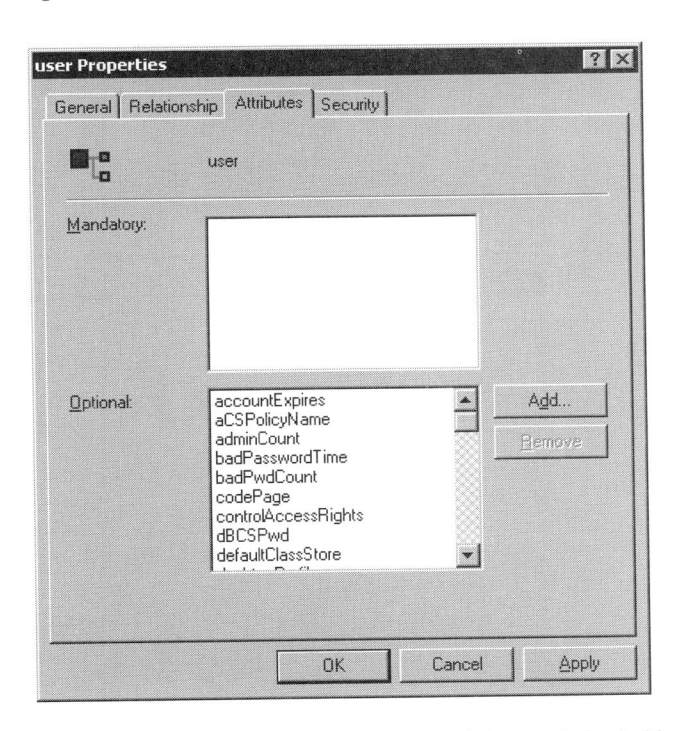

Fig. 14.1. In this window you can view mandatory and view/add optional attributes of an object class

3. Click **Add** and choose a new attribute in the **Select Schema Object** window (multiple select is not possible). Click **OK**.

4. Until you click **Apply**, you can remove the attributes, which have been added incorrectly. When the selection is done, click Apply and close the window.

5. Point to the root in the tree pane and select **Reload the Schema** to write the changes from the memory cache to disk.

Now you can open the **Properties** window for a user in the **ADSI Edit** snap-in and verify whether the new attribute(s) has appeared in the list of optional properties. Either this snap-in or a custom script can be used for setting the values of that attribute.

Creating a New Class

The script presented below creates a structural class inherited from — *is a subclass of* — the *Person* abstract class. Objects of the new class can be created (instantiated) in organizational units (the *possible superiors*). The *mustContain*, *defaultSecurityDescriptor*, and *adminDescription* properties are not mandatory in this case. (Remember that an object of a new class always inherits all attributes of both its own and parent classes.)

Listing 14.22. newClass.vbs — Creating a New Structural Class

```
Dim objSchema 'As IADsContainer
Dim objRootDSE, objNewClass 'As IADs
Dim strSchemaContext 'As String

Set objRootDSE = GetObject("LDAP://RootDSE")
objRootDSE.GetInfo
strSchemaContext = objRootDSE.Get("schemaNamingContext")
' Binding to the Schema on the Schema Master:
Set objSchema = GetObject("LDAP://" + strSchemaContext)
objSchema.GetInfo

' Creating an attribute object
Set objNewClass = objSchema.Create("classSchema", _
                                  "CN=MyCorp-TEST-MyClass")
objNewClass.Put "cn", "MyCorp-TEST-MyClass"
objNewClass.Put "lDAPDisplayName", "myCorp-TEST-MyClass"
objNewClass.Put "governsID", "1.2.840.113556.1.5.7000. ... .1"
objNewClass.Put "objectClassCategory", 1 'ADS_CLASS_CATEGORY_STRUCTURAL
```

continues

Listing 14.22 Continued

```
' ADS_PROPERTY_APPEND = 3
objNewClass.PutEx 3, "possSuperiors", Array("organizationalUnit")
objNewClass.Put "subClassOf", "2.5.6.6" 'Person
objNewClass.PutEx 3, "mustContain", Array("name", "description")
objNewClass.Put "defaultSecurityDescriptor", _
            "D:(A;;RPWPCRCCDCLCLOLORCWOWDSDDTDTSW;;;DA)" + _
"(A;;RPWPCRCCDCLCLORCWOWDSDDTSW;;;SY)(A;;RPLCLORC;;;AU)"
objNewClass.Put "adminDescription", "My-Test-Class"

' Committing the changes:
On Error Resume Next
objNewClass.SetInfo
If Hex(Err.Number) = 0 Then
   WScript.Echo "The class has been successfully created!"
ElseIf Hex(Err.Number) = "80072035" Then
   WScript.Echo "Error (LDAP_UNWILLING_TO_PERFORM)"
ElseIf Hex(Err.Number) = "80071392" Then
   WScript.Echo "Error (LDAP_ALREADY_EXIST)"
Else
   WScript.Echo "Error:" + Hex(Err.Number)
End If

Set objSchema = Nothing
Set objRootDSE = Nothing
Set objNewClass = Nothing
```

To configure the *defaultSecurityDescriptor* property, use the Security Descriptor Definition Language (SDDL) (see the Platform SDK) or use the default value shown in the listing. This security descriptor provides the following default (i. e. directly defined, without inherited) permissions on objects of the new class:

- Authenticated Users — **Read**
- Domain Admins — **Full Control**
- System — **Full Control**

Using the Created Class

Normally, you can create objects of a custom class by using either the **ADSI Edit** snap-in or a script only. For our sample class, the procedure will be the following:

1. Open the **ADSI Edit** snap-in and select an OU (since the only superior of the sample class is *organizationalUnit*), where the new object will be created.

2. Click **New | Object** in the context or in the **Action** menu. Select the class from the list.

3. Enter the name of the new object and the values of all mandatory attributes (directly defined or inherited). You may also click **More Attributes** and define the values of necessary optional attributes.

4. Click **Finish**. The new object will be created.

You can also make possible appearing of a custom class in the UI of the **Active Directory Users and Computers** snap-in. See details in the "ADSI Edit snap-in" section (Example 2) of *Chapter 4, "Domain Manipulation Tools"*. (You might need to restart administrative snap-ins if you have done any schema changes concerning appearance of objects in the UI.)

PART V

APPENDIXES

Appendix A. Web Links

Appendix B. The LDAP and WinNT Providers Support of ADSI Interfaces

Appendix C. IADsTools Functions

Appendix A
Web Links

General

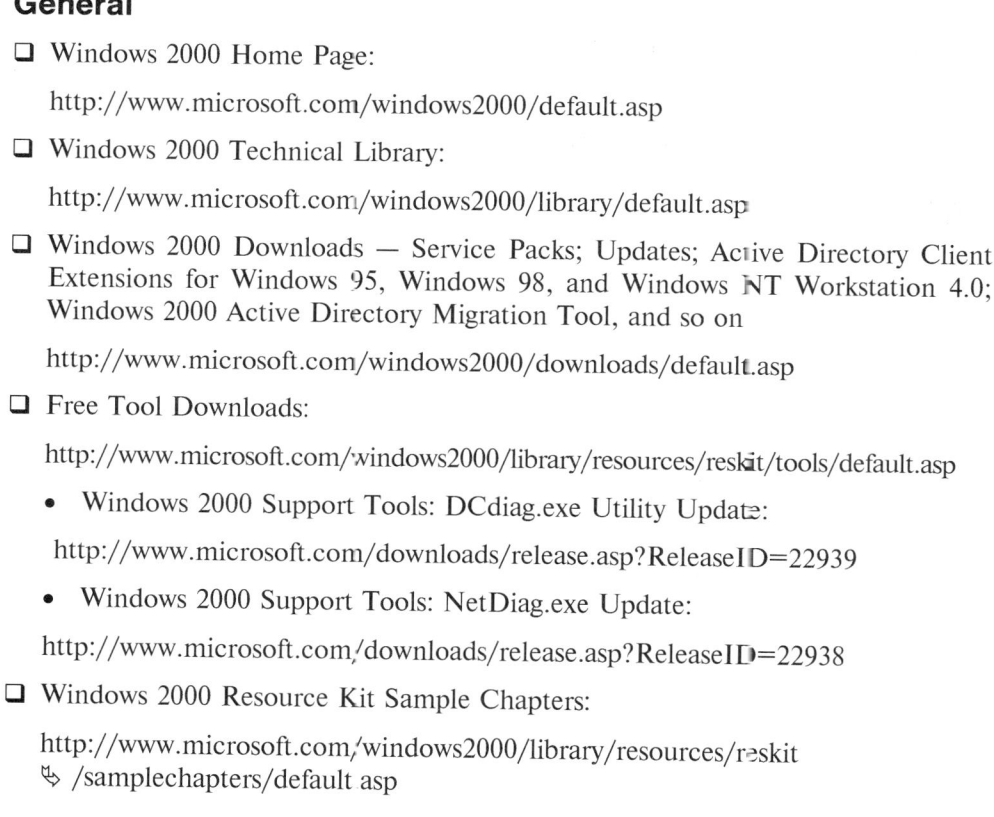

- Windows 2000 Home Page:

    http://www.microsoft.com/windows2000/default.asp

- Windows 2000 Technical Library:

    http://www.microsoft.com/windows2000/library/default.asp

- Windows 2000 Downloads — Service Packs; Updates; Active Directory Client Extensions for Windows 95, Windows 98, and Windows NT Workstation 4.0; Windows 2000 Active Directory Migration Tool, and so on

    http://www.microsoft.com/windows2000/downloads/default.asp

- Free Tool Downloads:

    http://www.microsoft.com/windows2000/library/resources/reskit/tools/default.asp

    - Windows 2000 Support Tools: DCdiag.exe Utility Update:

        http://www.microsoft.com/downloads/release.asp?ReleaseID=22939

    - Windows 2000 Support Tools: NetDiag.exe Update:

        http://www.microsoft.com/downloads/release.asp?ReleaseID=22938

- Windows 2000 Resource Kit Sample Chapters:

    http://www.microsoft.com/windows2000/library/resources/reskit/samplechapters/default.asp

ADSI

- Active Directory Service Interfaces Overview (links to resources and downloads):

    http://www.microsoft.com/adsi

    It is advisable to download the *updated version* from the Microsoft Platform SDK page. You can select and download only the necessary files:

    http://www.microsoft.com/msdownload/platformsdk/setuplauncher.asp

- MSDN Online Windows Development Center:

    http://msdn.microsoft.com/windows2000/

    Online documentation — click Platform SDK Documentation/Networking and Directory Services/Directory Services/Active Directory Service Interfaces.

- Public newsgroups:

    microsoft.public.active.directory.interfaces

    microsoft.public.platformsdk.active.directory

    microsoft.public.platformsdk.adsi

VBScript

- Microsoft Scripting Technologies (JScript, VBScript, WSH, etc.):

    http://msdn.microsoft.com/scripting/

- Script Debugger 1.0

    http://msdn.microsoft.com/scripting/debugger/

Windows Script Host (WSH)

- WSH 5.5 for Windows 9x, Windows NT, and Windows 2000:

    http://msdn.microsoft.com/scripting/windowshost/

Appendix B
The LDAP and WinNT Providers Support of ADSI Interfaces

The following table lists all interfaces (42 in total) supported by either the LDAP or WinNT provider, or by both of them. The last column indicates one of 10 categories to which the interface belongs. First of all, get acquainted with the *core* interfaces.

Interface Name	LDAP	WinNT	Category
IADs	**Yes**	**Yes**	**Core**
IADsAccessControlEntry	Yes	No	Security
IADsAccessControlList	Yes	No	Security
IADsClass	Yes	Yes	Schema
IADsCollection	No	Yes	Persistent object
IADsComputer	No	Yes	Persistent object
IADsComputerOperations	No	Yes	Dynamic object
IADsContainer	**Yes**	**Yes**	**Core**
IADsDeleteOps	Yes	No	Utility
IADsDomain	No	Yes	Persistent object
IADsExtension	Yes	Yes	Extension
IADsFileService	No	Yes	Persistent object
IADsFileServiceOperations	No	Yes	Dynamic object
IADsFileShare	No	Yes	Persistent object
IADsGroup	Yes	Yes	Persistent object
IADsLargeInteger	Yes	No	Data Type
IADsLocality	Yes	No	Persistent object
IADsMembers	Yes	Yes	Persistent object
IADsNamespaces	**Yes**	**Yes**	**Core**
IADsO	Yes	No	Persistent object
IADsObjectOptions	Yes	No	Utility

continues

Appendix B: The LDAP and WinNT Providers Support of ADSI Interfaces

Continued

Interface Name	LDAP	WinNT	Category
IADsOpenDSObject	**Yes**	**Yes**	**Core**
IADsOU	Yes	No	Persistent object
IADsPathname	Yes	Yes	Utility
IADsPrintJob	No	Yes	Persistent object
IADsPrintJobOperations	No	Yes	Dynamic object
IADsPrintQueue	Yes	Yes	Persistent object
IADsPrintQueueOperations	Yes	Yes	Dynamic object
IADsProperty	Yes	Yes	Schema
IADsPropertyEntry	Yes	Yes	Property Cache
IADsPropertyList	Yes	Yes	Property Cache
IADsPropertyValue	Yes	Yes	Property Cache
IADsPropertyValue2	Yes	Yes	Property Cache
IADsResource	No	Yes	Dynamic object
IADsSecurityDescriptor	Yes	No	Security
IADsService	No	Yes	Persistent object
IADsServiceOperations	No	Yes	Dynamic object
IADsSession	No	Yes	Dynamic object
IADsSyntax	Yes	Yes	Schema
IADsUser	Yes	Yes	Persistent object
IDirectoryObject*	Yes	No	Core/Non automation
IDirectorySearch*	Yes	No	Core/Non automation

* — Non-Automation clients only!

Appendix C
IADsTools Functions

The complete list of the functions (183 in total) that are implemented in the IADsTools DLL is placed below. Use context search to find the description of a fufunction in the iadstools.doc file.

AddPerformanceCounter()
ADSPNMappings()
ADStayOfExecution()
BridgeHeadName()
CheckDNForSpecialChars()
ClearPerformanceCounters()
ClearUserCredentials()
ClientSiteName()
ClosePerformanceData()
ConvertDNSToLDAP()
ConvertErrorMsg()
ConvertLDAPToDNS()
DCAddress()
DCAddressType()
DCListEntryComputerObject()
DCListEntryDnsHostName()
DCListEntryHasDS()
DCListEntryIsPDC()
DCListEntryNetBiosName()
DCListEntryServerObject()
DCListEntrySiteName()
DCName()
DCSiteName()
DirectPartnerFailReason()
DirectPartnerFailReasonText()
DirectPartnerGuid()

DirectPartnerHighOU()
DirectPartnerHighPU()
DirectPartnerInConflict()
DirectPartnerLastAttemptTime()
DirectPartnerLastSuccessTime()
DirectPartnerName()
DirectPartnerNumberFailures()c
DirectPartnerObjectGuid()
DirectPartnerSyncFlags()
DirectPartnerTransportDN()
DirectPartnerTransportGuid()
DSABridgeHeadTransport()
DSABridgeHeadTransportCount()
DSAComputerPath()
DSAConnectionAdminGenerated()
DSAConnectionEnabled()
DSAConnectionName()
DSAConnectionNotify()
DSAConnectionNotifyOverride()
DSAConnectionReasonCode()
DSAConnectionReasonCount()
DSAConnectionReasonPartition()
DSAConnectionServerName()
DSAConnectionTwoWay()
DSADNSHostName()
DSAInvocationID()

Appendix C: IADsTools Functions

DSAMailAddress()
DSAObjectGUID()
DSAOptions()
DSASchemaLocation()
DsGetDcList()
DsGetDcName()
DsGetSiteName()
EnableDebugLogging()
GCName()
GetActiveDirectoryProperties()
GetBridgeHeadsInSite()
GetChangeNotifications()
GetConfigurationNamingContext()
GetDefaultNamingContext()
GetDirectPartners()
GetDirectPartnersEx()
GetDomainNamingFSMO()
GetDSAConnections()
GetDSAProperties()
GetGCList()
GetGPOs()
GetGPOSysVolVersion()
GetGPOVersion()
GetGuidForServer()
GetHighestCommittedUSN()
GetInfrastructureFSMO()
GetInterSiteTopologyGenerator()
GetInterSiteTransports()
GetIPConfiguration()
GetMetaData()
GetMetaDataDifferences()
GetNamingContexts()
GetObjectFromGuid()
GetObjectGuidForServer()
GetPartialNamingContexts()
GetPDCFSMO()
GetPerformanceData()
GetRDNForObject()
GetRegistryData()
GetReplicationUSNState()
GetReplicationUSNStateEx()
GetRidPoolFSMO()
GetSchemaFSMO()
GetServerFromGuid()
GetServersInSite()
GetServersInSiteWithWritableNC()
GetSiteForServer()
GetSiteLinkBridgeProperties()
GetSiteLinkBridges()
GetSiteLinkProperties()
GetSiteLinks()
GetSiteList()
GetSiteProperties()
GetSubnets()
GetTrustRelationships()
GetWritableNCsForServer()
GPOGuid()
GPOName()
GPOSysVolVersion()
GPOVersion()
InitPerformanceData()
LastCallResult()
LastErrorText()
MetaDataDifferencesAttribute()
MetaDataDifferencesCount()
MetaDataDifferencesLastWriteTime()

MetaDataDifferencesObjectDN()
MetaDataDifferencesOrigServer()
MetaDataDifferencesOrigUSN()
MetaDataLastWriteTime()
MetaDataLocalUSN()
MetaDataName()
MetaDataServerName()
MetaDataSourceUSN()
MetaDataVersionNumber()
NamingContextName()
NetSendMessage()
NotificationPartnerAddedTime()
NotificationPartnerName()
NotificationPartnerObjectGuid()
NotificationPartnerSyncFlags()
NotificationPartnerTransport()
PerfCounterName()
PerfCounterValue()
ReplicaSync()
ReplicaSyncAll()
ReplPartnerGuid()
ReplPartnerInConflict()
ReplPartnerName()
ReplPartnerUSN()
ReturnedFlags()
ServerInSiteEntryName()
ServerInSiteEntryUUID()
SetDsGetDcNameFlags()
SetReplicaSyncAllFlags()
SetReplicaSyncFlags()
SetUserCredentials()
SiteEntryName()
SiteLinkBridgeEntryDN()
SiteLinkBridgeEntryName()
SiteLinkBridgeSiteCount()
SiteLinkBridgeSiteList()
SiteLinkBridgeTransport()
SiteLinkCost()
SiteLinkEntryDN()
SiteLinkEntryName()
SiteLinkEntryType()
SiteLinkName()
SiteLinkOptions()
SiteLinkReplInterval()
SiteLinkSiteCount()
SiteLinkSiteList()
SiteOptions()
SiteTopologyFailover()
SiteTopologyGenerator()
SiteTopologyRenew()
SubnetName()
SubnetSiteObject()
TestBind()
TranslateDNToNT4()
TranslateNT4ToDN()
TransportAddress()
TransportAddress()
TransportDLLName()
TransportName()
TreeName()
TriggerKCC()
TrustDirection()
TrustDomainName()
TrustNetBIOSName()
TrustType()

Glossary

Authoritative restore — a type of restore operation in Windows 2000 domains in which the objects of the restored directory subtree are treated as authoritative, replacing all copies of these objects that exist in a domain or in the forest. To make a normal restore authoritative, use the NTDSutil tool. See also *Non-authoritative restore*.

Authoritative server — a DNS server that registers resource records for a domain and is allowed to resolve queries about the names stored in the appropriate zone. The authoritative server is specified in SOA and NS records for this zone.

Authoritative zone — a DNS zone that contains resource records related to a domain name. The right to resolve this domain's names is delegated to that zone.

AXFR — a kind of DNS replication, where the *entire* zone file is transferred between name servers. The only possible zone transfer type in Windows NT 4.0 DNS. See also *IXFR*.

Caching name server — doesn't contain any zone files and is only used for improving DNS performance in local networks. The caching server can store a resolved query and quickly respond to subsequent queries from clients by using cached information without addressing the remote authoritative servers.

Cross-reference object — the Active Directory object that stores information about "external" directory objects and services, e. g. about an object that belongs to another domain (and, therefore, is stored in another directory partition).

Delegation — a method for distributing the workload among several name servers within the Internet or a domain. A name server may itself have the right to resolve queries for domain names, or can delegate some of the authority to other servers. This right is stated in the appropriate authoritative zones (with SOA and NS records).

Directory partition — a unit of replication in Active Directory, a part of directory namespace. There are at least three directory partitions: the schema, the configuration, and domain. Every domain controller holds two former partitions and its own domain partition. So, the forest of 5 domains will contain 7 directory partitions: one schema, one configuration, and 5 domains. The domain partition is replicated only in a given domain. The schema and configuration are replicated through the whole forest. The global catalog contains a subset of attributes of all domain objects.

Directory System Agent (DSA) — a core Active Directory service that manages the directory information stored on a hard disk.

Distinguished Name (DN) — the name that uniquely identifies an object within Active Directory. DN consists of the relative distinguished name (RDN) of the object and a set of parent objects' RDNs, e. g.
`CN=dc1,OU=Domain Controllers,DC=domain,DC=com`.

DN — see *Distinguished Name*.

DNS — see *Domain Name System*.

Domain — 1. **DNS domain** — any tree or subtree that is a part of DNS namespace. DNS naming starts with the *root domain* represented as "." (period). 2. **Windows 2000 or Active Directory domain** — a group of computers and other network resources that can be administered as a whole. The security parameters (policies) of one domain don't affect other domains and are not affected by them.

Domain Name System (DNS) — de facto Internet standard used for registering a computer's friendly names and IP addresses. DNS has a hierarchical structure of names that form a single namespace called the domain tree. DNS is by nature a static service, but later realizations (RFC 2136) describe a dynamic method of updating DNS information (recourse records). In Windows 2000, DNS is a *must-have* service, and if configured incorrectly, can generate many problems with authentication, administering, etc.

DSA — see *Directory System Agent*.

File Replication Service (FRS) — a standard Windows 2000 Server service used for replicating system policies and logon scripts stored in System Volume (SYSVOL). FRS also replicates data sets defined by the Distributed File System (DFS).

Forwarder — a DNS server that can continue resolving the client query if the client's preferred server couldn't answer the query. A typical example is the ISP's DNS server configured as a forwarder on a local DNS server.

FQDN — see *Fully Qualified Domain Name*.

FRS — see *File Replication Service*.

Fully Qualified Domain Name (FQDN) — a DNS name that uniquely identifies a computer on the network and consists of the computer (host) name plus all names in the domain tree starting with the root domain. An FQDN name reflects the hierarchy of all host's parent domains. For example, the FQDN for a `host1` that is a member of the `department` in the `company` will be `host1.department.company.com`.

Globally Unique Identifier (GUID) — a 128-bit (8-byte) number that is automatically generated for referencing objects in the Active Directory. Here is an example of GUID: 7050f604-9f15-4536-a592-76d5af2e3487 (32 hex digit).

GUID — see *Globally Unique Identifier*.

Host — a computer or other TCP/IP network resource with a unique name and IP address. Hosts can communicate one with another in a network using their IP addresses or some name resolving system (such as DNS or WINS).

Incremental zone transfer (IXFR) — a kind of DNS replication, when *only the modified* resource records of the zone file are transferred between name servers. This zone transfer type is supported in Windows 2000 DNS (in addition to AXFR). See also *AXFR*.

Iterative query — one of two methods used by DNS servers to resolve queries (see also *Recursive query*). If a DNS server can't answer the query itself, in iterative mode it returns to the client a referral to another DNS server that could contain the answer. This approach minimizes the workload on the DNS server and transfers it to the client itself.

IXFR — see *Incremental zone transfer*.

Master server — same as *Authoritative server*. Master servers will be either primary or secondary; this depends on the method of obtaining zone data.

Name server (NS) or **service** — a service that resolves friendly names (DNS or WINS) to IP address(es). Name servers store all information about the namespace. In Windows 2000, name services are widely used for locating sites, domain controllers, Global Catalog servers, and many other network resources.

Namespace — a list of available named objects that forms a hierarchical tree. An example of a namespace might be the folder structure on a hard disk. For name services, the DNS namespace is hierarchical, while the WINS namespace is flat.

Non-authoritative restore — the normal restore operation in Windows 2000 domains. The objects restored from backup media can be updated with new object copies stored on other domain controllers. See also *Authoritative restore*.

Primary master server — the master server that can be used for direct updating of zone information. The primary master is the source for replicating the zone file to other (secondary) DNS servers.

Primary zone — a directly updateable store for DNS resource records that belong to that zone. Can be considered as an analog of the domain PDC's database, replicated to all other replicas (BDCs).

RDN — see *Relative Distinguished Name*.

Recursive query — one of two methods used by DNS servers to resolve queries (see also *Iterative query*). If a DNS server can't answer the query itself, in recursive mode it becomes a resolver to another DNS server, retrieves the answer from them, and passes it to the waiting client. In this mode, the DNS server performs all the work in finding the final answer.

Relative Distinguished Name (RDN) — the name uniquely identifies an object within a directory container. In a sense, SAM account names can be regarded as RDNs in the domain container. The same RDN may be repeated in a naming tree (in a domain or in a forest), but must be unique in a particular chain of parent names, i. e. distinguished names cannot be repeated.

Resolver — a DNS client that submits the queries to name servers and receives IP address(es) that correspond(s) to a requested name. Windows 2000 resolver also performs the caching and some other "intellectual" functions.

Resolving — in DNS or WINS, the process (and mechanism) of finding a host IP address using its name, or vice versa. This process has two participants: a client issues a request to a name server, and this server returns the appropriate information.

Resource record (RR) — an element of the DNS database. A group of RRs make up a DNS zone. Depending on their purpose, resource records vary by type: there are A, PTR, CNAME, SRV, MX and other records.

Root zone — a zone that contains the DNS root domain.

Round robin — a method of establishing load balancing across servers or services. Using this approach, it is possible to register *several* IP addresses for one computer in DNS, so every subsequent query to a name server will be resolved with a different address.

Secondary master server — a master that can't itself perform zone updates and renews its data only as a result of zone replication from primary masters.

Secondary zone — a read-only copy of the primary zone, updated from it with zone transfers. It is used for DNS load distribution and fault tolerance. Can be considered as an analog of domain BDC's database that contains the information replicated from the master store (PDC).

Security principal — a user, security group, or computer account.

SOA — see *Start of Authority*.

SRV record — a resource record type used for registering and locating well-known TCP/IP services. Very important for Windows 2000 domains, because such records are used to locate domain controllers, sites, and global catalog servers.

Start of Authority (SOA) — for DNS, a resource record that specifies the domain's authoritative name server. The required first record in all forward and reverse zone files.

System state — system state is used for backing up and restoring system-specific information including Active Directory. On domain controllers, it consists of the registry, class registration database, system boot files, Active Directory database files, and SYSVOL volume.

Time-To-Live (TTL) — a time interval of caching a resource record on a client side (in the resolver) or on a name server.

Tombstone — a "hidden" Active Directory object that is removed from the directory but not yet entirely deleted.

TTL — see *Time-To-Live*.

Update Sequence Number (USN) — a 64-bit counter that is used for tracing replication changes between Active Directory domain controllers. Each domain controller increments its current (highest committed) USN at the start of each object update transaction.

UPN — see *User Principal Name*.

User Principal Name (UPN) — the standard naming format for logging on to Windows 2000 domains: `user@domain.com`. Consists of a user logon name and a *UPN suffix* that by default is equal to the domain name where the user account is registered. To simplify logging on, additional UPN suffixes can be used for *all* users in the domain tree. These suffixes are not required to be valid DNS domain names, e. g. such UPNs as `user@corpName` or `user@local` can be used.

USN — see *Update Sequence Number*.

Windows Name System (WINS) — a naming service that permits clients to get the IP address(es) corresponding to the requested NetBIOS name. Since clients can register or release their own names, WINS is a dynamic service in contrast to *standard* DNS.

WINS — see *Windows Name System*.

Zone — a part of DNS database stored on a name server. Zone is an element of DNS domain namespace and DNS database.

Zone transfer — the process of copying a DNS zone file from the primary master to the secondary master(s).

"How to...?"

This index, divided into themes, will help you to find where the answer to a specific practical question is located in the book. It is often difficult to locate the information you need in a certain situation, even if this information is contained in the book.

General Issues

...convert an error code to text description, 226
...convert time values stored as Large Integers into readable format, 196; 225
...find an Active Directory object by its GUID, 231

Active Directory Installation and Configuration

...configure Active Directory to use a non-Microsoft DNS server, 46
...delete a domain controller, 61
...delete a non-existing domain, 270
...delete orphaned (non-existing) domains or domain controllers, 182
...install a Windows 2000 DNS Server, 42
...install Active Directory, 50
...install an administrative snap-in on a client computer, 126
...install a domain controller, 50
...uninstall Active Directory, 61
...verify the DNS Configuration, 44; 53
...set the DNS Suffix of the computer, 64

Active Directory Domain Administration

...add a client computer to a Windows 2000-based domain, 65
...administer another domain, 122
...delegate some administrative tasks to a user or group, 145
...enable auditing of Active Directory objects, 148
...find an operation master, or transfer (or seize) an FSMO role, 137; 185
...find all groups of a specific type in a domain, 286
...find published resources, 136
..."hide" Active Directory objects, 85
...logon interactively to domain controllers, 60
...publish a shared printer or folder in Active Directory, 135
...search in Active Directory from client computers, 128
...verify that a domain controller is acting as a Global Catalog server, 36
...verify that a server is acting as a domain controller, 36

Active Directory Maintenance

...back up Active Directory, 152
...check the Active Directory database file, 178

...compress the Active Directory database file, 176
...move Active Directory database and/or log files to another location, 175
...restore Active Directory, 152
...shut down a remote computer, 196
...test a domain controller, 168

Active Directory Replication
...check replication, 171
...compare directory replicas on different DCs, 205
...determine what information has not been replicated from one DC to another, 209; 219
...disable replication for a DC, 224
...initiate replication between domain controllers, 142; 216
...list DCs that have replication connections with a specified DC, 213
...monitor replication traffic, 33
...see all replication connections of a server, 215
...see the changes that have been made on a DC from specific moment of time, 221; 351
...see when replication is completed, 30
...verify whether ACLs on a directory object are replicated among domain controllers, 298
...view deleted Active Directory objects (tombstones), 245
...view which attributes are replicated to Global Catalog, 17

Active Directory Security and Group Policies
...determine who has access rights on a specific AD object, 290; 295
...find all policies (GPOs) in a domain, 232
...refresh the user or machine group policies, 141
...set access permissions on an AD object from the command prompt (or in batch mode), 296
...troubleshoot group policies, 306
...verify a secure channel, 191
...verify inheritance of ACLs, 298
...view the names of GPOs existing in the domain, 315

Program Access to Active Directory
...create a number of Active Directory objects, 364
...implement a paged search from an ADSI script, 333
...import, export, or modify AD objects in batch mode, 252
...modify (extend) the Active Directory schema, 105; 261; 334; 381
...modify an attribute of an Active Directory object, 232; 262; 346
...modify attributes of a number of directory objects, 262; 346
...promote a DC to a Global Catalog server from the command prompt, 224; 368
...view membership in a group, 263; 363

INDEX

A

AccountDisabled, 362
ACL, 290; 295; 298
ACLDiag.exe, 290
Active Directory Browser
  (AdsVw.exe), 233
Active Directory Installation Wizard,
  55; 61
Active Directory Migration Tool, 274
Active Directory Service Interfaces
  (ADSI), 324
ActiveX Data Objects (ADO), 330
Administrative limits, 18
Administrative Tools, 76
ADMT, 277; 282. *See Active Directory
  Migration Tool*
ADO. *See ActiveX Data Objects*
ADSI, 388. *See Active Directory Service
  Interfaces*
ADSI Edit, snap-in, 18
ADsSecurity.dll, 377
ADsSystemInfo, 328
ADSTYPE, 352; 355
ADsVw.exe, 128; 233
Advanced Features mode, 84
answer file
  Active Directory installation, 62
attribute, 9; 326
attribute syntax, 12
attributeID, 334
attributeSchema, 334
attributeSyntax, 335
audit, 148
authentication, 329
authentication (LDAP), 15
auxiliaryClass, 335

B

Backup, 150
BDC, 26; 66; 145
Binding, 329

C

Canonical Name, 14; 92
change notifications, 28
ChangePassword, 361
child domain
  creating, 57
class
  abstract, 9
  auxiliary, 9
  structural, 9
Clonegg.vbs, 279
Cloneggu.vbs, 279; 283
Clonelg.vbs, 279
Clonepr.dll, 279
Clonepr.vbs, 279; 286
ClonePrincipal, 277
computer accounts
  managing, 268
Configuration, partition, 242
controls. *See LDAP controls*
Create, method, 360
CSV, 263
CSVDE.exe, 252; 263

D

DCdiag.exe, 53; 168
DCpromo.exe, 50
Debugger: see *Microsoft Script Debugger*

Default Domain Controllers Policy, 60
defaultNamingContext, 12
Default-Query Policy, 180
defaultSecurityDescriptor, 335
Delegation of Control, 293
Delegation of Control Wizard, 145; 293
Delete, method, 367
Deleted Objects, container, 245
demotion, 61
DFS: see *Distributed File System*
Directory Information Tree (DIT), 10
Directory Service Restore Mode, 150; 173
Distinguished Name (DN), 13
Distributed File System (DFS), 204
DIT, 13. See *Directory Information Tree*
DN: see *Distinguished Name*
DNS, 20; 40; 53; 58
DNScmd.exe, 44
domain controller
   additional, 57
   creating, 50
   testing, 168
domain members, 64
Domain Naming Master, 27
dommon.exe, 162
DRA Pending Synchronizations, counter, 34
DRA Sync Request Made, counter, 34
DRA Sync Requests Successful, counter, 34
DsACLs.exe, 295
DsaStat.exe, 205
DumpFSMOs.cmd, 138

E

Enumerating, 329
event log
   diagnostic levels, 34
   Directory Service, 30; 34
Export of Active Directory information, 252

F

File Replication Service (FRS), 204

Filter option
   in a snap-in, 88
filtering (ADSI), 329
Find option
   in a snap-in, 90
Flexible Single-Master Operation (FSMO), 26; 137
forest root, 22
FQDN: see *Fully Qualified Domain Name*
FRS, 29; 35; 145. See *File Replication Service*
FSMO, 137; 185; 267. See *Flexible Single-Master Operation*
full computer name: see *Fully Qualified Domain Name*
Fully Qualified Domain Name (FQDN), 14

G

Get, method, 330
GetInfoEx, method, 330
Global Catalog, 26; 35
Global Catalog Promotion Complete, registry value, 37
Globally Unique Identifier (GUID), 14
governsID, 335
Group Policy Object (GPO), 111
   replication of, 29
   troubleshooting, 306
GPOTool.exe, 30; 314
GPResult.exe, 306
Groups, method, 363
GSSAPI, 20
GSS-SPNEGO, 20
GUID, 14. See *Globally Unique Identifier*
guid2obj.exe, 231

H

highestCommittedUSN, 12

I

IADs, 328

Index

IADsAccessControlEntry, 377
IADsAccessControlList, 377
IADsContainer, 328; 360; 366; 367
IADsDeleteOps, 367
IADsGroup, 364
IADsOpenDSObject, 328
IADsProperty, 330
IADsPropertyEntry, 350
IADsPropertyList, 350
IADsSecurityDescriptor, 377
IADsTools, 339; 392
IADsUser, 361; 362; 363
Import of Active Directory information, 253
Infrastructure Master, 26
interface (ADSI), 327
interfaces
   core, 328; 390
isGlobalCatalogReady, 12; 37; 352
isMemberOfPartialAttributeSet, 335
isSingleValued, 335
isSynchronized, 36; 352

K

Knowledge Consistency Checker (KCC), 300
Kerberos, 20
Kerberos Distribution Center (KDC), 300
Kerberos tickets, 300
KerbTray.exe, 300
KList.exe, 302

L

LBridge.cmd, 145
LDAP: see *Lightweight Directory Access Protocol*
LDAP controls, 16
   Return Extended Distinguished Names, 246
   Show Deleted Object, 245
   Tree Delete, 249
LDAP
   dialect, 330
   policies, 180
   ports, 20
   queries, 89
   referral, 14
   search, 15
   URL, 14
lDAPDisplayName, 335
LDIFDE.exe, 252; 258
Ldp.exe, 36; 37; 238
Lightweight Directory Access Protocol (LDAP), 8

M

MaxPageSize, 241; 243
mayContain, 335
memberOf, 363
Members, method, 364
metadata, 251
method (ADSI), 327
Microsoft Script Debugger, 341
migration
   inter-forest, 277
mixed mode, 27; 67
ModifyLDAP.vbs, 18; 19; 181
MoveHere, method, 366
movetree.chk, 275; 276
MoveTree.exe, 273
movetree.log, 276
multi-valued properties, 347; 354; 356
mustContain, 335

N

native mode, 27; 67; 274
NetDiag.exe, 197
NetDom.exe, 67; 138; 266
NETLOGON, 35
netlogon.dns, 20
new forest
   creating, 56
New Taskpad View Wizard, 80
new tree
   creating, 57
NLtest.exe, 36; 37; 190
NTDSutil.exe, 19; 27; 36; 141; 154; 173
NTFRSutl.exe, 204

O

Object Identifier (OID), 10; 334
objectSid, 272
OID: see *Object Identifier*
OidGen.exe, 334
OLE DB, 331
oMSyntax, 335
originating DSA, 220

P

Paged Search, 243
Parent, method, 371
PDC, 26
PDC Emulator, 26; 29
Performance counters, 33
permissions
   granting and removing, 296
   on an AD object, 290; 295
   schema defaults, 294; 297
poledit.exe, 162
possSuperiors, 335
promotion, 50
property, 326
   operational (constructed), 330
Provider
   LDAP, 390
   WinNT, 390
provider (ADSI), 326
publishing printer, 57
Put, method, 330
PutInfoEx, method, 330

Q

Query option
   in a snap-in, 101
   in AdsVw.exe, 236
Query Policy, 18; 241
Querying Active Directory, 128

R

RDN: see *Relative Distinguished Name*
Referral, 14

Referrals, 241
   chasing, 242
Relative Distinguished Name (RDN), 13
Relative Identifier (RID), 277
Remote Administration, 125
Remote Administration Scripts, 161; 325
RepAdmin.exe, 143; 212
Replication, 27; 171
   internal errors, 35
   logging events, 228
   managing, 228
   monitoring, 30
   normal, 28
   scheduled, 28
   urgent, 29
replication metadata, 220; 251
ReplMon.exe, 30; 139; 144; 155; 226
replPropertyMetaData, 251
restore
   authoritative, 152; 153; 154
   non-authoritative, 152; 153
   primary, 152; 153
RID: see *Relative Identifier*
RootDSE, 10; 20; 36; 37; 239; 350
RPC, 201
RPC ping, 201
RPingc.exe, 202
RPings.exe, 202
Run as different user, checkbox, 121
RunAs, 120; 122

S

SAM account name, 14
SASL: see *Simple Authentication and Security Layer*
schema, 151
   abstract, 333
   extending, 261
   modification, 105
   Schema partition, 333
Schema Master, 27
SchemaDiff.vbs, 338
SchemaDoc.exe, 338
schemaNamingContext, 12
SDDL: see *Security Descriptor Definition Language*

Index

search filters, 17
Search.vbs, 230; 287
searchFlags, 335
Searching Active Directory, 244; 330
Secure Channels, 191; 269
security descriptor, 250; 295
Security Descriptor Definition Language (SDDL), 385
Security Identifier (SID), 277
seizing of role, 137
SetPassword, 361
ShowAccs.exe, 166
showInAdvancedViewOnly, 335
shutdown, 196
Shutdown.exe, 196
SID, 272. See *Security Identifier*
SIDHist.vbs, 279; 284
sIDHistory, 272; 284
SIDWalk.exe, 166
SIDWalk.msc, 166
Simple Authentication and Security Layer (SASL), 20
snap-in
   Active Directory Domain and Trusts, 193
   Active Directory Domains and Trusts, 93; 141
   Active Directory Schema, 104; 141
   Active Directory Sites and Services, 28; 92; 143
   Active Directory Users and Computers, 82; 130; 140
   ADSI Edit, 18; 98
   Group policy, 111
SQL dialect, 330
SRV records, 20
srvmgr.exe, 162
subClassOf, 335
subSchema, 333
System Monitor Control, 33
system provider (ADSI), 326
System State, 150
System Volume, 204
SYSVOL, 35; 145; 155. See *System Volume*

T

Terminal Services, 125
The local policy of this system does not permit you to logon interactively, message, 60
tombstone, 151; 245
tombstoneLifetime, 151
tree root, 22
trusts, 193
   creating, 68; 70; 72
   managing, 269
   verifying, 70

U

unattend.doc, 63
unattended installation, 62
UPN, 94. See *User Principal Name*
User Principal Name (UPN), 13; 94
userAccountControl, 67
Users, Groups, and Computers as Containers, mode, 87
USN, 351
usrmgr.exe, 162

V

verinc, parameter, 155
version number, 155

W

well-known RID, 277
well-known SID, 278
Windows 2000 Administration Tools, 104; 126
Windows 2000 DNS Server, 40
Windows 2000 Resource Kit, 160
Windows 2000 Support Tools, 160
Windows Script Host (WSH), 324; 325
WSH, 389. See *Windows Script Host*